EXPLORING THE PARANORMAL

PERSPECTIVES ON BELIEF AND EXPERIENCE

EDITED BY GEORGE K. ZOLLSCHAN, JOHN F. SCHUMAKER & GREG F. WALSH

PRISM · UNITY

ACKNOWLEDGEMENT

This book was started and nearly brought to completion during the time that the three editors were together at the Warrnambool Institute of Advanced Education. W.I.A.E is to be thanked for lending its support to the venture. We also acknowledge the efficient typing help rendered by Wendy Jacobs, Pauline Johnston, Naomi Levin, and Maureen McKay.

Particular thanks are due to one of our editorial team, Greg Walsh, who did most of the work on the Preface and the Section Introductions.

Published in Great Britain 1989 by

PRISM PRESS
2 South Street
Bridport
Dorset DT6 3NQ

and distributed in the USA by

AVERY PUBLISHING GROUP INC.
350 Thorens Avenue
Garden City Park
New York 11040

and published in Australia 1989 by

UNITY PRESS
6a Ortona Road
Lindfield
NSW 2070

1 85327 026 1

Copyright © 1989 George K. Zollschan, John F. Schumaker & Greg F. Walsh

Reprinted 1989

Printed and bound in the Channel Islands
by The Guernsey Press Limited

CONTENTS

Preface

At the end of the Eighteenth Century the scientific community in England and the rest of Europe was astounded by reports emanating from the newly established British colony of New South Wales (Australia) about the discovery of an animal called platypus or ornithorhyncus, as it was later renamed. So unusual and improbable were the descriptions of this animal that naturalists dismissed the reports from down-under as absurd. The reports generated heated debate because they suggested the existence of a creature which defied and upset long established zoological classifications.

The platypus was a strange mix of reptilian and mammalian features. Its feet were webbed and clawed like those of a reptile. It had a large flat beak like a duck. Yet its small body had a coat of fur which indicated that, like mammals, and unlike reptiles, the platypus was warm-blooded. Moreover, the female platypus possessed milk-producing glands with which to suckle its young. Even more confounding was the news that this mammal-like creature laid eggs! But when the eggs were hatched the young platypus was not left to fend for itself as any young reptile must do, but rather to feed on the milk of its mother. Indeed, it was only after one of these warm-blooded creatures was shot and its carcass transported from the rivers of eastern Australia, where the platypus is found, to zoologists in London for closer inspection, that the skepticism of scientists and a strong suspicion of fakery and fraud gave way to acceptance of this new zoological phenomenon.

Just as reports of the platypus generated skepticism and raised questions of fraud and trickery in science last century, so too do claims about paranormal phenomena today. This book is about the study of paranormal beliefs and experiences. All contributions are original to the volume, and as such, they will add to the growing fascination for this topic already shared by academic and lay reader alike.

There are other resemblances with the platypus which may strike the reader. Although the study of what might loosely be called paranormal phenomena is spread between a number of disciplines, most books in the area have tended to represent the point of view of a particular discipline be it parapsychology, anthropology, or philosophy. By setting out to present a truly interdisciplinary collection of chapters within the framework of this volume, we are combining the work of different species of scholars in much the same way as the platypus combines the characteristics of different life forms. Even more confounding is the fact that both believers in alleged paranormal phenomena and disbelievers are represented.

Before too much emphasis is placed on the Australian origin of the volume, however, it should be pointed out that contributors are drawn from North America and the British Isles as well as from Australia. Nevertheless, we can say that all of the editorial work was done in Australia and that an uncommonly large proportion of the chapters for an international volume were done by academics resident in Australia.

We have mentioned three characteristics of the book which deserve some further comment. They are: the subject matter, namely the paranormal; the interdisciplinary character of the contributions; and the fact that both believers and non-believers in the paranormal are represented. Let us take each of these characteristics and clarify the intention of the book by discussing them in more detail.

What is meant by the expression "paranormal phenomena"? To the man in the street such phenomena are simply "weird" or strange occurrences which go beyond our present understanding of normal sensory perception or the bringing into effect of desires and intentions without the kind of actions normally considered necessary. The phenomena involved can be grouped into two categories: (i) extra-ordinary ways of knowing; and (ii) extra-ordinary ways of acting.

Extra-ordinary ways of knowing include:

Telepathy, that is an alleged capacity of one mind to communicate information to another across time and space.

Precognition and *postcognition*, that is the acquisition of information about some future or past event by a mind.

Remote perception, that is the acquisition of information by a mind from an inanimate object — for example, through clairvoyant means.

Extra-ordinary ways of acting include;

Psychokinesis, that is the apparent ability to create physical effects without the use of any known physical process — as in spoon bending at a distance.

Out-of-body experiences, that is a sense of being able to leave one's body and view it from the outside — as often reported by persons who have been near death.

Healing, that is extra-ordinary abilities to cure ailments in cases where known medical procedures are unable to achieve results.

Common to all of these experiences is the challenge they represent to our perception of what is "normal". One of the purposes of this volume is to explore these experiences and discuss their implications for the perception of reality which prevails in the modern scientific world. But in the course of this attention is drawn to the fact that terms like "normal" or "usual" imply assumptions and meanings which presuppose a certain period of history or a certain culture. What is regarded as normal or usual in one period or culture, can be regarded as abnormal, unusual, or paranormal in another.

The term "paranormal" itself is most closely associated with the field of parapsychology. The boundaries of what are considered to be paranormal in that field have been strictly defined by para-psychologists. One of the contributors to this volume, Michael Thalbourne, has actually compiled a glossary of terms for use in parapsychology. Our desire is to broaden the debate and to include specialist areas other than parapsychology. This means the use of a wider definition of the term "paranormal" to include miraculous events as defined by religion, outstanding creativity viewed as "miraculous", and instances of what may be interpreted as collective delusion.

There is another way in which we can construe the paranormal. This is to think of it as referring to belief and experience which fall outside the explanatory ambit of current scientific thought, both popular and specialized. Such a definition would include areas such as astrology, numerology, Ufology, stories about missing ships and aircraft in the Bermuda Triangle, and various superstitions. As our definition of the paranormal does not extend as far as to include these, there is no discussion of these areas in the volume.

The study of paranormal beliefs and experiences can be app-roached from a number of academic disciplinary perspectives. These include psychology, philosophy, psychiatry, sociology, biology and anthropology. A second purpose of this volume is to overcome the fragmentation that has generally characterized research into the paranormal from these varied and disparate points of view. In particular we are concerned to build a bridge between prevailing scientific orientations and the study of the paranormal. We deem this important not only from the point of view of the possibility of shedding further light on areas of 'unusual experience' but also to provide an opportunity to review and question the adequacy of scientific method as presently understood.

At the same time we will take this opportunity to present ongoing research and current theoretical formulations. Needless to say we hope the juxtaposition of different points of view and disciplinary backgrounds in this volume will provide new ideas for readers whatever their stance on the question of the paranormal may be. As such we very much hope that the volume will open up new avenues for further investigation.

Right from the beginning this volume was envisaged as an interdisciplinary effort intended to stimulate discussion and dialogue between persons with different academic backgrounds and interests. The recent tendency to term 'unusual' capacities, experiences or beliefs as paranormal leads one to the view that the bulk of research and writing in the area has been done by parapsychologists. However, mention of the example of witchcraft as studied by anthropologists is sufficient to demonstrate that interest and expertise in the area extends well beyond the field of parapsychology. The awareness of this led to a decision by the editors to invite persons of varied backgrounds to contribute to the volume. As a result, we are able to bring together chapters written by philosophers, a psychoanalyst, a medical researcher, students of religion, sociologists, an anthropologist, as well as parapsychologists and psychologists.

In addition to tapping into the variety of skills offered by different specialists the book does not represent a 'party-line' on the validity or authenticity of paranormal claims and experiences. Indeed on the contrary, we looked for contributions from individuals on both sides of the paranormal debate. As it happens most of the chapters are from persons who accept the validity of some claims for paranormal claims and capacities. But skeptics figure in the volume, particularly in Section IV.

What is more, we are convinced that the best way of ensuring a fruitful debate between experts from such varied sources is to request authors to make their contributions accessible to the intelligent lay reader. In responding to this request the authors have sought to minimize, as far as possible, the use of specialist jargon. Needless to say, there is a large public of non-specialists out there including many who claim experience of the paranormal who may benefit from this.

Despite the somewhat bold ambitions and the inevitable limitations in size, we have been able to organize the contributions in such a way as to give the book an overarching coherence and structure. This has been achieved through dividing the book into four sections each of which has an editorial introduction. The first section entitled *Explaining the Paranormal* contains chapters which provide a general orientation to the subject. The second section entitled *Experiencing the Paranormal* looks at gateways through which access to paranormal experience can be obtained. The third section entitled *Researching the Paranormal* reports on different kinds of research which have a bearing on paranormal phenomena, experiences, and beliefs. Finally, the fourth section entitled *Debating the Paranormal* provides room for evaluation and argument concerning the authenticity and validity of claims for and against the paranormal.

Any division obviously contains some elements of arbitrary choice. The virtues of this particular way of organizing chapters in the volume is clear. It provides backbone and structure. Every single one of the diverse viewpoints represented finds a proper niche. Elements of arbitrariness inevitably persist, particularly in the assignment of the chapter to one or another of the sections. For example, not all the research papers in the volume have found their way into Section III. Stewart's research into Bigfoot sightings was located in Section IV because of the essential skeptical thrust of his line of argument and the contribution this makes to the overall debate in that section. Indeed, most chapters include some overview of research pertinent to the focus of their particular subject matter. There is overlap between the material in Sections I and IV. For example, all five chapters in Section I are concerned, to a greater or lesser extent, with discussion about assumptions underpinning various perspectives on the paranormal. Similar discussions about assumptions and their limitations are present in the contributions of Irwin, Flew, and Beloff in Section IV.

Some problems that becloud all reports of paranormal claims include the intrusion of deliberate trickery or fraud; the problem of coincidence or accident; and the problem of suggestibility. Our editorial opinion as to the weight and significance of all of these factors is divided. Zollschan and Schumaker present their views in their respective chapters. Walsh is of the view that not all paranormal claims can be accounted for by chance or illusion whether that illusion has its origin in sleight of hand, or mere psychological propensity. Several of our contributors discuss these problem areas from their own particular points of view in their respective chapters.

Many other issues surface in the course of the presentations included in the volume. The reader will note the contentiousness of these issues and the energy with which they are debated by the contributors. Behind all the points of contention in the book is an underlying issue. This concerns the relationship between science and the paranormal.

Science is about the study of regularities, that is to say, the study of events which are strictly repeatable. It appears to be in the nature of the paranormal to be sporadic, elusive, and unpredictable. On the assumption, which not all the editorial team shares, that some paranormal claims are valid, the possibility must be considered that historical rather than scientific methods are appropriate for accounting for their manifestations. Around the turn of the Century the German philosophers Windelbandt and Rickert argued that the social sciences, partly because of the alleged inherent lack of regularity of social events, would lend themselves to an historical approach. As yet, no agreed resolution has been found between those who advocate a view of the social sciences as generalising (that is as "science") or as particularising (that is as "history"). There exists the possibility that the argument that Windelbandt and Rickert made with respect to the social sciences may apply with even greater force to the study of the paranormal. In the end we should keep our minds open to the possibility that science may have relatively little to offer the study of the paranormal and to the viewpoint put by Tolstoy that science gives no answer to the only question that is important to us: "what shall we do and how shall we live".

SECTION I

EXPLAINING THE PARANORMAL

This section offers a number of frameworks for understanding paranormal belief and experience. They include the psychological, the philosophical, the psycho-historical, and the social. None of the five contributors in the section have any argument with the existence of paranormal phenomena. The issue which concerns them all is what is the best explanation of paranormal occurrences. Thus each chapter is concerned with implications of the study of the paranormal for established scientific procedures of investigation.

In Chapter 1, Charles Tart argues on the basis of contemporary psychological and anthropological findings that our very perception of the world is limited and shaped by a variety of filters. The limits thus imposed on mental functioning act as tacit assumptions about reality which have something of a self-fulfilling character. For science to cope with what are currently considered paranormal events these tacit and implicit forms of our knowing and grasping reality must be made explicit.

Stephen Braude, a philosopher who accepts the evidence for paranormal phenomena as being genuine, argues in Chapter 2 that individuals can influence the outcome of events by their intentions in a way that does not fit within the current assumptions of the physical or social sciences. In Braude's view, posing the hypothetical possibility for the existence of such a capacity provides a superior explanation of paranormal events than that provided by alternative formulations; in particular the notion that there can be backward causation in time.

Jule Eisenbud, a psychoanalyst, presents an historical overview of psychical research in Chapter 3. He is highly critical of a "kill the messenger" attitude toward reports of the paranormal which has prevailed in the sciences. In particular, he criticizes the failure to recognize the possible inadequacies of established scientific perspectives on causality and nature. This in turn has resulted in a failure to integrate the scientifically accepted view of man as revealed to him by his senses on the one hand, and a view of man as a creature of unexplained capacities and potentials as revealed by psychical research, on the other. Eisenbud argues that paranormal capacities are best studied using psychoanalytical rather than established para-psychological procedures.

The task of relating established science and the study of the paranormal is taken on more fully in Chapter 4 by George Zollschan. Zollschan seeks to locate the study of the paranormal in a philosophy of science by postulating an extension of Popper's three world thesis to a four world model. Particularly important in this chapter is Zollschan's discussion of creativity as comparable to paranormal experience. Like other contributors in the section, Zollschan wrestles with the problem of providing an explanatory framework in which both scientific method and matters which presently elude such method can be sensibly discussed. The Jewish mystical tradition provides some pointers for such a framework.

The final chapter in the section by Julie Howell questions assumptions implicitly made by social scientists when studying religious experience. Howell's criticism of prevailing social scientific approaches concerns the following assumptions: that there is an "objective" material world; that mind is generated by brain; that mind is an internal symbolic dialogue; and, finally, that minds can know only through the senses. In evaluating and rejecting each of these constraining assumptions, Howell opens up an opportunity for providing a radical alternative for investigating the paranormal in social life. In effect, she asserts that human experience can take place in ways other than through verbal and symbolic modes.

Looking at the group of chapters in this section as a whole, they appear akin to variations on a theme. In a nutshell, the theme is that current constraints on thought must be overcome in order to permit investigation of the full range of human capacities and experiences.

CHAPTER 1

HIDDEN SHACKLES: IMPLICIT ASSUMPTIONS THAT LIMIT FREEDOM OF ACTION AND INQUIRY

Charles T. Tart

Gautama Buddha taught (see, e.g., Goldstein & Kornfield, 1987) that a primary characteristic of life was suffering. Few have disputed this.

The Buddha also taught that this suffering was created by our ignorance, attachment, and aversion, and that most or all suffering could be overcome. To put it strongly, some *pain* is inevitable in life, but the *suffering* is optional.

To take this idea beyond an abstract ideal and begin to overcome the largely hidden shackles that constrict us and cause unnecessary suffering, we must examine the psychological nature of our lives. This chapter focuses on the negative, the constricted, mechanical nature of our lives, on the theory that clear diagnosis is helpful to working on a cure. We have many, largely implicit assumptions or habits of mind that unnecessarily constrict us: I will discuss the functioning of such implicit assumptions in general. Space limitations preclude discussion of specific assumptions common in our culture, but this can be found elsewhere (Tart, 1975a, or 1983a, chapter 2), as can some suggestions for working on cures after the diagnosis is made (Tart, 1986a). I have also kept the level of detail low in order to draw a general picture: documentation of most of the material in this chapter is available in most general texts on perceptual and cognitive psychology.

Understanding the effects of implicit (and explicit) assumptions on our experience and behavior is particularly important in studying the range of phenomena we loosely label the 'paranormal'. This book is aimed at a scientifically educated audience who, presumably, will evaluate the evidence for and against various aspects of the paranormal in a rational way. I have spent a great deal of time in my career doing this, as well as conducting experimentation in the area. That is, I have functioned as a scientist, dedicated to ideals of objectivity and rationality.

I have also functioned as a *psychologist* during this time, a student of my own and others' behavior and psychological processes.

'Unfortunately', I have found that almost none of the arguments between proponents and opponents of the paranormal are truly rational.
There are hidden assumptions, attitudes and emotional forces behind
the arguments on both sides that subvert the ostensible rationality of
the argument.[1] I characterized this above as 'unfortunate' in quotes. It
is unfortunate in many ways, but the widespread subversion of the
ostensibly rational, scientific process is, in another way, quite fortunate
if we let it remind us that we are dealing with much more important
issues than whether there are some anomalous communication and
action channels we do not yet understand scientifically, and *if* we then
try to expand our understanding in a way that does justice to the
emotional and spiritual needs we have as human beings.

The paranormal can indeed be the tip of the spiritual iceberg, as
many hope and many fear. Dealing irrationally with experimental
results about the paranormal when the real issue is often about our
spiritual nature is neither efficient nor genuinely scientific.

This chapter is an intellectual and psychological treatment about
the effects of hidden assumptions on us, primarily their cognitive
effects. It does not adequately deal with their emotional and spiritual
effects, as that would take several books in itself. Elsewhere I have
begun some of this expanded inquiry (Tart, 1970; 1972; 1975a; 1975b;
1977; 1979; 1981; 1983a; 1983b; 1983c; 1984; 1986a; 1986b; 1987).
Hopefully this chapter will help promote a personal and social
clarification of some issues.

While planning to deliver a lecture on the nature of the assumptions
we make as Westerners at a symposium some years ago, I thought I
would demonstrate how uncomfortable we are when people don't act
according to our assumptions by standing at the microphone after my
introduction and not saying a word for ten minutes. I found, however,
that while I could understand the importance of such a demonstration
in the privacy of my study, when I stood there with five hundred
people assuming I would talk, I couldn't stand it and started talking
after only one minute.

The importance of examining assumptions has become especially
clear to me because I have been involved in cutting edge areas of
research that have *forced* me to look at some of the assumptions we
make. I have been involved, for instance, in research on various
altered states of consciousness, where the mind temporarily works in a
quite different fashion than it ordinarily does. If we look closely at the
different patterns of functioning in altered states, we see that there are
different assumptions about the way the universe works being made
and different logics inherent in such states. Even though these altered
assumptions and logics may seem 'nonsensical', 'mystical', or 'weird'

from the viewpoint of our ordinary, consensus consciousness (Tart, 1986a), we nevertheless have to examine them.

My research on altered states has also forced me to look at Eastern thought as some of it has dealt with altered states of consciousness for hundreds of years, whereas it has been a largely ignored topic among western scientists. Although I cannot understand, much less literally believe everything I read about in Eastern writings, I take it as a valuable source of stimulation. But in trying to comprehend Eastern thought I constantly find myself thinking things like 'How can they possibly conclude something like that? What is behind that? This is ridiculous! Isn't this just primitive superstition?'

In particular, in 1973 and 1974 I put together a volume, *Transpersonal Psychologies* (Tart, 1975a or 1983a), in which I asked several authorities who were adept in various spiritual disciplines, to write about their spiritual/religious systems primarily as *psychologies* rather than as spiritual systems. I had to do a lot of editing of their chapters to harmonize styles, so I was immersed in the material. This constantly forced me to see different ways of looking at the world which did not make sense from my Western point of view. I knew my contributors were highly successful, intelligent people, but they kept writing the most nonsensical things! Since it was hard to believe that intelligent people believed enormous amounts of nonsense, I started examining the assumptions I was bringing to my editing. Enormous numbers of assumptions, largely implicit, came to the surface in this struggle.

What we will focus on in this chapter is the nature of knowledge and the nature of assumptions, and the role assumptions play in our everyday, as well as in our scientific life.

It is hard to adequately convey just how much implicit assumptions, hidden assumptions, hidden *shackles* control us. When I mentioned my *Transpersonal Psychologies* chapter on common Western assumptions to a colleague a few months after writing it, he naturally asked me what some of those assumptions were: to my embarrassment, I could not consciously remember a single one of them! I shall try to illustrate some of the problems that implicit assumptions create on both a personal and societal level and on a scientific level. I have also discussed these problems from a different perspective elsewhere (Tart, 1986a) as a Western perspective on the Indian idea that we live in *maya*, a state of illusions.

The Nature of Knowledge

What does it mean when I say I know something, 'I *know* X'? At a simple level, it might mean that I have had previous sensory experience with X. I have touched it, I have looked at it or heard or tasted it, I have been exposed to it previously. It might also mean, a little more complexly, that I recognize X as *familiar*, I have had a variety of experiences involving X. With more complexity, 'I know X' could mean not only that I am familiar with it but that I have put a mental or verbal label on X, representing it with a symbol. 'X is a hammer,' for example. Note that labeling is a satisfying cognitive act: at that point of labeling, curiosity and inquiry often stop. Once we have a name for something, we feel comfortable.

At a more advanced level, by saying 'I know X', I mean that I can recall how X has interacted with other things, how other things have affected it, so whenever I see X in similar conditions I can then make useful predictions about how X is going to react. I have seen unsupported objects drop numerous times, for example, and I am willing to predict from those observations that if I let go of some object that I have never tried letting go of before, it will fall.

We can take the sense of knowing something even further. In knowing X, we can mean that we have a mental symbol or representation of it and we can connect this symbol with other mental symbols or memories of experiences in novel ways. By saying 'I know X' I mean that I can reason about and logically extrapolate what may happen in a novel situation involving X, Y and Z, even though I have never observed X, Y and Z interacting before. This is what we call logical thinking. We use, as it were, an internal mental representation and some rules we have learned about what to do with these mental representations to transcend the limits of our actual experiences. Jean Piaget (1952), the well-known psychologist who studied cognitive development in children, called this ability *operational thinking*. Once we have symbols for various aspects of reality, we can use purely symbolic, logical kinds of operations to predict outcomes that transcend our specific previous experience. Operational thinking is a highly evolved form of human thought.

The most evolved form of operational thinking, according to Piaget, is called *reversibility thinking*. This is the ability to hypothetically consider any state along a continuum of possibility as potentially equal to any other state and to then return to that the same state from which the proposed operation began. That is, reversibility thinking is the ability to seriously, openly and logically consider *anything* with *all* of our inherent capacity.

For example, suppose I asked us to consider the optimal way to introduce widespread cannibalism of infants into society as a practical solution to the overpopulation problem. If we had our potential for reversibility thinking fully developed, we should be able to come up with several excellent, logical and practical schemes for achieving that goal. Whenever I ask people to think about this, however, I notice actions that suggest that no one is going to give that proposal any further thought! But in a fully developed human being, from this purely cognitive point of view, we ought to be able to think about *anything* with all our faculties. Then we ought to be able to come back, unaffected, to our starting point, to then say something like, 'All right, I've worked out a perfectly logical and creative plan to introduce infant cannibalism but in terms of my (unaltered) values and beliefs that is not something I would like to implement.' Then we should be able to drop the idea without in any sense being permanently changed as a result of thinking about it.

Hidden Assumptions

This is the point where we have to start considering assumptions. If we look up assumptions in various dictionaries, they will define it as the act of taking something for granted. We assume something is true. *It is not a matter of whether it actually is true or not*, we just simply assume that it is true. Before I step up on a lecture platform, for example, I implicitly assume that it is solid and will hold my weight. I almost never consciously think that its solidity is a *hypothesis* that I should check out empirically before I risk stepping on it, it is just an implicit assumption. Usually it works out.

Such implicit assumptions are legion and, as I will explain in greater detail below, they are not just *cognitive* assumptions. Many are also emotionally charged assumptions that result in strong explicit or implicit feelings about their topics. As well as cognitive and emotional assumptions, there are sensory assumptions that are built into the way we perceive the world around us. There are bodily assumptions built into the way we carry and move our bodies and into the postures we assume. All these assumptions that we take for granted, that we forget we are assuming, that have become just habitual, that have become implicit assumptions, are things that put severe limits on reversibility thinking. Pearce (1973; 1974) argues, rather convincingly, that while reversibility thinking becomes available by the time children are around eight or so years old, in most adults it is almost totally lost by the time they are twelve. That is, we no longer can think about *anything* with all our capacities; many topics are taboo. If we do happen to think about a taboo topic, we cannot just drop it afterwards and not be permanently changed by it, able to come back to our starting point.

Logics

Let us consider the following statement:

$$2 + 2 = 4$$

If I ask whether this statement is *true*, everyone would say it was. Why is it true? We tend to think it is true because that is the way the world is. After all, if we have two apples and add two more apples to them, we have four apples.

Actually $2 + 2 = 4$ because of assumptions. We assume certain things are true, we define certain operations for working with those assumptions as valid and we come up with a *logic*. We come up with a set of rules for how to think about things. The particular logic system used in this example is called arithmetic. Modern philosophy recognizes that *any* logic is a self-contained system. Whether something is logical in the system does not depend on how things function in the outside physical world.

It may matter on a practical, physical world level. If I came up with a system that said $2 + 2 = 5$, I may be able to logically justify it, but it won't be terribly useful in counting apples. But as a logic system we could justify it totally. The logical system of thought called Cabalistic Addition, for example, says that any time we have a two digit number, we add the two digits to get a single digit number because single digit numbers represent the real and hidden forces that rule the world. So if we want to add 8 and 5, first we add $8 + 5 = 13$, then we add the 1 to the 3 and get 4, the important answer. It is a perfectly logical system. It wouldn't be practical to apply to the counting of apples, because if I had eight apples in one hand and 5 in the other, it is going to be hard to convince me that I have 4 when we finish the counting operation. From one perspective, that just shows I am stuck in the surface layer of reality, unable to deal with the important aspects of life! So some logic systems seem better in terms of interpreting sensory experiences than others, but basically any logic, any system of rationality is based on simply assuming certain things about the nature of reality and how we validly operate on those things. Then *being logical* means that we follow the rules we have set in accordance with that.

Everyday Logic

I can explain the arbitrary nature of any logic, and we may intellectually follow the argument and agree with it, but in terms of our everyday behavior, this is not the way we function.

Figure 1 is a diagram from my *States of Consciousness* illustrating a concept psychologists call the naive view of perception and, by analogy, the naive view of thinking. For our purposes here, I will refer to it as the implicit operating assumption for how we ordinarily deal with the world. It assumes that there is a real world out there, a cat in this case. There are real light waves that send the stimuli into our eyes and hence to our brains. Inside our minds (which are generally assumed to be 'inside' our brains) we get faithful reproductions of whatever there is in the outside world. This is the operating assumption we make: just about every time we look at anything in the world around us, we see it in accurate detail.

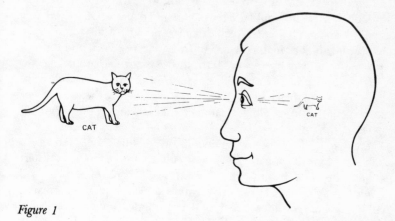

Figure 1

Now the basic operating assumption of the naive view of perception has a corollary. If we start thinking about how we get to the truth or improve our knowledge, the corollary is that knowledge is external to us, waiting to be discovered outside us. If we want to see what is around the corner, the obvious and logical thing to do is to walk around the corner and look. We will get there, we will see what it is, we will get a clear representation in our mind. The same kind of operating assumption applies by analogy to thinking. We all tend to implicitly assume that there is *a* logical way of rationally thinking. Our neighbors don't always think that logical way, they are illogical sometimes, especially on subjects like politics. But basically there is a single right way to think and if we simply apply that right way of thinking to problems, we are going to solve those problems and come up with reasonable answers.

These views are too simplistic and misleading in vital ways. Perception does not take place in this simple minded way, and there is no simple, given logic, such that if we just think according to the inherently correct rules we are bound to arrive at *the* truth. We have an immense amount of psychological data showing that the processes of perception and thinking are considerably more complicated.

Human Potentials

The findings of anthropology are of great value in helping to liberate us from the unnecessary limitations of the naive view of perception and thinking. We come into this world as human beings and that means there is a wide spectrum of potentials that *could* be developed. Many of us, when we were born, had the *potential* to run a four minute mile, to speak Chinese, to learn to cook well, to be 'possessed' by friendly spirits who would teach us songs and dances to share with our friends, and even master really exotic and 'mystical' accomplishments, like higher mathematics. But we were not born and did not grow up in isolation, we were born into a particular culture.

For our purposes we can define a culture as a group of people who, in the course of their history, have come to recognize the existence of some (but far from all) human potentials. Among those human potentials that they know about, they define some of them as good. There is an active encouragement of those potentials. When you are a baby and look at your mother in our culture, for example, and start saying the sound 'ma', that sound gets a lot of smiles and reinforcement. There are other potentials known about in a particular culture that are considered bad. When your little baby starts throwing the carrots all over the place, he is not as likely to get all those smiles and 'Good baby, Mommy loves you' reinforcements. Thus a culture ends up actively cultivating some potentials and actively inhibiting others because it does not want them to be developed. These cultivated potentials, in so far as they become habitual, in so far as they become automatic, act as implicit assumptions.

Figure 2, also taken from my *States of Consciousness* (Tart, 1975; 1983) is a schematic of the enculturation process in more detail. We will focus here on the little dots which represent human potentials we come into the world with: there were a multitude of them and they were relatively unorganized. Through the influence of our parents and later our teachers and peers, some of those potentials were developed, some of them were lost. As we became adults they gradually became systematically organized.[2] When we get old the potentials become disorganized, especially if we accept our Western cultural myth that we are supposed to get senile just because we are old. The point is we have lost many of the potentials we were born with, perhaps permanently. Some other potentials have remained as latent possibilities. The developed potentials become taken for granted, they become the implicit assumptions that have us in their power.

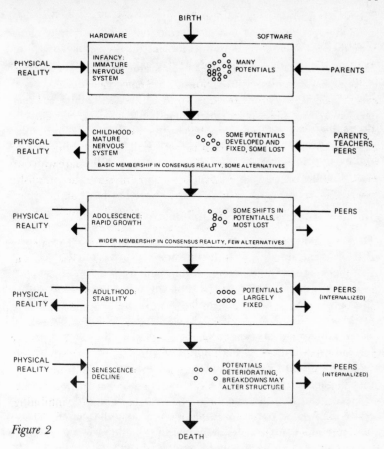

Figure 2

Let us look further into the idea of *implicitness* of assumptions.

In practicing science we make many assumptions, but we try to make them *consciously*. We might assume, for instance, that all processes in the universe are symmetrical. Then it follows that if we observe a positive particle resulting from some reaction, we ought to see a negative particle if we look for it. *If an assumption is conscious, we have the power to test and see if it leads to useful outcomes.* On a more everyday level, if I consciously assume that the tabletop I am writing on is solid, then it follows that if I bang my hand down on it I will feel a certain kind of sensation, and if I bang it really hard it will be painful. I can bang my hand down on it now at various speeds and test the consequences of my assumption. Ouch! It works quite well!

When an assumption becomes implicit, once it falls below the level of consciousness, it may continue to affect our behavior. But it affects it in a way such that we probably never test it. An acquaintance once recounted a wonderful example of this. He was in a cafe once and wanted to get out on the attractive terrace he could see through large windows. He spent several minutes looking unsuccessfully for a door, because the large glass structures he had at first thought were doors would not open. He pushed and pulled to no avail. He was ready to leave when someone finally came from the terrace, and he realized the glass structures were *sliding* doors. If our experiences have been with doors that push open or pull open and that perceptual and motoric habit/assumption becomes implicit, we can become trapped by a sliding door. Unless circumstances happen to jolt us out of that assumption.

Implicit, Automatized Assumptions Are Dangerous

Here is another example that you can try out as an exercise. Assume that life is meaningless, that the universe was just created by chance, that there is really no inherent meaning in life, that there is no point looking for meaning. Try to hold this attitude constantly as you go through an ordinary day. You will probably find that it is 'true'! The world will give you multitudes of events every day. Most of them won't seem connected in any way and if you don't make the effort of looking for patterns within it, if you hold on to your *experimental* assumption that there is no inherent meaning in things, things will indeed seem meaningless. You will be 'right'.[3]

Here we are making a *conscious experiment* of holding and studying the effects of an assumption. But many of the assumptions we already have were not conscious decisions on our part, they were forced on us in the course of enculturation by parents, society and life events, and they have become implicit, non-conscious. Our parents may have passed on assumptions about the meaninglessness of life, for example, and we may experience many meaningless events. Because that's the way the world is, or because of our assumptions? If we don't realize we are operating on the basis of multiple assumptions, we can't test them.

I have known some people, for instance, whose personality dynamics were such that although they complained a lot about suffering they actually got important secondary gains out of it. I have always been amazed at the number of tragedies the world seems to bring to their lives. They get far more than their fair share of tragedies! They do things that, in subtle (and sometimes not so subtle) ways, affect their world in a way that is going to validate their tragic assumptions, yet they seem to have no idea that they are doing a lot to create the world they experience.

Implicit assumptions are dangerous. That is the main theme of this chapter. When an assumption becomes implicit, so we don't know we are making it, then we forget to test (and retest and retest) it to see how well it continues to work. Then we are slaves to that assumption.

Another way of saying this is that our views and assumptions become *automatized*. They become automatic machinery that is operating in the background of everything we do, slanting our perceptions, decisions, and actions (Deikman 1966; 1976a; 1976b). In learning something initially we had to learn all the steps of the process consciously. The first time we learned how to ride a bicycle, for instance, we had to pay a lot of attention to what we were doing. There were many separate skills we had to learn and integrate. Once we learned to ride, we almost never think about all those component skills. We just get on a bicycle and start riding, with all the requisite skills operating automatically. In fact, it gets to the point, where its extremely difficult to *de*automatize them.

Deautomatization can be done. We can with effort break down our automatic patterns, rediscover what the steps are, what are the assumptions we are making. But it is not easy. Psychotherapy, for instance, illustrates how great efort must often be applied to uncover and deautomatize assumptive patterns that are making our lives miserable.

The Complexity of Perception: Constructing a World

Let us go back to the question of perceiving and thinking and take a more realistic view of what is actually going on that the earlier, naive view of Figure 1 showed. Figure 3 schematizes the process, given our present psychological knowledge. This diagram is much more detailed than the naive view, yet hardly begins to cover the true complexity of everything we know about perception.

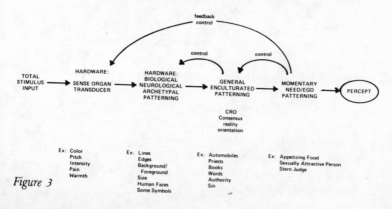

Figure 3

First a stimulus reaches our sense organs. Our sense organs are transducers to turn the energy of sound, light, pressure, etc., into nerve impulses, a form of energy that our nervous systems can process. In a sense, certain 'assumptions' are built into our sense organs. The eye, for instance, imposes limits on what we can see. It is sensitive to a very small portion of the electromagnetic spectrum. We can't see infrared, we can't see ultraviolet light. That puts limits on us right at the beginning of the perceptual process, limits that are going to affect the way we perceive and think about the world. Those may be generally useful limits. If the eye were more sensitive to infrared, for instance, we might not have as good visual acuity as we do now because we would start seeing a haze in our visual field, due to the heat of our own bodies. Useful or not, the important point is that there are assumptions built into sensory processing. Here we have an assumption that the 'visual' part of the electromagnetic spectrum is more important than the infrared part. That is not always true, of course: infrared vision would be helpful in the dark.

Our visual system is useful to illustrate assumptions that are, to use a popular computer analogy, 'hardwired'. Color, for example, is something that gets accentuated in the eye by the physical structure of the eye itself. We would perceive and think about a different world if we saw only black and white. Edges of things are perceived more readily than their surfaces: there are neurological mechanisms in the eye and visual system that enhance contrast. Angles are more likely to be perceived under difficult seeing conditions. All this selectivity is happening totally automatically, we have no control over it. These are assumptions built into being a human being. We can do something about these limits if we know something about them, either through instrumental aids or training ourselves, but they ordinarily have a totally implicit influence on us.

The nerves from our sensory organs go to brain areas that are also hardwired. Certain assumptions about the optimal way to process a certain kind of signals are built in. If we watch what newborn infants look at in a varied stimulus environment, for example, we will find they spend a lot more time looking at human faces or objects resembling faces than at any other kind of objects. This is not the result of prior experience with faces, but the hardwired assumption that human faces are a lot more important than anything else in the environment. This is an adaptive assumption in most cases, but nevertheless it is a bias. As another example, visual information is processed so it appears as background and foreground. That is actually a sophisticated processing of information. We didn't realize how sophisticated it was until we tried to create artificial intelligence programs to try to tell a machine how to distinguish foreground and background! But it is done automatically for us as a hardwired assumption.

The Enculturation of Perception

Beyond the hardwired assumptions affecting perception, we find what I am calling the general enculturated patterning of information processing. This is the way we have been conditioned and taught to readily and automatically perceive certain things that the culture values and to be less sensitive or perhaps even almost blind to things that a culture doesn't value. For example, in the area of speech we quickly learn to pay considerable attention to certain kinds of speech sounds that are prominent in the language of the people around us and we don't pay much attention to other speech sounds. The way we find this out, to our disappointment, is when we try to learn a foreign language as an adult and find it difficult to just hear differences in sound between various words in that language.

Our culture assumes that certain kinds of stimuli are important and teaches us the immediate recognition it considers important. When we see something with four wheels, a windshield, a top, and a pair of headlights, we usually don't sit there and consciously think 'Four wheels . . . a windshield . . . headlights . . . Hmmm, could it be a tractor? No, tractors don't usually have windshields, it must be something else . . .' We recognize it *immediately*, automatically, as an automobile. This is a part of our learned perceiving that has been totally automated. This automated, instant perception goes on to handle much more complex percepts, so we might instantly recognize a priest, or someone who is 'obviously' an authority, or a 'sinner'. Such experiences are actually complex judgements, based on interlocking sets of assumptions, but they have become so automated and so fast, that to us they seem like simple perceptions.

The Consensus Reality Orientation

Ronald Shor (1959; 1962; also in Tart, 1969, pp. 239–256), theorizing about the nature of hypnosis, created a useful conceptualization of this aspect of our minds. He postulated that there was a *generalized reality orientation*, the *GRO*, always active in the background of our mind. We are seldom aware of it explicitly. In a sense, everything we have been taught about is readily available in the background; it is seldom obvious to ordinary consciousness, but it is always there to interpret whatever happens to us. Stimuli that reach us call up the relevant aspects of this learned set of knowledge/assumptions. It is because the

GRO is there that we can recognize things immediately, know the appropriate things to do and so forth. In various altered states the GRO fades into relative non-functionality, thus allowing experience to take on new, unusual qualities. The functioning of the GRO and the automatic allegiance we give to it is what Castaneda (1971; 1972) reports his teacher don Juan as calling *doing*.

I have found it necessary to modify Shor's concept, as he wasn't adequately recognizing the limits imposed by being enculturated in a *particular* culture. In Figure 3 I've called it the *consensus reality orientation*, the *CRO*. The CRO is that pattern of immediately available information, interpretations, perceptions, labels, emotional reactions and so forth that was created by and fits the particular culture we were raised in, the culture's consensus as to what is important.[4] If we were raised in a puritanical culture, for example, we could 'perceive' sin at the drop of a hat. It is important to emphasize how much this process is experienced as simple *perception* of the way the world *is*, rather than as the complex set of judgements, based on implicit assumptions, that it is.

There are practical limits to the arbitrariness of cultural construction of perception with regard to perceiving physical reality: we have to survive in the physical world. Since most of our time as adults is spent in a complex social world, however, rather than dealing with basic physical reality, the usual world of our experience can be a quite arbitrarily constructed one. I have dealt with this at length in terms of its psychological cost under the concept of *consensus trance* (Tart, 1986a).

There is still another important class of factors determining the construction of our perceptions, namely the immediate need state of our egos. If we are hungry and we take a walk around the block, we are much more likely to notice the restaurants than the shoe repair shops. It is just the opposite if we need our shoes repaired. If we are sexually needy, we are much more likely to notice that someone is 'really' sexually attractive (and perhaps 'provocative') to us than if we are not sexually needy.

To summarize the perceptual process, then, there is an enormous range of input that comes in from the world around us, including that from other people. It is narrowed down immediately by the characteristics (hardwired assumptions) of our sensory receptors. It is narrowed down further to reflect our culture's assumptions about the world by the CRO process. Then it is often further narrowed to what is relevant to our needs of the moment. This tiny fraction of the original data reaching us is what we will perceive as what we naively think is what is 'really' happening. But perception is actually a semi-arbitrary construction of *hypotheses*, given a set of assumptions, about what is out there, based on our particular life histories.

Dealing with the Known and the Unknown

The automatized, implicit, semi-arbitrary construction of perception can be quite useful when we are dealing with the *known*. If my wife sends me to the store to buy a loaf of rye bread, it is useful to me that I have automated, implicit processes that let me recognize a loaf of rye bread instantly when I see it on the shelf, buy it and go home, instead of being in the store and thinking 'bread, that's an oblong thing', so I look around for oblong things (of which there are many), but then remember, 'Bread is usually wrapped, in cellophane, so it has got to be oblong things, wrapped, with shiny highlights on the surface.' We can go on and on. When dealing with the known, *when dealing with the things we have been prepared for, automatization can be a marvelous labor saving device*. When dealing with the unknown, changes that we are not prepared for, automated processes can be maladaptive.

After we perceive something, we think about it. Let us look at basic thinking, schematized in Figure 4. I have shown sequential or associative thinking. We think about one thing, that leads us to an intermediate deduction, which in turn leads to a further deduction and so forth. I have drawn heavy arrows to indicate the *probable* way our thoughts are liable to go, from whatever the perceived input problem is to the first deduction, to the next deduction, etc., to the final conclusion we reach. At just about every step in such a thinking process there are alternative ways we *could* think about the situation, alternative memories we *could* draw on in understanding it. But given our conditioning and enculturation, we are likely to think of certain kinds of things and unlikely to think of other kinds of things. If I say what is the first word that comes into your mind when I say 'Red' I would guess that you probably would respond with some kind of color as an association, or some familiar object that is red colored. You probably wouldn't come up with an association of, say, 'Shoe heels.' We give psychological word association tests of common words, and if we get many unlikely associations, we are likely to wonder if the testee is 'mentally ill' or otherwise 'deviant'.

So in any thinking process there are many steps where we can go off in a different, culturally unlikely way: that direction could lead to another unusual direction at the next step, and we might come to an unusual (by our cultural standards) conclusion, or decide that the outcome we reached wasn't useful. But, given our cultural conditioning and the assumptions about what makes sense, what is

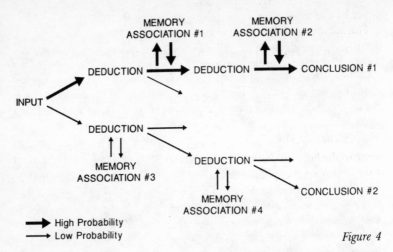

Figure 4

appropriate, 'sane', 'logical' to think about, our responses are likely to be 'normal', predictable.

If we look at the whole thinking process, then, we start out with constructed sensory inputs (a culturally biased way of perceiving) to some kind of situation (formulated in terms of biased, cultural norms). We don't understand or know how to deal with the situation, so we consult our memories of our previous experiences and knowledge (themselves culturally biased). If the situation is still not clear we try to get more information, we take another look. Again we are selectively perceiving: the box labeled 'input processing' in the figure refers to those automated assumptions, the CRO, that give us only a fraction of our knowledge, a fraction that, by cultural standards, is supposed to be relevant. By the time we go on to finally evaluate something in a way that 'makes sense', we are recapitulating, in many ways, the selections of our culture as to what is good, what is sensible, what is human.

This is why Pearce (1973; 1974) claims that the capacity for *reversibility thinking* is practically totally inhibited in most people by the time they reach their teens, as we discussed earlier. The capacity for reversibility thinking develops early. Children are capable of operational thinking by the age of 5 or 6, and beginning to develop their capacity for reversibility thinking. So that is the time we start their formal 'education' to thoroughly train them about what is (by our standards) *important* to think about and what is *bad* and what is *crazy*, lest they sit around and daydream or get involved in 'weird', anti-social ideas. By the time most kids are in their early teens, most of the assumptions of the culture have not only been transmitted to them, they have largely become automated. Many teenagers rebel, of course, at least in our society, but they often rebel along lines implicitly laid down by the particular assumptions of our culture.

Thus assumptions that have become implicit block our ability to think in a completely open manner, impairing our problem solving ability. There is a classic demonstration of this in an old psychology experiment. Imagine you are in a small room with two ropes hanging from the ceiling. There is nothing else in the room but a table in the corner. On the table is a hammer and a bag of nails. Your task is to tie the two ropes together.

You grab one rope and try to walk over to get the other, but you come to the end of your reach and find you can't quite reach the other rope. If you are like people who tried this before, there are all sorts of things you can then do. You can try reaching for the other rope with your foot, or you can try a running start. You can drag the table to a spot between the ropes and stand on it, but find you still can't reach it. In fifteen minutes to half an hour, most people never find a way to tie the two ropes together.

Some people will pick up the hammer and a nail and make semi-conscious pounding motions: they obviously want to hit the nail with the hammer, but that is of no use in tying the ropes together, no matter how satisfying it might be to hammer a nail!

The solution to the problem is a matter of overcoming a common assumption. The assumption is that a hammer is something you pound nails with. This is true: a hammer *is* something you can pound nails with, but a hammer is more than that. A hammer is a *weight*: if you have a weight and a rope, you can make a *pendulum*. Then the solution is simple. You tie the hammer on to the end of one rope, start it swinging, run over and grab the other rope and as the first one swings back, grab it and then tie the two ropes together. What you have to overcome is a lifetime of conditioning/assuming that a hammer is what you drive nails with.

The Active Nature of Assumptions

As I discussed assumptions so far, there has been one major element lacking. My analogies have tended to represent our assumptions as sort of passively lying arund, waiting for a particular stimulus situation to come along before anything happens. This is not the case: our minds are not sitting around passively waiting for something to come along to give them something to think about. Anyone who has ever sat down and watched his or her own mind for five minutes will realize that the ordinary mind is a three ring circus. There are at least three acts going on, some of them are subtle, some not so subtle; acts get changed, sometimes every few seconds; some of them happen faster than we can adequately watch. Our minds are hardly passive. Our ordinary minds, in one way, are constantly searching for input, trying to keep fear and anxiety at bay on the one hand and entertain themselves on the other.

As a part of that searching for entertainment, we may go out and find compatible companions or find tasks to do and keep ourselves constantly busy. This is a common pattern in our society today, to keep constantly busy so that there is never a 'dull moment'. Indeed, our culture offers more opportunity for distraction than has ever existed before. If we can't find external things to keep us busy, we usually generate fantasies to keep the busyness up. 'The next time I see so and so I am going to say such and such to her and that is just going to impress her!' 'Wait until I tell this joke to somebody.' Or, if we have a more depressive bent, we can think about catastrophes that are likely to occur. And on and on it goes.

Our capacity for operational thinking, unfortunately, frequently gets used in the service of generating fantasies, probably a lot more than it gets used solving real problems. We keep our minds constantly active that way. Since our fantasies reflect the consensus reality of the world we have been enculturated into, we exercise our assumptions and keep them fresh.

An Unsurprising Life in an Unsurprising World?

The long term result of enculturation and the automatization of assumptions can be represented by a 'wheel of life' diagram, as shown in Figure 5. The central wheel represents a person, the little geometrical figures around the rim of the wheel represent relatively permanent kinds of structures or assumptions, a readiness to perceive reality in certain prestructured ways, to act in certain prestructured ways, to experience in certain prestructured ways. The wheel does not have a solid rim, there are gaps in it for experience to come in, and when experience comes in, it tends to activate particular assumptions so that we think about them, experience them, and act on them in an approved way. These interlocking assumptions and reactions represent what our personality or our ordinary state of consciousness is.

This wheel of our being rolls on through life. But what life? Life is not lived in isolation, it is lived within the consensus reality that surrounds us, it is lived in a culture.

What is a culture? In an important way, a culture is a set of *prearranged* incidents, a culture is a conspiracy against change, against surprise. A culture is a situation in which, ideally, we can depend on

Figure 5

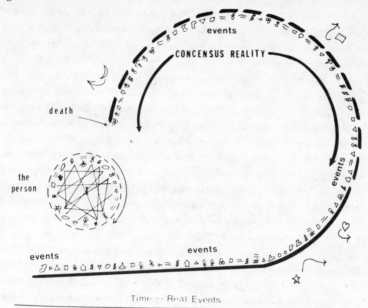

people and 'trust' people. What does trust people mean? It means that they won't do anything totally unexpected. It means that they are as rigidly enculturated and conditioned as you are and react in predictable ways. We may not like what they do, but their actions are not outside the range of what we are prepared to perceive.

So while I drew time's arrow in Figure 5, I have shown the culture, as curling back on itself in a sense, to represent the mutual conspiracy in a culture to eliminate change.

Look carefully at the symbols that are in this wheel representing the personality and those representing culture. In this idealized situation, nothing happens out in the culture that we are not prepared for. That is we already have psychological structures, sets of assumptions, built in to handle any situation that we are going to need in life. This is a way of viewing the recurring fantasies people have about the 'good old days', when everybody was supposedly happy and functioned well in society because everybody knew their place and stayed in it: that is, the cultural conspiracy against change and the unknown was supposed to have worked.

As a small demonstration of the power of consensus reality, I once showed this slide at a lecture but had deliberately misspelled consensus as 'concensus'. It made many people uncomfortable. Couldn't a learned professor spell correctly?

At this point, if you have gotten the feeling that I may not be talking about people but about robots or automatons, that is a good feeling to get. I won't push the analogy too far here (but see my *Waking Up*, 1986a) but enormous amounts of data from modern psychology indicate that, by and large, we are like robots in too many ways. A situation comes along, we perceive it through constructed, conditioned structures/assumptions and associations, and reactions are automatically called up that involve further, largely implicit assumptions, and, in a very real sense, we have a *mechanical* reaction to things.

So we can almost leave *consciousness* out of this particular model. I find it vital to put it back in, but that is a crucial developmental task we do not have space to discuss here, not something that just happens by itself (Tart, 1986a). But in a too real sense, most of our reactions are automated, conditioned, habitual. Most of the time we are operating on implicit assumptions in a deterministic, mechanical way, and it is hard to do much about it. This mechanicalness is, I believe, what is meant by the Indian concept of *maya* or the Buddhist concept of living in *samsara*, 'living in illusion'. We live in a small, too constricted version of what we could be as human beings. The task and adventure of enlarging our reality is the realm of psychological and spiritual growth, a topic too vast to go into in this chapter. Hopefully this understanding of the mechanicalness of the human condition will be of use in inspiring some to transcend the hidden shackles that imprison us. If we do not, we will continue to suffer needlessly, for in spite of any culture's attempts to avoid surprises, reality is matter of continual change.

Footnotes

1. Lest the reader who identifies strongly with his or her own rationality be offended by this statement, I do not exempt myself from such irrationality: indeed, I usually assume there are irrational and a-rational factors influencing my ideas and actions and try to find out what they are in order to compensate for and adequately work with them. I recognize the appropriateness of other factors than cold rationality (see Tart, 1986a), but try not to confuse them with it.
2. I was tempted when creating this diagram of adulthood to draw it as a square, but I thought that would be pushing the analogy just a little bit too hard!
3. If you do this experiment and find it too depressing, try the opposite one of assuming there is meaning in every event on another day to cheer yourself up. But realize you may be primarily seeing the results of your assumptions, not the true nature of reality.
4. We will treat culture as relatively homogenous here, but certainly complexities are introduced by subcultural variations as well as deviations from enculturation norms in individual families.

References

Castaneda, C. (1971), *A Separate Reality: Further Conversations with don Juan*. New York: Simon & Schuster.

Castaneda, C. (1972), *Journey to Ixtlan: The Lessons of don Juan*. New York: Simon & Schuster.

Deikman, A. (1966), De-automatization and the mystic experience. *Psychiatry*, *29* 329-343.

Deikman, A. (1976a), Bimodal consciousness and the mystic experience. In P. Lee, R. Ornstein, D. Galin, A Deikman, & C. Tart, *Symposium on Consciousness*. New York: Viking. pp. 67-88.

Deikman, A. (1976b), *Personal Freedom: On Finding Your Way to the Real World*. New York: Grossman.

Goldstein, J. & Kornfield, J. (1987), *Seeking the Heart of Wisdom: The Path of Insight Meditation*. Boston: Shambhala.

Pearce, J. (1973), *The Crack in the Cosmic Egg*. New York: Simon & Schuster.

Pearce, J. (1974), *Exploring the Crack in the Cosmic Egg*. New York: Julian Press.

Piaget, J. (1952), *The Origins of Intelligence in Children*. New York: International Universities Press.

Shor, R. (1959), Hypnosis and the concept of the generalized reality orientation. *American Journal of Psychotherapy*, *13*, 582-602.

Shor, R. (1962), Three dimensions of hypnotic depth. *International Journal of Clinical and Experimental Hypnosis*, *10*, 23-38.

Tart, C. (Ed.) (1969), *Altered States of Consciousness: A Book of Readings*. New York: Wiley.

Tart, C.T. (1970), Transpersonal potentialities of deep hypnosis. *J. Transpersonal Psychology*, *2*, 27-40.

Tart, C.T. (1972), States of consciousness and state-specific sciences. *Science*, *176*, 1203-1210.

Tart, C.T. (Ed.) (1975a), *Transpersonal Psychologies*. New York: Harper & Row.

Tart, C.T. (1975b), Samsara: a psychological view. In T. Tulku (Ed.), *Reflections of Mind*. Emeryville, California: Dharma Press. pp. 53-68.

Tart, C.T. (1977), Beyond consensus reality: Psychotherapy, altered states of consciousness, and the cultivation of awareness. In O.L. McCabe (Ed.), *Psychotherapy and Behavior Change: Trends, Innovations and Future Directions*. New York: Grune & Stratton. pp. 173-187.

Tart, C.T. (1979), Science and the sources of value. *Phoenix: New Directions in the Study of Man*, *3*, 25-29.

Tart, C.T. (1981), Transpersonal realities or neurophysiological illusions? Toward a dualistic theory of consciousness. In R. Valle & R. von Eckartsberg (Eds.), *The Metaphors of Consciousness*. New York: Plenum pp. 199-222.

Tart, C.T. (Ed.) (1983a), *Transpersonal Psychologies*. El Cerrito, California: Psychological Processes. (reprint of 1975 edition).

Tart, C.T. (1983b), Initial integrations of some psychedelic understandings into everyday life. In L. Grinspoon & J. Bakalar (Eds.), *Psychedelic Reflections*. New York: Human Sciences Press. pp . 223-233.

Tart, C.T. (1983c), The controversy about psi: two psychological theories. *J. Parapsychology*, *46*, 313-320.

Tart, C.T. (1984), Acknowledging and dealing with the fear of psi. *Journal of the American Society for Psychical Research*, *77* 133-143.

Tart, C.T. (1986a), *Waking Up: Overcoming the Obstacles to Human Potential*. Boston: New Science Library.

Tart, C.T. (1986b), Psychics' fear of psychic powers. *Journal of the American Society for Psychical Research*, *80*, 279–292.

Tart, C.T. (1987), Altered states of consciousness and the possibility of survival of death. In J. Spong (Ed.), *Consciousness and Survival: An Interdisciplinary Inquiry into the Possibility of Life Beyond Biological Death*. Sausalito, California: Institute of Noetic Sciences. pp.27–56

CHAPTER 2
EVALUATING THE SUPER-PSI HYPOTHESIS

Stephen E. Braude

Introduction

For the past few years, I have been urging that we take seriously what some call the *super-psi hypothesis* (e.g. Braude, 1986, 1987). Both abstract and empirical considerations suggest that psi-functioning in human beings may be considerably more extensive and controllable than its laboratory manifestations make it appear to be. Indeed, there are good reasons for thinking that psi might play a pervasive role in everyday affairs, and that it might operate on a very large scale. Not surprisingly, many have opposed this point of view, and their resistance has occasionally been as fascinating as the issues themselves. Sometimes dissenters marshall arguments so transparently weak that one can't help but think their opposition is motivated by more than mere intellectual disagreement. Nevertheless, the major objections at least raise interesting issues concerning the substance of the super-psi hypothesis and its proper means of evaluation. In this paper, I shall address these arguments and issues, and thereby attempt to clarify further the super-psi hypothesis.

Sketch of the Hypothesis

Every so often one will catch parapsychologists speculating on the possibility of extremely refined or highly sophisticated psi, or psi on a grand scale. And usually, they refer to this as *super-psi*. For example, the literature on survival often surveys the merits of so-called super-psi explanations. These are intended to account for the evidence for survival in terms of seemingly virtuosic psi on the part of living agents (e.g., Eisenbud, 1983, chapt. 14; Gauld, 1982). Another type of super-psi explanation has been offered in connection with the evidence for precognition. If one — plausibly — rejects the possibility of retrocausation, then ostensible precognitions can be interpreted in terms of ordinary forward causation and very high-level ESP or PK (Braude, 1986, 1987; Eisenbud, 1982).

Of course, it is far from clear what the term 'super-psi' is supposed to mean. But that is hardly surprising; it is not clear what 'super' means. As with other normative terms, it can be used loosely and apparently relativistically. What is super for one person may not be for another. Nevertheless, some fundamental features of the concept of super-psi are fairly easy to pin down. Initially, one might think that 'super-psi' denotes large-scale paranormal events. But in fact, most would agree that large-scale psi effects may not be instances of super-psi. The exceptions tend to be cases involving the transitivity of causes. For example, a very small psi event might initiate a causal chain that terminates in a very big effect, and that might or might not count as a case of super-psi. Hence, our classification of the case is not simply a function of event-magnitude. Rather, it has to do with matters of control and refinement.

Consider an analogy. Suppose that, while walking along a mountain ridge, I unwittingly dislodge a small stone which falls down the mountain side onto a railroad track, derailing a train that just happened to be passing along at that time. In virtue of causal transitivity, it is correct to say that *I* caused the train to derail. But nothing I did was impressive. The derailment is not something I achieved, or for which I could be held culpable. All I did was to dislodge a stone, and even that was unintentional. By contrast, suppose that I *wanted* to derail the oncoming train, and that to accomplish that end I threw a nearby stone the great distance onto the track below, at just the exact position and the exact time necessary to derail the train. Now that *would* be an achievement, and it would be analogous to at least one conceivable type of super-psi, in which a small psi effect is cunningly or expertly calculated or coordinated to have a large-scale result. Suppose, for instance, that I managed to cause an apparently precognized mine collapse by paranormally affecting a very small section of the mine support system, which I clairvoyantly determined to be that system's sole weak link.

Of course, it might also be super-psi if I paranormally produced a massive shock wave that collapsed the mine and surrounding mountain, even if the shock wave was a non-directed PK-effect (a kind of uncontrolled psychokinetic flailing about), and the mine just happened to collapse as a result. Hence, super-psi could conceivably be large-scale and unrefined. Furthermore, it could also be small-scale and refined. Suppose, for example, that one's business competitor used ESP to steal a vital secret formula, or that he used PK to erase nothing but that formula from the competition's paperwork and computer discs. If these achievements count as instances of super-psi (as claimed by many), it would be in virtue of their precision and accuracy.

Hence, it seems that super-psi is either psi of an exquisitely-controlled or refined nature, or else psi of great magnitude (whether refined or not). Of course, this definition remains (inevitably) somewhat vague. It will not help us conclusively to classify certain types of frequently reported phenomena. For example, some might question whether object levitations or materializations of the sort reported in the turn-of-the-century mediumistic literature are large-scale or refined enough to qualify as instances of super-psi. They might consider such phenomena to be impressive, but reserve the honorific term 'super-psi' for something even more outstanding. (One might wonder, however, whether there are *any* plausible criteria for regarding psi phenomena as substantially more outstanding than, say, a lifelike materialization.) In any case, borderline cases are to be expected, and should not prevent us from dealing profitably with some important and interesting issues.

Consider, first, the reasons for taking seriously the possibility of super-psi, if only as a mere working hypothesis. Since I have explored these reasons in detail elsewhere (Braude, 1986, 1987), I shall now merely outline them very briefly. To begin with, the theoretical alternatives to super-psi sometimes pose problems of a far more serious nature. With regard to precognition, for example, the only possible types of psi explanations are, on the one hand, the retrocausal analysis, and on the other, what Eisenbud calls the 'active' analysis (i.e., in terms of refined ESP and PK). But since the retrocausal analysis seems to be deeply unacceptable for several reasons (Braude, 1986, Eisenbud, 1982), and since the active analysis does comparatively little damage to our received scientific or broader conceptual framework, the only alternative psi explanation will require an appeal to super-psi. Similarly, a super-psi explanation may be the only way to avoid the conceptual errors of the retrocausal and observation–theoretic accounts of PK experiments with pre-recorded targets (Braude, 1979, 1988). Furthermore, an appeal to super-psi may lend an unrivalled degree of systematicity to our understanding of certain sets of events, events that would otherwise remain mysterious, unexplained, or simply unrelated (Eisenbud, 1970, 1982, 1983). Although we may not be *forced* to appeal to super-psi in such cases (unlike those just mentioned), we cannot, in the interest of explanatory adequacy, neglect that option.

A more abstract reason for taking super-psi seriously has (like others) been articulated by Eisenbud for some time. Given our present state of ignorance concerning the nature of psi, we must (at the very least) entertain the possibility of extensive psi once we grant that it might assume more moderate forms. In the case of PK, for example, since we have no idea how agents affect remote physical systems, we have no grounds for assuming that PK effects are inherently limited in

magnitude or refinement. Since we don't understand how even the
smallest-scale PK seems to violate the usual constraints on influencing
other physical systems, we can't set limits in advance on how far those
apparent violations may go. In fact, not only might we have to
entertain the possibility of extensive psi, we might have to entertain the
possibility of *unlimited* psi (at least in principle). The only way we could
ever be entitled to insist that psi effects have inherent limits would be
on the basis of a thoroughly developed and well-supported full-scale
psi theory, one that embraces the *totality* of available evidence for psi
(not just laboratory evidence), and explains how or why psi functions
both in and out of the lab. But at present, no decent theory forbids
large-scale or super-psi (most simply ignore it), and certainly no
scientific theory renders any form of psi improbable (Braude, 1986,
1987). At our current level of understanding, super-psi is as viable as
puny psi.

In fact, the super-psi hypothesis even has a kind of empirical
support. The turn-of-the-century evidence from physical mediumship is probably the very best evidence for psi of any kind. But that
evidence shows that psi effects may be far more varied, elaborate, and
refined, than those suggested by superficial interpretations of
laboratory studies. Granted, most people (parapsychologists included)
dismiss the evidence, often with a disdainful flourish. But I submit that
their arguments betray either an ignorance of the evidence or
confusions on key issues (see Braude, 1986, for a sustained defense of
this claim). A clear-headed and well-informed appraisal of mediumistic
evidence forces us to accept the reality of numerous dramatic
phenomena, by comparison to which laboratory psi seems both
boring and inept. But once we've accepted the reality of mediumistic
phenomena, we should be all the more reluctant to rule out the
possibility of still more dramatic, refined, or wide-ranging psi-
effects.

Supposed Objections

The traditional attacks on the super-psi hypothesis vary widely in their
degree of profundity, and none seem successful. But nearly all raise
important issues. Hence, we should be able to get a more robust feel
for the super-psi hypothesis by considering how it survives these
various attacks.

(1) *There is no evidence for super-psi*. The problem with this objection lies
in its tacit assumption about what the evidence for super-psi would
look like. Very generally, the assumption seems to be that if super-psi
occurred, we'd know it if we saw it. In other words, the assumption is

that occurrences of super-psi in daily life will be conspicuous, or easily identifiable as such, and that they will not blend in smoothly with, or be masked by or indistinguishable from, the network of surrounding normal events. But that assumption is clearly indefensible. For one thing, there need be no observable difference between (say) a heart attack or a plane crash caused normally, and one caused by PK. The only difference may be in their unobservable causal histories. Nor must ESP-acquired information carry a marker that identifies it as such, distinguishing it (say) from thoughts we regard as random, or perhaps as internally generated inspirations. But even more important, the assumption ignores the possibly important connection between the conspicuousness of a psi-event and the context of needs and interests in which it is produced.

In fact, both this objection and the next overlook possible links between psi functioning and other organic capacities. In particular, they fail to address the possibility that psi plays a role in everyday life, and that its manifestations might be intimately linked to a complex web of desires and concerns, as well as to idiosyncracies of the agent's overall psychology and belief system. And that is no small oversight. After all, there is no reason to think (a) that psi-functioning occurs only when parapsychologists are trying to induce it, or (b) that its manifestations in those contexts will be indicative of the role or limits of spontaneous psi. Indeed, unsolicited occurrences of ostensible psi-in-life are what drove researchers into the lab in the first place, and those manifestations are considerably more varied and apparently more virtuosic and refined than laboratory psi. Hence, one would think that any psi-theoretician worthy of the title would have something to say about the possibly broad role and specific applications of psi in its *natural* setting, away from the artificial constraints and contrived needs of laboratory experiments. Even mediumistic seances encourage displays of psi (e.g., materializations, object levitations) that might be quite different from its manifestations in more humdrum everyday situations. Although seances are perhaps less artificial than laboratory experiments, they are still highly ritualized or structured settings. Hence, we should also be wary of taking seance-room psi to be paradigmatic of spontaneous psi-in-life.

It is more reasonable to suppose that if super-psi occurs, and plays a role in ordinary life, then (like other organic capacities) its manifestations will range from the dramatic and conspicuous to the mundane and inconspicuous. It is also reasonable to assume that psi can be triggered either consciously or unconsciously, and that its effects can range from beneficial to lethal (Braude, 1987). Those who argue that there is no evidence for super-psi must, at the very least, give good reasons for believing that psi would not have these characteristics, and that it would accordingly be discontinuous with practically every other cognitive, intentional, or volitional function.

But of course, if psi does have these characteristics, then not only might its everyday instances naturally escape our attention, it might even be in our interest *not* to notice them. In some cultures, the possibility of daily and even large-scale psi, including lethal or malevolent psi (e.g., hexing) is a familiar feature of an overall world view. Members of those cultures accept the possibility that human agency is responsible for a wide range of occurrences, including those which more 'civilized' persons tend to attribute to impersonal causes. But within modern industrial societies, such 'magical' thinking threatens the world view with which most of us are comfortable. Granted, some are willing to entertain the possibility of physically influencing various states of affairs, especially when the effects are salutary — for example, in the realm of healing or (as with proponents of Transcendental Meditation) crime reduction. But few of those consider equally seriously the potential for pernicious uses of the same power. And it would hardly be surprising if many of us deny even the possibility of beneficial psi, because we grasp and fear that it is logically bound up with the possibility of consciously or unconsciously harmful and malevolent psi. Hence, for most of us, it might be psychologically advantageous if psi were to occur covertly, or at least appear to be beyond our control. In that case, we could conveniently feel like mere bystanders to events we might have helped shape (see, e.g., Eisenbud, 1982).

Those who argue that there is no evidence for super-psi are also guilty of a more general methodological error, sometimes noted in non-parapsychological contexts. For example, in connection with the evidence for UFOs, P.A. Sturrock discusses the dangers of what he somewhat misleadingly calls *theory-dependent* arguments (1987, p. 93). He writes,

> . . . if we entertain the hypothesis that the phenomena may be due to an extremely advanced civilization, we must face the possibility that many ideas that we accept as simple truths may, in a wider and more sophisticated context, not be as simple and may not even be truths.

The point applies equally to the possibility of extremely refined or large-scale psi. We must not rule out a novel or world-view altering hypothesis on the basis of arguments or interpretations of data that presuppose the denial of the hypothesis. For example, the super-psi hypothesis holds that psi might be sneaky and naughty. It might be triggered unconsciously; it might be in our interest for it to work surreptitiously; and it might be used to fulfill our least admirable needs and interests. Hence, we cannot evaluate the super-psi hypothesis by presupposing that psi will always be conspicuous and well-behaved.

(2) *There is evidence against super-psi.* This objection assumes two different forms. According to the first, the evidence strongly suggests that, although psi may be impressive, it has limits well below the realm of the super. And according to the second, the evidence *demonstrates* that super-psi does not occur. Let us consider these in turn.

(a) The first version of this objection has been clearly articulated by Anderson (1987). He writes,

> D.D. Home made objects weighing some hundreds of pounds move and sometimes levitate, but he never made a house fly or visited a distant friend by means of that peculiar power of locomotion. Nor has any other physical medium exhibited phenomena that would lead us to suppose such feats within the realm of accomplishment . . . Like other human abilities, we may not be able to state *a priori* just what the limits of PK may be, but it seems a safe bet on empirical grounds that they will not far exceed the virtuosic manifestations recorded with PK superstars like Home. (p. 10)

This argument is problematical for several reasons. First, it assumes, unjustifiably, that psi phenomena occurring within the peculiar dynamics of physical mediumship are paradigmatic of psi phenomena in radically different contexts. As we observed earlier, we are not entitled to suppose that the best examples of mediumship indicate what non-mediums may do, or what forms psi would take, in situations where needs, interests, and overall belief systems of the agent are different, and where no one is on the lookout for psi. Hence, we cannot assume that D.D. Home (or any other medium — e.g., Carlos Mirabelli; see Braude, 1986) represents the best psi can do *outside* of a certain set of conditions appropriate to a seance or associated with mediumship generally.

The varieties of classic mediumistic phenomena may have been influenced, first of all, by the psychology of the medium — e.g., the medium's normal capacities and interests, and of course the medium's conceptions of psi and its place in nature. Home thought the 'power' was strongest in dim light (and under the seance table), even though phenomena frequently occurred in relatively bright light (and away from the table). Palladino thought a 'cabinet' facilitated the production of phenomena, and in her case, perhaps it did. Moreover, Home apparently had the ability to psychokinetically produce musical performances on untouched instruments, and it seems to have been continuous with his normal musical abilities. By contrast, Palladino, who had no normally developed musical skills, never produced more than apparently random sounds on nearby instruments. And perhaps more importantly, both Home and Palladino genuinely felt that discarnate spirits caused their phenomena. Hence, it is not surprising that mediumistic phenomena took forms appropriate to spiritualistic beliefs and attempts at communicating with the deceased.

Moreover, it may be that a literal belief in mediumship is conducive to a certain type of *conspicuous* psi occurrence. Indeed, that would help explain why physical phenomena declined in magnitude and refinement during the early part of this century. As the spiritualist movement waned, an increasing number of people (including the mediums themselves) took seriously the deeply intimidating possibility that the phenomena were caused by ante-mortem human agency. Many began to suspect that mediums were psi *agents* rather than facilitators of (or vehicles for) post-mortem influence. But of course that radically changed the psychodynamics of mediumship, and raised issues of personal responsibility for phenomena, both in and out of the seance room, which convinced mediums needn't confront. A genuine medium would not have to feel responsible for the outcome of a seance. From the medium's perspective, both failures *and* successes depend on the skill of the ostensible communicator and the quality of the 'connection' between the two worlds. And most important, convinced mediums would not have to fear either the omnipotence or the omniscience of their own thought, especially outside the safe confines of the seance room (see Braude, 1986, for a more detailed discussion of these issues).

The belief systems of the *investigators* may also have helped determine the forms taken by mediumistic phenomena, once again most clearly in the case of physical mediumship (but see Eisenbud, 1983, chapt. 14, for a possible example of experimenter influence on the content of communications in mental mediumship). It is certainly suggestive that the engineer, W.J. Crawford, reported phenomena of the sort that engineers in particular would appreciate. The ectoplasmic phenomena of his medium, Kathleen Goligher, operated just like a cantilever when levitating a table. By contrast, physiologists such as Richet and Schrenck-Notzing observed ectoplasmic phenomena that behaved more organically than mechanically. It would have been interesting to see what results Richet, for example, would have obtained with Miss Goligher, or Crawford with Eva C. (see Braude, 1986, for a survey of these mediums and their investigators).

The second problem with Anderson's argument concerns another apparently unwarranted assumption. Anderson seems to be saying that the best evidence is for the existence of phenomena still a long way from super-psi. For example, he claims that it's 'a safe bet on empirical grounds' that the best psi 'will not *far* exceed' (emphasis added) that of the great mediums. It is unclear, however, what Anderson's tacit measure of qualitative distance is here. If Anderson is concerned only with the magnitude of the effect (e.g., levitating a house as compared to a table), it is true we have no direct mediumistic evidence for effects of that size. But we must also remember that large-scale effects of different, and possibly more relevant, sorts might occur surreptitiously in less contrived or ritualized human contexts. On the other hand, if Anderson has in mind the refinement or sophistication of mediumistic phenomena, then it is no longer clear why mediumistic phenomena would be radically different from presumed occurrences of everyday super-psi. According to what criteria would musical performances on untouched instruments, or materializations of lifelike hands, be less impressive than causing a detailed sequence of events to conform to an ostensibly precognitive dream?

This last point is reminiscent of an observation made by Richet, concerning materialization phenomena. Many have objected to full-figure materializations on the grounds that they are inherently more incredible than other PK phenomena (including partial material-izations). The reason, presumably, is that a full-figure materialization is inherently more impressive than the other phenomena — in fact, so much so as to be beyond belief. But Richet, quite rightly, demurred.

> it is as difficult to understand the materialization of a living hand, warm, articulated, and mobile, or even of a single finger, as to understand the materialization of an entire personality which comes and goes, speaks, and moves the veil that covers him. (Richet, 1923/1975, p. 491)

(b) The second version of objection (2) is perhaps even less convincing than the first. Its general strategy is to argue that if super-psi occurred, then many things would be different from the way they are. For example, some argue that if large-scale lethal PK were possible, then given the enormous amount of hostility in the world (conscious and unconscious), few people would be alive or intact today. Moreover,

> a monster, such as Hitler, who provoked so much ill-will, could not have survived for any length of time . . . [But] far from suffering as the result of being the target of so much hatred, Hitler was exceptionally lucky in his career and was only finally overpowered at a prodigious cost in lives and by a stupendous world-wide effort. (Beloff, 1985, p. 114)

Similarly, one might argue that if our thoughts can be benignly efficacious, people would be generally happier than they are.

But this argument is exceptionally weak. As I've noted elsewhere (Braude, 1987), even if psi is theoretically unlimited in refinement or magnitude, it might be severely curtailed in practice. To begin with, most (if not all) of our abilities or capacities are situation-sensitive; the manner and degree to which they are expressed depends on numerous contextual factors. For example, our capacity for circulating blood, digesting food, or remembering what we've read is not constant or uniform over time. It varies with our mood, health, age, time of day, etc., and in general can be impeded or enhanced in many ways. Even virtuosic abilities are vulnerable to various influences. For example, the performance of a great athlete can be hindered by injury, illness, temporary loss of confidence, preoccupation with personal problems, and great opponents (or weak opponents having a great day). Similarly, a great comedian's ability to be funny can be undermined, countered, or neutralized in a variety of ways and to varying degrees. Analogously, one would think that no matter how extensive, refined or virtuosic psi-functioning might be, it, too, will be subject to actual case-by-case limitations.

Presumably, then, hostile psi would be subject to various constraints, just like normal forms of hostility. It would be embedded within an enormously complex web of interactions, psi and nonpsi, overt and covert, local and global, and would be vulnerable to equally potent interferences, or checks and balances (including psychic defenses) within that network. Obviously, we often fail in attempting to fulfill our normal malevolent desires. We can be defeated by guilt, incompetence, outside distractions or interference, or adequate defenses. Similarly, in the case of hostile psi, we must entertain the possibility of an exceptionally broad range of countervailing factors, including psychic interactions that we will never know about. If we do not think in these terms, we will simply not be taking the possibility of hostile — or more generally, super-psi seriously. In fact, we would be committing the mistake noted by Sturrock, and in addition we would be failing to place the operation of psi within a real context of competing needs and interests.

Hence, Hitler's success in surviving the paranormal influences of worldwide enmity could be explained in terms of an extensive network of competing or crisscrossing causal chains. For one thing, Hitler had his admirers as well as his detractors — perhaps even among those who denounced him openly. And for another, Hitler would presumably have made his own contributions to the underlying network of causal influences, and might have mounted his own defenses or undertaken evasive tactics. Furthermore, any interests, feelings, and intentions having specifically to do with Hitler would have been embedded within a much larger network of equally potent interests, etc., either irrelevant or indifferent to Hitler's welfare. But then numerous additional competing influences might have fortuitously neutralized attempted psychic attacks on Hitler's life. Analogously, even the world's most accomplished assassin might be thwarted by a vast range of ongoing processes having nothing to do with his particular mission — for example, a flat tire, delayed train, lost luggage, icy roads, elevator malfunction, a migraine headache, upset stomach, or a mugger. In order to deny these possibilities, one would have to argue (quite implausibly) that attempts at psi-influence can never be interfered with (even by other comparable psi influences), and that the psychodynamics of paranormal hostility are radically different from those of normal hostility.

(3) *The super-psi hypothesis is non-falsifiable*. If nothing else, this objection has the virtue of being true. But it is of little interest theoretically, and it certainly does not undermine the super-psi hypothesis. If super-psi can be inconspicuous and pervasive, and if we cannot specify antecedent limits to its degree of magnitude or refinement, then I grant that we cannot generally falsify hypotheses positing its operation. The conspicuous phenomena of physical mediumship, however, might be an exception. Granted, even in these cases many hypotheses cannot be shown conclusively to be true or false — for example, the hypothesis that negative results were due to psi interference from the investigator (or a mildly interested person living on a Tibetan mountain top), or (in some cases) that the medium paranormally produced concordant hallucinations in all the sitters (rather than, say, a genuine but ephemeral materialization), or that the medium paranormally produced phenomena strongly suggesting fraud rather than psi. But if we are willing to appeal to higher-level theoretical criteria for choosing one hypothesis over another, we can reduce the problem of hypothesis selection to more manageable proportions. For example, we can effectively weigh some psi hypotheses against the sceptical hypotheses of fraud, malobservation, and misreporting (e.g., hypotheses positing psychokinetic or telepathic phenomena in the cases of Home and Palladino — see Braude, 1986).

That is why one should not make too much of the non-falsifiability of psi hypotheses. Even if hypothesis H is non-falsifiable, there may still be other grounds for deciding between H and rival hypotheses — for example, higher-level pragmatic considerations concerning theoretic systematicity, explanatory fecundity, and conceptual cost. Besides, the non-falsifiability of an hypothesis may simply reflect the intractable nature of the phenomenon in question, rather than a theoretical deficiency, or the fact that the phenomenon does not exist. Widespread, large-scale, and inconspicuous psi *would* be the sort of phenomenon whose existence might never be conclusively demonstrated or disproved. But in that case we would have no choice to accept the cards dealt us by nature. It would be indefensibly presumptuous to insist that nature operate only in ways amenable to the preferred methods of science.

In fact, if we rely rigidly on Popperian falsifiability and other analytical or theoretical techniques drawn from the 'hard' sciences, we will have to reject perfectly acceptable everyday hypotheses concerning the mental lives of ourselves and others. But not only do we constantly evaluate such hypotheses against competing hypotheses, our psychological survival depends on it. It is by means of such a process that we *reliably* determine whom to confide in, how to speak to other people (e.g., which issues to avoid, what 'tone' to take), whom we can rely on in times of stress, etc. And clearly, the ability to do this consistently requires a mastery of a certain kind of theoretical activity. Indeed, some of us are much better able than others to hypothesize about peoples' intentions, desires, needs, interests, capacities, etc. And although no such hypothesis is strictly falsifiable, many are highly justifiable on pragmatic grounds. That is demonstrated by the way they successfully guide our dealings with other people.

Of course, the uncertainty of hypothesizing about super-psi is generally greater than the uncertainty of our conjectures about ordinary psychological regularities. There may not even be as many psi-regularities, or they may be generally far less conspicuous. Or perhaps very few of our psi efforts successfully negotiate the complex underlying network of competing interests and interactions in which all such attempts would be embedded. Nevertheless, we can speculate about how super-psi *might* manifest — that is, what sorts of events or regularities it might help explain.

What should we say, for example, about people who seem to be remarkably lucky or unlucky? No doubt many cases of luck or misfortune can be easily explained by reference to familiar processes. But other cases seem to have no obvious explanation, especially when streaks of luck or misfortune continue for a while. Some people seem consistently to have a knack for making speculative business or investment decisions, whereas others seem regularly to fail at this activity. Some (but not others) seem repeatedly to operate within a surrounding maelstrom of chaos or disaster, and of these some always seem to be victims, while others seem always to escape unharmed. Why are these sorts of regularities sometimes strikingly long-term? Why is it that the lives of certain people are always filled with annoyances and difficulties, apparently not of their own making, while those of others are relatively trouble-free in the same respects? Why do some people repeatedly have difficulties with the postal service, mail-order companies, bank computers or personnel, automobiles, appliances, or other purchases, while others seem never to have such problems? I am not suggesting that there are simple answers, or any answers, to these questions. And I certainly don't recommend that we automatically assume that psi is operating in such cases; streaks of good or bad luck might still be fortuitous. But if psi functioning does operate in the world on a day-to-day basis, one might expect it to manifest in these ways. Hence, it might be worthwhile to undertake depth-psychological studies of the lives of lucky and unlucky people, and look for connections between their good or bad fortune and such things as their self-image, hidden agendas (possibly self-destruction) and relations with others. Granted, no definite conclusions will emerge from such studies; as we've seen, super-psi hypotheses are unfalsifiable. But in some cases a psi hypothesis might be particularly enlightening or suggestive in the way it systematizes an otherwise motley array of unconnected occurrences, or makes sense out of otherwise seemingly paradoxical features of a person's life.

Another possible stage of operation for everyday psi is the scientific laboratory. It would be transcendentally foolish to think that laboratory PK, for instance, operates only in connection with parapsychological laboratories. Quite apart from the way psi might function outside a scientific framework, one can't suppose that the only machines susceptible to PK are those designed to test for such influence. Hence, for all we know, PK might play a role in the gathering of conventional scientific data. This is especially plausible when we consider the possibility of experimenter-psi, and the fact that in conventional areas of science, a great many scientists jointly expect or hope for certain specific kinds of results. Of course, once again, we can't be certain that psi contributes to the results of ordinary scientific experiments. But for all we know, those groups of scientists could form an effective united subject pool.

The one area where I believe we have no choice but to posit the operation of super-psi is in the analysis of ostensible precognition. In cases where no normal explanation seems to work, the only alternative psi explanation involves positing the operation of retrocausal processes (Braude, 1986, Eisenbud, 1982). And that option, I believe, is conceptually intolerable. By contrast, positing super-psi is merely pschologically disconcerting.

References

Anderson, R. (1987). Review of S.E. Braude, *The Limits of Influence: Psychokinesis and the Philosophy of Science*. *Parapsychology Review*, Nov.–Dec.: 9–11.

Beloff, J. (1985). Review of J. Eisenbud, *Parapsychology and the Unconscious*. *Journal of the Society for Psychical Research* 53: 111–114.

Braude, S.E. (1979) *ESP and Psychokinesis: A Philosophical Examination*. Philadelphia: Temple University Press.

Braude, S.E. (1986). *The Limits of Influence: Psychokinesis and the Philosophy of Science*. London & New York: Routledge & Kegan Paul.

Braude, S.E. (1987). 'Psi and Our Picture of the World'. *Inquiry* 30: 277–294.

Braude, S.E. (1988). 'Death by Observation: A Reply to Millar'. *Journal of the American Society for Psychical Research* 82: 273-250.

Eisenbud, J (1970). *Psi and Psychoanalysis*. New York & London: Grune & Stratton.

Eisenbud, J. (1982). *Paranormal Foreknowledge: Problems and Perplexities*. New York: Human Sciences Press.

Eisenbud, J. (1983). *Parapsychology and the Unconscious*. Berkeley, California: North Atlantic Books.

Gauld, A. (1982). *Mediumship and Survival: A Century of Investigation*. London: Heinemann.

Richet, C. (1923/1975). *Thirty Years of Psychical Research*. New York: Macmillan; reprinted, New York, Arno Press.

Sturrock, P.A. (1987). 'An Analysis of the Condon Report on the Colorado UFO Project'. *Journal of Scientific Exploration* 1: 75-100.

CHAPTER 3

TO BE OR NOT TO BE HUMAN: A CAPSULE BACKSTAIRS HISTORY OF PSYCHICAL RESEARCH

Jule Eisenbud

All indications point to the fact that early humans held a view of themselves and the world radically different from the one held in historical times. In prehistoric times, according to this view, there was basically no conception of causality apart from human volition, in fact no conception at all of anything like causality in the abstract. Extrapolating backward from our earliest records and from the observations on preliterate peoples of travellers, missionaries, and anthropologists of the last two centuries or so, whatever happened was, for good or ill, the result of someone's wish to have it happen. However, at some unknown point in prehistory, perhaps the most significant development in human consciousness had its beginning. This was the externalisation of the will — and the putative causes of things — into agencies outside the self.

It is likely that the earliest manifestation of this trend was in relation to the returning spirits of the dead, who dutifully carried out the evil thoughts projected onto them by the living (a story in itself). As the process of externalisation spread, rocks, trees, and early man-made objects came also to be thought of as imbued with a mystical power to cause things to happen. This was embodied in the concept of mana, or one of its numerous equivalents. Traces of this magical view of the world can be seen today in certain funerary customs (e.g., food offerings to placate the dead), the widespread notion of the evil eye and, on the benevolent side, the power ascribed to religious relics. But by the time of the ancient Greeks, such beliefs had already begun to be looked upon as mere superstition as a materialistic view of the world took over and evolved into progressively refined models of how things *really* came to happen.

A persistent problem, however, was how to regard events that seemed not to happen in conformity to prevailing materialistic, or, latterly, scientific ideas. It became plain even from the time of the ancients that what would be regarded today as non-conforming, anomalous events — essentially those subsumed currently under the rubrics of telepathy, clairvoyance psychokinesis and precognition — would keep turning up, generation after generation, with notable consistency.

The solution to this problem has essentially not changed in historical times. This was, first, to insist, as did the great Roman orator Cicero, that there was no problem, that the anomalous things alleged to happen did not happen. Second, if the first solution was found weak or otherwise wanting, to simply disregard the problem. Thus, up to the very present, our scientific, or establishment, theories of how things work show little reflection of the possibility that our conventional ways of regarding causality and nature might, at the very least, be radically inadequate and incomplete. Man is viewed still as being in touch with what goes on about him solely by means of five senses which bring him different kinds of information via a brain that processes and stores this information. His senses and his brain enable him to adapt to an ever changing environment which is around him but in no significant manner of him; and he can alter this environment only by muscular action or indirectly through information conveyed by his brain and muscles to other living entities, or to products of his own contrivance which are simply extensions of these.

Conventional philosophy and psychology have never resolved certain anomalies in theories of knowledge and behaviour based upon this view, but these too, like the aberrant facts themselves, have, except for a rare dissident here or there, been ignored.

Attempts to deal systematically with certain officially aberrant facts of human cognition and behaviour began in the 1870s with the research into the extraordinary capacities of Daniel Dunglas Home carried out by the English scientist William (later Sir William) Crookes (Crookes, 1889–90, 1974). Scores of witnesses attested to observing Home affecting his physical environment in ways not explicable in terms of the accepted views of human capacities. These included levitations of tables, chairs (sometimes with people in them), and other objects, and of Home himself. On several occasions, moreover, an accordion specially purchased by Crookes was seen floating about in good daylight and, under conditions rendering contact with the keys impossible, playing well-known tunes. Crookes also investigated the controversial materializing medium Florence Cook who, he claimed, produced living forms in ways completely unaccountable in conventional biological terms.

A decade or so later, in 1882, the Society for Psychical Research was formed in Britain. Its purpose was to collect and investigate anomalous occurrences in the extraordinary realm hitherto neglected by science, mainly, to begin with, dreams and apparitions bearing an inexplicable correspondence to external events (Gurney, Myers and Podmore, 1918). Experiments were also conducted in areas such as clairvoyance and thought transference, while investigations were made of the abilities of specially endowed subjects, who were allegedly able to effect their physical environments in inexplicable ways or who claimed to be in communication with discarnate entities.

The impressive body of data amassed over several decades by this dedicated group of investigators, as well as by colleagues in Europe and in a Society for Psychical Research formed in 1885 in America, made it plain that science could continue to ignore the anomalous so-called psychical side of man only by not living up to its professed objectives. This became inescapably clear as more sophisticated techniques of experimentation and data evaluation developed by J.B. Rhine in America (Rhine, 1935) were applied and extended by investigators all over the world. These statistically grounded tech-niques were, despite early flaws arising from the novelty of their applications, in conformity with the highest standards of scientific procedure.

The view of man derived from this classical period of psychical research — or parapsychology, as it came to be called — was expressed in such pioneering works as Myers' *Human Personality and its Survival of Bodily Death* (1904), Richet's *Thirty Years of Psychical Research* (1923), and Rhine's *The Reach of the Mind* (1947). The picture of man as a windowless monad, a mechanical crawler upon the face of the earth, like a machine endowed merely with the superior power supply and control mechanisms of life, was challenged. Man was viewed now as a creature of still unexplained capacities and potentialities in a world not entirely the same as that revealed to him by his senses and their contrived deputies.

However, the two sides of man — that accepted by science and that revealed by psychical research — remained somehow unintegrated, as did the two worlds in which man functioned. There was the man of everyday experience, anchored in the crude frame of his earthy instincts and animal heritage, and there was the man of special, almost godlike gifts and potentialities — the world of the senses, as it were, and another, different world beyond the senses, a world mysteriously controlled by forces seemingly apart from the world of ordinary causality and physically embodied beings. The two sides of man appeared to have little to do with each other and the two worlds remained precisely that: two worlds. Occasionally, and for no very discernible reason, a window would mysteriously open in the monad that was man revealing a world 'out there' that was wholly apart from the world in which he worked, played, procreated and in general foraged for the satisfaction of his needs.

For reasons not entirely clear, this picture, still widely extant today in the field of physical research, seems to engender an implicit religiosity in many of those who adhere to it. Man is seen as an evolving species but there is a vague promise that he will rise above the material framework of his existence and achieve a 'spirituality' in line with a still barely glimpsed but hardly to be doubted destiny. The unusual capacities discovered in him are seen not as an integral part of his functioning in the everyday business of life — from an adaptational point of view neither higher nor lower, more or less need-inspired than the earthlier aspects of his functioning and behaviour — but as isolated flashes of some mysterious potentiality bearing promise of a state of existence to come. All this is vaguely associated with the ultimate triumph of good over evil, of man's 'spiritual' over his dark, sinister, sexual and aggressive side. Fostered by an almost deliberate culling of case material to support it, this view shows man as so concerned with the fate of his fellow man that he is able to breach his otherwise sense bound isolation to reach out empathically over space and time to get bad news, which is mostly what he gets in his premonitions, dreams and apparitions.

The onesidedness of the theoretical preconceptions in terms of which material was gathered to support this implicit point of view made it difficult to conceive of man as other than passively involved in the sometimes fatal misadventures of his fellows. Case material of a less benevolent kind which abounds in the annals and folklore of people the world over — of curses, spells, and incantations to bring about the destruction of an enemy and perhaps the sexual surrender of his wife, was ignored, as was the philosophical problem of precognition which, faced squarely (see later), make it imperative to take such material into account. Thus, just as science managed systematically to avoid aberrant data *in toto*, establishment psychical research managed somehow to avoid bringing into the picture data and theoretical considerations that might not fight the view of man evolving upward into higher spirituality. The result was that psychical research grew into — and has remained *para*psychology, beyond and outside the psychology of everyday existence, and with a huge investigative bias against *in vivo* observation of spontaneously occurring material.

It is not surprising that the first major departure from this rather inhuman classical parapsychological view was inaugurated by the observations of psychiatrists. In 1921 Wilhelm Stekel, a Viennese psychoanalyst, reported a number of patients' presumptively telepathic dreams which indicated that the dreamers did not concern themselves with events of major proportions but with everyday experiences out of which dreams are ordinarily fashioned. Stekel (1921) maintained that the paranormal acquisition of information revealed in these dreams arose not chiefly out of empathic concern over the misfortunes of loved ones but more often out of hate, discord and jealousy. In the following year, Sigmund Freud (1955b) showed that fortune-tellers were apt to pick up the repressed unconscious wishes of their clients, and that these wishes could sometimes be murderous.

Both Stekel and Freud extended their observations over the next few years. Stekel, besides emphasizing the type of ordinary, everyday emotional linkages in telepathic interactions, showed that information paranormally received need not be consciously apprehended as such. For example, a person might experience a bodily pain or other symptom rather than a veridical vision or dream at the precise moment of being betrayed by a spouse (Stekel, 1943). Meanwhile Freud showed, in a penetrating analysis of a possibly telepathic dream, that the laws by which the dreamer attempted to cope with a conflictful situation by his use of paranormally acquired information were no different from the laws that governed other areas of his unconscious mental life (Freud, 1955a). He also showed that a patient in treatment could become paranormally sensitive to material of concern to the analyst, and that the reaction that was evident in the patient's associations — jealousy, in the instance reported — could be related dynamically to this material just as if the patient had acquired conscious knowledge of it (Freud, 1964).

Other investigators also extended these observations in the years following (Eisenbud, 1949). The picture emerging from the cumulative data showed man's paranormal capacities to be very much in the service of his adaptional needs — that paranormally acquired information could, for example, be woven into the texture of dreams not only in the same manner as normally acquired information but also for the same purposes, namely, the resolution of conflict situations by the magical (if only fantasied) manipulation of the internal and external environment. Such information, moreover, could be shown to be utilized in a symbolic manner in dreams, just as ordinary information was apt to be, the element fire, for example, symbolizing sexual arousal, the element water symbolizing birth, royalty a parent, and so forth. Sometimes elements such as newspaper headlines, or radio or telephone communication, would suggest that extraordinary, i.e., paranormal, processes were being used (Eisenbud, 1970). In addition, data from waking life confirmed Stekel's observation that paranormal processes are capable of conditioning not only all areas of thought and awareness but also our deepest levels of bodily functioning. Indeed that almost any type of symptom, from disturbances of the musculoskeletal system to disturbances of the cardiovascular respiratory system, could be a reaction to external events apprehended in a presumptively paranormal manner (Eisenbud, 1970). A group of such cases was reviewed by Stevenson (1970), a psychiatrist at the University of Virginia.

It goes without saying that observations of the sort just cited, as well as those cited earlir, could never be arrived at by statistical and allied experimental procedures, since they are completely outside the province of such means of investigation. And indeed, it is precisely because they lack the cachet of the laboratory that such data tend, moreover, to be sequestered from the mainstream of thought in parapsychology.

An area that has latterly been receiving some attention I have dubbed 'the psychic pathology of everyday life' (Eisenbud, 1970), after Freud's pioneer study (under that title) of unconscious determinants of errors, accidents, slips of the tongue and other so-called parapraxes (Freud, 1960). The possible role of psi in certain of these occurrences was extended to include psychokinesis (Eisenbud, 1972). On the cognitive side, such psi-conditioned behaviour has been termed 'psi-mediated instrumental responses' or, acronymically, PMIR (Stanford, 1977).

Perhaps the best conditions under which to study such responses are during pschoanalytic treatment where, several times a week, persons candidly report the day's happenings, along with their thoughts, dreams, feelings and fantasies. In this situation it is sometimes possible to piece together event sequences in which one person can be construed as manoeuvring another, by paranormally mediated unconscious suggestion, to carry out an act which will benefit him (the party of the first part) but for which, under the circumstances, he will appear, at most, to be an innocent bystander (Eisenbud, 1970).

Although such things have apparently always been recognized in the annals and folklore of mankind, they have only comparatively recently been approached experimentally. In 1886 the French psychiatrist Pierre Janet initiated a flurry of reports on hypnosis and suggestion at a distance by an account of his own witnesses experiments on *le sommeil a distance* (Janet, 1986 a, b). In the 1930s the subject was investigated on the quiet by Russian investigators who, however, were able to report their skilfully instrumented procedures only during the political thaw several decades later (Vasiliev, 1976).

Significant theoretical applications based upon these investigations have been slow in coming. But since certain types of occurrences involving paranormally mediated influence of one type or another may sometimes be construed as possibly leading to harmful consequences (Eisenbud, 1982), an obvious and inevitable question is: to what extent does such a postulated kind of interaction, unconsciously brought into play as part of an individual's adaptive armamentarium, take place on a 'silent', unobtrusive level, where it might never be brought to light in the normal course of events. Indeed, given man's normally short (and seemingly growing shorter) fuse, and his virtually unlimited proneness to mischief and mayhem, this question, if an extended psi hypothesis is entertained at all, cannot long be evaded.

Nor can one much longer evade the manifold possibilities unfolding from the psychic photography, or thoughtography, of Ted Serios and others (Eisenbud, 1967, 1975, 1977a, b). If, as appears to be the case, these persons are able unconsciously to manipulate silver chloride molecules into astonishingly intricate patterns by mental means, it is inconceivable that latent in all humans is the capacity to engineer a wide variety of biological and physical systems into patterns that would take their place in the broad spectrum of everyday occurrences. Although the conditions necessary to bring such patterns to actuality might remain largely obscure, this would be no more the case, except for our habitual preconceptions, than with all seemingly spontaneous happenings.

The logically and philosophically called-for implications of such a state of affairs have been persuasively argued by Braude (Braude, 1985, 1987), who sees, as does the present author (Eisenbud, 1982), that a virtually unlimited psi capacity, deployed on an unconscious and active level, would at least enable us to make some sense of the hard data of precognition. In fact, if anything ought to coerce us into facing the full range of possibilities of psi functioning, however threatening, it is the difficult problems posed by these data. This is especially true since, Braude (1986) has shown, the concept of retrocausation, uncritically accepted by generations of parapsychologists, turns out to be philosophically bankrupt.

These considerations, if taken seriously and applied at large, might seem to threaten a return to something like Levy-Bruhl's magic world of the primitive, a return literally with a vengeance, since once the door is opened to all the possibilities implied in such a picture, no one could ever feel safe, as Levy-Bruhl pointed out in his classic discussion of 'home bred bewitchment' (1933), from the 'evil eye' (open or shut) of a family member or neighbour.

It need hardly be emphasized, however, that this way of viewing things does not include other aspects of man's ineradicably ambivalent nature. Manifold possibilities, such as dangers miraculously averted or paranormal healing, may clearly be related to psi-mediated or psi-conditioned occurrences on the other side of the ledger. Such an approach, however, at least gives us a coherent basis for understanding the origin and development of science's irrational materialistic warp and in fact its implacable 'kill the messenger' attitude toward the discipline which threatens to expose some of the tools at the disposal of man's unconscious aggressions. This alone may turn out to be not the least valuable fall-out of contemporary trends in psychical research.

References

Braude, S.E. (1985), *The Limits of Influence: Psychokinesis and the Philosophy of Science*, London/New York, Routledge & Kegan Paul.

Braude, S.E. (1987), 'Psi and our Picture of the World', *Inquiry*, 30, 277–294.

Crookes, W. (1874), 'Notes of an enquiry into the phenomena called spiritual during the years 1870–1873'. *Quarterly Journal of Science*, January.

Crookes, W. (1889–90), 'Notes of seances with D.D. Home'. *Proceedings of the Society for Psychical Research*, Vol. 6, 98–127.

Eisenbud, J. (1949), 'Psychiatric contributions to parapsychology: a review', *Journal of Parapsychology*, 13, 247–262, in Devereux, G., (ed.) (1953), *Psychoanalysis and the Occult*, New York, *International Universities Press*.

Eisenbud, J. (1965), *The World of Ted Serios*, New York, Morrow.

Eisenbud, J. (1970), *Psi and Psychoanalysis*, New York, Grune and Stratton.

Eisenbud, J. (1977a) 'Paranormal photography', in *Handbook of Parapsychology*, (Ed. B. Wolman), New York, Van Nostrand Reinhold, 414–443.

Eisenbud, J. (1977b) 'Observations on a possible new thoughtographic talent'. *Journal of the American Society for Psychical Research*, Vol. 71, 299–304.

Eisenbud, J. (1982) *Paranormal Foreknowledge*, New York, Human Sciences Press.

Freud, S. (1955a), 'Psychoanalysis and telepathy', vol. 18, *Complete Psychological Works*, Standard Edition, London, Hogarth Press.

Freud, S. (1955b), 'Dreams and telepathy', Vol. 18, *Complete Psychological Works*, Standard Edition, London, Hogarth Press.

Freud, S. (1960), *The Psychopathology of Everyday Life*, Vol. 6, *Complete Psychological Works*, Standard Edition, London, Hogarth Press.

Freud, S. (1964), 'Dreams and occultism', Chapter 30, *New Introductory Lectures on Psycho-Analysis*, Vol. 22, *Complete Psychological Works*, Standard Edition, London, Hogarth Press.

Gurney, E., Myers, F.W.H. & Podmore, F. (1986), *Phantasms of the Living*, London, Trubner. Abridged (1962), New Hyde Park, University Books.

Janet, P. (1886a), 'Note sur quelques phenomenes de somnambulisme. *Revue Philosophique de la France et de l'etrangere*' Vol. 22, 190–198. Trans. Report on some phenomena of somnambulism. *Journal of the History of the Behavioural Sciences*, Vol. 4, 1968, 124–131.

Janet, P. (1886b), 'Deuxieme note sur le sommeil provoque a distance et la suggestion mentale pendant l'etat somnambulique.' *Revue Philosophique de* la France et de l'Etrangere, Vol. 22, 212–223. Trans. 'Second observation of sleep provoked from a distance and mental suggestion during the somnambulistic state.' Journal of the History of the Behavioural Sciences, Vol. 4, 1968, 258267.

Levy-Bruhl, L. (1933), Primitives and the Supernatural, Chapter VI, New York, Dutton.

Myers, F.W.H. (1904), Human Personality and its Survival of Bodily Death, New York, Longmans, Green & Company. Abridged edition, New Hyde Park, University Books, 1961.

Rhine, J.B. (1935), Extra-Sensory Perception, Boston, Bruce Humphries.

Rhine, J.B. (1947), The Reach of the Mind, New York, William Sloane Associates.

Richet, C. (1923), Thirty Years of Psychical Research (Trans. Debrath, S.), New York, Macmillan.

Stekel, W. (1921), Der telepatische Traum, Berlin, Johannes Baum Verlag.

Stekel, W. (1943), The Interpretation of Dreams, (2 Vols), New York, Liveright.

Stanford, R.G. (1977), 'Conceptual Frameworks of Contemporary psi Research', in Handbook of Parapsychology (Ed. B. Wolman), New York, Van Nostrand Reinhold, 823–858.

Vasiliev, L.L. (1976), Experiments in Distant Influence, New York, Dutton.

CHAPTER 4

VARIETIES OF EXPERIENCED "REALITY" AS REVERBERATIONS FROM FOUR WORLDS

George K. Zollschan

Introduction

It is difficult to devise explanations which do justice to the entire range of human experience within a particular unitary explanatory framework; say, for instance, that of natural science (materialism, physicalism). Explanations based on a number of diverse frameworks each viewed as autonomous and irreducible to another framework are of greater effectiveness in throwing light on wider ranges of events without forcing us to cope with anomalous results or sweep certain inconvenient findings under the carpet. Popper's three world postulate was devised to optimize explanatory effectiveness in various areas of philosophical concern. Popper claims, in other words, that the postulations of three different autonomous realms (or "worlds") enables us to propose satisfactory explanations for problems otherwise unsatisfactorily explained.

The position held in this chapter is supportive of the notion that the simultaneous adoption of more than one apparently self-contained framework is a useful strategy of explanation. However, I shall maintain that Popper's three world postulate still excludes from consideration ranges of important experiences or events. The four world postulate to be presented here helps to correct these deficiencies. I hasten to add that Popper is on record as having no objection to the postulation of more than three worlds (Popper, 1979, p. 107). While the present discussion cannot avoid some critique of Popper's doctrine it is primarily intended to expand it so as to include a fourth, neglected, world. Within the context of this volume the events and experiences which require a fourth autonomous explanatory framework are paranormal events and experiences. For the purposes of this chapter discussion of the paranormal will focus on sources of creativity viewed as paranormal capacity; for it is in this context that Popper's three world postulate most obviously calls for a fourth explanatory framework.

As a kabbalist I note that a postulate of four worlds is not original. It traces its influence to the kabbalistic community of Safed in the Sixteenth Century and particularly to Cordovero and Luria who number among its outstanding figures. The notion itself can be traced to earlier sources (Scholem, 1961, p. 272). In this kabbalistic doctrine the worlds range from nearness to the divine to the lowest of the worlds; that of nature. Specifically the four kabbalistic worlds are as follows:

Atziluth (literally, "nearness"). This is the world of divine emanation which may be experienced by some select persons as an ethereal feeling.

Beriah (literally, "creation"). It would be mistaken to take this world as the source of human creativity. Various commentaries about the contents of this world describe it in terms consistent with calling it the world of symbols.

Yetzirah (literally, "formation"). This is often described by medieval kabbalists as the world inhabited by angels. Since angels are the carriers of divine intentions (one per specific intention) it is safe to treat this world also as the world of human intentions.

Assiyah (literally "making") is generally accepted as the world of nature and, in humans, of natural impulses.

It will become abundantly clear in the course of this chapter that the worlds of *Assiyah*, *Yetzirah*, and *Beriah* respectively correspond closely to an interpretation of Popper's Worlds 1-3. *Atziluth*, the kabbalistic fourth world, is the world of divine emanation. This world can surely also be described as the world which harbours, or generates, divine inspiration. Both the outstandingly creative and the paranormal can be interpreted as divinely inspired without much difficulty. When discussing this fourth world, however, I shall shift from the idiom of the Lurianic kabbalists of Safed to that of another writer from the same period; namely the Maharal of Prague.[1] This is done primarily because of the availability in English of some of the Maharal's comments on what I call my fourth world.

The issue of inspiration may perhaps require an additional word. Positing an explanatory realm entirely of its own for inspiration as such implies that it is an experience, or a process, somehow discontinuous from processes and experiences capable of explanation by "normal" means; that is to say, by types of explanatory patterns adopted and accepted with respects to Worlds 1-3. The current raging dispute about whether paranormal powers exist at all suggests, at any rate to a person who has experienced their effectiveness, that individuals who are devoted to normal explanatory patterns wish to deny the very existence of paranormal phenomena for that reason. Those who are simply not willing to throw the evidence for paranormal phenomena out of the window must accept the notion that, for the present at any rate, some autonomous paranormal explanatory frame is necessary. With respect to creativity, the issue is not quite as simple. It is possible to see creativity as merely a continuation, in extreme form, of ordinary and generally observable ingenuity and inventiveness. Such a point of view may be described as "rationalistic" and corresponds to Popper's position.[2] On the other hand, one can take the opposite point of view and see the extraordinarily creative as a miraculous manifestation of inspiration from an unexplained source. The latter position is taken in this chapter.

The argument of the chapter is developed in the following way. After a personal reflection, Popper's three world postulate is briefly presented. Thereafter, Worlds 1–3 are discussed in a manner intended both to be compatible with Popper's own distinction and with the overall intentions of my own argument. World 4 will be presented as an autonomous realm posited so as to repair systematic deficiencies which appear consistently across each of Popper's three worlds.

A Preliminary Reflection:

Gunnar Myrdal (1944, esp. pp. xli–xlviii and 71–86; 1969) has made the point that the attempt to obtain objectivity in social research is aided rather than impeded by "coming clean" about one's own values, beliefs, and opinions. Adopting a spurious objectivistic attitude enables researchers to smuggle unrecognized valuations into their procedures and reports.

When considering the paranormal I would certainly concur with Myrdal's advice to social scientists, particularly as regards the question of belief. Belief or disbelief in paranormal phenomena seems to be entrenched in many people as a fundamental principle comparable to a religious creed. Let me begin, therefore, by heeding Myrdal's sage counsel and revealing the evolution of my own attitudes and beliefs with respect to paranormal (or allegedly paranormal) phenomena.

As a youngster who moved around from one culture and sub-culture to another in my early years, I developed a precocious (and entirely well founded) skepticism about what people told me. This skepticism received formidable reinforcement when I became first a student of, and then research assistant to, the eminent philosopher of science, Sir Karl Popper, in London. At the same time, I inherited from my maternal grandfather in Vienna a considerable interest in, and insight into, the field of Jewish mysticism.

The skepticism and mysticism coexisted, and continue to coexist, in me without excessive tension. In earlier years I saw kabbalistic manipulation of numbers, letters, words, and sentence structures as a royal road for freeing creativity in thinking.[3] That was the situation around twenty years ago when I met a so-called "clairvoyant" (actually, an amateur practitioner of precognition) in a social situation. This man foretold a number of events in my life, including the exact date of "receiving" my doctorate.[4] I was not in the habit of consulting soothsayers and, after writing the prophecies down in my diary, forgot about the encounter until several of them had actually eventuated.

There is no known way in which it is possible to give an exact statistical evaluation of the chance that these predictions were simply lucky guesses; I judge it to be infinitesimal. What is more, certain of the prophesied events could not possibly have been "normally" influenced by my own conscious or unconscious actions. The exact date at which my oral doctoral defence was scheduled, for instance, was entirely outside my personal control.

After several of these foretold events actually occurred (not all of them did) my curiosity was aroused and I consulted a number of self-styled clairvoyants. I must report, partly to my disappointment and partly to my own relief, that their ministrations were quite worthless as predictions. That fact in itself, however, serves to strengthen my conviction that the prophecies of the amateur oracle I had met by chance had to be more than just incredibly lucky guesses. If "professional" guesses were invariably off target my friendly — entirely unremunerated — amateur simply could not have scored several bull's-eyes by engaging in guessing games.

In the intervening time (and, as far as I can tell, uninfluenced by the above events) I have become more seriously involved as a practising kabbalist and have had the privilege of witnessing certain kabbalistic masters display "powers" of healing and of precognition. I have also been interested to note that such healing and, particularly, precognitive capacities seem to be somewhat sporadic in their effectiveness.

I hope the foregoing remarks have served to throw some light on my personal attitude to the paranormal. Accepting the reality of paranormal capacities and events certainly makes it a lot easier for me to account for works of genius, particularly in the field of music. My youthful ambitions to become a composer were thwarted by the combined lack of both talent and opportunity. However, I have always felt it possible to reconstruct imaginatively the activity and ideation that goes into a "normal" musical composition. What I would define as a composition of genius eludes such reconstruction. It contains eruptions of ideas which I can represent to myself only as coming from "another world". Let us proceed, therefore, to examine a philosophical approach which makes it possible to consider the explanation of events within the context of a model containing more than one world.

Popper's Three World Postulate and its Deficiencies:

As a springboard for a discussion of varieties of experienced reality, Popper's three world postulate serves a useful purpose. Viewed in the context of its explanatory intentions, the three world postulate fails on careful examination to account for human creativity; particularly as revealed in the invention of scientific theories or creation of works of art. I shall ask the reader to entertain with me the hypothesis that the mysterious point of origin of creativity or inventiveness is also the source of paranormal capacities and experiences.

Perhaps the best way to introduce the three world postulate is to let Popper speak for himself. In one of the earliest published expositions: World 1 is "the physical world or the world of physical states"; World 2 is the "mental world or the world of mental states"; and World 3 is mysteriously and grandiloquently introduced as "the world of intelligibles or of *ideas in the objective sense*" (Popper, 1979, p. 154). Popper's mysterious World 3 becomes more understandable when one looks at what he describes to be its contents and origins. In early expositions the contents are theories, arguments, and problems. In later writings Popper expands this list to include symbol systems such as mathematics and languages (Popper and Eccles, 1983, pp. 41-47) and even "tools, institutions, and works of art" (Popper, 1982, p. 187). In origin, World 3 is described as being man made.

If we translate Popper's ·description of these three realms into simpler terminology, *World 1* turns out to be the *world of nature*, *World 2* the *domain of subjective knowledge*, and *World 3* the *realm of culture*. Indeed, the later cited works betray Popper's dawning realisation that earlier expositions of World 3 were somewhat narrow, concentrating solely on the "logical and intellectual province of World 3" (Popper, 1982, p. 187); on culture, as it were, spelled with a capital "K".

Having benefitted from the translation the reader may well wonder what the fuss is all about. To be sure, it takes a certain single-mindedness of purpose to rediscover culture all by oneself in an intellectual environment (the London School of Economics) where one is surrounded by able and noisily articulate anthropologists and other social scientists. However, in all fairness, it must be pointed out that Popper had displayed an acute appreciation of science as a social enterprise before he concocted the three world postulate in his sixties.

Criticism and testing by observation are the cornerstones of Popper's philosophy of science. In his account of the historical evolution of scientific discovery, criticism of myths and later of theories emerges in some cultural traditions. Theories, of course, are no more than myths which have acquired a more systematic and explicitly explanatory character. Later in such traditions criticism by appeal to observation (in other words, *testing*) becomes incorporated into the scientific tradition (see, Popper, 1962a, pp. 120–135). What is new about the three world postulate, as far as Popper is concerned, is that cultural myths and rituals, once decently evolved into theories and testing procedures, gain status as realities in their own right. They become entirely independent of the thought processes of this or that particular scientist. Furthermore, World 3 objects (i.e. ideas, theories etc.) display an intrinsic logic of their own, quite independently of the intentions of those who create them. Thus the numerical conventions of mathematics, for instance, display inherent features not even guessed at by the clever people who invent or set up numbering systems.

The discovery of cultural reality independently of this or that culture bearer can hardly be credited to Popper. Additionally, the fact that cultural techniques, beliefs, and values are highly consequential for human existence has been noted by anthropologists and sociologists since the earliest beginnings of their disciplines. For example, Durkheim wrote in 1895 that "the systems of signs I use to express my thoughts, the system of currency I employ to pay my debts, . . . the practices followed in my profession, etc., function independently of my own use of them" (Dukheim, 1964, p. 2). Singling out the special sub-culture of science adds nothing to Durkheim's jaded sociological insight. More important than the issue of originality of the World 3 concept is the role it plays in Popper's philosophical system as a whole. In this connection the peculiar status of World 2 must be considered.

Popper's World 2, the world of individual subjectivity, is something of an orphan planet in the three world postulate. He views it as no more than the "mediator between the first and the third world" (Popper 1979, p. 156). Perhaps World 2 can better be described as a sort of eccentric moon in orbit around two planets, namely the "objective" worlds 1 and 3. Or, to bring the metaphor down to a sub-lunar level, Popper sees the subjective scientist in orbit between the laboratory, where he/she interacts with the world of nature, and that corner of the college senior common room frequented by colleagues from the same discipline, where interaction with the relevant scientific sub-culture takes place. Any ideas our peripatetic scientist might conceivably have are considered as derivative from the sub-culture.

In a later work with Eccles, Popper develops the three world postulate to support arguments for mind–body dualism and for "downward causation" from subjective intentions to physical processes occurring in the brain. Here again, intentions which are treated as activating the brain machinery are seen very much as creatures or repositories of the world of culture. Popper confesses here that "it is easier to understand how we make World 3 objects than it is to understand how we understand them, or grasp them, or 'see' them" (Popper and Eccles, 1983, p. 44).[5]

I am not in disagreement with Popper's contention that the subjective grasping of a cultural object (like a language or bicycling skills) is a bit like re-inventing it. However, the comparison is vague and stands in need of careful conceptualization. A reasonable conclusion one might draw from the notion that each individual has to remake culture, so to speak, would be that each person carries within and carries out a different, idiosyncratic, version of culture. Such a line of reasoning would lead one to place much greater importance and autonomy on World 2 than Popper cedes to it. The discussion of World 2 below will explain why he is so opposed to subjectivity.

Popper's distrust of anything smacking of the subjective spills into his treatment of scientific or artistic inspiration. Thus he offers the opinion that "most investigations into the psychology of creative thought are pretty barren" (Popper, 1982, p. 48) and rejects psychoanalysis, the most fertile field for such investigation, as inherently untestable and therefore unscientific (Popper, 1962a, pp. 35-36).[6] I remember hearing him speak in lectures and seminars about "leaps in the dark" as providing imaginative theories and ingenious tests. In later years his attitude to such leaps changed and he views any reference to them as irrationalistic (see Lakatos, 1974, p. 255; also Popper, 1962b, vol. ii, pp. 380-381). One suspects, however, that Popper would also have to take the same view regarding the most recent advances in physics which are discussed in the following section.

World 1: The World of Nature

Ziman has made the assertion that the ". . . fundamental principle of scientific observation is that all human beings are interchangeable as observers". In other words, independent observers can agree on observations of nature; such observations, to use his words, are "perceptually consensible". The assumption of such consensibility leads him to assert that "there is nearly universal consensus concerning . . . the natural domain" (Ziman, 1978, p. 120).

Ziman would have to agree that the consensibility assumption is, of course, limited by the presence in human populations of persons with perceptual impairments such as deafness or blindness. The assumption is further weakened by differences between persons in the acuity of their senses and of the problem that different degrees of sensual acuity could, among other things, reflect training and, therefore, culturally transmitted features.

Despite these difficulties, one would have to agree that the consensibility assumptions must underlie any discussion of human observations of the world of nature viewed as objective and unitary; at least as a rough approximation. In the absence of consensibility one would have to submerge the world of nature into that of subjectivity or, in other words, postulate a different world of nature for each observer.

If we are willing to accept that notion of a unitary and objective natural world, therefore, it is legitimate to assert that such a world presents itself in the first instance to pre-scientific or non-scientific man as shared perceptual experiences of given natural environments. Universally significant features of such natural environments include such elements as climate and terrain as also of the flora and fauna populating the terrain.

Here we come to the next difficulty. Characteristics attributed to the identical natural environment are subject to historical and cultural variation. Mountains, for instance, only become viewed as features of natural beauty and grandeur under the influence of romanticism in Europe. Prior to that they were perceived rather as sources of danger and obstacles to travel. In order to sustain the consensibility assumption one needs to add a further assumption (equally subject to question) that actual natural features like mountains are apprehended by the senses in similar ways irrespective of their overlay of cultural evaluations.

Yet another difficulty concerns the availability of terms in a particular language to capture environmental features. Certain primitive cultures, for instance, have terms for only severely limited numbers of colours in their languages. The question arises here as to how — or even whether — colours without names are perceived by members of the culture. Nameless colours (like the nameless joys and fears so prevalent in Western cultures) may conceivably be perceptually consensible but they are not, to use another of Ziman's expressions, "communicably consensual". In the absence of communicable consensuality their status as sensations is philosophically vexatious.

Even if we set aside the difficulties facing Ziman's consensibility assumption mentioned above, we would have to agree that members of pre-scientific cultures, as well as non-scientists in scientific cultures, gain but a provincial and localized conception of the world of nature. As Niels Bohr pointed out ". . . the task of science is . . . to extend the range of our experience . . ." (cited in Feyerabend, 1981, vol. 1, p. 17). Strictly regarded, the world of nature must include all existing "environments" apprehensible by the sense either directly or through the mediation of scientific instruments. The moment we liberate the notion of a world of nature from the constrictions of this or that specific environment proximate to the perceptions of members of a particular human group, we invoke scientific as distinct from naive perceptions of nature.

Scientific examination of the world of nature, of course, does much more than merely extend the number of directly perceivable natural environments as these present themselves to naive observers. Scientific instruments reveal sectors of nature completely imperceptible without their use as well, of course, as remote environments in which human beings could not possibly survive. We need not be concerned, in this context, with technical questions regarding possible distortions introduced by the instruments themselves. For our present purposes it is sufficient to note that Ziman's consensibility notion is proposed as an argument for obtaining reliable knowledge of nature through "instrument readings" as much as through unaided observation. A fair measure of agreement between different scientists on observations obtained by such readings makes it possible to subject theories about nature to testing and to map the contours of the natural world. Of course, besides extending the range of experience science aims at providing an optimally coherent and unitary conception of experience.

It is of considerable interest that the world of nature as revealed by contemporary physics is not merely remote from unaided perception but inaccessible to intuitive human understanding — even by physicists themselves! Instrument readings as such must remain closely tied to naive perception. What the readings convey (or reliably appear to convey) is beyond the grasp of human conception. The very notion of "nature" becomes transformed, in modern physics, from an image of tangible and familiar surroundings to a vertiginous abyss of mathematical abstractions; abstractions which are logically coherent and explanatorily powerful but beyond the grasp of metaphorical or imaginative representation. To a lesser extent, but still quite significantly, the same tendency may be found in genetics and in other advanced scientific specialisms. The more science advances in its power to generalize and to provide consistent and coherent explanations, the more it eludes direct representation by the human intelligence.

One must hasten to add that for any ordinary application it may be possible, or even necessary, to operate at levels of abstraction far below those which stem from pursuit of the scientific goal to provide explanations of the greatest possible generality and power. In many applications of physics, as in bridge building for instance, Newton's laws are a sufficiently good approximation to be perfectly usable; even though they have been decisively refuted and replaced by Einstein's theory. It would be possible to assert, indeed, that Einsteinian principles would be confusing to the bridge builder and could even be seen as inapplicable to bridge building in any direct sense. The level of conceptualization required for bridge building is quite different from that required to provide a unified and coherent explanation of the nature of the cosmos as a whole or for phenomena in sub-atomic nature.

Indeed, one can give examples where even pre-scientific principles are adequate both for explanation and for the successful attainment of specified physical tasks. Imagine a theoretical physicist whose hobby is carpentry. For this person as physicist, the "substantiality" of solids (such as planks and beams of wood) consists of electrical repulsions. Yet, when wielding saw, plane, and sandpaper in making a table our hobbyist can be (one might almost say, needs to be) totally disregardful of electrons and protons. It is entirely possible for such a person to be both physicist and carpenter without suffering from what psychiatrists call a "split personality". The understanding that there are different levels of adequate explanation, calling for drastically disparate types of conceptualization, is quite general among modern persons.

If we return to explanations at the highest level of generality, however, the picture that emerges is as surprising and bizarre as the wildest claims made by believers in paranormal powers and events. Of course, it differs from such claims in being subject to rigorous mathematical formulation and often of testing and confirmation. In order to reveal some of this picture to non-physicists I have decided to select a recent book by Paul Davies (1984) to represent contemporary physics. Davies has the double advantage of being both a reputable physicist and an excellent, lucid, popularizer of the most abstruse notions. I should emphasise that his presentation of contemporary physics does not necessarily and always represent a consensus of thinking among contemporary physicists.

The Cosmos as presently in existence, is viewed as having come into being in a "big bang". Physical laws, as presently understood, refer to the Cosmos in its present state of expansion which began after the first instant of the explosion.[7] Space and time are inherent characteristics of this Cosmos and cannot sensibly be said to exist "outside" it or to have existed before it came into being. The matter to be found in this spatiotemporal universe consists of large numbers of sub-atomic particles which are themselves immaterial in any conventional sense of the term. These particles vary in, and can be classified, according to their mass, electric charge and spin. Some of them are extremely evanescent and their existence is theoretically deducible from four forces postulated as operating in the universe. These are gravity, electro-magnetism, the weak force (accounting for particle decay in radiation) and the strong force (holding protons together against the repulsion of their electric charge).[8]

A major challenge faced by contemporary physics is to formulate a unified theory accounting for all of these four forces within the same conceptual formulation.[9] This can be done by dimensionalizing space-time. Einstein's, by now familiar, four-dimensional block universe in effect dimensionalizes gravity and accounts for its associated inverse square laws of attraction. In 1921 Kaluza suggested that the electromagnetic force could be accounted for by adding a fifth dimension. By mathematical extension of this line of reasoning Davies (p. 164) asserts that eleven dimensions provide the simplest possible account of space-time in such a way as to unify the four forces.

Forces operating between particles, and changing the description of such particles, are described as messenger or "virtual" particles. Thus a neutron encountering a neutrino transmutes into a proton and an electron (Davies p. 119) through exchange of a messenger particle (W-). The existence of force fields in a vacuum suggests that "empty space is a seething ferment of virtual particles" (Davies, p. 105). Indeed, Davies suggests that particles themselves "are only minor disturbances bubbling up over the background sea of activity" (p. 191) and goes on to explain the big bang itself as arising out of an excited vacuum state; the vacuum state, so to speak, transmuting into a state containing particles. Under this description the Judeao-Christian notion of creation *ex nihilo* (out of nothing) becomes a literal explanation. Davies leaves unclear how one can conceptualize a vacuum (which, after all, is empty *space*) before space itself exploded into existence. His speculations, for what they are worth, are to be found on and around page 202 of his book.

Finally, subatomic particles do not really exist as separate entities in their own right. Matter cannot be understood from the examination of given particles in isolation. Only the total ensemble of particles in the entire Cosmos may be considered "real". Thus ". . . observation in quantum physics is not just . . . a means of accessing information existing in the real world . . . the equations of quantum physics explicitly encode the act of observation" (Davies, pp. 39–40).

Obviously, my evanescent distillation of contemporary physics has more shock value than informative content. It will have fulfilled its purpose if the general reader is persuaded that contemporary scientific thinking at its cutting edge stretches ordinary intuition beyond its furthest limits. Almost incredibly, its bottomlessly abstract formulations have led to the invention of a multiplicity of gadgets in everyday industrial and even domestic use!

The processes whereby the naive shared perceptions of persons about nature which obtain prior to science have become transmuted into both powerful and useful — though intuitively incomprehensible — explanations have been studied by scholars in the areas of history and philosophy of science. A variety of conditions in the course of the development of science have been suggested which invite or encourage the invention of new hypotheses. Interestingly enough, the actual operations whereby bold and new hypotheses are invented elude explanation.

World 2: The World of Subjectivity (Intentions)

The small amount of attention that Popper devotes to the world of subjectivity stems from an aversion to what he calls "psychologism"; an aversion displayed long before he announced his three world postulate. In his first characterization of psychologism he describes it as the "doctrine that all empirical sciences are reducible to sense perceptions" (1959, p. 93). He then uses his general argument against inductive observation to reject the doctrine. Furthermore, he is rather emphatic in excluding the conception or invention of scientific theories or any other types of ideas (musical themes; dramatic plots) from the ambit of philosophy of science. The latter is concerned with the logic of scientific discovery. Psychology may concern itself with questions about the conditions of inspiration but there is no such thing as a "logical method for having new ideas' (1959, p. 32). Though he ascribes the task of studying inspiration to empirical psychology, one gets a strong feeling that he believes any effort to attempt to discover the sources of inspiration to be a vain one.

In later discussions of psychologism Popper shifts the meaning somewhat to make it refer to the notion that social events are "reducible to the laws of human nature" (1961, p. 152). Much as he rejects the earlier version of psychologism in favour of a logic of scientific discovery he rejects the latter in favour of interpretations of social events by what he calls *situational logic*.

Interestingly enough, Popper's arguments regarding logic of the situation guiding social action was anticipated by Max Weber, who states that the "rational deliberations of an actor . . . do not become a bit more understandable by taking 'psychological' considerations into account" (Weber, 1947, p. 108). Elsewhere, Weber distinguishes between meaningful action and merely reactive behaviour (1947, p. 32). Yet Weber's approach is explicitly concerned with the construction of models of *subjective* meanings and intentions of individuals. Interpersonal relations are viewed by him as guided by mutual interpretation (or misinterpretation) of the meanings and intentions held by others with whom one relates. The logic of social situations, for Weber, consists in large part precisely of the reciprocal understanding of intentions.[10] It is always construed as being based on the subjective understanding of individuals. Thus clearly, Weber gives a prominent role to subjectivity whilst distinguishing the latter from psychologism. Indeed, he discarded psychologism for exactly the opposite reasons that Popper states. Weber thought of psychology as a "natural science and hence not accessible to the application of subjective categories" (Parsons in Weber, 1947, p. 25). Thus we find Popper throwing away subjectivity with the bathwater of psychologism as he construes it, while Weber rejects his own construal of psychologism because it fails to do justice to subjectivity!

In order to clarify the issue, a few words on contemporary psychology are appropriate at this point. Schools of thinking in psychology range in their views from total rejection of subjectivity (behaviourism) to the featuring of subjectivity as a central issue. Between these two extremes is a wide spectrum of intermediate positions whose coloration, unfortunately, gets somewhat mixed because of the promiscuous tendency of some psychologists to borrow ideas and terminologies from the two extremes of the spectrum while failing to provide a clear conceptual basis for their syncretistic formulations.[11] It would be rash to claim that no clearly conceptualized positions at all may be found which avoid either embracing or totally rejecting a subjective viewpoint but, viewed from the point of view of subjectivity, the two extremes of the continuum call for brief description.

Operant Conditioning, the contemporary behaviourist position, is that all activities start as random muscular twitches. Such twitchings produce behavioural emissions such as movement of limbs and noises from the larynx. Such emissions are called "operants". Behaviour is shaped by the environmental "reinforcement" and "extinction" of such operants. Reinforcement and extinction are themselves defined by whether specifiable emissions of operants increase or decrease. Differences of behaviour as between different individuals are accounted for by differential histories of reinforcement. Verbal behaviour, like any other, is shaped in the way described.

The total erradication of World 2 is not as unproblematic as behaviourists seem to indicate. Descriptions of complex conduct simply cannot proceed without the attribution of some guiding rationale to the activity in question. Even if we consider a type of activity in which muscular movements themselves are prominently featured, for instance a gymnastic display, the conduct itself is indescribable, quite simply, because it is not perceived (or perhaps even perceivable) as a jumble of muscular movements but as a "gymnastic display". What makes it this is beyond the grasp of behaviouristic explanation.

The subjectivistic position in psychology, at the other extreme, views human action as governed by purposes, intentions, goals and the like. Here the complication is that conscious and rational activity guided by intentions provides few specifically psychological problems. However, subjective psychologies attribute intention-like character-istics to apparently irrational activities (as well as inabilities to act) and view these as unconsciously motivated. In effect, the psychologist or psychiatrist argues that the person (or "patient") whose behaviour is viewed as problematic acts "as if" he/she had a particular intention or goal, or better, several conflicting intentions.[12]

Weber confined his own analysis to consciously intended actions and I shall try not to burden this discussion of World 2 too heavily with various problems associated with the attribution of a rationale to irrational behaviour. Indeed, I shall return to psycho-analytic interpretations when discussing World 4. Instead I will conclude discussion of World 2 by dwelling briefly on the modern philosophy of action. For the sake of brevity I shall focus on von Wright's lively and interesting discussion (1971, 1976). Von Wright's formulation has the incidental advantage of laying out very clearly the relationships between World 2 and Worlds 1 and 3.[13]

Von Wright conceives of action as having an "inner" (or subjective) and an "outer" aspect. The inner aspect consists of the actor's intention; the outer aspect consists of three types of "phases". The three phases are: 1) a muscular activity by the actor ("antecedent"); 2) a physical event which the muscular activity brings about ("result"); and 3) sometimes one or more effects of the result ("consequences"). For example, a lady flips a switch (antecedent), thus turning on the electric light (result), which enables her to continue reading the newspaper and startles the cat (consequences). Von Wright's central claim is that the various phases of the outer aspect of an action can be explained if, and only if, they are subsumed under a common intention. One would understand the switch-flipping action of the lady in our above example as "turning on the light with the intention of being able to continue reading". Of course, the action could have unintended consequences such as "startling the cat".

The relationship between subjective intention and processes in the world of nature is provided by the second (result) phase of the outer aspect of the action. Flipping the switch closes an electric circuit thereby harnessing a natural process (the flow of electricity). Some might object that electric circuits are human artefacts and, therefore, mediate between directly occurring natural processes and the muscular activity. The objection is correct to the extent that electric circuits, like all human artefacts, embody intention in their very design. However, one could easily change the example so as to avoid reference to artefacts. The lady, for instance, might pick up a flat stone and place it in the middle of a shallow brook in order to step to the other side without getting her feet wet. Here no previously existing artefact is necessary to illustrate Von Wright's notion of the outer aspects of an intention.

Though von Wright is not absolutely clear on the following point, one might add that it is also possible to formulate intentions which require no outer manipulation of physical objects. Thus one can inform, or persuade, or even coerce others merely by speaking to them. Here the muscular activity (speaking) results in no physical event outside of itself. Nonetheless, the muscular activity can bring about consequences in the state of mind and consequent activities of other persons. If claims for the existence of psychokinetic action were valid, it would even be possible to bring about consequences (both in the mental states of others *and* in nature) without any muscular activity. In such a case, however, I should be inclined to locate the relevant intention in World 4 rather than in World 2. More central to von Wright's pre-occupations is the belief that the notion of causation in the world of nature arises out of actions; that is to say, the kinds of actions in which scientists engage in the course of experimentation. He thus concludes that our notions about cause and effect in Popper's World 1 are dependent upon actions emanating from Popper's World 2.[14]

A few words are necessary on the inner aspect of the action; on the intention itself. Von Wright believes that intentions can be explained by reference to the *practical inference schema* which he adapts from

Anscombe and, more remotely, from Aristotle's views of deliberation. The irreducibly simplest version of such a practical inference schema is the following:

MAJOR PREMISE: A intends to bring about x
MINOR PREMISE: A considers he cannot bring about x unless he does y
CONCLUSION: Therefore A sets himself to do y.

Now, of course, not all actions are fully intentional and consciously deliberate. The practical inference schema, however, is pivotal for the explanation of all action (Von Wright, 1976, p. 394).

The above statement of the practical inference schema is couched from the actor's point of view. In other words it is in the first person. It assumes that deliberate action necessarily must follow a certain line of reasoning. The matter is complicated in two ways. First there must be a belief on the part of the actor that a means (or appropriate action) to the goal exists and that he is capable of instantiating that means. Secondly, the actor may be aware of different means (actions) sufficient for reaching the goal. In the latter case one can merely say that the actor will necessarily select one of these functionally equivalent actions (Smith and Zollschan, 1980, p. 12). Yet even when one bears these complications in mind, the postulate of first person practical inference strikes one as barren, particularly when it is separated from von Wright's programme to pose it as an alternative to causation in nature.

Personally, I would agree with Dewey (1933) that the flow of consciousness in most people is sporadic and episodic. Habitual routines govern most of our lives and emerge in thought only when they are interrupted or disrupted. Similarly, I feel, practical inferences become consciously articulated only under circumstances in which either routine activities are frustrated or in which novel intentions arise.

In that connection it is of considerable interest that philosophers of action usually choose the most banal and uninteresting types of action for analysis — the types of action indeed, that hardly qualify for conscious attention at all. Their featured actors are forever flipping light switches, or opening windows, or taking dogs for a walk. Even von Wright's apparently dashing and original intention of getting some caviar (1976, p. 396) pales into routine when one realises that he is Finnish (and therefore, one might infer, regularly eats ladles full of the stuff for breakfast). While the banality of intentions discussed by the philosophers may serve the function of lending apparent simplicity and clarity to their arguments, they are also instrumental in concealing a central question about intention; namely, "how are intentions formed?". Such a banishment into limbo of intention formation from the analysis of intentions reveals the most serious flaw of purely subjectivist explanation in coming to grips with action, and, in particular, with original or unusual action.

World 3: The World of Symbols

The reader is reminded that, for Popper, World 3 is the world of culture and symbols. What lends particular interest to the practical inference schema as applied by von Wright and discussed in the previous section of this chapter is that it can be translated into second person and third person formulations. To a greater or lesser extent such formulations depend upon their intelligibility of what is known about the socio-cultural context in which they occur. For example, the act of depositing a cheque in one's bank account would be very puzzling for a person (whether observer or, for that matter, actor) who knows nothing about banks or their mode of operation.

The second person perspective illuminates the process of under-standing another's intentions. It can also apply to the analysis of one's own intentions under circumstances where one stops to ask oneself "why am I doing this?" The third person perspective can form the basis of a theory of practical efficacy so as to provide a solid foundation for the study of situational logic; a type of study which, hitherto, has been evoked only progamatically.

Third person practical inference fits directly into Popper's World 3 without too many problems. For that reason it will be discussed first. Von Wright (1963) suggested that there is a sense of 'objective' practical necessity that may be formulated by a third person practical inference schema. The following form of it provides a felicitous formulation of what is meant by situational logic.

MAJOR PREMISE: A intends to bring about x
MINOR PREMISE: Unless A does y he cannot bring about x
CONCLUSION: Therefore A must do y *or* fail to bring about x

The conclusion of a third person practical inference specifies that an actor must perform some specific action or fail to achieve his goal. It does not specify what action will actually be attempted by the actor. It is therefore capable of being falsified. A third person practical inference is falsified either if the actor performs an action at variance with the one prescribed and succeeds, or, if the actor performs the prescribed (supposedly necessary and sufficient) action and fails.

As a case in point, one needs only to consider a third person practical inference regarded as axiomatic as recently as the end of the Nineteenth Century, as follows:

MAJOR PREMISE:	A intends to fly
MINOR PREMISE:	Unless A is lighter than air (or is lighter than air when combined with a balloon) he cannot fly
CONCLUSION:	Therefore A must make himself lighter than air or fail to fly.

It may be objected that this example refers to World 1 rather than to World 3. Such an objection is partially valid since technology at any given stage of development is an interface between Worlds 1 and 3. However, the example could just as easily refer to what, in any given historical period, is considered practically efficacious in achieving a particular social or interpersonal goal, as for example: ritually declaring a couple to be "man and wife"; making an audience laugh; inducing a soldier to fight; or seducing a woman.[15] Technological as much as interpersonally practical nostrums for the achievement of aims can fairly be described as being social or socio-cultural in character. Within given social contexts practical efficacy depends as much on established conventions and rules for bringing about an outcome as on the physical feasibility of doing so.

Understanding the intention of another is also capable of being stated in the form of a practical inference schema as follows:

MAJOR PREMISE:	A does y
MINOR PREMISE:	y is an action A considers necessary to bring about x
CONCLUSION:	Therefore A intends to bring about x.

The above form of practical inference corresponds, in the second person, to von Wright's account of first person and third person practical inference (Zollschan and Smith, 1981, p. 7). In other words it may be described as "intersubjective". It implies that the observer attributes a precise intention to the action y. Such an attribution is equivalent to giving the activity a rationale or investing it with meaning. At this point I leave open the question of direct conscious or unconscious intuition of another individual's intentions. Where authentic, such direct intuition would correspond to a World 4 process.

On the other hand the observer may be asking the question "why is A doing y?" within a frame of reference committing the same observer to find an intention x which renders y an appropriate action, or at least an action which makes some sort of sense. Thus the second person perspective permits the analysis of the attribution of intentionality to behaviour where the precise intention x constitutes a puzzle to be solved rather than merely as a datum to be perceived.

The moment that a second person practical inference becomes problematic in this way, intention x is posed as an hypothesis rather than as a simple attribution. What is interesting about hypothetical second person practical inferences is that they can refer either to World 2 or World 3. In other words, certain second person practical inferences are subjective (or perhaps better "intersubjective") in that they refer to the observer's purely personal knowledge of the actor. Other second person practical inferences are "objective" in that they draw upon what can loosely be called "culturally shared" assumptions. Some examples of the types of hypotheses which might be brought to bear in second person practical inference are featured below:-

i)   B (the observer himself or someone he knows well) does y to bring about x and A is like B in that respect.

ii)   The observer knows A very well and his special circumstances or history dispose him to bring about x.[16]

iii)   The observer knows A well and he habitually (or repeatedly) does y to bring about (or try to bring about) x.

iv)   A has been told by C that y will bring about x (and A believes C).

v)   y is a necessary condition for bringing about consequence x in the light of a theory of practical efficacy.

vi)   y is typically done by persons of a certain type (which characterizes A) for bringing about x.

It should be noted that hypothesis (v) is a form of the minor premise of third person practical inference differing only in that it does not assume the premise to be necessarily true. Auxiliary minor premise (vi) rests upon some social typology (e.g. of age groups, classes, occupations, ethnic groups, etc) and assumes that individuals of a given type will engage in "typical" (i.e. type specific or type appropriate) behaviour. A limiting case where (v) and (vi) overlap concerns the actions of handicapped persons who can either be types (i.e. "the blind", "the paraplegic"), or viewed as engaging in particular actions because these actions are practically efficacious under the special conditions of the handicap. Painters who paint with their feet may generally be assumed to have something "wrong" with their hands.[17]

Inspection of the types of hypotheses listed above indicates both that they may range from subjective to socio-cultural and, also, that the distinction between the subjective and the socio-cultural is not absolutely definite. The lack of absolute precision in drawing a line between the two worlds leaves the door open for attempts to reduce one to the other. Such attempts must engage our attention.

First let us examine the reduction of World 3 to World 2. Popper accuses previous theorists of knowledge for this shortcoming and, some of the time, Weber reads as though he were construing the socio-cultural world purely in intersubjective terms. The issue in question here concerns the degree to which any so-called "culturally shared" assumption can, indeed, be shown to be generally shared by persons designated as being carriers of the culture under consideration. Surprisingly little research has been done on this problem and I suspect that different members of any given society have quite startlingly different slants on what are assumed to be shared cultural perspectives. Nonetheless, most carriers of any culture do have a sort of recipe knowledge of things to be done and conventions to be followed which enables them to interact routinely with other carriers of the same culture. To return to the discussion at the beginning of this section, most middle-class people in the non-communist industrialized world "know" how to cash a cheque, though the depth and extent of their personal understanding of the operation of the banking system might be subject to considerable variation. Certainly, the members of any given society use more or less the "same" language. All of this does suggest the autonomy of a cultural realm which is not reducible simply to subjective behaviour.[18]

Alternatively, it has recently become fashionable to reduce World 2 to World 3. Here the argument hinges largely on the existence of languages which people have in common. Any rational activity, it is argued, must be linguistically elaborated. Thus even a first person practical inference requires "habits of mind" which are socially acquired. Though Popper specifically features the world of subjectivity as an autonomous one in his three world postulate there is just a hint that he, himself, may be inclined to a subtle form of reductions to World 3. At any rate, he is intriguingly silent on the topic of subjectivity except as a link between Worlds 1 and 3.

Yet it is beyond doubt that any instantiation of World 3, even if it consists only of grasping a symbol such as a written word or sentence, can only occur through an individual person's activity. What is more, different individuals in the same society, or even the same sub-section of the society, may construe the identical symbol in different ways. This suggests, in turn, that one must cede the autonomy of a subjective realm which is not reducible simply to culture.

There is an approach which permits a non-reductive treatment of World 2 and World 3 as autonomous realms. Symbolic Intercationism, a sociological school of thought, propounds the view that both *society* (World 3) and *self* (World 2) arise out of communication by symbols. Here it is unnecessary to elaborate the symbolic interactionist position beyond the notion that one can differentiate between self and society (or culture) even though both arise out of symbolic interaction between individuals. All that needs to be assumed if this view is taken is that both World 2 and World 3 are composed of the same elements, so to speak. What is of particular interest in this context, however, is that symbolic interactionism bases its analysis on the assumption that symbols have come into existence. Nothing like a coherent theory of symbol formation or, perhaps better, "symbol creation" is proposed.

Thus, just as the analytic philosophy of action lacks a theory of intention formation, so symbolic interactionism can throw little light on symbol creation. Neither of these approaches even tries to provide a convincing account of creativity.

World 4: The World of Inspiration

Certain features about each of Popper's three worlds have been revealed which indicate that the three world postulate is incomplete. On first appearance World 1 seems to yield itself directly to naive perception. But as scientific knowledge grows, this apparently familiar world becomes explainable only by the most abstract models of thought. How the scientific mind can leap to these abstractions is left unexplained. Similarly, World 2, the world of personal knowledge and subjective intentions, leaves the ends or goals of activity unexplained unless it trivializes them. World 3, finally, is a world composed of more or less shared symbols. Here again the three world frame of reference limits understanding by failing to explain the creation of new symbols. I believe that a four world frame of reference is needed to overcome these deficiencies.

For the sake of convenience I shall call this fourth world the World of Inspiration. What is notable about the three other worlds is the sense of a symbolic barrier between the acting self and the medium in which it operates. Each of these three worlds corresponds to a sort of knowledge predicated on limitations or boundaries. The world of nature presents an order in which no "miracles" are permitted; the subjective world is confined within the limitations of practical reasoning; and the symbolic world accepts pre-existing symbols as being akin, in a sense, to established facts of nature. Predictions in each of these three worlds depends absolutely on the boundaries which set defined limits on the processes occurring with them.

The World of Inspiration on the other hand, is a separate autonomous world in which possibilities are unbounded. It is fluid and contains no defined limits. Because of the openness of possibilities within this fourth world its direct description is, in principle, impossible. World 4 is inherently veiled and inaccessible to the observer in the sense that, like a "black hole" in cosmology, one cannot describe what is going on within it. It has to be inaccessible in this way because any direct description would bind and entrammel it in established explanations and symbols which are foreign to it. The existence of this world can be inferred only from its interaction with the other three worlds. Such interaction occurs whenever there is a leap towards profounder and more accurate explanations in World 1; a spontaneous breakthrough of original intentions in World 2; or the development of new symbolic forms in World 3.

What is more, I suggest that apparently "paranormal" capacities and experiences, as well as genuine mystical experiences, find their source in World 4 just as World 4 is also the source of irruptions of novelty or creativity in the other three worlds. This is not because I believe that the paranormal or the mystical is necessarily the same as the creative but because none of these are trammeled by pre-existing limitations of space or time; convention or causality. Hence the paranormal and the mystical, as well as the creative belong to the World of Inspiration. What is more, I see particularly heightened instances of creativity as being nothing less than paranormal or "miraculous" in character. The depth and originality of some outstandingly creative works — Beethoven's late string quartets, for instance — to my mind contain some of the same qualities as a true prophecy or an extraordinary feat of psychokinesis.

The difference between the extraordinarily creative and the genuinely paranormal is that in modern societies creative works are significant and enduring while paranormal feats are sporadic and leave little mark. But the reader should be reminded that in certain cultures and at certain historical periods prophecy and the working of miracles or witchcraft play a significant and even decisive role.

As indicated, World 4 is a dark planet; a world of concealment. The nearest characterization of it that I have found is by R. Yehuda Loew, the Maharal of Prague. The Maharal works with a two world postulate in which his notion of the world of nature includes all of Popper's three worlds. His other world — he calls it the world of Nivdal or the "separate" world — corresponds to my World 4. Evidently, the paranormal capacities of R. Loew were highly developed. A fable (if it was just a fable) developed around him that he actually breathed life into a figure of clay (the Golem of Prague) and used this homunculus for the protection of the Prague Ghetto. Personally, I am very skeptical of the tale. I do not think that paranormal capacities of such majestic power are available to mere humans. However, the very notion of a figure of clay being infused with life provides a representative anecdote of the function of World 4 in my four world postulate.

R. Loew distinguishes between the intellectual who comprehends and grasps the natural world and the prophet who is in contact with what I call World 4. Experience of World 4 he describes as "empirical" much in the same way as external vision of a material object is empirical. For this reason the prophet is called a "seer". He must necessarily have some experimental connection with the object of his prophecy.[19]

A moment of reflection reveals the truth of this insight. If World 4 is unbounded by the limits of human thinking and classification it necessarily can only be experienced like some inward equivalent of a direct experience in the external world. One might say that it is formless and chaotic like the heavens and earth at the beginning of the first day of creation in the Biblical account. The chaos permits of direct experience. However, it only acquires boundary and form in interaction with the other three worlds. In such interactions it provides bold new hypotheses to explain natural phenomena (World 1); the specific content of novel intentions (World 2); and new symbols (World 3).

If the necessity for postulating a fourth world is accepted and if it is agreed that this world can be directly experienced, the problem of study and description remains acute. Obviously, World 4 can yield itself only to indirect study in its interaction with the other three worlds. The interaction of World 4 with the other three worlds has been glimpsed, from one particular perspective, in the psychoanalytic study of the personalities of particularly creative persons and/or of the special circumstances in which creativity is triggered in persons who are not normally creative.[20]

What becomes clear from the examination of psychoanalytic case histories and from theoretical evaluations of such case histories is that the core of creativity consists of the capacity to engage in untrammeled free association. For effective creative expression other things too are needed. Mainly these consist of some appropriate talent and disciplined commitment to the creative task.[21] Kohut (1971, pp. 208-316) suggests, additionally, that creative episodes in people's lives occur at a time when deep wounds to their self esteem ("narcissistic injuries") are healing.

The conclusion one may draw from psychoanalytic accounts of creativity is that free association provides a connecting link between World 4 and the other three worlds. As inchoate inner sensations grope towards expression and form, new conscious motives and symbols and explanations become vitalized and realized. Furthermore, since contact with World 4 is experienced deep within the self, a strong sense of (often wounded) self love coupled with more or less periodic bouts of self acceptance is an additional condition of creative potential. I would suggest that persons whose narcissism is dissipated in the course of their personal development by love of others will free associate in symbolically more conventional and less fluid ways.[22]

Persons with paranormal capacities, experiences, and beliefs have also been studied by psychoanalysts. Chapter 3 in this volume contains a contribution by one of them. However, I am not aware of any real convergence of thinking in the psychoanalytic studies of creativity and of the paranormal. If the autonomy of World 4 is recognized and if paranormal as much as creative capacities find their origin in this world, then the personality characteristics of "psychics" and the special circumstances in which "psychic" episodes are triggered deserve careful study. Moreover, if the basic proposition advanced in this chapter concerning the autonomous character of the four worlds is accepted, reductionist attempts to find explanations of the paranormal in the natural, subjective, or symbolic worlds are bound to lead into a blind alley.

Conclusion

In this Chapter I have sought to revise Popper's three world postulate by proposing a fourth world of inspiration. The chapter should be read strictly as an exploratory attempt to relate the study of the paranormal to an established philosophy of science. It is in the nature of explorations to raise issues and questions. Inevitably there are many loose ends and tying these up will require much further effort. At any rate, it cannot be said of this preliminary effort that the loose ends have been tucked beneath the carpet.

As a final thought I offer the suggestion that my four world postulate can provide the basis for overcoming barriers to fruitful discussion posed by world views based exclusively on one or another of the four worlds. Materialism and physicalism focus on World 1; subjectivism on World 2; cultural determinism and ordinary language cultism on World 3; and romanticism as well as mysticism on World 4. A system comprising four worlds can encourage the type of discussion of currently entrenched ideologies which makes their transcendence virtually inevitable. The trick can only be pulled off, however, in a full discussion of interactions between the four worlds. In this preliminary discussion of the model my intentions, of necessity, have been much more limited.

Footnotes

1. The acronym "Maharal" stands for a Hebrew expression which may be translated as "our master, Rabbi Loew". In Jewish circles R. Yehuda Loew ben Bezalel of Prague is known under this acronymic appelation.

2. Though Popper has had a variety of interesting things to say about creativity in the course of his publications, the principal view that one gets is that creativity consists of a particularly rapid rate of emission of ideas. Of course, this assumption has to operate under the proviso that such ideas are not randomly scattered in all directions but focused on the subject in which the creativity is being exercised. This leaves the unanswered problem of providing an explanation of what fosters the conditions under which such a proviso can be satisfied.

3. The reader is referred to a book by David Bakan (1958) in which he traces Freud's thinking back to kabbalistic sources. In particular, he refers to Abraham Abulafia's method of using association as a way of meditation. This method is remarkably similar to "free association" in psycho-analysis.

4. I interpret the date of receiving my doctorate as the day of making my oral defence of the dissertation and receiving the customary "congratulations Dr. Zollschan" rather than the official date of actual conferral.

5. Popper's practice of appropriating old ideas in the social sciences and passing them off as his own provides itself with a sort of alibi in this equation of "understanding;" and "making". Above I have mentioned how he plays the role of a new Columbus rediscovering the notion of culture. He himself states (Popper, 1979, p. 107) that his argument concerning the autonomy of culture finds its origin in a much earlier work. Here we find a statement in criticism of Marx's historical materialism that "ideas may revolutionise . . . economic conditions" (Popper, 1962b, Vol. ii, p. 108). One really wonders whether Popper can really have been unaware of Weber's classic elaboration of this very point (Weber, 1958). Certainly, he does acknowledge the expression "methodological individualism" as finding its roots in Weber's thinking. (Popper, 1962b, vol. 22, p. 324.) Elsewhere, he piously attributes a well-known and widely quoted talmudic saying to his second cousin once removed, J. Popper-Lynkeus! (Popper & Eccles, 1983, p. 3.)

6. Grünbaum's magisterial critique of the epistemological foundations of the psycho-analysis, though raising doubts about the capacity of free association in clinical situations to yield adequate tests for psycho-analytic theory, dismisses Popper's criticism as indicating "insufficient command or scrutiny of its logical contents rather than a scientific liability of psycho-analysis" (Grünbaum, 1984, p. 113).

7. The Cosmos does, however, contain "black holes" in which established laws of physics do not operate.

8. Complicated and expensive machinery, such as nuclear accelerators, are used to confirm the existence of such particles.

9. Unification of the electro-magnetic force and the weak force has been accomplished by the Weinberg-Salam theory of 1967.

10. Popper's accusation that Weber's characterization of sociology is essentialistic in nature (1962b, vol. II, p. 216) is nothing less than grotesque. In fact Weber provided a situational analysis of social relationships which is incomparably superior to Popper's later attempt.

11. A prominent case in point is Bandura's 1974 presidential address to the American Psychological Association. While accepting Skinner's notions of "conditioning" he proceeds to depict this process as "subject to the intervening influence of thought" and even places "evaluative capacities" alongside cognitive ones as regulators of action additional to primordial "reinforcements" in themselves. As a result of these expectations and evaluations people produce consequences rather than merely suffer them; or, in Bandura's terms, they engage in "self-reinforcement" (Bandura, 1974, pp. 859-860). A brief description of reinforcement is provided below.

12. For a fuller account of this interpretation of subjectivistic psychology, the reader is referred to some of my previous published work (Zollschan, 1964; Zollschan and Gibeau, 1964; Zollschan and Smith, 1981).

13. Von Wright's version of intentionalism lends itself well to my purposes without worrying about his own primary intentions for adopting his position. His own major pre-occupation is to distinguish between causal and teleological (i.e. intentionalistic) explanation and to argue against the conception that both natural causes and human intentions can be subsumed under what he calls the general covering law model of explanation. Indeed, he suggests that the practical inference schema (to be discussed below) provides an alternative to the covering law model; an alternative, in fact, which provides the social sciences with a distinct model of explanation. Whether or not the social sciences require a different explanation model than other sciences is not an issue directly addressed in this chapter.

14. Indeed, this idea of dependency of directed observation on intention is a weaker version of the more radical principle adopted by phenomenology; namely, that perception (or rather, mental constitution) of objects and events itself depends upon the activity of directing attention upon the latter. Brentano, and after him Husserl, actually termed such object-constituting activity "intention". Subjective intention in the phenomenological sense, however, is not easily subsumed under the practical inference schema. For that reason I shall confine my arguments regarding "perception" to the second person attribution of intentions.

15. Smith and Zollschan (1980, pp. 20-21) have suggested a research technique for testing theories of practical efficacy to take its place besides ethnomethodology. Ethnomethodological procedures are designed to test implicit taken-for-granted social assumptions by violating these. Similarly, one could test theories of practical efficacy by giving research subjects tasks intended to challenge the minor premises of third person practical inferences in social contexts. Much unsuspected information might be gleaned by following such a procedure. One may add that originality consists, in large measure, of such challenges to accepted theories of practical efficacy.

16. This sort of premise assumes background knowledge of an actor which explains his idiosyncratic actions. Take a person who consistently avoids getting married under circumstances where marriage would appear to be a reasonable course of action. The personal background of one person (for instance, the situation in his parental home) may incline him to prefer bachelorhood in preference to his ingrained expectation of becoming a tormented husband. Another person might avoid getting married because

this would limit his capacity to exploit sexual opportunities. Compare this example with Weisman's discussion of the statement in a psychoanalytic situation: "Before I'd get married, I'd rather be a bachelor" (Weisman, 1965, pp. 55-56).

17. An additional complication with second person practical inference about the action of handicapped persons is that such inference may be of a privileged rather than a public character. That is to say, the observer may be able to explain pecularities of behaviour (such as painting with the feet) not because this is a collectively recognized solution for painters with no hands, or with functionally defective hands, but because he knows that the actor intends to paint and is unable to do so using his hands. In such a case I would class the hypotheses as being of type (ii) rather than types (v) or (vi).

18. Berger and Luckman (1967, pp. 70-85) present an interesting Robinson Crusoe model of social reality construction in which two persons from entirely different cultures (stranded, say, on a desert island) will develop routines of interaction. If these people had children or if there were newcomers to the island they would be faced with an already existing social reality. Thus what may begin as purely intersubjective acquires an autonomous reality of its own for additional members.

19. (See Maharal, 1980). The three introductory sections of this work are available in translation (Maharal, 1979, esp. p. 4).

20. Psychoanalytic theories and investigations also have influenced some psychological comparative studies.

21. In view of limitations of space in this chapter I cannot expand here on sources from which I have drawn for reaching this conclusion. My review of psychoanalytic theories of creativity was done as part of the work on my doctoral dissertation which reviewed theories and reports by Arieti, Bellack, Greenacre, Kubie, Rank, Storr, and others (Zollschan, 1978).

22. Kohut believes that narcissism does not necessarily have to become transmuted into what psychoanalysts call "object love" but can continue to undergo growth and development in its own right (Kohut, 1984, p. 47). That both narcissism and object love can develop together in the same person is illustrated very clearly by J.S. Bach who was both majestically creative (with a highly narcissistic dramatic flair) and a devoted and tolerant husband and father.

References

Bakan, D., (1958), *Sigmund Freud and the Jewish Mystical Trudition*, Princeton, N.J., Van Nostrand.

Bandura, A. (1974), "Behaviour Theory and Models of Man", in *American Psychologist*, XXIX, pp. 859-869.

Berger, P. and Luckman, T. (1967), *The Social Construction of Reality*, Harmondsworth, Penguin.

Davies, P. (1984), *Superforce: The Search for a Grand Unified Theory of Nature*, London, Heinnemann.

Dewey, J. (1933), *How We Think*, Boston, Heath.

Durkheim, E. (1964), *Rules of Sociological Method*, (Transl. Solovay, S.S. and Mueller, J.H.), Glencoe, Illinois, Free Press.

Feyerabend, P.K. (1981), *Realism, Rationalism and Scientific Method: Philosophical Papers, Volume 1*, Cambridge, Cambridge University Press.

Grünbaum, A. (1984), *Foundations of Psychoanalysis*, Berkeley, University of California Press.

Kohut, H. (1971), *The Analysis of Self*, (Monograph No 4, The Psychoanalytic Study of the Child), New York, International Universities Press.

Kohut, H. (1984), *How Does Analysis Cure?*, Chicago, University of Chicago Press.

Lakatos, I. (1974), " Popper on Demarkation and Induction", in Schilpp, P.A., *The Philosophy of Karl Popper*, La Salle, Illinois, Open Court, pp. 241-273.

Maharal, (1979), *The Book of Divine Power: Introductions* (translated, annotated, and illustrated by Mallin, S. in collaboration with Carmel, A.), Jerusalem, Gabriel Beer.

Maharal (1980), *Sepher Gevurot Ha'Shem* (Hebrew), B'nei Brak, Israel, Yahadut Press.

Myrdal, G. (1944), *An American Dilemma*, New York, Harper & Row.

Myrdal, G. (1969), *Objectivity in Social Research*, New York, Pantheon.

Parsons, T. (1947), Introduction to Weber M., *The Theory of Social and Economic Organization*, New York, Oxford University Press.

Polanyi, M. (1962), *Personal Knowledge*, Chicago, University of Chicago Press.

Popper, K.R. (1959), *The Logic of Scientific Discovery*, New York, Basic Books.

Popper, K.R. (1961), *The Poverty of Historicism*, (corrected version), London, Routledge & Kegan Paul.

Popper, K.R. (1962a), *Conjectures and Refutations*, New York, Basic Books.

Popper, K.R. (1962b), *The Open Society and its Enemies*, (4th Edition, 2 vols.), New York, Harper.

Popper, K.R. (1979), (rev. ed.), *Objective Knowledge*, Oxford, Clarendon.

Popper, K.R. (1982), *Unended Quest*, Glasgow, Collins.

Popper, K.R. and Eccles, J.C. (1983), *The Self and its Brain*, London, Routledge & Kegan Paul.

Scholem, G.G. (1961), *Major Trends in Jewish Mysticism*, New York, Schocken Paperback.

Smith, T. and Zollschan, G.K. (1980), "Strategies in the Explanation of Action", Paper read before Section 27 (Sociology), 50th Congress of the Australian and New Zealand Association for the Advancement of Science, Adelaide (Unpublished).

Von Wright, G.H. (1963), "Practical Inference", in *Philosophical Review*, LXXII, pp. 159-179.

Von Wright, G.H. (1971), *Explanation and Understanding*, Ithaca, Cornell University Press.

Von Wright, G.H. (1976), "Replies", in Mannien, J. and Tuomela, R. (eds.), *Essays in Explanation and Understanding*, Dordrecht, Reidel.

Weber, M. (1947), *The Theory of Social and Economic Organization* (transl. Henderson, A.M. and Parson, T.), New York, Oxford University Press.

Weber, M. (1958), *The Protestant Ethic and the Spirit of Capitalism*, (transl. Parsons, T.), New York, Scribner.

Weisman, A.D. (1965), *The Existential Core of Psychoanalysis*, Boston, Little Brown.

Ziman, J. (1978), *Reliable Knowledge*, Cambridge, Cambridge University Press.

Zollschan, G.K. (1964), "Beyond the 'Reality Principle'" in Zollschan, G.K. and Hirsch, W. (eds.), *Explorations in Social Change*, Boston, Houghton Mifflin, and London, Routledge & Kegan Paul.

Zollschan, G.K. (1978), "A Critical Examination of Theories of 'Development', with Special Reference to Underlying Motivational Assumptions", thesis submitted to the University of London in fulfilment of the requirements of the degree of Doctor of Philosophy (Unpublished).

Zollschan, G.K. and Gibeau, P. (1964), "Concerning Alienation: A System of Categories for the Explanation of Rational and Irrational Behaviour", in Zollschan, G.K. and Hirsch, W. (eds.), Boston, Houghton Mifflin, and London, Routledge & Kegan Paul.

Zollschan, G.K. and Smith, T. (1981), "Practical Reasoning in Sociological Explanation", Paper read before Section 27 (Sociology), 51st Congress of the Australian and New Zealand Association for the Advancement of Science, Brisbane (Unpublished).

CHAPTER 5
THE SOCIAL SCIENCES AND MYSTICAL EXPERIENCE

Julia Day Howell

Records of all human communities include reports of people experiencing 'other worlds' or occasionally observing 'this world' operating in a non-lawful fashion. Since their inception the social sciences (anthropology and sociology) have known in general terms what to do with these reports. They have read them as poetically or insanely distorted statements about the 'real world'. (Here the 'real world' must be understood as the world as it ordinarily appears to us, and naively attributed some ultimate factuality.) The poetic distortions are sometimes charitably cast as useful, as when Durkheim (1968) sees a totem as a mythical representation of the solidarity of the clan that celebrates it, or when Malinowski (1948) points out the psychological support rituals provide South Sea islanders in fearsome situations. A more severe judgment is reflected in characterizations of extra-ordinary experiences as insane distortions, as when Devereux (1956) labels a shaman's ascent of a sky ladder in pursuit of a lost soul a psychotic episode. The experiences are then judged to represent breakdowns in adaptive information processing about the real world. Somewhat less severe judgments are embodied in characterizations of such experiences as mere neuroses. We see this in Marx's (1955) reflection on the value of religious feeling as an artificial but still useful means of healing the alienation of workers, or in Freud's (1959) view that the formless world of bliss reported by mystics is a fantasy recollection of the unproblematic environment of the womb, resorted to by weak people when they are unable to face reality.

Asserting that social scientists have known since their inception what to do with the præternatural is another way of saying that social science explanations of extraordinary experiences inevitably fall within the limits of certain assumptions about the world and how we know it. Violation of these assumptions pushes an explanation into the realm of the implausible and warrants its dismissal from serious consideration at scholarly meetings and before editorial boards. The naive realism that underlies such judgments on the plausibility limits of theory, however, has become increasingly unjustifiable in recent years as developments in other disciplines, most notably psychology, neuroscience, physics and philosophy, have challenged the assumptions upon which the social sciences were founded. It is time, then, to examine these assumptions and re-evaluate the plausibility limits for the social sciences of the paranormal. To initiate this project I offer the following summary of assumptions underlying mainstream anthropological and sociological theorizing:

1. That there is an objective material world of tables and chairs 'out there'. For social scientists who model their work on the hard sciences (the positivists) this is held as a testable (and, to their satisfaction, amply substantiated) proposition; for those who reject the model of the hard sciences and see their work as translation and explication (the phenomenologists) this is held as a gut feeling (except by the theologically inspired and the few who have experienced powerful altered states).

2. Deriving from the first assumption, the second holds that mind is generated by brain. Some circularity is admitted in the case of psychosomatic illness (mind may affect body), but this does not alter the predominant direction of causal flow asserted: from brain to mind.

3. 'Mind' *is* the internal dialogue (as identified, for example, by George Herbert Mead). That is to say, mind is the flow of words we use to describe what we see going on and to imaginatively discuss it with others 'inside our heads'. Here we move beyond the realm of the commonsensical and of unspoken, academically unformulated assumptions, into the realm of propositions set forward by social scientists as discoveries. In anthropology and sociology, following on from social psychology, these are taken as fundamentally unchallenged discoveries.

4. Deriving from the second assumption is the fourth, that mind is bound by the physical parameters of the body. Therefore:
   (a) Experience is essentially individual; it is shared only as mediated experience via the body's sensory mechanisms and via the symbolic systems of human communication.
   (b) Experience is bound by the time-space coordinates in which the body moves.

From these assumptions it follows that all experience, even extraordinary experience of other worlds, of other-worldly beings or sensations, or of this-worldly objects behaving in non-lawful ways, is really a distortion of the objective reality we know through our senses in ordinary states of mind. Explanation in the social sciences, then, should logically take the form of relating the distortion to its actual referent in the world as ordinarily known. The referent may be a social process or a psychological process, or it may even be an understanding of the world, a formulation of what it means to be a creature of limited understanding with limited control over the world. But whatever the particular tactic, the strategy is the same: the otherness of some experiences that occasionally dawn upon people's lives is recast as part of this world, the world as ordinarily known.

All the assumptions identified above may well hold, yet the way they have been held on to has been the way of believers clinging to a creed. And indeed, if we examine the origins of these assumptions we find that the social science strategy has been shaped by the opposition it was constructed to defeat: the religious systems that legitimated the monarchies of eighteenth and nineteenth century Europe. In combatting a creed, the social sciences have allowed their own biases to turn into one. We can see how this happened: They needed to replace the 'divine order' that justified monarchy with a 'natural order' equally universal, powerful and compelling. Ordinary reality had to take the place of divine truth. It had to give access to knowledge of that order to the laity, which meant that the use of Reason and the empirical method had to replace consecration into a special condition in which a unique Revelation could be interpreted. And it had to banish from the natural order intrusions of 'supernatural' occurrences that would threaten its explanatory power and require recourse to clerics. The assumptions we have identified forwarded these purposes and undergird the study of all aspects of social life. The social sciences of religion (a category into which people in the premodern world would have placed what we call the paranormal, as would many people still today) also took over from the Christian churches their historically peculiar conception of what religion is about: namely belief in certain propositions about the nature of the universe. This, together with the assumption that mind is nothing but talk, has limited the social sciences' capability for understanding paranormal experience.

Yet the social sciences need not hold these assumptions indefinitely as articles of faith. Neither monarchy nor hegemonic Christianity any longer threaten republicanism, the political programme the early doctrines of social science were designed to support. The cost of opening the assumptions up to examination is not what it used to be. And if there is anything to the claim that a science of social life is possible, then these assumptions must be examined. This, then, is what I propose to undertake in a preliminary way in what follows. The discussion shows that recent developments outside the social sciences bring into question each of the assumptions outlined above. There is good reason to doubt all of them. The implications of this for work within the social sciences are enormous: we can look forward to entirely new strategies for understanding the place of the paranormal in social life.

Reevaluating Assumption One: The Objective vs The Subjective World

Since the time of Max Weber social scientists have been wary of making too literal a comparison between the study of social life and the study of the physical world. Weber (1969: 29–58) cautioned that people, after all, do not respond to each other automatically, as for example, bodies do to the gravitational attraction of the earth. They interpret the actions of others according to what they think are plausible intentions and choose their responses from among their own alternatives as they see them. The intellectual heirs of Marx and Durkheim (with some recent exceptions) have taken this caution lightly, and have proceeded to identify constraints on human behaviour imposed by the social situations in which people find themselves, like being poor, or living in an urban environment, or being female or belonging to a particular ethnic group. Their studies show not that all people of such social categories act in particular ways but sometimes more members of a category act in a certain way than you would expect by chance. For example, Lewis (1971) found that people who went into trance in the societies he studied were likely to be socially disadvantaged. In the picture they paint of the social world social categories have a kind of objective reality; they cause behaviour. Descriptions of the social world are built up out of observations of what people do and what people say, out of behaviours that supposedly anyone in the same situation could see or hear. Such behaviours are taken to be objectively real, in contrast to 'inner experiences' which cannot be validated by an 'outside' observer. Researchers in this 'positivist' tradition nowadays all acknowledge that they cannot be perfectly objective in their study of this 'reality' because personal interests bias selection of problems, of material relevant to solving those problems and of frameworks for analysing those problems. And the 'truths' gleaned are provisional, always subject to further testing. But the real world is out there somewhere, even if we cannot know it with perfect exactitude. Furthermore, it is the only credible source of understandings for behaviour. So it is that all other-worldly experiences and non-lawful events in this world must be seen as deriving from or referring to the 'real' world, and studies of the præternatural are studies about communities' beliefs, not about the varieties of non-ordinary experiences.

Another tradition of social analysis (phenomenology) takes Weber's caution much more seriously. It abandons all effort to explain the social world as an objective reality in favour of describing what people construe it to be, and the meaning they find in it. And it develops the view that everything we see, feel, hear — all our perceptions — are moulded by our expectations. These expectations are in turn shaped by the cultures in which we grow up, especially by the language we use to interpret experience, but also by our intentions towards others and the world. So we do not see some objective, external reality, but rather a product of the interaction between our senses and our expectations. This line of argument has been reinforced of late by studies in the psychology of perception. However, it has had little impact on the plausibility limits imposed on interpretations of præternatural experiences. Perhaps this is because phenomenologists in the area of social analysis themselves tend to keep two sets of books: one for academic descriptions of other cultures and one for everyday life. For practical purposes the common sense western world which most of us understand in terms of our four assumptions is real. The work of the phenomenologist helps them explain to themselves how other people can believe the unlikely things they do, but we all know when the natives are fooling themselves. Also, the phenomenologists have not been concerned with varieties of interior experience, even though this might be expected given their stand that the subjective and objective realms interpenetrate. Rather they have busied themselves with descriptions of traditions, with what is verbally shared and commonly known to groups of people, and also with what people expect to happen rather than with what is actually experienced.

There is reason for the phenomenologists to be more consistent, and for other social scientists to question more deeply their assumption that an objectively real world can explain præternatural experiences. The phenomenologists' appreciation of the subjective nature of all experience should also be taken as an invitation to explore more fully the range of inner experience people have and study this in its own right.

Assumption Two: The Mind–Body Problem

Closely related to the first assumption, that there is an objective world out there, is the second assumption that there are objectively real objects, namely brains, that produce our thoughts and more broadly, our minds. Evidence abounds in clinical and experimental neurology of linkages between brain functioning and experience: people with fevers sometimes see or hear things that others around them do not see; lesions and traumas to parts of the brain are associated with predictable changes in peoples' abilities to understand and interact with others; and certain mind-altering drugs produce distinctive changes in awareness. And much is known about the way sensory stimuli are related to perception. No one denies there are important linkages between brain and mind. But what these linkages are, and whether or not one is justified in concluding that mind is produced by the brain is open to much debate.

That debate has been reopened on fundamentally new terms in recent years as a result of revolutionary developments in cognitive psychology and neuroscience that have enabled scientists such as Penfield (1976) and Pribram (1986) to challenge the long-established philosophers' dictum that empirical studies of brains have nothing to teach us about the mind/brain issue. Among the goals that have stimulated the reopening of the mind/brain issue is the search for mechanisms that link brain and mind.

This search began from the understanding that brain and mind are different kinds of entities, along the lines Descartes understood them: The brain is the kind of thing that has 'extension' (res extensa) or takes up space (it is a material object in other words). In contrast the mind, being thought (res cogitans), has no localization in space (it is, in other words, immaterial). This Cartesian view entered modern investigations into mind/brain relations through the work of Ernest Mach (1914). He reasserted Descartes' 'dualist' view and tried to resolve the problem of how qualitatively different entities, mind and brain, could interact by asserting that they have similar structures. Positivists, as we have seen, declared one of these entities, the mind, of no interest because its operation is not open to external observation and validation. With new findings from neuroscientific investigations into the way brains process information, however, minds once more have become a subject of much interest. While one response to the new information available on brain functioning has been to revamp the dualist view, as for example Eccles and Popper (1977) have done,[1] others have found this unsatisfactory.

Both the philosophical embarrassment caused by these theories that seek to link two entities of different kinds and new understandings of brain functioning have prompted the neurosurgeons Wilder Penfield and Karl Pribram (each in somewhat different ways) to abandon the old 'dualistic' views in favour of some kind of 'monism'. Clearly, as Pribram observed (1986, p. 509), the 'drives' and 'forces' that popular psychology pictures operating in our bodies are not in any obvious sense material. But interestingly, neither are the processes that he and other neuroscientists identify as the stuff of brain functioning. Recourse is quickly made by them to information processing concepts, and the mode of processing has little to do with the strategies with which we customarily deal with the 'material world'.

The discovery that memories are not localized in the brain has also caused Pribram to doubt the view that mind and brain are different kinds of entities on the dualistic model. Memories are actually distributed across the brain, much in the way information is distributed on holographic film. The encoding and reading out of information by the brain, according to Pribram, resembles the processes (the Fourrier transforms) through which information is recorded in and reconstructed from holographic film. The brain, as he puts it, acts as a 'spectral analyzer' (1986, p. 517). This new model contrasts radically with the previous concepts of brain functioning that liken it to the operation of lenses. Pribram, following Bohm (1971, 1973) poses the contrast this way:

'Lenses focus, objectify and draw boundaries between parts. Lenses particularize. Holograms by contrast are distributive, unbounded and holistic' (1986, p. 517).

As has been widely observed, many of the non-common-sensical qualities of mystical experiences are modelled by holograms and by the holographic like functioning of the brain (Wilber, 1982).

None of what has been said points unambiguously towards any particular conception of mind/brain relationships, although the notion of brain generating mind as argued by Mach has been shown to have serious weaknesses. Against his dualist views stand a variety of monist views that do not see brain and mind as wholly distinct nor portray brain as always generating mind. Thus Penfield (1976) has expressed doubt that the physical apparatus of brain can wholly account for mind. David Bohm, a physicist, has developed the holographic model and characterized mind and brain as parallel 'explications' of an 'implicate order', a deep level of reality which is unknowable to us except by implication through the study of the patterned phenomena that manifest from it (1973, 1980). Pribram (1986) follows Bohm in opting for a model that takes neither the mental nor the physical as prior, or indeed as ultimate substances. His model relates the 'world of ordinary experiences' (where mind and matter are experienced as dualities) to a deeper order of reality ('characterized by descriptions akin to those of the experiences of mystics') through the spectral transform (Pribram 1986, p. 518).

For present purposes, then, we can identify two models of mind/ brain relationships that are worthy of adoption as a basis of social scientific study: Penfield's and the Bohm model as adopted by Pribram. Penfield is willing to consider (like the Hindu Advaita philosophies) that mind actually thinks into existence the body it appears to have, along with the world as ordinarily perceived. But this mind can also think other thoughts. Amongst those other thoughts social scientists could place dreams, deep sleep and ecstatic visions, without cause necessarily to understand the non-ordinary experiences as anything but the processes of thought itself. According to Bohm's and Pribram's way of thinking, both mind and what we perceive as matter affect one another because they are parallel unfoldments of the same process. But mind is not in principle limited to the knowing of the material world, that is, to perceiving differences in 'material things' and analyzing them. Mind is in principle unlimited, capable of experiencing in the holographic mode. In this case the social scientist must once again be chary of over hasty attribution of non-ordinary experiences to 'material' causes. The interaction between mind and brain in this model might well justify materialist explanations of paranormal experiences in some cases, but other experiences would have to be accepted as experiences of 'what is'.[2]

A more cautious approach for social scientists and psychologists is mapped out by Nelson (1988), who while sympathetic with Bohm, urges us to leave aside all questions about where reality lies in our study of non-ordinary experience and take as the primary issue the subjective nature of all experience. While Bohm's model of 'what is' suggests that there may well be some empirical referent for the most extraordinary experiences of wholeness that mystics have, it can be demonstrated (as reasonably as anything else can be demonstrated) that people do have such experiences — and many other kinds of non-ordinary experiences as well. A science of the præternatural, then, can be based on the analysis of the conditions under which experiences of different types (including of 'ordinary reality') are likely to occur. No question of interpreting one kind of 'world' in terms of another arises because one deals only with multifaceted descriptions of states. The shaping of experience around symbolic concepts and physiological inputs is capable of being incorporated into the analysis as aspects of experience, rather than as 'more real' entities to which the description of the experience reduces.

Assumption Three: Mind As The Internal Dialogue

All of the failed attempts to transcend the reduction of religious experience to the social or pathological have done so because that which experiences — the mind, the self — is covertly assumed to be a play of symbols. Mind is understood to be a construction of sense perceptions into units prefigured by one's culture and a manipulation of those symbols. Symbols mark out 'reality; into discrete objects, including the self, and so the self and the world appear as assemblages of bounded entities. This is the 'mind, self and society' (or world) as Mead (1934) portrays it, and also as it is portrayed (with a variety of different terminologies) in behavioural psychology and in the psychoanalytic tradition. Given this view of mind, all experience, no matter how extraordinary, must be in the final analysis *of* the social world because mind is an endless interplay of symbols. There are, however, alternative models of mind that make a place for experiencing that does not flow through symbols. The Hindu and Buddhist traditions have long held that such a mode of experiencing is possible. Indeed many yogic and Buddhist techniques of opening the awareness to non-ordinary experiencing purposefully disrupt the internal dialogue.[3] However it is only recently that psychologists have taken non-verbal modes of experiencing seriously, perhaps because mystical practice is once again occupying significant numbers of westerners and surveys are showing that dramatic spiritual experiences, even in Western countries, are far too common to be understood in terms of abnormal psychology (Hay and Morisy, 1978; Hay and Heald 1987).

Among the more useful of the new models of mind that include a component of non-verbal experiencing are those of the psychiatrist Arthur Deikman and that of the psychologist Charles Tart. Deikman (1982) asks us to observe a fundamental distinction between 'awareness' and the objects of awareness, which are traditionally (in psychiatry) considered to be the world of self. The different schools of psychiatry variously emphasize what he calls the 'thinking self', the 'emotional self' or the 'functional self' (the awareness of oneself as an actor in the world, largely constructed through observations of the body in its physical context). All of these traditional foci of therapy, he argues, can be considered aspects of an 'object self', a superordinate category that must be recognized in contrast to an 'observing self' that consists of awareness of all else. That this 'observing self' is not one part of the object self observing another he demonstrates by recalling the Advaitist exercise of asking 'Who am I?' and by citing the experience of meditators who learn to move from awareness of objects to contentless awareness. Here is a model of mind that 'contains' both what is involved in discursive thought (Mead's mind) *and* mind that is *not* but is still aware. The significance of this for studies of religious experience should be clear: we should not assume that experience always flows wholly through the discursive mind (the 'object self'), and so we must specify the limits of the applicability of models of extraordinary experience that are based on this understanding of mind.

Deikman also provides a model that suggests how experience can shift from that modality dominated by the conception of oneness as an object self into one more conducive to awareness of 'awareness': by changing one's *intention* from that of operating on the world for the benefit of the object self (instrumental activity) to 'receiving from the environment' (Deikman 1982, p. 71). In the 'receptive mode':

> '. . . past and future drop away and sensual attributes dominate over the perception of form and verbal meaning. Analytic thought tends to cease; attention becomes diffuse and boundaries blur. The separate self dissolves, permitting the experience of connection or merging into the environment' (Deikman 1982, p. 71).

By modelling a not wholly discursive mind *and* by specifying how each mode of mental functioning is engaged Deikman enables us to study præternatural experiences without casting them as products of social forces or as symbolic statements about the everyday world. But it is not clear exactly how the 'receptive mode' of experience should map onto præternatural experiences, and in particular, onto experiences in dramatically altered states of consciousness. Deikman's examples of receptive mode functioning include listening to music, sexual involvement and other everyday activities. Any of these can certainly be invested with special meaning, but *as described* they do not point unambiguously towards the feeling of 'otherness' that we know people claim for certain experiences, particularly those they label religious. Undoubtedly we should recognize varieties of self-designated religious experience, both in Deikman's object mode and in his receptive mode, that can be adequately described in social, ego-psychology and symbolic terms. But there is a remainder: those where people feel what Nelson (1988) has called an 'ontic shift' or 'reality shift',[4] a sense that they are no longer dealing with the world as it is ordinarily known, and that this new state is fraught with significance.

To describe these shifts, we need to specify other operations. Deikman (1969) has gone some way towards this, but not the whole distance. He extends the concept of 'deautomatization' developed by Gill and Brenman (1959) to explain how mystical states are accessed. In ordinary exprience action is carried out in large part automatically, that is, without our attention to every step in the process. This leaves attention free to engage in discursive thought and to scan the environment for threats or opportunities that might require a change of response pattern: that is Hartmann's (1958) 'automatization' of activity. We can, however, 'deautomatize' the way we operate by refocusing our attention on the fine details of one action or upon one or a few features of our environment. This is normally done at the cost of attention to discursive thought, that is, to the internal dialogue, and the result is that we slip from the active style of relating to the world into the receptive mode (Deikman 1969, p. 31). If this deautomatization is directed at a single percept (e.g., the blue vase in his experiment, or the mantra in Transcendental Meditation), rather than at some activity such as learning to drive a car, the subject is likely to have experiences similar to those reported by mystics — experiences characterized by intense realness, unusual sensations, unity, and trans-sensate phenomena (Deikman 1969, p. 35).[5]

Of central value in Deikman's deautomatization concept is its focus on deployment of attention and on interruption of standard patterns of information processing by redeployment of the attention. Virtually all triggers used in inducing altered states of consciousness can be interpreted as operating in this way. In order to do so we need to introduce Fischer's (1971) concept of levels of arousal. The various kinds of altered states, Fischer argues, can be characterized by the levels of arousal of the central nervous system: extraordinarily high levels of arousal ('hyperarousal') are associated with trance dances and possession states; especially low levels of arousal ('hypoarousal') are associated with yogic and mystic states. We can see that hyperarousal techniques (e.g. repetitive dancing or drumming) draw attention to the kinetic or sound percept which by its repetition interferes with the scanning for significant differences and discursive thought that constitute 'ordinary reality'. Hypoarousal techniques also interfere with the construction of ordinary reality through discursive thought. However they do it by drawing attention away from the environment, away from the flux in which we seek to identify opportunities and threats, and fixing the attention instead upon a single object (see Hutch, 1984a, b). This is most useful, but the model does not account for the discontinuity in experience associated with the sense some people have of a reality shift. It also brings in the necessary assumption that brain functions generate mental states.

To account for the sense some people experience of a reality shift Tart's notion that consciousness manifests in discrete states (d-SoC) (both altered and ordinary) is crucial (Tart, 1972, 1975). Tart noted that when people experience a change of state the total system of experiencing (memory, time sense, body awareness, etc.) undergoes a radical reorganization. Between states no system functions; hence the change of state is a quantum-like leap (1975, p. 14). While there are, of course, variations within states, the states tend to be stable, because of 'loading stabilization', 'negative feedback stabilization', 'positive feedback stabilization', and 'limiting stabilization' (various ways of keeping attention engaged in habitual ways) (Tart, 1975, p. 5).

Nelson (1988) provides us with a model of the conditions under which movement across d-SoCs is likely to occur without bringing in the assumption that brains always cause mental events. His analysis identifies both personality factors and 'operations' (activities, physical and mental) that are associated with experiences of reality shift. Those who reported one or more of such experiences tended to have high capacities for becoming absorbed in their environment or an activity, to be more open than non-experients to new experiences, to be especially emotionally reactive, and to be less likely than others to deny personal shortcomings. The operations most strongly associated with experiences of reality shift were absorbed attention to an object or contemplative exercise, change in stress levels and removal from social participation.

In sum, there is no dearth of models of mind that incorporate a component or mode of non-verbal and/or non-ordinary experiencing. It is essential to note at this point, however, that not all, or even most experiencing in altered states of consciousness is free of symbolic content or even words. Thus the degree of encoding of extraordinary experience must be acknowledged as variable from one state, and perhaps from one experience, to another.

Assumption Four: Mind and Body Boundaries

We have now disposed of Assumption One in favour of the view that all we experience is (ultimately) subjective. Also, examining Assumption Two, we have seen that strong arguments have been made to the effect that mind generates brain or is, like brain, generated by some higher order non-material process. And we have dealt with Assumption Three (that minds are the internal dialogue), introducing alternative models that include non-verbal experiences. All these points serve to undermine explanations of non-ordinary experiences that derive them wholly from the social world, but leave a place for partial explanations in terms of social needs and/or symbolic meanings in most cases. But one topic remains to be dealt with: Assumption Four, that minds know only through the sensory mechanisms of the bodies in which they arise and to which they are therefore limited. What the social scientist has at issue here are not explanations of the higher regions of mystical experience but accounts of supernatural healing and super-normal feats such as form the standard catalogue of Indian *siddhis*.[6] Such special capabilities are also widely claimed in other traditions. One is in danger here of appearing to come to the defence of cheap tricksters, which is a less dignified form of foolery than defending misguided noble-mindedness. No matter. There are clear implications in the line of argument developed to this point — and now also a wealth of empirical findings from reputable sources — that require that the issue be addressed.

It is our discussion of mind/brain relationships that is relevant here. If it is the case that mind generates body, rather than the other way around, or that mind and body are parallel but semi-independent explications of an implicate order, then mind need not be limited to knowing through the body's sense organs. In the Penfield or Advaitist models, mind could simply think other thoughts (in a solipsistic universe) or could know other minds and their thoughts directly. Virtually the same would hold true for the Bohm and Pribram forms of monism, except that one would posit more physical constraints from, or perhaps simply interaction with, body. How minds interact would certainly have to be determined, but the fact that this has not yet been done need not detract from the possibility of its being done. We have to acknowledge, in short, a logical possibility.

That this possibility is a probability is strongly indicated from a number of directions. The most significant of these is the maturation of parapsychology into an acknowledged scientific discipline that has been able to substantiate a variety of psi-phenomena with reasonable standards of replicability (Reinsel, 1982).[7] All the psi-phenomena (extrasensory perception, psychokinesis, precognition) by definition, involve the crossing of body boundaries by mind without recourse to sensory cues.[8] It would be out of place to review parapsychological research in detail when reviews of the subject are readily available, but it is worth noting that explanations of psi-phenomena in the more obvious materialistic terms have been dismissed. Most frequencies of the electromagnetic spectrum have been ruled out as carriers of psi information, and the invariability of psi-phenomena at different distances and over time implies that no known form of physical energy is involved (Reinsel 1982, p. 165).

Another data base that suggests the independence of mind from the body's sense organs under some circumstances is the Grof's LSD and holonomic clinical files (Grof, 1976, 1985). The holonomic therapy (patterned breathing techniques, relaxation, and holographic music) induces altered states of consciousness similar in range to LSD, but does so, significantly, without drugs. The LSD itself, Gros asserts, does not generate a 'toxic psychosis' essentially unrelated to how the psyche functions under normal circumstances (1985, p. 30). Grof's clinical data on altered states of consciousness thus induced say something about the potentials of normal minds. These potentials include certain paranormal phenomena such as apparent recollection of perinatal experiences (some of which the Grofs have been able to corroborate in detail) along with mystical states that violate the normal time-space parameters of experience. Recollection of one's birth has been excluded from psychiatry[9] (which otherwise encourages regression through free association and dream analysis up to but not including birth) on the grounds that the child's nervous system would be too immature at that time to record information in retrievable form. In any case the reported viewing of details of the birth not visible to the child challenges normal science interpretations of the data.

Similar data come from thanatology, specifically from the study of near death experiences (see Moody, 1975; Ring, 1980; Zaleski, 1986). The ability of some resuscitated patients to recall not only what was going on around them when they were clinically dead, but to report on the disposition of objects not visible to them from where their bodies lay (Sabom, 1982) presents the same challenges as the perinatal experience data of the Grofs. Reviewing the literature on this topic the psychologist Ring has concluded that the phenomena cannot be interpreted within the Newtonian–Cartesian paradigm and he attempts to develop an alternative along neutral-monistic lines.[10]

In the parapsychology literature there are suggestions of a connection between psi-phenomena and experiencing in a non-verbal mode. Parapsychologists have found that recipients (those attempting to receive non-sensory transmissions of information) perform better if prepared with relaxation and other techniques such as are ordinarily used by meditators to clear their minds of verbally structured thoughts (Reinsel 1982, p. 160).

We must now look at the implications of psi-phenomena for the social scientific study of religion. (We need not limit the field of applicability to præternatural *experience* in this case.) While it is undoubtedly the case that straight out trickery is employed in many examples of purported spiritual healing and demonstrations of supernatural powers (as it is in sales, love, politics and everywhere in life), and while it is also undoubtedly true that psychic healing can in many cases be explained by ritually and otherwise symbolically induced placebo or psychosomatic effects (see McGuire, 1985), on the basis of the sort of evidence presented above I think we shall also have to acknowledge the possibility that a percentage of cases of spiritual healing and other examples of supernatural powers are in fact genuine. Indeed the concept of 'supernatural' (Tylor's [1971] classic marker of the religious) will have to be rethought. Insofar as it means 'spurious' or 'illusory', we shall not be able to apply the term to the religious categorically, although it may remain appropriate for references made to traditional symbols by people in ordinary states of consciousness or for wholly ritualized imitations of dealing in the præternatural.[11] Insofar as the term 'supernatural' means *outside* of that which is understood by science to be part of the material world . . . well, what more needs to be said at this point?

Conclusions

None of the assumptions normally implicitly made by social scientists when they study experiences of 'other worlds' and of non-lawful events in 'this world' can be accepted without question. The alternatives to those assumptions here presented suggest that human experience can take place in modes other than the verbal and otherwise symbolic. Further, it is likely that experience in non-verbal, non-symbolic modes sometimes violates the boundaries of what we ordinarily, but with little justification, take to be separate material objects. This means that those who would explain religious and other extraordinary experiences, as well as spiritual healing and supernatural powers, must at least acknowledge the limitations of the explanations they give in terms of social motives and symbolic communication. It would be even better to demarcate the data to which those explanations do and do not legitimately apply. This is like asking social scientists interested in the social functions of food exchange and the symbolic uses of food to acknowledge that food does after all have nutritional value. And it is useful for the sociology of foods to identify which foods are really 'junk foods' and which have something nutritionally important in them.

Footnotes

1. See the brief discussion of Eccles and Popper's position in Zollschan's chapter in this volume.
2. Compare this position to that of Koepping (1978).
3. Many of these states, though it can be argued not all (see Almond 1982, pp. 166–173 and Wainwright 1981, pp. 18–22, as against Katz 1978, pp. 22–74) are shaped by the symbolic tradition of the practitioner.
4. See Nelson's chapter in this volume on the concept of 'reality shift', or in his original terminology 'ontic shift'.
5. These he proceeds to explain reductively, falling back upon a psychological explanation. The need for that reduction depends, however, upon what stance one takes on the mind–brain issue (Assumption Two). The model need not be adopted along with the reductionistic interpretation.
6. *Siddhis* are supernormal powers credited to Indian yogis.
7. A useful sociological study of the status of parapsychology as a science is provided by McClenon (1984).
8. The mind/body opposition here should be read as though in inverted commas, as we may not be talking about different entities.

9. Memory of the fostering intrauterine environment does, of course, figure in Freud's theory of personality, but not memory of the birth process. However, Rank's (1929) heterodox Freudian theory does make birth trauma the critical experience in personality formation.

10. Against this interpretation see Blackmore (1982); she, however, acknowledges that the Sabom (1982) data cannot be explained within her framework (Blackmore 1988, p. 10). Her argumentation also rests on Assumption Two, without question or justification.

11. As, for example, probably much of Iban shamanic ritual (see Jensen, 1974) and the Balinese Brahmana's ritualized samadi in which he manifests Siva for the purpose of making holy water (see Hooykaas, 1966).

References

Almond, Philip (1982), *Mystical Experience and Religious Doctrine, An Investigation of the Study of Mysticism in World Religions*, Amsterdam, Mouton.

Blackmore, Susan (1982), *Beyond the Body*, London, Heinemann.

Blackmore, Susan (1988), 'Visions Beyond: A Life Changing Drama', *The Weekend Australian*, May 14–15. Reprinted from *New Scientist*.

Bohm, D. (1971), 'Quantum Theory as an Indication of a New Order in Physics. Part A. The Development of New Orders as Shown Through the History of Physics', *Foundations of Physics* 1, 359–381.

Bohm, D. (1973), 'Quantum Theory as an Indication of a New Order in Physics,. Part B. Implicate and Explicate Order in Physical Law', *Foundations of Physics* 3, 139–168.

Bohm, D. (1980), *Wholeness and the Implicate Order*, London, Routledge and Kegan Paul.

Deikman, A. (1969), 'Deautomatization and the Mystic Experience' *in* C.T. Tart, ed., *Altered States of Consciousness, A Book of Readings*, New York, John Wiley.

Deikman, A. (1982), *The Observing Self: Mysticism and Psychotherapy*, Boston, Beacon.

Devereux, G. (1956), 'Normal and Abnormal: the Key Problem of Psychiatric Anthropology' *in* J.B. Casagrande and T. Gladwin eds., *Some Uses of Anthropology: Theoretical and Applied*, Washington.

Durkheim, Emile (1968/1915), *The Elementary Forms of the Religious Life*, New York, The Free Press.

Fischer, R. (1971), 'A Cartography of the Ecstatic and Meditative States', *Science* 174, 897–904.

Freud, S. (1959/1907), 'Obsessive Actions and Religious Practices', *in Collected Works*, 9, London, Hogarth Press.

Gill, M. and Brenman, M. (1959), *Hypnosis and Related States: Psychoanalytic Studies in Regression*, New York, International Universities Press.

Grof, Stanislav (1976), *Realms of the Human Unconscious: Observations from LSD Research*, New York, E.P. Dutton.

Grof, Stanislav (1985), *Beyond the Brain; Birth, Death and Transcendence in Psychotherapy*, Albany, N.Y., State University of New York Press.

Hartmann, H. (1958), *Ego Psychology and the Problem of Adaptation*, New York, International Press. .

Hay, D. and Heald (1987), 'Religion is Good For You', *New Society* 17.

Hay, D. and Morisy, A. (1978), 'Reports of Ecstatic, Paranormal and Religious Experience in Great Britain and the United States — A Comparison of Trends', *Journal for the Scientific Study of Religion* 17 255–268.

Hutch, Richard (1984a), 'An Approach to Consciousness Studies: Experiential Religion', *The Australian Journal of Transpersonal Psychology* 4, 177–201.

Hutch, Richard (1984b), 'Consciousness Research in the Psychology of Religion', *in* R.A. Hutch and P.G. Fenner, eds., *Under the Shade of a Coolibah Tree*, New York, University Press of America.

Hooykaas, Christiaan (1966), *Surya-Sevana: the Way to God of a Balinese Siva Priest*, Amsterdam, Noord-Hollandsche U.M.

Jensen, Erik (1974), *The Iban and Their Religion*, Oxford, Clarendon Press.

Koepping, Klaus-Peter (1978), 'Toward a Hermeneutics of Religious Experiences; Some Comparative Notes on the Ethnography of Psychedelics', *Religious Traditions* 1, 9–38.

Lewis, I.M. (1971), *Ecstatic Religion. An Anthropological Study of Spirit Possession and Shamanism*, Harmondsworth, Penguin Books.

McClenon, James (1984), *Deviant Science: The Case of Parapsychology*, Philadelphia, University of Pennsylvania Press.

McGuire, Meredith B. (1985), 'Religion and Healing', *in* P. Hammond, ed., *The Sacred in the Secular Age*, Berkeley, University of California Press.

Mach, E. (1914), *The Analysis of Sensations and the Relation of the Physical to the Psychical*, Chicago, Open Court.

Malinowski, Bronislaw (1948), *Magic, Science and Religion and Other Essays by Bronislaw Malinowski*, Glencoe, Ill., The Press Press.

Marx, F. and Engels, F. (1955), *On Religion*, Moscow, Foreign Languages Publishing House.

Mead, George Herbert (1934), *Mind, Self and Society from the Standpoint of a Social Behaviorist*, edited by Charles W. Morris, Chicago, The University of Chicago Press.

Moody, R. (1975), *Life After Life*, New York, Bantam.

Nelson, Peter L. (1988), *The Technology of the* Præternatural, An Operational Analysis and Empirical Study of the Psycho-Phenomenology of Mystical, Visionary and Remote Perception Experiences, Ph.D. Dissertation. Department of Studies in Religion, University of Queensland.

Penfield, W. (1976), *The Mystery of the Mind*, Princeton, Princeton University Press.

Popper, K.R. and Eccles, J.C. (1977), *The Self and Its Brain*, Berlin, Springer-Verlag.

Pribram, Karl H. (1986), 'The Cognitive Revolution in Mind/Brain Issues', *American Psychologist* 41 507–520.

Rank, Otto (1929), *The Trauma of Birth*, New York, Harcourt Brace.

Reinsel, Ruth (1982), 'Parapsychology: An Empirical Science', *in* Patrick Grim, ed., *Philosophy of Science and the Occult*, Albany, N.Y., State University of New York Press.

Ring, Kenneth (1980), *Life at Death: A Scientific Investigation of the Near Death Experience*, New York, McCann and Geghegan.

Sabom, Michael (1982), *Recollections of Death*, London, Corgi.

Sacks, Howard (1979), 'The Effect of Spiritual Exercises on the Integration of Self-Esteem', *Journal for the Scientific Study of Religion* 18, 46–50.

Tart, C.T. (1972), 'States of Consciousness and State-Specific Sciences', *Science* 176, 1203–1210.

Tart, C.T. (1975), *States of Consciousness*, New York, E.P. Dutton.

Tylor, Edward B. (1971), *Primitive Culture. Researches into the Development of Mythology, Philosophy, Religion, Language, Art and Custom*, 2 vol., London, John Murray.

Weber, Max (1969), *Basic Concepts in Sociology*, New York, Greenwood Press.

Wilber, K. ed. (1982), *The Holographic Paradigm and Other Paradoxes, Exploring the Leading Edge of Science*, Boulder, Co., Shambhala.

Zaleski, Carol (1986), *Otherworld Journeys*, Oxford, Oxford University Press.

SECTION II

EXPERIENCING THE PARANORMAL

People vary considerably in the extent to which they report experiencing the paranormal. This may reflect their circumstances, their attitudes, or other personality factors. Evidence exists to suggest that access to paranormal experience can be facilitated in a number of ways. Each of the contributions in this section discuss circumstances and methods which can prompt experience of the paranormal. These include the use of drugs, near-death experience, mysticism, meditation and certain child–parent relationships.

Ronald Conway reports on the clinical use of the drug LSD to obtain partial or complete access to what he prefers to term a 'transpersonal' experience: that is an experience of transcending one's personal identity, history and social frame of reference. Although his evidence is anecdotal, Conway argues that 'there indeed appear to be paranormal ways of knowing and seeing which transcend the intellectual repertoire of the individual subject and give access to awareness not available to normal intellectual or sensory input'.

Gary Groth-Marnat examines paranormal experiences associated with the condition of being near death. Included is discussion of telepathy, out-of-body experiences, precognition, and an increase in psi-phenomena following the near-death experience (NDE). Without understating the importance of NDEs, Groth-Marnat points out that they have the distinct disadvantage that they cannot be studied directly but rather are dependent on retrospective self reports. By contrast with Conway, Groth-Marnat concludes that it is unlikely that the study of NDEs will contribute to validating the objective reality of paranormal phenomena.

The next two chapters approach the paranormal from the angles of mysticism and meditation. For Ralph Hood in Chapter 8 the failure to take both mysticism and the paranormal seriously is less an empirical than a conceptual problem. In other words, mystical experiences may be more common than people actually register and report. Hood outlines the 'unity thesis' which puts forward the notion that mystical experiences reflect a common human reality. However, this is perceived and expressed by the experiencing person in ways consistent with his or her culture and personality.

Another technique for obtaining access to paranormal experience is meditation. Roderick Bucknell in Chapter 9 describes Buddhist meditative experiences which are without verbal or visual content. He refers to a number of steps of ever more refined states of 'contentlessness' leading to 'contentless non-experience' and ultimately to a state of 'pure unconsciousness'.

The final chapter in the section is concerned with paranormal experiences which are activated by breakdowns in bonding relationships at a family or social level. Richard A. Hutch relates belief in the paranormal to a capacity for uncanny experiences generated to counter the 'derailment' of bonding relationships, particularly between mother and child.

The list of gateways to paranormal experiences discussed in this section obviously is not exhaustive. They do provide, however, good examples of the sort of activity or circumstances that are thought to facilitate paranormal experience. The issue of the validity, as distinct from the authenticity, of the experience is still an open one. A wider range of paranormal experiences is reviewed in Chapter 12 by Peter Nelson.

CHAPTER 6
LYSERGIC ACID AND TRANSPERSONAL EXPERIENCE

Ronald Conway

Most of the significant therapeutic reporting concerning psychedelic drugs and their effects dates prior to 1975. This is due to the world-wide reaction against LSD in response to the U.S. hippie counter-culture misuse of the substance since 1963 and its traffic in the illicit drug scene. This reaction reached a level of such unwarrantable bias and intensity that professional use of LSD therapy and research has been all but paralysed for over fifteen years. The ideological warfare over LSD, and the treatment of evidence concerning the real versus alleged dangers of its use, could be a subject for a sociological study in itself. This is a study from which both illicit users and many badly misinformed anti-drug crusaders might well emerge with equal discredit. Throughout the entire history of pharmacology it would be hard to nominate a substance more praised or damned from hearsay. One suspects that one reason for this is the capacity of LSD to alter human consciousness in ways which suggest that Western official adherence to a crude bio-physiochemical model of mind has proven quite inadequate to explain all the phenomena which arose from psychedelic experiences.

The writer does not propose to detail here all the physical and mental manifestations arising from LSD. The accidental discovery of Lysergic Acid Diethylamide by Albert Hofmann in the Sandoz Laboratories of Switzerland in 1943 did not lead to much serious professional appraisal until the mid-fifties and a useful summary of work in this early period is provided by Caldwell (1968, pp. 3–18). During this early period LSD was given experimentally to many distin-guished writers, scientists, philosophers and theologians. A period of quite optimistic wonderment ensued, leading to the increasing enthusiasm for the use of LSD by psychiatrists and clinical psycho-logists in various avenues of psychotherapy. The later furore over the distribution of LSD to students by Leary and Alpert on the Harvard campus at the inception of the American hippie cult soon obscured the great value of much therapeutic work done with the aid of LSD be-tween 1960 and about 1964. After this period legal supplies of the sub-stance began to run out and most therapeutic work was abandoned.

Those readers interested in the therapeutic uses of LSD might consult Abramson (1967), Caldwell (1968) Grof (1975). For one of the best symposia from the orthodox scientific community concerning the various therapeutic, research, legal and societal issues touching psychedelic drugs, the reader could consult Hicks and Fink (1969). Suffice it to note that LSD and its much milder, shorter-acting analogue, Psilocybin, found numerous rewarding applications in the hands of resourceful clinical workers. Hoffer reported substantial success with chronic alcoholics in Canada, Sandison claimed encouraging gains with intractable non-psychotic personality disorders in the U.K., while Grof (1975) produced some extraordinary research into memories and traumas surrounding birth (or peri-natal experience) during his years in Prague. This writer (Conway 1968) worked either directly or indirectly as part of a team with over a hundred and forty cases of obsessive and/or obsessive-compulsive neurosis, principally males, between 1964 and 1972. He found that median doses of LSD accompanied by intensive directive analysis frequently resolved many of the ambivalent conflicts underlying this stubborn neurotic syndrome. At least some measure of permanent improvement occurred in the majority of cases. It was during work in the clinical setting and during a series of personally experienced legal LSD 'trips' that the writer underwent certain transpersonal experiences and also recorded these as well as those reported by therapeutic subjects.

Rather than use the term 'paranormal' in connection with psychedelic drug-activated experience, the term 'transpersonal' is more appropriate in that it suggests more precisely a broad three-fold distinction the subject customarily experiences between (1) bodily and perceptual sensations (2) ego-centred personal experience and (3) experience *transcending* one's personal identity, history and social reference frame either partially or completely. It is this third category of experience which is of most relevance here. Almost invariably, however, it is necessary for the subject to have gone through the first two gradations of experience before he/she can encounter the third. LSD is not even a 'drug' in the usually understood sense of the word. The base dose is in micrograms and it would be more appropriate to describe its action on the brain as that of a biochemical catalyst which evokes almost as many different shades of experience as there are users. The cortex stages the setting for the subject's experiences when the substance itself is at the point of excretion. Hence, only the broadest generalisations can be made by the use of cross-sectional research. Those experiences common to almost all randomly chosen subjects are usually the most superficial and of least scientific and philosophical interest — increased pulse-rate, pupillary dilation, sensory disruption and distortion and low-level hallucination, etc. Meanwhile the previous 'mental set' and resistances of the subject act as a kind of lodestone to which any experiences beyond this level tend to be anchored. In therapy, this mental set is merely the point of departure for any useful work. It must invariably be broken through if the subject is to benefit. It is in the 'upper' or 'lower' reaches beyond such a breakthrough that the most profound transpersonal and transcendent experiences usually occur.

It follows from such considerations that *qualitative*, in-depth investigation is much more fruitful when studying psychedelic phenomena. As with all paranormal and transpersonal experiences, such phenomena are unequally distributed in the general population and it makes for poor economy of effort to be constantly striving for normative predictions. In common with workers such as Dr. Stanislav Grof, possibly the foremost world authority on the outer reaches of LSD experience, this writer believes that all normal human subjects are potentially capable of penetrating the same altered states of consciousness. This potential, however, is draconically limited by factors of curiosity, intellectual capacity, fear of psychosis, emotional freedom, and, above all, our socio-cultural conditioning. The cultural conditioning of the past four centuries in the West has been essentially tied to a faith in data from the outer physical environment to the detriment of inner reflective, meditative and introverting behaviour. Hence almost half of all LSD subjects do not experience much beyond extravagantly-coloured ego-centred sensations unless there are unusual factors such as bereavement, personal need, a powerful spirit of enquiry, or the administration of a high 'psycholytic' dose of LSD. Such a dose helps to temporarily demolish the conventional mind-set of developed communities. Indeed, many of the most remarkable anecdotal experiences under LSD have been stumbled upon rather than sought, usually when the subject is least resistant or anxious. Noted authority Sidney Cohen has been quoted as observing wryly: 'Some people are just too insensitive to experience much beyond a highly-coloured sensory binge. You don't get water out of a dry well'.

Barr and Langs (1972, pp. 89–140) have provided a useful grouping of the most common subject reactions. These can be compressed into the first two physical and 'ego-grounded' categories but the authors (typically of reductionist workers) either ignore the third category states or lump them together with other so-called 'hallucinatory' and 'regressive' experiences. Barr and Lang appear to tease out five main groups:

(a) Those with high self-esteem and intelligence whose fantasy life 'improves' under LSD.

(b) Those with low-integration and schizoid tendencies who regress badly under the substance and have 'bad trips'.

(c) Obsessive, highly-integrated personalities whose denied fears and hostilities and repressed sensuality tend to surface under the catalytic action of the substance.

(d) Those of low intelligence who become fascinated with bodily sensations and have rather intoxicated, primitive reactions with strong visceral, sexual or reproductive content.

(e) Rigidly high 'achievers' on whose defences the drug makes little useful impression of any kind.

The writer accepts the existence of these broad groupings from his own professional experience. However, they are mainly true of low dose sessions with subjects having little professional guidance. One must stress that LSD is merely a powerful *agent* in consciousness expansion. Without the dimension of patient/subject sensitivity and some genuine therapist flair these five categories of reduction are about all that one might expect.

For charting the third state transpersonal realm one must turn to less methodologically rigid authors such as Masters and Houston (1966) and, of course, scientific workers of daring, persistence and originality such as Grof. The following test of transpersonal experiences possible under psychedelic induction, of course, rarely refers to those had in their pure form. Very frequently (but not always) there is an element of distortion and confusion of inner imagery and a tendency toward fleeting and unstable transitions from one state to another. (These latter are frequently susceptible to some clinical control by a median dose of nicotinic acid.)

(A) Expansion of Consciousness in Time:

(1) Regression to natal and foetal experiences.

(2) Racial and ancestral experiences.

(3) Consciousness of inorganic matter and 'earth consciousness'.

(4) Sense of oneness with planetary and universal life ('space travel').

(B) Consciousness of Organic and Cellular Functions:

i.e. Conscious participation in one's own separate organic functions from organ down to cell.

(C) Extension of Experience into Higher Transcendental Realms:

(1) Entry into world of Jungian archetypes — the Great, Mother, The Wise Old Man, the Hero, Hermes the Trickster et al.

(2) Intuitive understanding of Universal Symbols — the Cross, Buddha, the Virgin Mother et. al.

(3) Awareness of 'Chakras' and 'Kundalinic' energies.

(4) Mediumistic experiences. Acquisition of knowledge and information without objective means.

(5) 'God-consciousness'. Awareness of 'superconscious' forces and, 'cosmic mind' and a sense of the transcendental unity of all manifestations.

I have borrowed this list with several minor alterations from Grof (1975, pp. 156–7) as it is the most comprehensive so far published. Most sensitive subjects with adequate intelligence and without conscious mental resistance experience one or more of these substates and phenomena during LSD sessions, even when they are attained only fleetingly and with limited ego-comprehension of their significance.

In the writer's experience, most anxious clinical subjects are likely to have some transpersonal experiences in either a vague, limited way or to wrestle with them in a state of panic as a preconceived pseudo-psychotic experience. However, with the aid of a resourceful professional guide, inductees are helped to see that many of the more disturbing images and sensations experienced are no more than symbolic inflations of their personal fixations, or derive from archetypal scenes or figures with the typical Janus-face of both malign and benign aspects. The well-adjusted, intelligent subject is more likely to have transpersonal or transcendental experiences without excessive perceptual or emotional 'pollution' than a neurotic or disturbed person whose apprehensions frequently 'muddy the pond'. Hence the preliminary mental set of the subject is of great importance in either limiting or expanding the range of phenomena he/she will experience.

The sceptical enquirer invariably raises the question of suggestibility. Do subjects experience what they *expect* to experience, and can such experience be induced by experimental suggestion? The answer to the first part of the question is 'no', provided that it is understood that the central focus of experiences can be affected or distorted by strong emotional currents and desires. Subjects *cannot* govern or predetermine what they 'see' in any defined way. As for suggestibility, the contrary condition is usually the case. Most clinical subjects invariably reject, often impatiently, any suggestions which 'are out of phase' with what they undergo, while non-clinical reactions tend to follow the same pattern.

Thus, only two conclusions remain concerning the nature of LSD-prompted phenomena. Either they help the person tap into non-objectified levels of reality which are really 'there', or there is some latent fund of genetically-encoded 'hallucination' of which all subjects partake to some degree. The latter conclusion is at least as hard to sustain as the former.

Specific Transpersonal Experiences

This writer has detailed his own significant transpersonal experiences elsewhere (Conway 1984, pp. 193–198). In brief, they included a fully 'vivified' evolutionary sequence of consciousness from the sensations of amoebic life upward through the reptilian, mammalian and human upward to a sense of cosmic awareness and a vivid sense of participation in universal human experience. Vivid participation, in historical scenes, even to the sense of smell, was also experienced. However this may have been partly a function of the subject's prior interest in history. Perinatal experience (common in sensitive subjects) was also undergone. The writer felt all the sensations of late foetal life and also of issue through the birth canal. Following the method of Grof, these experiences were carefully checked against the known details of one's actual physical birth and proved essentially correct. The writer also experienced transexual phenomena such as being in labour, having a uterus and female genitalia. (This is also common in the experience of many normal subjects, confirming the bisexual and androgynous nature of our biological inheritance in a striking way.)

Finally, the writer experienced quite a 'high' religious/trans-cendental experience of great purity with complete freedom from imagery and sensory distortion. This was a total sense of the ineffable, a sense of union with God, or corresponding to the samadhic state of eastern mysticism. The eventual fading of this sublime experience was one of the most regretful occasions of the writers' entire life.

Two transpersonal 'telegenic' or telepathic experiences in each of two therapeutic subjects are so remarkable as to be worth reporting. A young railway worker with no more than two years of technical/high school was being treated for a form of sexual deviation by LSD-aided analysis. At one point he sat up in bed and asked for a pencil and pad. He inscribed upon it three lines in obscure characters, stopped and lost track of what he was doing. The characters were later identified as the first phrases of an ancient Vedic prayer in Sanskrit. The subject was as oblivious of their origin as his helpers until they were eventually deciphered by a scholar. The second instance occurred in the treatment room of a large Melbourne public hospital. The subject treated, a young woman, asked to leave her bed and two workers accompanied her to the window where she looked out across two broad avenues of heavy motorised traffic. Immediately opposite was a large and long parked haulage van. The subject remarked 'there is a little girl on a tricycle on the other side of that van'. The presence of such a girl on the concealed sidewalk beyond was improbable in such a spot. Yet shortly afterward there did indeed emerge from behind the concealing van a small girl slowly pushing a tricycle. Since the subject could hardly have possessed X-ray vision, she was later questioned. She remarked: 'it came to me as a clear and sharp picture from inside my head.'

Needless to say, such isolated anecdotal incidents will invite scepticism as 'evidence' in the traditional sense, but *they did happen* and conventional explanations cannot suffice to explain them. There indeed appear to be paranormal ways of knowing and seeing which transcend the intellectual repertoire of the individual subject and give access to awareness not available to normal intellectual or sensory input. Even a small scattering of such cases among hundreds of LSD experiences give cause for wonderment and defy reductionistic explanations.

Perhaps the most common of all transpersonal experiences outside the remoter personal memories of the individual are those which Carl Jung called archetypes. Even today the Jungian postulate of a Collective Unconscious containing archetypal figures and symbols peculiar to the whole race or even of the whole of humanity is treated with scepticism by the hard-line empirical/behavioral schools of psychology. Yet thousands of archetypal experiences invoking both the malign and benign Great Mother, heroic and demonic figures (many of them lying outside the individual experience or memory of the person prior to their 'trip'), Wise Old Men, etc., continue to demonstrate that Jung was correct in divining a sub-stratum of unconscious human experience which is not normally accessible to our workaday mode of cognition. LSD experiences show a range and variety of genuine archetypal material which often fully transcend personal life experience, as Jung asserted over half a century ago.

It was found by the writer that at least 35% of all the therapeutic subjects studied by him had, at some time during a short series of psychedelic sessions, insights which dealt with material outside their own likely (or even possible) experience prior to therapy. Empathy or telepathy with favoured persons or events over distance, sophisticated knowledge of material beyond one's actual educational range, religious experience involving Christian, Buddhic or even pagan figures, feelings of blissful identification with racial, planetary or god-like experience were the main phenomena reported. Very frequently a complete transcendence of death and the normal fear of dying was experienced. In some cases there was much sensory distortion but most of these subjects eventually merged into a calm, contemplative state in which they reported a great expansion of their normal cognitive and emotive reference frame, believing themselves to be part of a greater human 'whole' than they were before.

Long-term reporting after 20 years indicates that some 20% of all subjects contacted indicated that the LSD experience had permanently changed their cognitive and emotional perspective to an extent which forbade them ever returning to what they regarded as the narrower reference frame of their lives before undergoing their psychedelic experiences. This can be most cogently summed up by one intelligent subject who wrote as follows: 'In previous years I believed only in what my five senses could verify. I was quite ego-absorbed and saw others as being essentially 'different' from myself. Now I believe I have discovered a common link between all human experience. At its summit there is a loving intelligence in which all our separate knowings converge and are enhanced. Beyond everything I have lost my dread of death and know that something within me will never pass away.'

References

Abramson, H.A. (1967), *The Use of LSD in Psychotherapy and Alcoholism*. New York, Bobbs-Merrill.

Barr, H.L., Langs, R.L. (1972), *LSD, Personality and Experience*. pp. 89–140, New York, John Wiley & Sons.

Caldwell, W.V. (1968), *LSD Psychotherapy*, New York, Grove Press.

Conway, R. (1968), *The Use of LSD in the Treatment of Personality Disorders*. Unpublished paper given to Conference of Australia and New Zealand Association for the Advancement of Science— May.

Conway, R. (1984), *The End of Stupor?* Melbourne, Macmillan Co. (Aust).

Grof, S. (1975) *Realms of the Human Unconscious: Observations from LSD Research*. New York, Viking Press.

Hicks, R.E. & Fink, P.J. (eds) (1969), *Psychedelic Drugs*. New York, Grune & Stratton.

Masters, R.E.L. and Houston, J. (1966), *The Varieties of Psychedelic Experience*. New York, Holt, Rinehart and Winston.

CHAPTER 7

PARANORMAL PHENOMENA AND THE NEAR-DEATH EXPERIENCE

Gary Groth-Marnat

During the past decade near-death experiences (NDEs) have received considerable coverage in the popular media as well as in scientific publications. A typical description of a person nearly dying includes a review of life events, an out-of-body experience, a sense of going down a tunnel perhaps accompanied by noises, arriving at a border or threshold, encountering a being of light, and finally experiencing a sense of re-entering their bodies. The vast majority of experiencers have a feeling of peace or calm. Either all of the above experiences might happen, or, more frequently, three or four of them. Most descriptions represent a blending of transpersonal, hallucinatory, and paranormal phenomena.

Whereas paranormal phenomena have frequently been associated with many altered states of consciousness (Krippner & George, 1986), NDEs are noteworthy in that paranormal phenomena occur with such frequency and variety. The ones most typically associated with NDEs are telepathy (especially with deceased friends or relatives), out-of-body experiences, precognition, and an increase in psi phenomena following the near-death experience (NDE).

Phenomenology of the NDE

During the late 19*th* century there was considerable interest in studying the visions which dying persons frequently reported in the hope that the observers could obtain a glimpse into possible post-mortem existence. These death-bed visions were accompanied by intense emotions and were usually of deceased relatives (Clarke, 1878; Cobbe, 1877; Hyslop, 1907). It was noted that sometimes the death-bed visions included a deceased relative that the dying person could not have known had died (Barrett, 1926; Cobbe, 1877; 1882; Hyslop, 1918). Such anecdotes were often used as evidence of the objective reality for survival and telepathic communication with the dead. More recent surveys of the death-bed observations of physicians and nurses have provided support for the belief that visions are not associated with sedation or delirium since they usually occur when the patient is in a clear state of consciousness (Osis & Haraldson, 1977). Usually previously deceased persons are seen by dying persons and half of them stated that the apparitions were going to take them to their death (Osis & Haraldson, 1977).

The past decade has resulted in researchers moving away from studying observers' reports of dying persons to interviewing actual survivors regarding their subjective experiences. The most familiar description of NDEs comes from Moody's (1975) publication of interviews with 150 persons who had either been clinically dead or who had come close to death. Typically the person would experience a variety of the following themes:

1. Peace, serenity, ineffability.
2. Noises (music, clicking, whistling, buzzing).
3. A sense that they had risen above their body and could observe details of what was going on below them.
4. Passing through a tunnel.
5. Encountering spiritlike persons (relatives, friends).
6. Encountering a being of light (often unidentified but sometimes referred to as a religious figure).
7. Life review.
8. Experience of a border region which could not be passed.
9. Reluctance to return to body.

In contrast to Moody's descriptions, Noyes (1971, 1972) organized NDEs into either encompassing resistance to dying (usually at the beginning of the experience), life review, and transpersonal experiences. Ring (1979) categorized NDE experiences into five unfolding sequential patterns which occurred with decreasing frequency (peace, body separation, entering the darkness, seeing the light, entering the light). Based on these categories, he developed a scale to assess the relative depth of the experience. Sabom's (1982) interviews with cardiac patients led him to divide NDEs into autoscopic hallucinations (out-of-body experiences), transcendental experiences, or a combination of the two (for a review, see Groth-Marnat & Schumaker, 1988).

The incidence of persons reporting NDEs is 0.7% within a university population (Locke & Shantz, 1983) but this would probably be somewhat higher if older age groups were to be assessed. Studies on the proportion of persons having had NDEs who have come close to death range between 22% and 43% (Locke & Shantz, 1983; Sabom, 1982; Thomas, Cooper & Suscovich, 1982). The proportion and depth of NDEs was highest among persons having serious illnesses such as heart disease and lowest among persons experiencing near fatal accidents (Noyes & Slymen, 1979; Ring, 1980).

Most persons report some paranormal phenomena during a NDE (Ring, 1980) and frequently there is an increase in openness to these phenomena following the experience (Greyson, 1983; Kohr, 1982). Greyson and Stevenson (1980) found that, of persons having NDEs, 75% reported out-of-body experiences, 49% reported seeing an apparition, 39% reported extrasensory phenomena, and 21% stated that they had been the subject of someone else's psychic experience during their NDE. This is consistent with more general studies on paranormal phenomena which suggest that the likelihood of psi phenomena is increased during altered states of consciousness (Krippner & George, 1986; 1975; Tart, 1978). The higher rate of psi phenomena associated with NDEs also corresponds to studies indicating a much higher number of visions in the dying (Osis & Haraldson, 1977).

Out-of-Body Experiences

Out-of-body experiences (OOBEs) are one of the most frequently reported and thoroughly researched areas of paranormal phenomena associated with NDEs. The OOBE is a subjective exprience in which experiencers describe their consciousness as having left their bodies. Often they describe having travelled to distant places and 'seeing' objects or events about which the person could not normally have known. During NDEs, people typically report looking down on their bodies and, if in situations such as surgery, give descriptions of the procedures used to resuscitate them. Ring (1979) found that 37% of people experiencing NDEs reported having an OOBE whereas Greyson and Stevenson (1980) reported a much higher rate of 75% in their sample.

Kastenbaum (1984) provides the following illustrative case of a person experiencing an OOBE following extensive surgery for a chest tumor.

I became aware that 'I' was no longer in my body. This was a little stranger than I was ready for, so I deliberately did not 'look back'. The fundamental rules of being now seemed up for grabs. An old image entered my mind, that of an anthropologist, an ethnographer, beginning to explore a new culture . . . I moved slowly around the room, speeded up, and slowed down again, experimenting with changing rates of motion very quickly . . . Then, more carefully, I moved nearer the walls and skimmed alongside. Finally, I worked up the courage to 'put my hand' on the wall and push gently. My hand seemed to enter the wall. I did it again and felt myself penetrating deeper into the wall. This was a little frightening. The absence of familiar restraints can be unsettling . . . It occurred to me, therefore, that maybe I was dead . . . Somehow I got back into my body. Very strenuously, I tried to get my chest to move. I tried very hard to breathe and expand my chest. If I could make someone notice, then I'd know I was not dead. I kept working on it for some time. I was aware that some figures had looked into the room at one point and decided I was 'still out', that is to say unconscious. Finally, I heard something like 'I think he's coming to.' (Kastenbaum, 1984; pp. 5–6).

The above case highlights the subject's sense of reality regarding the experience in that the OBE did not have the feeling of being a hazy drug induced half-conscious phenomena. There is also the necessity of learning different modes of functioning, the gradual realization of the possibility of death, the predominantly visual rather than auditory or tactile descriptions, and the struggle to return to the physical body.

Surveys of non-NDE OOBEs indicate that between 10% and 36% of the population report having had an OOBE (Blackmore, 1982a, 1982b, 1982c; Irwin, 1988). The occurrence of an OOBE does not relate to demographic characteristics (Palmer, 1978, 1979; Irwin, 1988; Kohr, 1983) or general psychological profile (Gabbard, Twemlow, & Jones, 1982) although reporters are likely to have better social skills and greater ability to become absorbed in imaginative activities (Irwin, 1981; Wilson & Barber, 1983). Most OOBEs are short, lasting one minute or less. Only 20% report having a second or astral body and the majority of persons see themselves as a 'blob' or point of consciousness (Blackmore, 1982a).

Comparisons of persons who report having experienced an OOBE with non-experiencers indicate experiencers are more likely to pursue different experiences, have novel goals, and be more accepting of death (Irwin, 1988). A greater belief in death and an afterlife was particularly evident in persons having OOBEs as a part of NDEs. This afterlife was typically perceived as being a reward and representing a benevolent eternity (Irwin, 1988). However, it is difficult to determine whether the OOBE component of the NDE was associated with these beliefs or some other element of the OOBE.

The frequent occurrence of OOBEs associated with the experience of dying has created renewed interest in the question of survival after death. The argument, at its simplest, states that if a person can leave their body during their lifetime then consciousness must not necessarily be dependent on biological processes and therefore one continues to survive in some form after biological death. In the past, parapsychological research has struggled with the same question by attempting to demonstrate objective perceptions of such things as events and numbers during the OOBE. For example, Tart (1967, 1968) requested trained subjects to self-induce an OOBE and report on a five digit number which was written away from their sight. One subject on 9 trials was unable to see the numbers whereas a second subject was able to accurately report all five digits on her fourth trial but was unable to return for followup testing. Other subsequent studies by other researchers have produced results which are suggestive of possible increased accuracy in OOBEs but are by no means conclusive (Mitchell, 1981; Osis & McCormick, 1980).

Numerous anecdotes of NDE experiencers accurately perceiving events which actually occurred during NDEs fill the literature. One of the few systematic studies to attempt to empirically verify objective events during NDE associated OOBEs was Sabom's (1982) comparison of the relative accuracy of persons who had undergone cardio-pulmonary resuscitation (CPR) and reported a NDE with a 'control' group of persons who had undergone CPR but did not report a NDE. The NDE group specified far greater and more accurate details than the control group and their details were beyond general knowledge of CPR and they were also able to report unique variations relating to their case. Objections might be that his patients were merely piecing together the events of the resuscitation through semi-conscious auditory recall. Sabom (1982) defends the objective accuracy of the OOBE recall by pointing out that the descriptions were primarily visual rather than auditory, the perspective was not at eye level but usually near the ceiling of the operating room, the details of the medical instruments were beyond what would be expected, and comparison with a non-NDE group indicated far greater knowledge of the resuscitation procedure.

The accuracy of observed events during an NDE associated OOBE is one of the strongest arguments for the objective (versus subjective) reality of NDEs. Most researchers skeptical of an objective explanation can provide explanations of OOBEs within a traditional positivistic model (see Blackmore, 1983; Seigel, 1980) with the exception of accounting for the reporting of accurate details by persons with OOBEs which would otherwise be impossible to know. However, evidence beyond numerous anecdotes and the small number of subjects reported by Sabom (1982) is needed. Future studies should include not only larger sample sizes but more sophisticated methodologies especially double-blind procedures and structured questionnaires. However, even if the accuracy of otherwise un-knowable details could be fully documented, the explanation for this phenomenon would still be debatable. Possibilities might include ESP or pre-mortem astral travel and may not necessarily prove survival after death. Thus, even if perception is accurate, there is no evidence that something actually leaves the body and that this something survives death.

Precognition Associated with Near-death Experiences

Ring (1982) found precognitive experiences present in a small number of subjects. All of these experiences occurred during deep, prolonged NDEs which included a life review and encounter with a higher being. The first category of precognitive experience was labelled as personal flashforwards since they involved events which had not yet occurred in the person's life. Sometimes they referred to the specific events in a person's life whereas others referred to general life design. The recall of the personal flashforward varied. In some cases the precognition would remain fully intact directly after the NDE whereas other persons would remember it only just prior to or even during the event itself. The following case began with a description of a NDE and included an encounter with various beings who conveyed to her details of what she and her family would be like in the future. She notes,

> . . . As I gained the knowledge of what our family would be like in the future, I could see, hear, and smell. Particularly striking was the smell of the salad I was producing (cucumber) mingled with the smell of evergreens growing around the house and the odor of freshly cut grass. Also I could detect my own cologne and soap from the shower my husband had vacated. This picture was only a glimpse, but it made one huge impression on me. I must have vowed right then and there never to forget it, because I certainly have not. (Ring, 1982, p. 50)

In a correspondence 22 years after the NDE the subject commented:

> 1. We look exactly like that right now.
> 2. Our kids look like that picture too.
> 3. The rapport in our family is now as I've already described (*in the NDE description*).
> 4. Our older daughter has been married, had two daughters of her own, and been divorced (*also as described in the NDE*).
> 5. Our home . . . could fit the description. I only wish I had paid more attention to the way the house was built. (Ring, 1982, p. 50)

In contrast to personal flashforwards Ring (1982) also provides a group of subjects who had prophetic visions pertaining to previews of the future state of the entire planet. These prophetic visions occurred during encounters with guides or beings of light and the contents of these visions were noteworthy in their consistency among all subjects. As in the personal flashforwards, recall of the vision varied from directly after the NDE to just before or during the event. For example one subject reported the following in association with her NDE:

> Three Mile Island. I knew it was going to happen! I don't know *why*. Three Mile Island stuck in my mind . . . I knew it was going to happen. I was telling Vicky . . . I told her it was going to happen, and do you know, two days later it happened. (Ring, 1982, p. 55)

In addition to specific events as described above, the prophetic visions also related to geophysical changes (earthquakes, volcanic eruptions), meteorological changes (warming of the atmosphere), nuclear war, and a new era of peace.

The validity of both personal flashforwards and prophetic visions is difficult to determine given the possibility that only positive reports are likely to be submitted. Reports in which the predicted event does not occur are probably dismissed as mere hallucination. Thus, the personal flashforwards reported to Ring might have been a combination of selective reporting, chance, and creative construction based on probable futures. Possible interpretations of the prophetic visions might be that the experiencers are responding to collective expectations or, as might be predicted from psychodynamic theory, they are projecting their fear of dying onto the world which has resulted in the frequent visions of destruction. An archetypal explanation would suggest that such visions are the expression of a sequence of symbols which helps the psyche to resolve conflict (Perry, 1974). Ring (1982) also proposes explanations derived from theoretical physics to account for accurate predictions such as the alternative futures theory in quantum physics.

Increased Psi Experiences Following NDEs

Most investigators have found that persons who have a NDE have significant changes in personality including greater self acceptance (Ring, 1984), increased concern for others (Flynn, 1982; Ring, 1984), greater orientation towards the present (Noyes, 1980), and reduced fear of death (Moody, 1975; Noyes, 1982; Sabom, 1982). Changes in attitude tended to be more frequent in persons who believed that, during the NDE, they were actually dying and who had also reported panoramic memory experiences (Greyson & Stevenson, 1980). An increase in paranormal phenomena following NDEs has also been noted (Greyson, 1983; Ring, 1984, 1986; Kohr, 1982).

Kohr (1982) found a positive correlation between the occurrence of NDEs and psychic and psi-related experiences but did not speculate whether this meant (1) that NDEs occur more frequently in persons sensitive to psychic phenomena, (2) the occurrence of the NDE caused greater attention to psi phenomena (but not an actual increase in frequency), or (3) that NDEs actually stimulate psychic phenomena in the lives of experiencers. In an attempt to answer these questions Greyson (1983) requested persons to estimate the frequency of psychic phenomenon before and after the occurrence of their NDEs. Since psi and psi-related events increased following NDEs, he concluded that

NDEs served to stimulate these phenomena. He also acknowledged that this finding could also be accounted for by the subjects selectively giving greater post-NDE attention to psychic phenomena. Specifically, Greyson (1983) found greater increases in waking ESP experiences, OOBEs, encounters with apparitions, and perception of auras. There was also an increase in both altered states of consciousness (mystical experiences, lucid dreams, and weekly dream recall) as well as psi-related activities (dream analysis and meditation).

NDEs as Evidence of Survival

Parapsychology has historically placed considerable effort into investigating the possibility that people survive biological death. Investigations have centered on mediumship, reincarnation, possession, non-NDE OOBEs, and hauntings and poltergeist disturbances (see Roll, 1984; Stevenson, 1977). Parapsychologists themselves are divided on the issue of survival. In reviewing evidence related to the above areas of investigation, Beloff (1983) concludes that seemingly valid arguments can be developed to either support or discount a survivalist position.

The past 10 years has seen a resurgence of interest in survival caused in part by interest in NDEs. Supporters of a survivalist position point out that NDEs occur across different cultures and are only minimally influenced by demographic characteristics such as age, religious beliefs, occupation, and expectation (Giovetti, 1982; Ring, 1980, 1982, 1986). They also cite cases of empirical verification of objective events during the OOBE phase of the NDE (Sabom, 1982) and numerous cross cultural similarities such as NDE descriptions in the *Tibetan book of the dead* (Becker, 1985; Evans-Wentz, 1960). Furthermore, supporters point out the difficulty traditional science has in either explaining the NDE itself or the personality changes following NDEs (Grosso, 1981).

Despite the above arguments supporting a survivalist position the most they can do is merely suggest survival rather than prove it. Perhaps central to this lack of clear proof is that clinical death (cardiac and respiratory arrest) does not equal complete biological death (usually measured by flat EEGs). If the people had truly died, then they would not come back to tell us about their experience. The NDE may be merely a glorious fade out before non-existence. This is similar to the 'Schroedinger's cat' paradox in theoretical physics; a cat is in a closed box and the lid is attached to a hammer which will kill the cat if it opens the box. Is the cat alive or dead? Since the only way to know is to open the box, the investigation itself creates the reality of death. The cat simultaneously exists in a situation of both life and death. Likewise, for a NDE to prove survival the person could never come back to tell us about it because then they would not have truly died.

Further difficulties in using NDEs to prove survival are the observation that only a minority of persons who come close to death actually report having had a NDE. Does this mean that persons reporting NDEs survive whereas others do not? It is implausible that some survive whereas others do not. A pro-survivalist might also point out that NDEs have been reported to have occurred during flat EEGs which suggests that brain activity was non-existent and therefore mental activity must be occurring independent of biological functioning. However, proving that the NDE actually occurred during the time of the flat EEG is nearly impossible as well as there being extreme difficulty in proving that there was not some form of unmeasured electrical activity somewhere in the brain which might have produced the NDE.

In order to prove survival it must be demonstrated that (1) something leaves the body and (2) that the something which leaves continues after complete biological death. Although NDEs are suggestive of survival they are not proof and, due to the paradox surrounding definitions of death, can probably never be proof. Thus, NDEs present parapsychology with an additional area for studying the possibility of survival but do not provide it with the much sought after proof.

Conclusions

The above review clearly underlines the importance of NDEs as an altered state of consciousness highly conducive to the occurrence of paranormal phenomena. In fact few, if any, altered states are likely to have the frequency and variety of paranormal events which occur with NDEs. These include OOBEs, apparitions, recognition, and being the subject of someone else's psychic experience during the NDE. NDEs also frequently result in increased psi experiences following the NDE and have made a significant contribution to the study of survival. However, NDEs have the distinct disadvantage that they cannot be studied directly but rather are dependent on retrospective self reports. There is at least the possibility that these reports may be biased in predictable but currently unknown ways. Whereas an altered state such as hypnosis or drug-related changes can be induced and methodologically studied under controlled conditions, NDEs, for obvious reasons, cannot. Thus researchers are largely reduced to tabulating percentages and studying correlational relationships.

Causal mechanisms must be directly inferred leaving open a wide number of interpretations for the data. A parapsychologist might look at empirical verification of objective events during OOBEs and document this as evidence of survival whereas another might interpret the same event as occurring due to telepathy. A more traditional scientist might explain the accuracy of recall as caused by a combination of good guesswork plus experimenter bias which was unconsciously reinforced by the interviewer.

As with the question of survival and its relation to NDEs, one may ask whether the study of NDEs contributes to validating the objective reality of paranormal phenomena. Parapsychology has been attempting to create clear proof of psi phenomena for over 100 years with the result being extensive volumes of research but with both believers and disbelievers. Although the study of NDEs provides extremely fertile ground for psi-related investigation, it is unlikely that this study, in and of itself, will resolve this now long-continuing debate.

References

Barrett, W.F. (1926), *Death-bed Visions*, London, Methuen.

Becker, C.B. (1985), 'Views from Tibet: Near-death experiences and the Tibetan Book of the Dead', *Anabiosis*, 5, 3–20.

Beloff, J. (1983), 'Three open questions', In G. Roll, J. Beloff, and R.A. White, *Research in Parapsychology 1982*, London, Scarecrow Press.

Blackmore, S. (1982a), *Beyond the Body*, London, Heinemann.

Blackmore, S. (1982b), 'Have you ever had an OBE?: The wording of the question', *Journal of the Society for Psychical Research*, 51, 292–302.

Blackmore, S. (1982c), 'OBEs, lucid dreams and imagery: two surveys', *Journal of the American Society for Psychical Research*, 76, 301–317.

Blackmore, S. (1983), 'Are out-of-body experiences evidence of survival?' *Anabiosis*, 3, 137–155.

Clarke, E.H. (1878), *Visions, A study of False Sight*, Boston, Houghton, Osgood.

Cobbe, F.P. (1877), 'The Peak-in-Darien: The riddle of death', *Littell's Living Age and New Quarterly Review*, 134, 374–379.

Cobbe, F.P. (1882), *Peak in Darien*, London, Williams and Norgate.

Evans-Wentz, W.Y. (Ed.), (1927/1960), *The Tibetan Book of the Dead*, Oxford, Oxford University Press.

Flynn, C.P. (1982), 'Meanings and implications of near-death experiencer transformations: Some preliminary findings and implications', *Anabiosis*, 2, 3–14.

Gabbard, G.O., Twemlow, S.W. & Jones, F.C. (1982), 'Differential diagnosis of altered mind/body perception', *Psychiatry*, 45, 361–369.

Giovetti, P. (1982), 'Near-death and deathbed experiences: An Italian survey', *Theta*, 10, 10–13.

Greyson, B. (1983), 'Increase in psychic phenomenon following near-death experiences', *Theta*, 11, 26–29.

Greyson, B. & Stevenson, I. (1980), 'The phenomenology of near-death experiences', *American Journal of Psychiatry*, 137, 1193–1196.

Grosso, M. (1981), 'Toward an explanation of near-death phenomenon', *Journal of the American Society for Psychical Research*, 75, 37-60.

Groth-Marnat, G. & Schumaker, J.F. (1988), 'The near-death experience: A review and critique', *Journal of Humanistic Psychology* (in press).

Hyslop, J. (1907), 'Visions of the dying', *Journal of the American Society for Psychical Research*, 1, 45-55.

Irwin, H.J. (1981), 'Some dimensions of the out-of-body-experience', *Parapsychology Review*, 12, 1-6.

Irwin, H.J. (1988/in press), Out-of-body experiences and attitudes to life and death. *Journal of the American Society for Psychical Research*.

Kastenbaum, R. (Ed.), (1984), *Is There Life After Death?*, London, Rider.

Kohr, R.L. (1982), 'Near-death experience and its relationship to psi and various altered states', *Theta*, 10, 50-53.

Kohr, R. (1983), 'Near-death experiences, altered states, and psi sensitivity', *Anabiosis*, 3, 157-174.

Krippner, S. & George, L. (1986), 'Psi phenomena as related to altered states of consciousness'. In B. Wolman, *Handbook of Altered States of Consciousness*, New York, Van Nostrand Reinhold.

Locke, T.P., Thomas, P. & Shontz, F.C. (1983), 'Personality correlates of the near-death experience: A preliminary study', *Journal of the American Society for Psychical Research*, 77, 311-318.

Mitchel, J.L. (1981), *Out-of-body Experiences: A Handbook*, Jefferson, N.C., McFarland.

Moody, R. (1975), *Life After Life*, Covington, GA, Mockingbird.

Moody, R. (1977), *Reflections on life after life*, Simons, Is., GA, Mockingbird.

Noyes, R. (1971), 'Dying and mystical consciousness', *Journal of Thanatology*, 1, 25-42.

Noyes, R. (1972), 'The experience of dying', *Psychiatry*, 35, 174-184.

Noyes, R. (1980), 'Attitude change following near-death experiences', *Psychiatry*, 43, 234-232.

Noyes, R. (1983), 'The human experience of death or, what can we learn from near-death experiences?' *Omega*, 13, 251-259.

Noyes, R. & Slymen, D. (1979), 'The subjective response to life-threatening danger', *Omega*, 9, 313-321.

Osis, K. & Haraldson, E. (1977), *At the Hour of Death*, New York, Avon.

Osis, K. & McCormick, D. (1980), 'Kinetic effects at the ostensible location of an out-of-body projection during perceptual testing', *Journal of the American Society for Psychical Research*, 74, 319-329.

Palmer, J. (1978), 'Deathbed apparitions and the survival hypothesis', *Journal of the American Society for Psychical Research*, 72, 392-395.

Palmer, J. (1979), 'Correspondence: More on deathbed apparitions and the survival hypothesis', *Journal of the American Society for Psychical Research*, 73, 94-96.

Perry, J. (1974), *The Far Side of Madness*, New York, Prentice-Hall.

Ring, K. (1979), 'Further studies of the near-death experience', *Theta*, 7, 1-4.

Ring, K. (1980), *Life at Death: A Scientific Investigation of the Near-death Experience*, New York, Coward, McCann & Geoghegan.

Ring, K. (1982), 'Precognitive and prophetic visions in near-death experiences', *Anabiosis*, 2, 47-74.

Ring, K. (1984), *Heading Toward Omega*, New York, Morrow, 1984.

Ring, K. (1986), 'Near-death experiences: Implications for human evolution and planetary transformation', *Revision*, 8, 75–85.

Roll, W.G. (1984), 'Survival after death: Alan Gauld's examination of the evidence', *Journal of Parapsychology*, 48, 127–148.

Sabom, M.B. (1982), *Recollections of Death: A Medical Investigation*, New York, Harper & Row.

Siegel, R. (1980), 'The psychology of life after death', *American Psychologist*, 35, 911–931.

Stevenson, I. (1977), 'Research into the evidence of man's survival after death: A historical and critical survey with a summary of recent developments', *Journal of Nervous and Mental Disease*, 165, 152–170.

Tart, C.T. (1967), 'A second psychophysiological study of out-of-body experiences in a gifted subject', *International Journal of Parapsychology*, 9, 251–258.

Tart, C.T. (1968), 'A psychophysiological study of out-of-body experiences in a selected subject', *Journal of the American Society for Psychical Research*, 62, 3–27.

Tart, C.T. (1978), 'Psi function and altered states of consciousness: A perspective', in B. Shapin & L. Coley (Eds.), *Psi and States of Awareness*, New York, Parapsychology Foundation, pp. 180–210.

Thomas, L.E., Cooper, P.E. & Suscovich, D.J. (1982), 'Incidence of near-death and intense spiritual experiences in an intergenerational sample: an interpretation', *Omega*, 13, 35–41.

Wilson, S.C. & Barber, T.X. (1983), 'The fantasy prone personality: Implications for understanding imagery, hypnosis and parapsychological phenomena', In A.A. Sheikh (Ed.), *Imagery: Current Theory, Research, and Application*, (pp. 340–387), New York, Wiley.

CHAPTER 8
MYSTICISM, THE UNITY THESIS, AND THE PARANORMAL

Ralph W. Hood, Jr.

The study of mysticism like that of parapsychology has been fraught with conceptual difficulties. To a large extent, both mysticism and the paranormal suffer less from a mass of relevant empirical literature, (equal in stature to any empirical literature in 'mainstream' psychology) than from an incompatibility with dominant paradigms of modern psychology. In this sense, the failure to take both mysticism and the paranormal seriously is less an empirical than a conceptual problem. As such, little is to be gained by the mere collection of additional empirical data. What is needed are conceptual models within which existing empirical data can be adequately addressed. As Wittgenstein (1958, p. 232) noted,

> The confusion and barrenness of psychology is not to be explained by calling it a 'young science' . . . for in psychology there are experimental methods and *conceptual confusion*.

Not surprisingly then, essays on mysticism and the paranormal often begin with conceptual arguments largely apologetic in nature, telling the reader why mysticism or the paranormal ought to be taken seriously. Such approaches have merit, and we shall partly follow this tradition out of the necessity to adequately treat mysticism. Our interest will be in articulating what we shall call the *unity thesis* in mysticism. The importance and precise nature of this thesis will be discussed below. For now, we can simply note that this thesis argues that despite wide differences in description and interpretation, mystical experiences refer to a common reality that nevertheless must always be culturally and individually expressed. This means that despite being identical in the particular sense to be explicated in this essay, mystical experiences nevertheless vary widely in description both within and without various traditions. The paradox to be made apparent, we hope, is that mysticisms do indeed reflect an 'identity in difference' that can both respect varying traditions and heresies and at the same time affirm a transcendent reality that is common to all these traditions and heresies. Furthermore, this claim is not without relevance to parapsychology as we shall make evident as the essay develops. Our initial task is to select an appropriate methodology within which what we have to say makes sense. This methodology, broadly speaking, is phenomenology. We wish to show initially what from other methodological perspectives appears surprising: the notion that mystical experiences are quite definite experiences, easily delineated, and indeed necessarily quite common. The problem, as we shall see, is less with persons who report mystical experiences, than with social scientists who are surprised by such reports.

Phenomenological Reflections on Mysticism

It is a curious irony that mystical experiences have a reputation of being rare, 'a bit strange' and certainly sharing the epithet of referring to something that is vague and at best ethereal. Not surprisingly, the earliest psychological literature on mysticism virtually equated mysticism with madness, a tendency which persisted among some psychologists despite all the empirical data to the contrary (Spilka, Hood, & Gorsuch, 1985; Chs. 8, 12).

Phenomenological investigations of mysticism quickly dispel the notion that mysticism is anything other than an experience rather easily identified throughout history, in all cultures, and with fairly precise criteria of recognition. Not at all a vague experience, reserved for those who cannot see clearly and with the pejorative connotation that some suggest! Indeed, just the opposite: it is an experience of immense clarity and precision, available to all, and so easily recognized as such that it is often ignored. If such claims seem perplexing, it is likely only due to a methodological commitment that seeks mystical experiences with procedures and concepts that will not do the job. It is, as if (as the proverbial tale goes) one sought one's glasses everywhere except where they truly are — resting nicely on one's own nose! It is this sort of claim that modern confrontations with mysticism have helped illuminate. Such efforts have largely been identified with phenomenological methods, but have long roots in the Western philosophical tradition, particularly in what Robinson (1981, p. 257) nicely refers to as 'methodological rationalism'. What these approaches share is the conviction that what is needed is not simply more empirical data but rather a rational, intuitive apprehension of the meaning of the data we already have. Indeed data that we already possess intimately within our very selves. As Stahl (1975, p. 123) notes, 'If mysticism is to be studied seriously, it should not merely be studied indirectly and from without, but also directly and from within'.

Earle's Mystical Reason

Recently Earle (1980) argued the position from within most forcefully. His argument is profound enough and of such immense value in illuminating mysticism that it ought to be read in its entirety. Yet the argument is not simply his, but has a long history. In simple terms it requires me to reflect upon the undoubtable fact that I am a conscious being whose very consciousness allows me to reflect upon all that I am not. What I am conscious of is something other than myself — whether that chair over there or any other perceived object, I stand in opposition to it. From the phenomenology of Husserl to the existentialism of Sartre the claim that consciousness is of something other than itself becomes a crucial starting point for mystical reflection.[1] What I am not allows me to seek what I am — and what I truly am cannot be any mere object of consciousness. Indeed, when I seek even myself in reflective awareness, I am not that self either. Here in phenomenological terms is a 'divestment' (itself a classic mystical technique) — a withdrawal in reflection from the objects of my consciousness — whether perceptual images veridical to some claimed objective reality or memories or imaginations presumable within my mind's eye and perhaps mere subjective fantasies. All this I can remove myself from, indeed must remove myself from to be aware of them. Precisely because I can do this throws into relief the I that I truly am, and this I is not an object of consciousness. This I is contentless, indeed never reflectively captured in itself, but simply aware that it is the ground of all else. As such, this I is not simply most truly me, myself as pure actuality, but also curiously one. Surely my 'I' of which I have immediate intuitive apprehension is a transcendental 'I' and as such is that unity or One that we all are.

   In the great traditions of the West this transcendental 'I' has often been equated with God (Earle, 1980, p. 72). Herein lies a phenomenological claim that parallels classic mystical claims to the realization of one's true self, to a merger with the absolute, or to that curious claim of the mystics that I and God are one. In James' (1958, p. 321) most succinct phrasing serving both to define and illuminate mysticism; 'The overcoming of all the usual barriers between the individual and the Absolute is the great mystic achievement. In mystic states we become one with the Absolute and we become aware of our oneness'. In Deikman's (1982, p. 3) words, 'the mystical tradition asserts the equation I (Real Self) = God,' or in Earle's (1980, p. 72) words, '. . . each transcendental I is God'.

   Furthermore, this mystical state is best sought not in presumably rare states of ecstasy or among what William James' called the 'religious virtuosos' but rather among the common experiences of everyone. It is everyday reality that is as truly mystical as any other and so we ought not to be surprised that among common people the report of mystical experience is indeed a frequent occurrence. So much so that Scharfstein (1973, pp. 63–70) can title an entire chapter, 'everyday mysticism'. This despite the fact that common persons living their everyday realities seldom argue phenomenology. Yet the persuasive nature of mystical experience is demanded by phenomenological reflection and simply would reflect inadequate empiricism if it went undetected by social scientists. As Earle (1980, pp. 5–6) asks:

> The truth is that, far from being inarticulate or lost in the ineffable, the mystics are almost too articulate, can hardly stop talking. In fact, their best texts are so expressive that readers hostile or not otherwise known for their sympathy to mysticism find themselves secretly understanding the whole business. Would that be possible if mysticism were confined to the abrupt or convulsive experiences, undergone, after all, by only a few?

The empirical study of mysticism has documented its commonality as indeed it must given these phenomenological reflections. However, before we note this empirical literature it will behove us to consider one more investigator within the phenomenological tradition.

Stace's Common Core

Probably no investigator has gained a greater stature in the contemporary study of mysticism than Stace. Here too, is an excellent example of careful phenomenological research. His Mysticism and Philosophy (1961) has drawn an entire volume of critical response by many of the foremost scholars of our day (Katz, 1978) and has served as the conceptual foundation upon which empirical measures of mysticism have been devised (Hood, 1975). In a very real sense most of the modern scholarship on mysticism centers around Stace's work. Stace draws from a wide variety of sources, traditional and otherwise, to seek the minimal core criteria that mysticisms seem to share. After careful selection of a wide variety of cases, Stace finds that the essential distinguishing core of all mysticism is an experience of unity — a oneness.[2] The nature of this unity or oneness is identified in two senses by Stace, leading to a classification of two types of mysticism, which may be but 'two species of one genus' (Stace, 1961, p. 131). One type of mysticism is an awareness that the multiplicity of all that is perceived is nevertheless one. This extrovertive mysticism is identified by a perceptual experience of unity and has little in common with the mystical reflection of Earle noted above. Yet as we shall note later, this extrovertive mysticism is of immense relevance to the unity thesis and cannot be ignored. For now we simply set it aside in favor of a discussion of introvertive mysticism which Stace suggests is what is most truly mystical for which extrovertive mysticism is perhaps but an incomplete version (Stace, 1961, p. 133).

It is often unappreciated that phenomenological reflection, appropriately conducted, can produce unanimity as much as any carefully conducted empirical research. In Stace's illumination of introvertive mysticism we find a firm compatibility with Earle's phenomenological reflections previously discussed. This is as it must be if the mystical consciousness is illuminated fairly to be what indeed it is. For Stace, introvertive awareness is an undifferentiated state of pure awareness, in which one's true self emerges. That mere empirical hypothesizing might miss what phenomenological reflection demands is well noted by Stace (1961, pp. 85–86):

> Suppose that, after having got rid of all sensations, one should go on to exclude from consciousness all sensuous images, and then all abstract thoughts, reasoning processes, volition, and other particular mental contents; what would there then be left of consciousness? There would be no mental content whatever but rather a complete emptiness, vacuum, void. One would suppose *a priori* that consciousness would then entirely lapse and one would fall asleep or become unconscious. But the introvertive mystics — thousands of them all over the world assert that they have attained to this complete vacuum of particular mental contents, but that what then happens is quite different from a lapse into unconsciousness, On the contrary, what emerges is a state of *pure* consciousness — 'pure' in the sense that it is not the consciousness *of* any empirical content. It has not content except itself (emphases in original).

Of course, the paradoxical recognition from mere empirical suspicions that the absence of all sensation produces not simply a nothingness, or a lapse into unconsciousness but a 'no-thing-ness' and a pure consciousness is precisely to be expected based upon Earle's phenomenological reflections. Here the point is obvious: what a mere empiricism suggests is impossible or paradoxical is revealed as fundamental and essential by phenomenological reflection. One's self suddenly emerges and is found to be what it always truly is, simply itself removed now from a world of estrangement, of things which it is not. In Earle's (1980, p. 44) terms it is the autophenomenal ego and this ego is identified with God or the Absolute. Herein lies the relationship between mysticism and reason that belies what only superficially are perceived as contradictory terms. The respective phenomenological analyses of Earle and Stace mesh nicely. Mysticism tends towards religious and metaphysical systems to explicate this newly realized self. Reason and mysticism are clearly not compatible as Bertrand Russell (1921) seemed to think. In Earle's preface to his otherwise curiously titled text, Mystical Reason (1980, p. xi):

> Mysticism is not in the least an affair of the irrational swooning, visions, and ecstasies, nor is reason an affair of drawing out long chains of argumentation about increasingly empty abstractions. Mysticism certainly loves its visions, and reason also exhibits itself in analysis, refutations, and formal deductions, and no doubt both have their peculiar functions and virtues. But that either should imagine these secondary phenomena to be its own very essence is a preliminary error which can be removed: mysticism deepens itself into an intuited identity of the self of the mystic and God, and reason plumbs itself into its own rational intuition of the identity of the transcendental ego which exercises reason, and absolute reality of which the transcendental ego is the consciousness (emphases in the original).

Enough has been said about the phenomenology of mysticism to assure the reader that one is confronted with an experience at once both profound and persuasive. An experience that upon appropriate reflection stands as foundational with respect to a psychology of self and one that suggest that psychological efforts to explain away mysticism are doomed a priori to failure. It makes forever non-problematic the by now well established fact that the report of mystical experiences is largely a normative phenomena, reported by at least a third of the population in America and Great Britain (Spilka et al., 1985, pp. 183–191). Indeed, given the phenomenological reflections above, the failure to identify persons who are mystical would be at best a serious instance of empirical myopia. Granted that commonality of the report of mystical experience as has been well established empirically and is mandated by phenomenological reflection, the relevance of the description of such experiences now becomes crucial for our concern with the identity thesis.

Interpretation and Experience

Within the conceptual literature on mysticism a well established principle is that interpretation and experience are intimately related and yet must be made as distinct as possible. That is to say, what one experiences is at least partly independent of the language within which experience is described. We readily grant that experience cannot ultimately be totally divorced from interpretation since even to recognize an 'experience' is itself interpretative. Yet it remains clear that varying interpretations can be given to otherwise quite similar experiences. This point has been both conceptually (Almond, 1982; Katz, 1969; Stace, 1960, pp. 31–38) and empirically (Bourque, 1969;

Back & Bourque, 1974; Hood, 1985) investigated with specific reference to mysticism. This point allows what Almond (1982, pp. 71–72) refers to as 'autobiographical criteria' for the assessment of mystical experiences and is the procedure meticulously adhered to by Stace in his analysis of the 'common core' to otherwise widely varying mystical descriptions. This principle demands that one focus upon the minimal phenomenological or experienced aspects of any purported mystical experience independent of the language within which that experience is expressed. The paradox is that one must use some language to describe an experience and indeed, to even make oneself aware that one has had an experience. The truth of this apparently troublesome paradox will shortly prove to be the key to unlocking the unity thesis we wish to support. In order to show this we need to return to Stace's distinction between introvertive and extrovertive mysticisms noted previously. Of particular relevance is the relationship between interpretation and experience within introvertive mysticisms.

Introvertive Mysticism and the Unity Thesis

There is little question that what Stace terms introvertive mysticism is what phenomenological reflections on mysticism reveal mysticism proper to be. This is mysticism in its highest or most complete form. Using Almond's autobiographical criteria noted above, persons do report this experience in widely varying contexts and settings and when they do the identity of the experience can be identified despite the wide differences in interpretation. Here we need not review this well established empirical fact (see Hood, 1985; Spilka et al., 1985: Ch. 8). What we must do is explore the meaning of this identity.

Perhaps James' (1961, p. 321) put this claim most strongly when he argued:

> In Hinduism, in Neoplatonism, in Sufism, in Christian Mysticism, in Whitmanism, we find the same recurring note, so that there is about mystical utterances an eternal unanimity which ought to make a critic stop and think, and which brings it about that mystical classics have, as has been said, neither birthday nor native line. Perpetually telling of their unity of man with God, their speech antedates language, and they do not grow old.

If we note carefully James' claim, it is that one cannot discount the theologies or interpretive schemes within these traditions. These clearly are different and presumably at least partly rooted in mystical experience. Their differences of interpretation must be noted least we become what Zaehner (1961, p. 198) called 'indifferentists'. What we can make note of is that the core experience of unity referenced by these traditions as an undifferentiated state of awareness must logically be the same. As Stace (1961, p. 203) forcefully put the point:

> . . . if the undifferentiated unity is the pure unity of the individual self, then there is no *principium individuationis* on which can be based a distinction between one pure self and another. Therefore, we cannot stop at the individual ego, but are logically compelled to pass on to a Universal Self.

Here phenomenology, logic, and empiricism unite in referencing an experience of pure awareness, devoid of content, in which the identity of the one must be accepted.

The problem emerges in stating what this one is. Copleston (1982) has passionately argued that reflection upon diversity and unity, necessitates metaphysical reflections for which philosophy cannot provide adequate answers. Hence, the meaningfulness of such reflection largely rests upon religious interests, particularly where metaphysics converges with mysticism. In a similar vein, Smart warns us that those who are too facile in equating variously described mystical experiences make the error of assuming they know an Absolute truth denied to others. In his succinct critique of the well known parable of the blind men and the elephant, where one is tempted to claim that each person's description is true insofar as it describes adequately a part of the elephant, Smart (1968, p. 132) reminds us that this can hold only if the reader experiences the entire elephant.

> We can describe the blind men hanging on to different parts of the same elephant as doing so because we see the elephant. The parable depends on the notion that we have eyes whereas the hangers-on are blind. In short, if one is in an advantageous position regarding the truth, one can say with confidence that others have only a partial view of it.

Smart's criticism is decisive insofar as any description claiming to unify otherwise diverse descriptions itself claims a truth open to debate. And this debate, of course, is interminable. Herein lies Copleston's (1982) claim that the issues of a transcendental unity cannot be adequately metaphysically resolved and the very meaningfulness of the questions fades with the loss of religious interest.

Both Smart's and Copleston's views can be illuminated instructively by a consideration of an issue within the Jewish mysticism tradition. Katz in arguing against the identity thesis articulates the opposition within the Jewish traditions of identifying any experience of unity as being one with God. He is correct when he states (Katz, 1978, p. 34):

> . . . the Jewish conditioning pattern so strongly impresses traditional

mystics (as all Jews) with the fact that one does not have mystical experiences of God in which one loses one's identity in ecstatic moments of unity, that the Jewish mystic rarely, if ever, has such experiences. What the Jewish mystic experiences is, perhaps, the Divine Throne, or the angel Metatron, or aspect of the Sefiroth, or the heavenly court and palaces, or the Hidden Torah, or God's secret Names, but not loss of self in unity with God.

Katz is right. The Jewish traditions do not foster a unity of self and God in any interpretative sense. But this is not to say that Jews therefore cannot experience introvertive mysticism. That they can is verified by the great Jewish mystic Buber (1965, p. 24) who clearly recognizes within his own experience an introvertive mysticism:

> Now from my own unforgettable experience I know well that there is a state in which the bonds of the personal nature of life seem to have fallen away from us and we experience an undivided unity. But I do not know what the soul willingly imagines and indeed is bound to imagine (mine too once did it) — that in this I had attained a union with the primal being of godhead. That is an exaggeration no longer permitted to the responsible understanding.

Here Almond's autobiographical criteria works well. Buber experiences this egoless state and his treatment of it shifts based upon commitment to a particular interpretative tradition. As such, the tradition makes of this experience what it must and that becomes part of a personal experience shaped as much by tradition as by the limiting nature of the experience itself. Here no facile identity of Jewish mysticism and Christian mysticism is possible as we must work at what Schuon (1975) calls the exoteric plane of differentiation. This is the necessary differentiation produced by different interpretative schemes maintained by various traditions. Yet the limiting case of what Schuon calls the esoteric dimension, that which is only referenced by the exoteric but never exhausted, remains one, identical. This is the pure undifferentiated state of introvertive mysticism clearly referenced by Buber. Katz's critique becomes a support of the unity thesis as it simultaneously correctly identifies differences within great exoteric religious traditions with respect to their interpretations of introvertive mysticism that nevertheless can be realized as identical in an esoteric sense. It is the paradox of the unity thesis that the sense in which this identity occurs can never be stated despite the fact of its recognition. In this sense there is a metaphysical or ultimately descriptive solution to the identity thesis, to the unity of the one and the many.

On the other hand, the refusal to accept any metaphysical or descriptive solution to the identity of mystical states is paradoxically the solution to the unity thesis we wish to support. For it is within traditions and linguistic communities that reference to such transcendent unity is maintained and the community protects only the reference. To do so it necessarily uses discursive language which at the proximate level is divisive and necessarily so. Each community or tradition is necessarily exoteric. Their language and descriptive metaphors forever define them apart from other traditions. Hindu, Christian, Jewish, or secular mysticisms are necessarily what they are described to be in their particularity and uniqueness. These create differences both in meaning and experience of mysticism insofar as it is interpreted and influenced by such traditions (Katz, 1983). Yet all references to an undifferentiated awareness necessarily must in their esoteric sense be identical. This point is logically required as noted by Stace's insistence that that which lacks a principle of differentiation must be identical with itself. This point is also phenomenologically illuminated as both necessary and essential by Earle's reflection on the transcendental ego. This point is reflected in empirical studies of mysticism in which basic experiential aspects of mysticism can be identified despite wide variations in description (Hood, 1985). It means, that what is identical in mysticism is a unity forever referenced in its diversity. Yet paradoxically, no statement of that unity, however coy, will be other than a metaphysical blunder. However, this does not mean that we need despair at efforts to study mysticism within contexts that identify their unity by their differences. We can note this by a consideration of Stace's extrovertive mysticism, in a way that adds a curious twist to Stace's own treatment of this mysticism.

Extrovertive Mysticism and the Unity Thesis

Stace's discussion of extrovertive mysticism is problematic. Even Stace (1961, 131) notes that it may be preparatory to or a less developed form of introvertive mystical experience. Both mysticisms make reference to a unity but with extrovertive experiences the unity is visionary — a 'seeing' of all things as one. In introvertive mysticism nothing is seen as the experience itself is contentless. The one is not seen. The self becomes identical with this one. In extrovertive mysticism, however, a unity is perceived. The many is seen as one, but the many maintains its distinct separate identities. There is little doubt that such experiences occur. Almost all writers on mysticism identify these experiences and note their troublesome difference from the unity devoid of content that is identified by Stace as introvertive. Furthermore, the fact that such experiences are actual perceptions suggest their relationship to parapsychological claims. Surely this 'sensing' beyond the normal, this perception of unity within a differentiated visual field is indeed a paranormal experience indicating a linkage between mysticism and the paranormal. What seems crucial here is whether or not extrovertive states precede introvertive states or follow from them. There is no firm empirical evidence on this issue but the problem is crucial. It suggests not only that some mystical experiences (extrovertive) are paranormal, but also, that other mystical experiences (introvertive) may facilitate paranormal powers. What we offer here is suggestive only but surely relevant to the unity thesis. For it is obvious that in extrovertive mysticism we have the experiential counterpart to the unity thesis, even if in a more restricted sense. Extrovertive mystics see the many as one; see the unity in diversity; actually experience in this restricted sense what the unity thesis proposes.

If what we have suggested with respect to the paranormal nature of extrovertive mysticism is correct, it may be that the distinction between Stace and Almond regarding the ordering of extrovertive mystical experiences can be resolved in a way that modifies both researchers. Stace (1971, p. 132) suggests that extrovertive mysticism may be a lower or less developed introvertive mysticism — hence suggesting one moves from extrovertive to higher introvertive states. Almond (1982, pp. 71–72) using his autobiographical criterion suggests that often extrovertive mystical descriptions are not actual experiences, but merely descriptions of the world following introvertive mystical states. In other words, after reaching a pure unitary consciousness, introvertive mystics describe the world as one without actually having that (e.g. extrovertive) experience. Clearly Almond is partly right in that many descriptions of extrovertive mystical experiences read like philosophical conclusions divorced from any actual extrovertive experience. An example might be the statement of Meister Eckhart quoted both by Otto (1932, p. 61) and Stace (1960, p. 63) as indicative of extrovertive mysticism: 'All that a man has here externally in multiplicity is intrinsically One. Here all blades of grass, wood, and stone, all things are One. This is the deepest depth.' Another example might be Chuang Tsu's (1974, p. 12) claim: 'That holy man with all his virtues looks on all the confusion of ten thousand things as one.' But here, using Almond's autobiographical criteria we have an inkling of a claim rooted in experience, a 'seeing'. Perhaps most forcefully, the actual experience of extrovertive mysticism is articulated by Zaehner (1957, p. 28) who correctly notes that extrovertive mysticism is often identified with the theological doctrine of pantheism but notes: 'It would be far more accurate to describe this experience as "pan-en-hen-ism", "all-in-one-ism", for that is what in fact experience tells us.' And there is doubt that the validity of this mode of perception, perhaps paranormal, is precisely that of any claim to sense perception. As James (1958, p. 324) put the issue:

> Our own more 'rational' beliefs are based on evidence exactly similar in
> nature to that which mystics quote for theirs. Our senses, namely, have
> assured us of certain states of fact; but mystic experience are as direct
> perceptions of fact for those who have them as any sensations ever were
> for us (emphasis added).

Here Almond's autobiographical criterion applies. James' reference is not to a belief of unity in multiplicity but rather to a direct
experience interpretable as fact. That some persons actually experience
this unity in multiplicity, often spontaneously, and without preparation can no longer be questioned. Others seem to achieve this power
to perceived unity in multiplicity following introvertive mystical
experiences. We suggest that following introvertive experiences,
mystics realize paranormal powers to perceive the world of multiplicity
as one and actually do so. Certainly the vast conceptual literature on
mysticism is replete with reports of paranormal powers among the
mystics. If we are correct, this is an empirically testable hypothesis in
the manner we have stated it. Of course, extrovertive and introvertive
mystical experiences can be related in other ways, and even be
independent. However, the spontaneity of many reported extrovertive mystical experiences as opposed to the careful and often hard
won cultivation of many introvertive mystical experiences suggest that
introvertive experiences are nourished best with metaphysical or
religious traditions that cultivate this 'inward way'. Extrovertive
experiences may be paranormal powers awakened in persons for a
variety of reasons and in a variety of contexts and whose objectivity is
provided by their being clearly perceptual in nature and referring to
objects united as one within the perceptual field.

Summary

We now can summarize the unity thesis in two senses, each of which
overlaps the other. Both paradoxically allow a unity in diversity. In
introvertive mysticism the diversity of this unity is necessarily entailed
by efforts to describe, recognize, and transmit the fact of such
experiences, which when realized are nevertheless paradoxically
identical. As Bucke (1961, p. 59) concludes, '. . . there is not instance of
a person who has been illumined denying or disputing the teaching of
another who has passed through the same experience.' Yet to describe
this illumination, to point to it, to make any reference to it at all
differentiates and creates the traditions within which such experiences
have meanings. In extrovertive mysticism as a possible paranormal
mode of awareness, an actual experience of the one and the many

occurs, most likely following introvertive awareness. As such the unity thesis suggests an often ignored linkage between the paranormal and the mystical (Bucke, 1961, p. 309) which surely is the outcome of what Cerullo (1982) has documented as the secularization of the soul within the parapsychological tradition. Perhaps the time for re-enchantment has come — for the union once again of the paranormal and the sacred.

Footnotes

1. For the purposes of this article Stace's additional criteria common to both introvertive and extrovertive mysticism are ignored as are his additional unique criteria for each of these mysticisms.
2. Obviously, Sartre (1957) would not permit a transcendental ego as does Husserl. However, this debate need not concern us here. In any case, even Sartre's (1956) en-soi-pour-soi could it exist would follow the analysis of the unity thesis presented in this chapter. For our purposes it is sufficient to note that Sartre accepts Husserl's intentionality of consciousness.

References

Almond, P.C. (1982), *Mystical Experience and Religious Doctrine*. New York: Mouton.

Back, K.W. & Bourque, L.B. (1970), 'Can feelings be enumerated?'. *Behavioural Science*, 15, 487–496.

Bourque, L.B. (1969), 'Social correlates of transcendental experiences', *Sociological Analysis*, 30, 151–163.

Bourque, L.B. & Back, K.W. (1974), 'Language, society, and subjective experience,' *Sociometry*, 34, 1–21.

Buber, M. (1965), *Between Man and Man*, New York: Macmillan.

Bucke, R.M. (1961; originally published, 1901), *Cosmis Consciousness, Secaucus*, New Jersey, University Books.

Cerullo, J.J. (1982), *The Secularization of the Soul*, Philadelphia, Pennsylvania: Institute for the Study of Human Issues.

Chuang Tsu, (1974), *Inner Chapters, Gia-Fu Feng & Jane English*, trans., New York: Vintage Books.

Copleston, F. (1982), *Religion and the One*, New York: Crossroad.

Deikman, A.J. (1982), *The Observing Self*, Boston: Beacon Press.

Earle, W. (1980), *Mystical Reason*, Chicago, Illinois: Regenery Gateway.

Hood, R.W., Jr. (1975), 'The construction and preliminary validation of a measure of reported mystical experience', *Journal for the Scientific Study of Religion*, 14, 29–41.

Hood, R.W., Jr. (1985), 'Mysticism' in P.E. Hammond, ed., *The Sacred in a Secular Age*, Berkeley, California: University of California Press.

James, W. (1961, first published 1902), *Varieties of Religious Experience*, New York: Mentor.

Katz, S.T. (1978), *Mysticism and Philosophical Analysis*, New York: Oxford University Press.

Otto, R. (1932), *Mysticism East and West*, New York: Macmillan.

Robinson, D.N. (1981), *An Intellectual History of Psychology, Rev. ed.*, New York: Macmillan.

Russell, B. (1921), *Mysticism and Logic and Other Essays*, London: Longmans, Green & Co.

Sartre, J.P. (1956), *Being and Nothingness*, H. Barnes, trans., New York: Philosophical Library.

Sartre, J.P. (1957), *The Transcendence of the Ego*, F. Williams & R. Kirkpatrick, trans., New York: Farrar, Straus, and Giroux.

Scharfstein, Ben-Ami (1973), *Mystical Experience*, Indianapolis, Indiana: Bobbs-Merrill.

Schuon, F. (1975, first published 1948), *The Transcendent Unity of Religions*, New York: Harper and Row.

Smart, N. (1968), *The Yogi and the Devotee*, London: Allen and Unwin.

Spilka, B., Hood, R.W. Jr., & Gorsuch, R. (1985), *The Psychology of Religion*, Englewood Cliffs, New Jersey: Prentice-Hall.

Stace, W.T. (1961), *Mysticism and Philosophy*, London: Macmillan.

Stahl, F. (1975), *Exploring Mysticism*, Berkeley, California: University of California Press.

Wittgenstein, L. (1958), *Philosophical Investigations, 2nd ed.*, G.E.M. Anscombe, trans., New York: Macmillan, 1958.

Zaehner, R.C. (1961), *Mysticism: Sacred and Profane*, New York: Oxford University Press.

CHAPTER 9
BUDDHIST JHĀNA AS MYSTICAL EXPERIENCE

Roderick S. Bucknell

Systematic study of the writings of mystics from a variety of traditions and historical periods has yielded an important, and to some extent controversial, generalization: mystical experience of the kind often called 'introvertive' is, in essence, a state of consciousness devoid of content, a 'contentless experience'.

This generalization has been discussed at length and argued for fairly convincingly by, among others, W.T. Stace (1960), J.R. Horne (1978), and P.C. Almond (1982). It has also had its critics, however. The idea that what the mystics attain might be essentially 'contentless experience' — a state of consciousness totally devoid of sensory input, memory, discursive thought, feeling, emotion, etc. — was early rejected outright by Rufus Jones (1909, p. xxxiv); and in recent times the notion has been severely criticised by S.T. Katz (1985, pp. 77–78). Thus, what some scholars confidently identify as the very core of introvertive mystical experience is dismissed by others as an impossibility.

The case for 'contentless experience', is most adequately presented by P.C. Almond in his book *Mystical Experience and Religious Doctrine* (1982). Building on the earlier work of Stace (1960), Smart (1965), and others, Almond develops the notion of contentless experience into a four-part hypothesis concerning the nature of introvertive mystical experience (Almond 1982, p. 174). He then goes on to suggest that this hypothesis might provide orientation for future research, proposing that it be systematically tested, against available data, by researchers specialized in the different religious traditions (p. 175).

Almond's proposal for a series of tradition-specific examinations of his hypothesis appears not to have been put into effect as yet. The present paper is therefore intended as a first contribution in this direction. The area of specialization in question is Buddhist *jhāna*, the system of graded meditative practice whereby the Buddhist prac-titioner cultivates mental calm and stability, as a foundation for the subsequent development of liberating insight. *Jhāna*, a particularly well documented example of a mystical discipline, will be examined in order to test Almond's hypothesis, and perhaps, in the process, throw further light on the nature of mystical experience in general.

The discussion begins with a brief résumé of Almond's hypothesis and its ramifications, and then turns to the subject of *jhāna*. The doctrinal foundations of *jhāna* are reviewed, with particular attention to the Sutta Pitaka account of the sequence of *jhānas* and their composition. Then a phenomenological account is given of the entire course of *jhāna* practice, from the point of view of the practising meditator. Next, doctrine and practice are brought together in a brief discussion of the apparent correspondences between the meditative stages of the phenomenological description and the *jhānas* of the textual description. This account of *jhāna* is then considered alongside Almond's hypothesis concerning introvertive mystical experience, with particular attention to its implications for the notion of 'contentless experience'. It is concluded that the evidence from *jhāna* generally supports the hypothesis, while also indicating a need to refine some aspects of it. Finally, attention is drawn to some further possible implications of *jhāna* for mysticism studies.

Almond's Hypothesis

Introvertive mystical experience, the type that Almond is particularly concerned to elucidate, is one of two broad types recognized in Stace's perhaps over-simple typology (Stace 1960, 60–62). Also sometimes called 'mysticism of introspection' or 'the inward way', it stands contrasted with extrovertive mysticism, 'the outward way'. As Stace puts it, 'the extrovertive experience looks outward through the senses, while the introvertive looks inward into the mind' (1960, p. 61). In the extrovertive experience the mystic, often without conscious effort, gains a totally new and transforming realization of the nature of the world and of his place in it; in the introvertive experience the mystic, usually in the course of pursuing a long and rigorous religious discipline, probes the dark, silent depths of his own inner self and thereby attains to a far more profoundly transforming realization.

Introvertive mystical experience is well exemplified in the following extracts from the writings of two great Christian mystics, the first from Jan van Ruysbroeck (1916, pp. 185–186), the second from Meister Eckhart (Blakney 1941, p. 201).

> The God-seeing man . . . can always enter, naked and unencumbered with images, into the inmost part of his spirit. There he finds revealed an Eternal Light . . . It [his spirit] is undifferentiated and without distinction, and therefore it feels nothing but the unity

> In this barren Godhead activity has ceased and therefore the soul will be most perfect when it is thrown into the desert of the Godhead, where both activity and forms are no more, so that it is sunk and lost in this desert where its identity is destroyed.

Such expressions as 'naked', 'unencumbered with images', 'un-differentiated', 'nothing but the unity', 'barren', 'desert', 'activity has ceased', 'forms are no more', 'identity is destroyed' combine to convey the idea of mental emptiness. It is, above all, the repeated occurrence of expressions of this kind that has led Stace and others to identify such statements by mystics as attempts to describe 'contentless experience' or 'pure consciousness' (Stace 1960, p. 110). References to doctrinal concepts, such as 'God' and 'Godhead', are attributed to retrospective interpretation: after the event each mystic interprets and describes his experience in terms of the familiar categories of his inherited religious tradition. Hence, according to Stace and others, the reports of introvertive mystics consistently point to a state of consciousness 'from which all the multiplicity of sensuous or conceptual or other empirical content has been excluded, so that there remains only a void and empty unity' (Stace 1960, p. 110).

Almond endorses this generalization. He therefore adopts, as the first component of his hypothesis, the proposition that at least some mystical experience consists in attainment of 'the contentless state' (1982, p. 175). By virtue of its very contentlessness, such an experience would be identical for all who attain it. This would account for the remarkable unanimity among mystics from diverse religious back-grounds, in their descriptions of the introvertive experience: it is the *same* experience for all mystics, in all cultures and in all ages.

At the same time, many accounts of introvertive experience indicate a state that is not truly contentless. The mystic often appears to have achieved only a partial emptying of consciousness. Almond covers this situation by postulating, as the second component of his four-part hypothesis, that the 'pure' or totally contentless state is the upper limit or 'limiting case' in an ascending scale of progressively less content-filled states (p. 175).

This leads naturally to two further related propositions, yielding, in effect, the following as the full statement of the hypothesis:

1. At least some mystical experience consists in attainment of the contentless state.
2. This state is the upper limit in an ascending scale of mystical experience, a scale of progressively less content-filled states.
3. Progress through this ascending scale of states, and attainment of the highest, totally contentless state, is the purpose of the contemplative path taught in some traditions.
4. Attainment of the contentless state occurs most commonly in the context of a set of doctrines appropriate to such attainment (Almond 1982, p. 175).

While Almond's hypothesis has considerable explanatory power, it is also vulnerable to certain criticisms. Most serious is Katz's criticism, mentioned earlier, of the central notion of 'contentless experience' (Katz 1985, pp. 77–78). Katz considers that a truly contentless psychological state would be indistinguishable from dreamless sleep, and would therefore be something very different from introvertive mystical experience. The mystical experience, being a conscious state, must have some content — from which it follows also that, contrary to what Almond supposes, every mystical experience must be to some degree conditioned by context, in particular by the mystic's traditional religious background. In other words, far from there being one universally identical peak mystical experience (Almond's 'limiting case'), there are as many different mystical experiences as there are mystics (Almond 1982, p. 128).

The notion of a contentless state of consciousness certainly raises a host of philosophical problems. Common sense suggests that if there is experience, i.e. if there is consciousness, then it must be experience *of something*, consciousness *of something*. Consciousness must, it seems, have an object; it makes no sense to speak of 'consciousness that is conscious of nothing but itself'; the notion of 'pure consciousness', or 'contentless experience' is self-contradictory. The keystone of Almond's hypothesis is, therefore, its most vulnerable point. In Almond's defence, however, it may be noted that the difficulty of imagining a contentless experience, or of resolving the seeming self-contradictoriness of the notion, is totally in keeping with mystics' consistent claims that their experiences are ineffable and have a quality of paradoxicality. Again, reasoned philosophical argumentation about contentless experience is itself of questionable validity, given that, *ex hypothesi*, such experience entails a major psychological paradigm shift.

As Almond points out, the proper way to evaluate his hypothesis is to test it against relevant data provided by the various religious traditions. It is therefore with this end in view that we now turn to an examination of Buddhist *jhāna*.

As a test case for any hypothesis concerning the nature of mystical experience, Buddhist *jhāna* is a most appropriate choice. Buddhism accords an important place to mystical practice and experience, so has an abundant literature on the subject, and a vigorous living tradition of practice. The textual accounts of *jhāna* describe a definite series of stages, emphasizing progressive elimination of mental factors, and therefore promise to be of use in evaluating or adumbrating the notion of contentless experience. Practitioners of *jhāna*, though usually reluctant to discuss their attainments, can be called upon to provide first-hand information on the experimental side of their practice. It is even possible for the more serious investigator to find supposedly competent teachers of *jhāna*, willing to guide him or her through the entire process. The choice of Buddhist *jhāna* for the present purpose is, therefore, well motivated. We consider first the doctrinal foundations of *jhāna*, the theory behind the practice. (See, e.g., Gunaratana 1980: Vajiranana 1962; Narasabho 1971; Griffiths 1983)

Doctrinal Foundations of Jhāna

As a Buddhist technical term, the Pali word *jhāna* (Sanskrit *dhyāna*, broadly equivalent to *samādhi* and *samatha*), denotes, according to context, either a certain class of meditative practices or the individual mental states attained during such practice. Satisfactory English equivalents are 'concentration' and 'stage of concentration' respectively.

The place of *jhāna* in the overall Buddhist soteriology is made clear in the familiar three-stage summary of the total path of practice: 'moral discipline — concentration — insight' (*sīla— samādhi — paññā*). The Buddhist aspirant who has become well established in the moral discipline (*sīla*), takes up the practice of concentration or *jhāna* (*samādhi*), as a preparation for the subsequent development of insight (*paññā*). *Jhāna*, then, is not an end in itself. What will bring the ultimate liberation is not *jhāna*, but the subsequent perfection of insight. Thus, Buddhist meditation is of two types: (1) meditation for calm (*samatha*, *samādhi, jhāna* — a practice common to all Indian religious traditions); and (2) meditation for insight (*vipassanā*, *paññā* — an exclusively Buddhist practice). Unfortunately, the distinction between these two levels of practice is frequently overlooked by scholars discussing Buddhist meditation in the context of mysticism. As R.M. Gimello reminds us (1978, p. 188), it is only *jhāna* (meditation for calm) that is in question in any comparison with other mystical traditions.

The textual accounts of *jhāna* present a superficial appearance of consistency and simplicity. The same stereotyped description seems to turn up again and again, not only throughout the Pali canon, but also in the corresponding sections of the Chinese canon. However, in reality the situation is not so simple. Closer examination reveals, within the Pali canon, not just one account of *jhāna*, but two significantly different accounts, which may be termed, after the collections in which they typically occur, the Sutta version and the Abhidhamma version. The seemingly slight differences between these two versions have in fact had far-reaching hermeneutical consequences. Since this is not the place for lengthy discussion of textual questions, it must suffice here to state baldly the one essential conclusion that emerges from careful analysis of these two versions of the *jhāna* doctrine: The Abhidhamma version (known to be the more recent of the two) can be shown, on the basis of certain internal contradictions and other features, to be very probably a product of scholastic meddling with the earlier Sutta version (cf. Bucknell & Stuart-Fox 1986, pp. 176–177, 226 n. 50). It is therefore on the Sutta version that the present discussion is based.

The standard Sutta account of the *jhānas* is often preceded by a brief, and indeed quite inadequate, description of the necessary practical preparations. It tells how the monk, wishing to practise meditation, goes to some quiet place such as the foot of a tree in the forest, adopts a cross-legged sitting position, and 'establishes mindfulness in front of him.' Just how the meditator 'establishes mindfulness' is not spelled out in the *suttas*; however, later commentaries describe the process in some detail as a resolute focusing of attention on some chosen sense object, most commonly the breathing (more fully described below). Through practising this focusing of attention, the monk in time attains the first *jhāna* — and it is here that the *jhāna* account proper begins.

The attainment of the first *jhāna* is described as follows (Trenckner 1964, p. 40, my translation; Horner 1967, p. 51).

> Separated, indeed, from sensuality, separated from unwholesome mental states, he attains and abides in the first *jhāna*, in which there are discursive thought (*vitakka-vicāra*), zest (*pīti*), and pleasure (*sukha*), and which is born of separation.

Here we encounter for the first time the serious problem of how to translate the Pali technical terms — serious because more is at stake than mere linguistic accuracy. The translations adopted here are necessarily to some extent provisional. For example, it may well be that 'zest' is not quite what is meant by the Pali term *pīti* in the context of *jhāna*. However, because many translators do render *pīti* as 'zest', and because this rendering is unlikely to be very wide of the mark, it will be provisionally adopted here.

The transition from the first *jhāna* to the second comes about, according to the textual description, through the 'suppression of discursive thought' and the establishing of 'inner tranquillity and oneness of mind'; and this fact is reiterated in the epithet 'born of concentration', applied to the second *jhāna*. Similarly the third *jhāna*, and then the fourth, is attained by loss of some component factor of the preceding *jhāna* and the establishing of the appropriate counter-vailing factor. The description reads as follows (Trenckner 1964, p. 41; Horner 1967, p. 52).

Through the suppression of discursive thought, he attains and abides in the second *jhāna*, in which there is inner tranquillity and oneness of mind, in which discursive thought is absent, and zest and pleasure are present, and which is born of concentration.

Through the fading away of zest, he abides in equanimity, mindful and discerning; and experiencing pleasure with the body, he attains and abides in the third *jhāna*, which the 'Noble Ones' refer to as 'abiding in equanimity, mindfulness, and pleasure.'

Through the relinquishing of pleasure and pain, through the previous disappearance of happiness and sorrow, he attains and abides in the fourth *jhāna*, in which pleasure and pain are absent, and equanimity, mindfulness, and purity are present.

The texts often, but not always, go on to describe a further four stages, not specifically referred to as *jhānas* (Trenckner 1964, p. 41; Horner 1967, p. 53).

Through the complete transcending of physical sensation, through the disappearance of contact-sensation, through non-attention to variety-sensation, aware that space (*ākāsa*) is endless, he attains and abides in the realm of the infinity of space (*ākāsānañcāyatana*).

Through the complete transcending of the realm of the infinity of space, aware that consciousness (*viññāna*) is endless, he attains and abides in the realm of the infinity of consciousness (*viññānānañcāyatana*).

Through the complete transcending of the realm of the infinity of consciousness, aware that there is nothing, he attains and abides in the realm of nothingness (*ākiñkaññāyatana*).

Through the complete transcending of the realm of nothingness, he attains and abides in the realm of neither perception nor non-perception (*n'eva saññā n'āsaññāyatana*).

Attainment of the realm of neither perception nor non-perception marks the end of the series.

Of the eight stages, the first four are referred to as the first to fourth *jhānas*, while the last four are treated as subdivisions of the fourth *jhāna*. However, following a terminology adopted in the later Abhidhamma texts, practitioners and scholars often refer to the first four as the *rūpa-jhānas* (the physical *jhānas*), and to the last four as the *arūpa-jhānas* (the non-physical *jhānas*). This terminology, based on the two different types of concentration object used (physical and non-physical), is convenient and will therefore be adopted here.

Analysis of the statements made, in the above account, about the composition of the several *jhānas*, and directly about the pre-*jhāna* state (the normal consciousness existing before the practice begins), yields the following tabular representation of the entire series.

Stage	Component Factors/Object		
normal state:	discursive thought	sensuality	pleasure/pain
rūpa-jhāna 1:	discursive thought	zest	pleasure
rūpa-jhāna 2:	one-pointedness	zest	pleasure
rūpa-jhāna 3:	one-pointedness	equanimity	pleasure
rūpa-jhāna 4:	one-pointedness	equanimity	purity
arūpa-jhāna 1:	infinity of space		
arūpa-jhāna 2:	infinity of consciousness		
arūpa-jhāna 3:	nothingness		
arūpa-jhāna 4:	neither perception nor non-perception		

The arrangement of this table is based on recognition of certain terminology synonymies and antonymies. Most importantly, 'one-pointedness' signifies absence of discursive thought, 'equanimity' absence of zest, and 'purity' absence of pleasure. Thus, as the table shows, progress from the normal pre-*jhāna* state through to *rūpa-jhāna* 4 consists in successive elimination of component factors, while progress thereafter consists in successive transformations of the object of the one-pointed attention.

In practice, the eight stages of *jhāna* are attained, one by one, over a long period, and only through great effort and persistence. However, once any particular *jhāna* has been mastered, it can thereafter be attained relatively rapidly when required. The texts occasionally refer to monks proficient in *jhāna* as passing rapidly through the series in either direction.

It will be evident from the above that the Sutta account of *jhāna* is quite inadequate as a guide for anyone actually wishing to put it all into practice. This inadequacy is made good by the wealth of detailed instructions available from two other sources. The first such source is the various meditation manuals (the most authoritative of which is the fifth-century *Path of Purity*, Tin 1971); the second, and perhaps more important, source is the living oral tradition, i.e. the teachings of practising meditation masters. It is to such sources, and of course also to the fruits of personal experimentation, that one must turn for information on *jhāna* as a living mode of spiritual practice.

Jhāna in Practice

The following account describes in particular the technique of 'mindfulness of breathing' (*ānāpāna-sati*), this being the best authenticated and most commonly used technique for the practice of concentration or *jhāna*. However, as will be pointed out, the description is, with only minor modifications, equally valid for other less widely used techniques (See Nanamoli 1973; Buddhadasa 1980; Narasabho 1971; Vajirnana 1962).

The practices described are typically applied in regular daily sessions, each lasting from half an hour to several hours, depending on the meditator's circumstances and inclinations. The meditator is usually advised by his teacher to begin by finding a quiet spot in which to practise. He is usually also advised to adopt a moderately austere mode of living for the duration of his meditation course, entailing sexual abstinence, simple diet, and the forgoing of all forms of amusement or distraction, including even textual studies. The meditator may be required to perform the traditional ritual of paying homage to Buddha, Dhamma, and Sangha; at the least, he will be advised to reflect on the value and purpose of the practice he is about to undertake, and thereby to place himself in an appropriate frame of mind.

Having completed these preparations, the meditator begins to practise mindfulness of breathing (or some similar exercise) in strict accordance with his teacher's instructions. He seats himself cross-legged on a cushion, holds his back erect but not stiff, closes his eyes, and begins concentrating on his breathing.

This involves focusing attention on the fine tactile sensation experienced at the rim of the right nostril as the breath passes in and out. That sensation is the concentration object; at each sitting attention must be focused on it and restrained from wandering. Invariably, however, attention does wander. After only a few breaths the meditator realizes, to his dismay, that instead of concentrating on the sensation at his nostril rim, he is involved in a train of thought having no apparent connection with the practice. He immediately returns attention to the concentration object and begins again, but before long the same thing happens. Repeatedly, despite all efforts to keep the mind fixed on the concentration object, thoughts arise; and the trains of mental imagery and/or verbalizing sometimes continue for a minute or more before the meditator realizes the digression and is able to cut them short. Only after long and persistent effort — over weeks or months, depending on individual temperament and the intensity of the practice — does success come. Finally, however, the dedicated meditator does succeed in keeping attention fixed on the concentration object for up to a minute without any thought arising.

With further practice the periods of full concentration and freedom from thought grow longer and more intense. The meditator becomes able to sit fully concentrated for many minutes together. With thought totally absent, there is no sense of boredom; the practice, which had formerly seemed dull and tiresome in the extreme, now seems irresistibly interesting. During this phase of the practice the meditator often finds his body making strange involuntary movements, such as a pronounced trembling, repeated jerking, or creeping goose-flesh. The meditation master reassures his student that reactions of this kind are common. They are by-products of the high-level of mental energy being developed, and have no importance other than as signs that progress is being made. The meditator must merely note their existence and resume his concentration practice.

Following this advice, the meditator finds that the odd movements eventually cease, and his facility in concentration improves accordingly. But before long a new effect appears, in the form of various delightful bodily feelings: a feeling of lightness as if the body were floating some distance above the seat, or a pervading warmth radiating like an aura from the body. The meditator may find that he can readily bring about an intensification of these feelings; however, the master warns against this. The pleasant feelings are once again unimportant by-products of the practice; the meditator must merely acknowledge their existence and return to the concentration object.

With further practice the delightful feelings subside in their turn, leaving nothing in consciousness but the concentration object. Formerly faint and barely discernible, the sensation at the nostril rim is now experienced vividly as a zone of intense tactile sensation. There is nothing else in consciousness. As far as the meditator is concerned the rest of his body is non-existent.

Further prolonged concentration eventually results in a strange transformation of the object. The zone of intense tactile sensation is replaced by a glowing area of light of similar shape and orientation, experienced inwardly as a vivid mental image. (The eyes remain closed throughout these experiences.) For example, if the zone of sensation at the nostril was experienced as crescent-shaped, the glowing area of light that takes its place is similarly crescent-shaped. This symbolic image (nimitta) is of variable colour, indeed the meditator finds that with practice he can to some extent determine its colour and brightness at will. Its size seems indeterminate, there being no other content of consciousness with which it might be compared. Having once developed a symbolic image, the meditator is instructed by his master to adopt it as his new concentration object. At each sitting he must begin by concentrating on the breath as usual, but as soon as the symbolic image appears, he must concentrate on that instead. This has the effect of causing the symbolic image to arise more rapidly each time, and, once arisen, to become progressively more vivid and stable.

The meditator continues practising in this way, until one day, without warning, his symbolic image suddenly disappears. Thus deprived of the only content of consciousness the meditator has the sense of having been suddenly cast into an infinite black vacuum — a strange and sometimes disturbing experience. He may, as a result, lose his composure, in which case he experiences an abrupt return to normal consciousness. However, the master gives reassurance, and advises his student to cultivate this state of mental emptiness, entering it whenever he can. In addition, he tells him to prolong its duration, by making a resolution to that effect at the start of each meditation session. Following these instructions, the meditator finds that the state of emptiness stabilizes and, as promised, lasts progressively longer.

In this state of emptiness, as at all previous stages of the practice, the meditator always remains aware of his condition; he retains a detached awareness of the condition of zero mental content. However, there eventually comes a time when even this residual consciousness abruptly ceases. The effect is as if the meditator had suddenly gone under total anaesthetic, or fallen into deep dreamless sleep. It cannot be said of this state that the meditator *experiences* it; what he does is *infer* it after the event. Just as one may infer, on waking, that one has been sound asleep for such and such a period of time, so the meditator infers, on returning to normal consciousness, and referring to a clock or some other reliable indicator of the passage of time, that he has been sitting in a state of total unconsciousness, and for how long. Without the aid of such external indicators of time, he would be convinced that the state had lasted only an instant; there is not even any after-effect in the form of physical fatigue, stiffness, or hunger, that might provide a clue.

With practice, the meditator may become able to sit in the state of unconsciousness for hours together. Many meditators insist that it is possible to determine in advance how long the state shall last, by making an appropriate resolution at the outset. Some masters consider that the aim should be to prolong the state to twenty-four hours, and a tradition exists that true adepts can remain in it for as long as seven days.

The meditator who has become proficient in attaining and maintaining this state of unconsciousness is likely to be told that he has 'completed the course'. This is not to say that he has reached the end of the Buddhist path of practice, but rather that he has gone as far as a master of *jhāna* can take him.

Discusssion with practising meditators and meditation masters confirms that the sequence of stages just described is typical and indeed largely predictable. Competent meditation masters are familiar with the sequence, and are thus able to reassure their students as each stage is attained, and guide them beyond it to the next.

However, there do exist two significant variations on the course of practice as described. The first has to do with the nature of the symbolic image. Though this is most commonly a visual image in various shapes and colours, it may be experienced as an auditory image 'heard' with the 'inner ear', and mental counterparts of the other sense modalities may also occur.

The second variation has to do with differences in the concentration object adopted at the outset. Some meditators prefer to concentrate on a visual object, such as a coloured disc, a Buddha icon, or a candle flame; or on an auditory object, such as the sound of dripping water or a *mantra* quietly chanted by the meditator himself. In the case of visual objects the practice has to be slightly modified, the meditator beginning with his eyes open rather than closed. The initial practice consists in gazing at the chosen object — for example, a clay disc — until unwavering concentration has been achieved. Next the meditator must imprint the form of the disc so thoroughly on his mind that he can, on closing his eyes, visualize it clearly in all its details. Then, having formed a clear mental image of the disc, the meditator concentrates on that until it is replaced by a symbolic image in the manner described above. Where the initial concentration object is a sound, such as that produced by dripping water, the situation is like concentration on breathing, though the symbolic image formed is likely to exhibit some kind of rhythmic movement (for example a regular oscillation in time with the sound). The case of a chanted *mantra* differs, however, because the meditator gives up chanting as soon as he can 'hear' the *mantra* inwardly, and concentrates on that auditory image instead. This auditory image subsequently gives way to a symbolic image as in the other practices.

Correlation Between Doctrine and Practice

When the sequence of meditative stages described above is compared with the sequence of *jhānas* of the Sutta account, a close overall correspondence becomes apparent. A thorough comparison would naturally necessitate detailed analysis and interpretation of the Pali terminology; but even a superficial comparison suffices to indicate that the correspondences are as follows (cf. Bucknell & Stuart-Fox 1986, pp. 177-178; Griffiths 1983, pp. 60-62).

* *Rūpa-jhāna* 1 (discursive thought, zest, pleasure:
Initial attempts to stop the flow of thought and keep attention focused on the breathing or other object are largely unsuccessful; however, these attempts do have the effect of eliminating emotional involvement in the contents of consciousness, by replacing it with concentrative energy (i.e. 'zest').

* *Rūpa-jhāna* 2 (one-pointedness, zest, pleasure):
Eventually the flow of thought comes to a stop, at first only briefly,
later for minutes together. This one-pointed condition is progressively
prolonged through increasing concentrative energy, which, however,
is likely to 'overflow; into involuntary bodily movements, such as
trembling, jerking, or gooseflesh.
* *Rūpa-jhāna* 3 (one-pointedness, equanimity, pleasure):
Through being merely noted, these bodily movements cease;
however, the meditator now becomes increasingly aware of delight-
fully pleasant feelings of lightness, warmth, etc.
* *Rūpa-jhāna* 4 (one-pointedness, equanimity, purity):
These feelings cease in their turn, leaving nothing in consciousness but
the physical sensation that is the concentration object.
* *Arūpa-jhāna* 1 (infinite space (*ākāsa*); cessation of physical sensation.
This is recognizable as a distinct stage only in the case of a visual object
or a chanted *mantra*.):
A perfect mental image of the original concentration object is formed
and retained; e.g. a mental image of the clay disc is 'seen' inwardly
after the eyes are closed. Thus physical sensation gives way to an
uninterrupted non-physical experience. (The term *ākāsa*, usually
translated 'space', denotes in other contexts the intangible medium in
which the four physical 'elements', earth, water, fire, and air, are said
to be contained. It is therefore possible that 'infinite space' signifies
here absence of earth, water, fire, and air, and thus refers to the
cessation of physical sensation that marks attainment of this *jhāna*.)
* *Arūpa-jhāna* 2 (infinite consciousness (*viññāṇa*)):
The perfect mental image of the concentration object (or, if arūpa-jhāna 1 is
lacking, the concentration object itself) is replaced by a stylized mental
counterpart of it, the symbolic image.
* *Arūpa-jhāna* 3 (nothingness):
The symbolic image disappears suddenly and without warning,
leaving an experience of total emptiness, an unchanging detached
awareness of an infinite black vacuum.
* *Arūpa-jhāna* 4 (neither perception nor non-perception):
Even the residual awareness of emptiness ceases, yielding a state of
total unconsciousness. The linguistic form of the term 'neither
perception nor non-perception' reflects the recognition, in Indian
logic, of four possibilities: 'It is,' 'It is not,' 'It both is and is not,' and 'It
neither is nor is not.' The fourth of these is arguably the one most
applicable to the meditative state in question here, since strictly
speaking the meditator has no way of knowing anything about the state
he is in. That there is, in this last *jhāna*, no awareness of anything — not
even of nothingness — is indicated by ᵗʰe absence of a counterpart for

the phrases 'aware that space is endless' and so on, that occur in the descriptions of the three preceding *jhānas*.

The above pattern of correspondences is not widely recognized among Buddhist scholars or practitioners. This is because it is based on the historically early Sutta version of the *jhāna* doctrine, while almost all other attempts, traditional and modern, to explicate the *jhānas* have been based on the later and slightly different Abhidhamma version. The meditative stages are naturally the same in either case; such differences as arise are differences in interpretation of the Pali terminology. While such questions of interpretation are of considerable interest in the context of Buddhist hermeneutics, they have no real bearing on the present discussion, and will therefore not be mentioned further.

The Jhānas and Almond's Hypothesis

Progress through the *jhāna* series consists in the refinement or elimination of one mental component after another until, with the attainment of the fourth *arūpa-jhāna*, nothing remains. The *jhāna* series therefore provides excellent material for an appraisal of the notion of 'contentless experience'.

Almond's term 'contentless experience', as also Stace's 'pure consciousness', denotes a state which, while totally empty of all sensation, imagery, etc., is nevertheless definitely a *conscious* state. In attempting to discover whether such a state is to be found among the *jhānas*, one naturally turns first to the upper end of the series. (Almond does so: 1982, p. 177.) It immediately becomes evident, however, that the fourth *arūpa-jhāna* or 'realm of neither perception nor non-perception' is not to be equated with the 'contentless experience'. This final *jhāna*, being a state of total unconsciousness, comes close to Katz's 'dreamless sleep', but does not tally with the concept of 'contentless experience'.

A more promising candidate is the penultimate stage, the third *arūpa-jhāna* or 'realm of nothingness.' From the textual description it is evident that this *jhāna*, despite its name, is not a state of *total* nothingness. The description includes the phrase 'aware that there is nothing' (*n'atthi kiñcī ti*), indicating that consciousness is still there. It is a consciousness of nothingness. In practical terms, there is consciousness or awareness of the 'infinite black vacuum' that results from the sudden disappearance of the symbolic image. At that stage in the course of practice, the meditator is totally without sensory input, imagery, feeling, or emotion of any kind, and yet remains conscious. Such a state is precisely what is understood by 'contentless experience': a state of consciousness which has no content or object. Clearly, then, the third *arūpa-jhāna* is to be equated with the 'contentless experience'.

This is the answer to Katz's major criticism. Regardless of what logical reasoning or native intuition may suggest, contentless experience *is* possible. The empirical evidence is, quite simply, that meditators practising within the Buddhist tradition of *jhāna* do regularly attain this state.

The above findings lend strong support to Almond's hypothesis. The first of the four propositions in that hypothesis states: 'At least some mystical experience consists in attainment of the contentless state' (Almond 1982, p. 175). On the basis of the evidence from Buddhist *jhāna*, it can now be affirmed that this proposition is valid.

There can now be no objection to the generalization, mentioned in the first paragraph of this paper, that what the classical introvertive mystics attained was, in essence, the contentless experience. From the perspective of *jhāna* practice, there is nothing puzzling about mystics' references to 'the dark night', 'the wayless abyss', 'nakedness of the soul', and 'rejecting all images'. The frequency of theistic terminology ('desert of the Godhead' etc.) is very reasonably attributed to retrospective interpretation (cf. Smart 1966, pp 78–81). Practitioners of Buddhist *jhāna* are no less likely than Christian or Muslim mystics to interpret their experiences in terms of prevailing doctrine. A meditator who has just succeeded in mastering a new stage in his concentration practice is very likely, on returning to normal consciousness, to conclude (possibly incorrectly) that he has attained this or that *jhāna*. The above section entitled 'Correlation between doctrine and practice' provides a particularly elaborate example of such retrospective interpretation. Once interpretation is distinguished from genuine description, the classical accounts of introvertive mystical experience are seen to be attempts to describe an experience devoid of content. That they are indeed descriptions of the contentless experience (otherwise 'the third *arūpa-jhāna*', or 'the realm of nothingness') can now be affirmed.

The second component of Almond's hypothesis is to the effect that the contentless experience is the limit in a scale of progressively less content-filled states. The evidence from *jhāna* appears to put the validity of this proposition in doubt. In the *jhāna* series, a perfect example of a scale of progressively less content-filled states, it is the second last stage (*arūpa-jhāna* 3), rather than the last (*arūpa-jhāna* 4), that corresponds to the contentless experience.

In retrospect, such a situation is precisely what one ought to have expected: there is yet another stage beyond contentless experience, namely 'contentless non-experience'; after pure consciousness comes 'pure unconsciousness'. However, this fact does not necessarily represent a flaw in Almond's hypothesis. The scale of states to which the hypothesis refers is one of diminishing *content*. In terms of an algebraic model, Almond's scale of states has to do with the changing values of the function 'Consciousness of X', as 'X' approaches zero. The claim is that, *contra* Katz, 'Consciousness' can remain even after 'X' has diminished to zero. It is this claim that is 'interesting' (and, for the same reasons, controversial), rather than the fact (already well known) that consciousness too can diminish to zero.

The verdict is, then, that the second proposition in Almond's hypothesis is valid, though a little misleading. It is misleading in seeming to imply that the stage-wise process of development in which the mystic/meditator is involved can go no further than the contentless experience.

That mystical writings frequently refer to the contentless experience, and not to the state of unconsciousness that may follow it, need not surprise. There is arguably little about the state of total unconsciousness that might lead a person to attach religious importance to it. By contrast, the preceding contentless experience cannot fail to impress the mystic/meditator as being in some way enormously 'significant'. This probably has much to do with the fact that the contentless experience naturally lends itself to doctrine-based interpretation; it is, by its very nature, likely to be taken as attainment of oneness with Godhead, or as realization of the identity of *ātman/ brahman*, or as liberation of *puruṣa* from *prakṛti*, etc., according to the mystic's religious background. These facts serve to explain why, in most mystical practice, the contentless experience is, as Almond's second proposition states, the 'limiting case'.

The third proposition of Almond's hypothesis is that progressive transcending of content-filled states, culminating ultimately in the pure contentless experience, is the purpose of the contemplative path taught in some traditions. If qualified as above, to the effect that the contentless experience is not the last, but rather the second last in the series, this proposition is certainly broadly true of the contemplative paths taught in Indian religions. For Buddhism — but probably not for Jainism or Hindu yoga— the transcending of content-filled states is only a means to a rather different end. The Buddhist meditator, having attained mental stillness through *jhāna*, moves on to another type of practice, insight meditation; but *jhāna* is, nevertheless, an indispensible part of the total course of practice.

In Indian religions the transcending of content-filled states is taught as a well-defined and centrally important path of practice; in the Semitic religions, by contrast, it is a by-way only sketchily outlined in the writings of those who have followed it. Many Christian contemplative practices have close Buddhist or Hindu parallels; for example, repeating the Jesus Prayer is functionally indistinguishable from the Hindu and Buddhist practices of *mantra* chanting, and is similarly conducive to elimination of mental content. (Incidentally, one can also find, in Christian mystics' accounts of their experiences, counterparts for the remarkable effects associated with the earlier stages of *jhāna*, such as involuntary bodily movements and pleasant feelings of warmth or of lightness.) Thus, although the Semitic religions have nothing comparable to the systematic programmes of consciousness-emptying that characterize the Indian religions, they do have in their mystical traditions, certain patterns of practice that conduce, whether by design or fortuitously, to the same transcending of content-filled states.

The fourth and final proposition in Almond's hypothesis states that attainment of the contentless state occurs most commonly in the context of a set of doctrines appropriate to such attainment. The interested researcher does not need to undertake a statistical survey to be convinced that techniques conducive to attainment of the contentless state are more widely practised in Buddhist and Hindu communities than elsewhere. In particular, in the Buddhist countries of southeast Asia the practice of *jhāna* is widespread, not only within the community of monks but also among lay-people. Success in attaining the various stages of *jhana* is not necessarily equally widespread. However, discussion with meditation masters and their students indicates that these stages are indeed attained by many dedicated practitioners — a situation that certainly has no parallel in Christian or Muslim communities. (Javanese Islam is an exception — attributable, however, to strong Hindu influence.)

One could name several factors as probably contributing to this situation, such as availability of competent teachers, community expectations, and ease of entry into a contemplative monastic order. But these all come down to one single factor, which is also itself by far the dominant factor, namely the soteriological significance ascribed to such meditative practice by the associated doctrine. In the received doctrines of the Indian religions, attainment of the contentless state is accorded a high place among the practices by means of which the goal of spiritual striving may be attained; by contrast, in the received doctrines of the Semitic religions, attainment of the contentless state has, to all appearances, no place. The causal connection between doctrine and practice is self-evident.

Conclusions and Implications

It has been shown that Almond's hypothesis concerning the nature of introvertive mystical experience stands up well when tested against the data provided by Buddhist *jhāna*. Similar tests against other contemplative traditions ought to be carried out, though it seems unlikely that they would yield a different result. Even if they did reveal differences in respect of certain details, that could in no circumstances weaken the principal claim made by Almond — along with Stace and other earlier workers — that at least *some* mystical experience consists in attainment of a contentless state of consciousness.

It is, of course, possible for a sceptic to question whether one can rely on Buddhist meditators' reports of their inner experiences. For the present it must suffice to answer that the reports of present-day Buddhist meditators are unlikely to be less reliable than the often barely intelligible writings of Christian or Muslim mystics of past ages, which constitute our major corpus of data about classical introvertive mystical experience. At the same time, it must be acknowledged that this question about the acceptability of data from introspecting meditators does raise some methodological problems.

There are a few other lines of investigation that should now be followed up as natural developments from the present study. One such line of investigation would examine, from the vantage point of the practising meditator, the nature and role of interpretation, both retrospective and incorporated, in mystical experience. Another would investigate, again from the meditator's privileged vantage point, the nature of extrovertive mystical experience; for a theory of mystical experience that leaves this more common, though less remarkable, type of experience out of account is to that extent inadequate. The second branch of Buddhist meditative practice, insight meditation, suggests itself as a source of potentially valuable material for such an extended investigation.

Finally, a thought on the 'religious' implications of the present discussion. Mysticism appears to have been demystified. Detached researchers have equated introvertive mystical experience with a series of unusual psychological states, states which are readily describable in terms of familiar mental functions (or absence thereof), and which can be induced by a systematic mental training that has no necessary connection with religion.

Seen from one point of view, this is a drastic devaluation of what was the most precious core of religion, and a sabotaging of what was the most telling evidence for the existence of 'the transcendent'. However, from another point of view it is precisely the opposite. The remarkable states of consciousness in question are themselves precious attainments, which cannot be explained away; and, insofar as these states go beyond the limits of ordinary mundane consciousness, they are themselves transcendent (whence the term Transcendental Meditation). The present approach to mystical experience can, therefore, be viewed as a process of sifting and refining, whose function is to separate out the pure essence of religion from among the clutter of doctrinal, mythological, and other dross that still tends to obscure it.

References

Almond, P.C. (1982), *Mystical Experience and Religious Doctrine*, Berlin, Mouton.

Blakney, R.B. ed. (1941), *Meister Eckhart*, New York, Harper & Row.

Bucknell, R. & Stuart-Fox, M. (1986), *The Twilight Language: Explorations in Buddhist Meditation and Symbolism*, London, Curzon.

Buddhadasa (1980), *Ānāpānasati (Mindfulness of Breathing)*, trans. by Nagasena, Bangkok, Sublime Life Mission.

Chalmers, R. (1977), *The Majjhima-Nikāya, vol. III*, London, Routledge & Kegan Paul.

Gimello, R.M. (1978), 'Mysticism and Meditation' *in* S. Katz ed., *Mysticism and Philosophical Analysis*, London, Sheldon Press, 170–199.

Griffiths, P. (1983), 'Buddhist jhāna: A form-critical study', *Religion* vol. xiii, 55-68.

Gunaratana, H. (1980), A Critical Analysis of the Jhanas in Theravada Buddhist Meditation. Doctoral thesis, The American University.

Horne, J.R. (1978), *Beyond Mysticism, Studies in Religion* Supplements, 6.

Horner, I.B. trans. (1967), *The Middle Length Sayings, vol. III*, London, Luzac & Co.

Jones, R.M. (1909) *Studies in Mystical Religion*, London, Macmillan.

Katz, S.T. (1985), 'Recent Works on Mysticism', *History of Religions*, vol. XXV, 76–86.

Narasabho, S. (1971), *Buddhism*, Bangkok, Mahachulalongkorn Rajavidyalaya.

Nanamoli (1973), *Mindfulness of Breathing*, Kandy, Buddhist Publication Society.

van Ruysbroeck, Jan (1952), *The Spiritual Espousals*, London, Faber & Faber.

Smart, N. (1965), 'Interpretation and Mystical Experience', *Religious Studies*, vol. I, 75–87.

Stace, W.T. (1960), *Mysticism and Philosophy*, London, Macmillan.

Tin, P.M. trans. (1971), *The Path of Purity (Visuddhimagga)*, London, Luzac & Co.

Vajiranana, M. (1962), *Buddhist Meditation in Theory and Practice*, Colombo, Gunasena & Co.

CHAPTER 10

UNCANNY EXPERIENCE IN PSYCHOANALYTIC PERSPECTIVE

Richard A. Hutch

In 1919, Freud wrote an essay called, 'The Uncanny'. Seemingly unrelated to the essay is another German word, *Heimlichkeit*. It is difficult to translate, but Freud's English translator thought that any correct translation would have to link the German word, meaning secrecy or privacy (as in the sense of 'hidden'), to the 'uncanny'. Bakan (1958), maintains it is telling that Freud used the word in his seventieth year to explain his special 'Jewish feeling' to the B'nai B'rith Lodge in Vienna which he had joined years earlier. Bakan quotes Freud to suggest that Freud was 'coming home' to himself. That is, he was returning to the roots of his self-understanding, and the feeling of doing so was an unusual one. Freud's personal origins lay deep within the culture of the Jewish mystical tradition: says Freud,

> Thus *heimlich* is a word the meaning of which develops towards an ambivalence, until it finally coincides with its opposite, *unheimlich*. *Unheimlich* is in some way or other a sub-species of *heimlich* (quoted in Bakan, 1958, p. 306).

Things were perhaps 'hidden', private and secret, but they also were not so private and not so secret at closer scrutiny. They could be weird and awful, or uncanny (*unheimlich*). For Freud, '... the "uncanny" is that class of the terrifying which leads back to something long known to us, once very familiar' (Freud, 1959, vol. IV, pp. 369–370). It is like returning home after being away a long time, and to find that things are as they were when you left even though you yourself have undergone great changes. It all seems weird, so familiar but at the same time also unfamiliar.

I should like in this paper to advance Freud's discussion of the uncanny by citing recent discussions of the psychoanalysis of narcissism and offering an illustration of an up-dated psychology of the uncanny taken from a classic tale of the supernatural by Henry James, Jr. Narcissism is either primary or secondary. Primary narcissism is simply body pleasure. It is exemplified by thumb-sucking, expelling or retaining faeces, and masturbation. Secondary narcissism refers to feelings of pride and self-esteem. These feelings arise during periods of ego-inflation. The inflated self is born of the interplay between the dynamics of 'mirroring' and 'idealizing' of the (m)other. These dynamics will be elaborated in our consideration of the uncanny. I shall argue that a psychology of the uncanny turns on the possibility of arrest at the secondary narcissism level, which makes difficult the preservation of the self when a person believes psychological jeopardy is imminent. One either caves in to narcissistic developmental arrest, in which case the uncanny results from negative or reactive psychodynamics, or one embraces the uncanny as a positive source of personal empowerment. While the former response is only regressive and leads to pathology, the latter is deliberate and creative and may transform consciousness in beneficial ways. Developmental origins of uncanny experiences and a general belief in the efficacy of paranormal phenomena usually stem from the *possibility* of failure of the relationship between a mother and an infant or young child, even though such a failure may not have actually occurred.

There can be a 'bonding' or 'communication' breakdown. Somehow the relationship could fail to adequately 'mirror' the young one's budding sense of self. Hence, the relationship could fail to support the child's growth toward autonomy. Reality becomes cold and unresponsive, or a dire 'threat' when it is perceived to respond at all to the fragile self. The uncanny, like imaginary companions, is psychologically created as a means of preventing communication breakdowns and, perhaps, also as a means of restoring the continuity to a person's self-concept and sense of being fully alive. Although it represents a stop-gap measure, a positive response to the uncanny can enrich living. The paranormal is grounded in a capacity for uncanny experiences. The possibility of failure of an internalized pattern of bonding with the (m)other-imago during adulthood is countered by paranormal experiences. Such experiences are displacements of the (m)other-child bond in its ideal form, in which communication breakdown is not evident. Paranormal experiences are generated so as to restore to the self feelings of omnipotence or, at least, a sense of connection to and communication with a reality other than a 'normal' one.

The Uncanny in Recent Psychoanalytic Discussions

Freud's *tour de force* on the psychology of the uncanny was reiterated by Bergler (1934), a faithful disciple who believed that the uncanny was a return of repressed trauma and libidinous wishes. How to get a hold on the war that raged between the life of the instincts and social morality was the issue. Bergler argued that the uncanny results from a loss of the distinction between imagination and reality. This occurs when repressed infantile complexes are revived or when primitive beliefs which had been transcended by education appear suddenly to be confirmed once more (Bergler, 1934). Sachs (1933) thought that the failure of ancient Greeks to invent the machine was a result of a narcissistic over-evaluation of the body. He connected this failure with uncanny feelings about machines and with the typical 'influencing machine' which many schizophrenics claim controls their thoughts, feelings and actions (Tausk, 1933).

Spitz (1963) mentions the uncanny effects he experienced on a visit to Mme Tussaud's waxworks in London. He explains these effects developmentally, owing to a child's increasing ability to discriminate between animate and inanimate objects. In a wax-works, perception and cognition temporarily shift to regressed modes. Kohut (1972) alludes to the uncanny in his discussion of Kleist's essay, 'On the Puppet Theatre'. He sees as important to his study of narcissism the theme of 'apprehensions about the aliveness of self and body, and the repudiation of these fears by the assertion that the inanimate can yet be graceful, even perfect' (Kohut, 1972). Perhaps this is why puppet shows hold children spellbound. They evoke the feeling of uncanniness. There is something familiar but also quite unfamiliar about puppets in motion. The work of Kohut and Spitz is most important in weaving together a new, up-dated psychology of the uncanny, and I shall rely on it in detail. Also, Bach (1975) provides an excellent summary of the depth-psychological approach to paranormal phenomena and outlines various cross-cultural theories about the uncanny (Bach, 1971, 1975; Bach & Schwartz, 1972).

According to Bach, two ideas are essential in any understanding of the uncanny, both crafted from the work of Kohut and Spitz on the psychoanalysis of narcissism. First, Kohut has shown that people who are prone to uncanny experience begin with a narcissistic personality profile in which the dynamic projection (or, in psychoanalysis, 'transference' phenomenon) of 'idealizing' and 'mirroring' are locked into the mother-child bond. The child creates out of its mother an 'ideal' fulfiller of all its needs. When these needs go unmet the child takes it as an insult and responds with denial, rage or false compliance. This serves to establish the child's narcissistic isolation which represents a bonding breakdown with its mother and the 'object-world' of society. Such a breakdown of bonding at this early stage becomes a protracted infantile trauma in the classic sense. It is always an unconscious impediment to full development, and a source of ritualized neurotic behaviour in adulthood.

With the dynamic breakdown between ideal and actual fulfillment of the child's needs in the mother–child bond actively in place, the projection of 'mirroring' occurs. This is the child's attempt to see in its mother a reflection of itself, a secure base from which to explore separation from the mother–child bond and to become an autonomous individual. This is its natural and proper fate. In the narcissistic personality the mirroring dynamic is tied directly to idealizing, but it also fails to accomplish its task. The adage, 'out of sight, out of mind', pertains here. If the mother fails to promote the budding self-coherence of the child, the youngster's isolation from the social world is increased. 'Not seen', the child grows up 'not seeing' social reality (parents, siblings, peers, etc.) accurately. Being 'not seen' means that the child grows up, as Bach states, with the 'typical narcissistic problem of a lack of belief in the continuity and substantiality of the self and in the continuity of the process of being alive; (Bach, 1975, p. 78). It is from this psychological context that the 'paranormal' or 'spiritual' realm emerges.

One might believe that a lack of belief in the continuity and substantiality of the self means that such a person fears death. This is not untrue. However, things are not exactly as ordinary logic would lead us to believe. A constant unconscious fear of death is present, but it is not the usual aging and dying process. Rather, the fear of death is equated with a sudden and catastrophic withdrawal of the life-supporting mirroring functions of the mother or the wider social world of the adult narcissistic personality type. A sense of continuity and substantiality of the self depends, ideally, on the regularity of events, the expectation of satisfactions, and the tolerability of frustrations. This is the environment necessary for building psychic structure and a sense of personal identity. Faced with the possibility of such a 'death', or the catastrophic possibility of a loss of the 'mirroring-other', a person conjures up aspiration, ghosts, ghouls, vampires, spirits, demons, energies, an 'ultimate' reality, and the like. By doing this one is able to seek refuge in an *alter ego* doubling process, or as Bach puts it, take out a 'kind of "life insurance" against ego dissolution' (Bach, 1978, p. 78). Thus, another world is created and filled with beings in which one's instinctual forces are both embodied and controlled.

Spitz explains the uncanny in terms of narcissistic personality development and the inclination to create 'doubles' as a means of fending off 'death'. If narcissistic projections of idealizing and mirroring are disrupted, a person will create 'doubles', and describe the relationship he or she has with them as 'uncanny'. This can lead to the child's defensive reaction to mother as well as the wider social world she initially represents. The unpredictability of being able to maintain narcissistic projections is experienced as being 'turned on and off'. The tables may be turned, as in the reaction of a child to be like its parent, and to 'turn the world on and off' at will. This kind of defensive reaction may include invoking an altogether different world of spirits which fends off the 'death' which in the ordinary world would be assured. Therefore, there is a direct connection between eerie, inhuman and 'uncanny' feelings and, as Bach says, 'persistent discontinuities of the self-experience such that the self-object world and the self do not remain continuously alive for each other' (Bach, 1975, p. 80). Spitz suggests that if the dialogue of bonding is disrupted in early childhood, it is likely that the disruption will be carried over into adulthood. Whether the uncanny is a symptom of pathology or a touchstone of personal insight and growth depends on the degree of skill one has developed in managing narcissism in mature and integrated ways.

Spitz (1964) described the 'derailment of dialogue'. He noted that monkeys raised on surrogate mothers fail to develop play or social relations. Spitz explained this on the basis of a missing factor in the inanimate surrogate mother, namely, the capacity to conduct a dialogue with the baby. This dialogue is not a verbal one. It is one of action and responses which take place in the form of a circular process within the dyad of monkey to monkey, of child to mother, and so on. Sometimes, and always in the case of narcissistic personality formation, dialogues derail:

> Behaviour patterns consist of an anticipatory, appetitive, and consummatory phase we call action cycles. Interrupting action cycles prior to consummation produces unpleasure in various forms, only one of which is anxiety . . . Consistent interruption of action cycles leaves a residue which is cumulative . . . These now will cumulate in their turn and lead to the disorganization and disruption of the compensatory attempts. The cumulation of this process is what I call *derailment of dialogue* (Spitz, 1964, pp. 760–775).

Inhibition and distortion of ego formation and psychic structure follow on from such a vicious circle of derailed dialogue in early childhood and young adulthood. Such persons fail to sustain the process of ongoing communication with the world. They feel as though they truly *exist* only when locked into the extremes of depression ('loss' of the unconscious 'ideal' mother image) or mania ('inflation' brought on by the unconscious 'mirroring' mother image). A capacity to appreciate the ordinary round of human existence seems lost to such persons.

Kohut (1971) portrays early psychosexual development as occurring in three stages: (a) a stage of autoeroticism or 'primary' narcissism, where the self and the other (usually the mother) are undifferentiated; (b) the stage of narcissism where a sense of self and the externality of the object world begin to form; and (c) the oedipal stage in which ego and object love become realities. Kohut dwells on the second stage, the stage of narcissism proper. According to Homans (1979), what distinguishes Kohut's work from Freud's is Kohut's belief that narcissism follows an independent line of development and that it does not simply collapse into the oedipal stage. On the one hand, narcissistic arrest or injury may freeze creativity, in which case uncanny experience expresses a reactionary or defensive psychodynamic manoeuvre. In such instances, the uncanny is usually negative and composed of frightening or 'spooky' experiences and the perceived threat 'death'. On the other hand, a fully developed narcissism reinforces the integrity of the self in a constructive or enhancing manner. Here the uncanny is experienced as positive, and it is often associated with genius and an empowered, potentially creative sense of self. The uncanny 'forces' of the former conception are to be avoided, but those of the latter become positive 'spirit guides' or 'intuitive directions' which are useful in living.

Thus, the narcissism of early childhood intrudes into adult life in the shape of narcissistic transferences, or projections in both negative and positive ways. This is especially so when one is arrested on the second stage of narcissism. An inability to differentiate between one's inner self and the externality of the object-world gives rise to a belief in a 'spiritual' or 'paranormal' realm of existence. This 'hyper-reality' is capable of over-riding daily routine at any moment. It can be accessed through traditional magical and religious practices, or it may access itself to the realm of every day living quite spontaneously as in 'taking possession' of a person.

The dynamics of narcissism create a system of perfection in the worldview of an individual, but often such a system turns out to be less than perfect. In the first stage of narcissism the baby experiences the mother without the 'I-you' differentiation (Kohut, 1966). This is infantile bliss and total 'perfection', akin to the paradisical imagery common to most religions. The necessary shortcomings of maternal care, however, upset this equilibrium, and a different system of 'perfection' emerges. The earlier system is replaced with a grandiose image of the self (the beginning of a coherent self) along with a powerfully idealized parent image (the beginning of a sense of 'the Other'). Optimal conditions of child care foster a transmutation of the second stage of narcissism proper. As Homans (1979) states, 'grandiosity in the self undergoes gradual disappointment and taming, so that the child begins to develop a wholesome and realistic sense of self-esteem and self-enjoyment. And, in the sphere of the idealized other, the parent imago gradually becomes internalized in the form of mature ideals, goals, and visions of what reality ought to be' (p. 40).

Two types of circumstances can trigger creative feelings of uncanniness. One is when an event is so unique or sudden to a person's life experience that it cannot be assimilated into pre-existing frameworks of understanding. So-called premature or 'crackpot' discoveries in science are included here because they cannot be fitted logically into an accepted canon of scientific thought. Paranormal psychology itself is often in this class of discoveries. Creative states of consciousness, which often involve narcissistic modes of functioning, are a second means by which uncanny experience can be triggered.

Henry James, Jr. and Creative Management of the Uncanny

We know that Henry's older brother, William James, was given to uncanny experiences. The most important experience, which he recorded in his famous book of 1902, *The Varieties of Religious Experience*, involved a materialization of the invisible shape of evil. It is a classic quotation. As he described its onset, James said that he had been in a state of 'philosophical pessimism and a general depression of spirits' when he stepped into a dressing room in his home in Cambridge, Massachusetts to procure some article:

> . . . suddenly there fell upon me without any warning, just as it came out of the darkness, a horrible fear of my own existence. Simultaneously there arose in my mind the image of an epileptic patient whom I had seen in the asylum, a black-haired youth with greenish skin, entirely idiotic, who used to sit all day on one of the benches, or rather shelves against the wall, with his knees drawn up under his chin, and the coarse gray undershirt, which was his only garment, drawn over them enclosing his entire figure. He sat there like a sort of sculptured Egyptian cat or Peruvian mummy, moving nothing but his black eyes and looking absolutely non-human. This image and my fear entered into a species of combination with each other. *That shape am I*, I felt, potentially. Nothing that I possess can defend me against that fate, if the hour for it should strike for me as it struck for him. There was such a horror of him, and such a perception of my own merely momentary discrepancy from him, that it was as if something hitherto solid within my breast gave way entirely, and I became a mass

of quivering fear. After this the universe was changed for me altogether (James, 1961, p. 138).

We have in this report two levels of psychological dynamics. On the one hand, all is as it seems for a young man in low spirits sitting about the house. There is nothing unusual about that. On the other hand, the uncanny wells up from within, and the dynamic of another realm seizes attention. There was the familiar and secret (*heimlich*) of James' low spirits while sitting at home. This was dramatically joined by the weird, the terrifying, the uncanny (*unheimlich*).

Henry James, Sr. also reported at one point having undergone sudden fear and trembling, believing that there was 'some damned shape squatting invisible to me within the precincts of the room, and raying out from his fetid personality influences fatal to life'. Within ten seconds the elder Henry felt himself 'a wreck', reduced, as he put it, 'from a state of firm, vigorous, joyful manhood to one of almost helpless infancy'. He remained glued to his seat for what seemed like an hour, during which time he was 'beat upon by an ever-growing tempest of doubt, anxiety and despair, with absolutely no relief from any truth I had ever encountered save a most pale and distant glimmer of divine existence' (Edel, 1982, p. 301). He abandoned the struggle and called his wife to help him. Later, he attempted to make sense of it all by associating with Swedenborgians, for whom similar 'vastations' of the soul were commonplace. Also, in the mix of the James family was sister Alice who wrestled with neuroses all her life. She was finally confined to the care of a friend and nurse who in our day would be recognized as her ageing lesbian lover.

Henry James, Jr. never fell into line with the rest of his family. He never underwent any similar sort of uncanny experience, let alone experiences so directly attached to foreboding and evil. He was a writer who absorbed from his family an intellectual fascination about the uncanny and turned his unique family background into a very successful literary career. Much of his career owed itself to his tales of the supernatural, which described human relations and the uncanny with striking precision. The creative edge Henry James had on his brother and on his father derived from the fact that he managed to 'turn the tables' on narcissism. He maintained distance from engaging in any personal sense of the uncanny in his everyday life. He did this in favour of creatively converting the fear of death (and evil) associated with the uncanny into the source of his literary art. As Bach might put it, he did not cave in to the incipient narcissistic sense of 'death'. He was able to 'get on top of it all', and to be the active agent and not one to subject himself to any pathology of the uncanny. He would skilfully conjure up the uncanny in his writings, instead of submitting to the lure of narcissism in his personal life. A would-be neurotic thus became a world-renowned writer. This was the uncanny harnessed at its creative best.

James was led to write stories about materialized ghosts and about super ghosts, which were gruesome and quasi-supernatural. The ghosts are embodiments of the uncanny. They actually were foils against which his literary genius was formed. His earliest tales of the 1860s are conventional. A second lot, including his most famous story, 'The Turn of the Screw', was written during middle age and when he was in a state of great anxiety and depression. In these stories James created his 'daylight ghost', the ghost that walks without the benefit of white sheets, blood stains, shrieks, unearthly noises, and other conventional Gothic elements. Intriguing phantoms and anti-phantoms, some demonic and others benign and comic appear in the last group of stories. Edel (1982) summarizes the nature of James' best tales of the uncanny in life. They are often 'without phantoms at all, but are wrought with an ambiance of "the strange and sinister embroidered on the very type of the normal and easy"' (p. 304). A closer association of *unheimlich* (weird, uncanny) and *heimlich* (private, hidden), as Freud postulated, could hardly be better illustrated. Having offered the case for Henry James, Jr. as a good illustrator of the uncanny, let us now turn to James' 1897 story, 'The Turn of the Screw', in order to see just how he accomplished this.

Pathological Management of the Uncanny: A Supernatural Tale

We could well ask, what happens if grandiosity fails to undergo sufficient disappointment and taming, and if wholesome and realistic self-esteem and self-enjoyment fail to eventuate? When we think of the protagonist of 'The Turn of the Screw' we realize that achieving a completed second stage of narcissistic development was probably not part of her lot in life. The story is about a haunted governess, the daughter of an English country parson and a woman for whom the uncanny is ever present, and some children. It is told by the young governess in a manuscript she left behind after her death. She says that she sees the ghosts of Peter Quint and Miss Jessel, two deceased employees of the estate where she is in charge of the children, little Miles and his sister Flora. On the face of it, the behaviour of the children is established as 'normal' in every sense of the term. Miles always wants to know when he is to return to school and be with his mates. Flora enjoys typical pastimes of little girls in the gardens and around the lake at Bly. Yet the governess makes the behaviour of the children seem sinister. She engages in projecting a supernatural realm inhabited by ghosts in order to fend off fears deep within herself. On the face of it all, things are not what they seem. The real 'turn of the screw', the particular twist of pain in the tale, is a product of what the governess does to the children and how they 'try constantly to accommodate themselves to her unearthly vision' (Edel, 1982, p. 305). This is a case of a narcissistic mother substitute who is the source of a 'derailment of dialogue' with two children. We can observe the dynamics by which she engages the children in her delusional drama, itself structured psychologically by the idealizing and mirroring projections of her narcissistic personality.

The plot is a simple one. An unnamed governess is hired in London by the bachelor uncle of the two young children, Flora and Miles, who reside at Bly, the uncle's country estate. Although the man wishes to care for his niece and nephew according to the desire of his deceased brother, the children's father, he wants nothing to do with the actual daily affairs of Bly nor with the education of the children. He will, however, pay all the bills. We learn that the governess is to be in full charge of the children and the rambling estate, aided by Mrs. Grose, the housekeeper, and several assistants and labourers about the place. The story revolves around two major facts. First, that Miles returns from boarding school to Bly having been expelled and told never to return. The reason for his expulsion is never clarified, and this itself establishes a 'derailment of dialogue'. The governess avoids making what would otherwise be normal, prudent enquiries about the reason for the expulsion of a youngster, whom she refers to as 'the little gentleman' and believes to be the perfection of innocence (Edel, 1971, p. 447). The second major fact is that the governess' predecessor, Miss Jessel, left Bly some time ago and had since died. The same eventual fate came to the children's uncle's valet, Peter Quint, who died when he fell off a cliff while on his way home from the local pub. Moreover, Miss Jessel was above the working class station of Quint, himself a 'base menial', and in spite of this was purported to be Quint's lover (Edel, 1971, p. 481).

If sustained ignorance about Miles' expulsion from boarding school suggests a 'derailment of dialogue' by the governess with the innocent children, then it is in the conjured daylight ghosts of Miss Jessel and Peter Quint, seen by the governess on ten occasions throughout the story, that the dynamic projection of 'idealizing' and 'mirroring' are evident. The story pits the governess against the children and Mrs. Grose, with the governess gradually being overtaken by a foreboding sense of a narcissistic 'death'. She senses the uncanny in visions of the ghosts of Quint and Jessel and finally takes extraordinary steps to force the children and Mrs. Grose to see things as she herself believes them to be. In the end, Flora and Mrs. Grose flee from Bly at the insistence of the governess, and in seeking to save Miles from 'evil' brings about his death. Does the real secret lie in the personal background of the governess which she refuses to see, not as daylight ghosts, but for what it actually is? Although we shall never know for sure, the governess illustrates a case of arrested development related to our updated psychology of narcissism. For her, the uncanny is a threat to be defended against. It is not regarded as an aide in living nor as a source of personal empowerment.

We could hypothesize that the governess in James' story hardly experienced optimal conditions of child care, and that the system of perfection she brought to Bly was split off from reality. This may have found unconscious expression in her sense of the uncanny, her visions, and her 'making over' of the children, whom in the end she thought were in league with the dead. If, as it appears, her narcissistic needs go gradually unembraced and untamed, her wish for an idealized powerful parent image may have become split off, or repressed, from reality. That the governess puts herself at the 'helm' of the household suggests the grandiose self at work. The governess alone presumes that her view of the situation must command the attention of all. She is unable to tame her grandiosity on the basis of feedback from the children and Bly staff. Arrested childhood development persists into adulthood. She remains 'derailed' in otherwise possible dialogue with those willing to help her and with the personal source of her torment.

Her wish for an idealized parent figure goes unfulfilled. The troubled woman unwittingly reverses the situation, and converts herself from the unfulfilled child into a benevolent and protective parent who battles against the evil parental images of the two conjured up ghosts. She attempts this with a skewed vision of the real demands placed upon her by the everyday facts of life at Bly. The governess becomes the heroine of goodness and presses her cause on the household. At the same time, she employs unconscious denial and narcissistic rage about her 'evil' developmental arrest each time she sights the ghosts of Peter Quint and Miss Jessel. The extent of her conflict could only lead to 'death', or the falling apart of her idyllic world at Bly. This was the screen upon which her inner conflict was cast.

Fearing that the ghosts were about to take possession of the souls of the children, the governess instructs Mrs. Grose to take the now ill

Flora and to flee from Bly and the evil forces which she alone envisaged there. Miles remained behind because, thought the governess, he was the special target of corruption and needed direct exorcizing ministrations. Miles' expulsion from school remained unexplained. Later, however, the governess believes that the expulsion was for wickedness. Just before departing Flora grows fearful of the governess and nestles into the folds of Mrs. Grose's dress for protection from accusations of complicity with Miles in evil. She comes down with a fever, this being the ostensible cause of the governess insisting that Flora be taken from Bly and from any further harm from 'evil'.

The governess wanted to bring out proof of Miles' corruption by the two Bly ghosts. However, she screened out the reality of her inner conflicts and instead seized on the issue of Miles' expulsion from school and pressed hard her enquiries. 'What then did you do?,' she asked. 'Well,' said Miles, 'I said things.' 'What *were* these things?,' raged the governess (Edel, 1971, pp. 547–549). At that very moment of high emotion a ghost appeared before her eyes. This was the governess' tenth and final sighting of a daylight ghost. She felt as though the room was filled with the taste of poison. Miles, fearing lest he participate in the governess' view, asked her, 'It's *he*? (Edel, 1971, p. 549). The governess was determined to have all the 'proof' she sought and challenged the frightened boy. She demanded to know, 'Whom do you mean by "he"?; Miles shouted, 'Peter Quint — you devil!' (Edel, 1971, p. 550). The youngster betrayed the demonic force that held the governess. She took it as confirmation that Miles had filled her ears with his 'supreme surrender of the name' of Peter Quint and that she had 'his tribute' for her 'devotion' to him (Edel, 1971, p. 550). The now thoroughly deluded woman had all the 'proof' that she needed.

Suddenly the governess grabbed Miles as if to protect him from the ghost of Quint. She lunged at Quint, perhaps mistaking the boy for the ghost, and exclaimed, 'but he has lost you forever!,' referring to Miles. Yet, the forces of conflict within her would not be separated. For a demonstration of what she believed to be part of her exorcism she said to Miles, 'There, *there*!,' pointing in the direction of the window where she saw the apparition (Edel, ed., 1971, p. 550). But frightened Miles was unimpressed by her 'proofs'. The governess pressed Miles harder to her person, seeking perhaps to bond with her fantasy of innocent perfection which she had long ago failed to achieve in fact in herself. But it was too late. Her persistent confusion of internal and external realities could not be exorcized from her tenuous sense of self. Her desperation and physical might grew too strong. Miles' heart stopped. With this died any hope of wielding any 'turn of the screw' of ' ordinary human virtue' at Bly (Edel, 1971, p. 539).

Conclusion

We see how the uncanny can be conjured up in a life through a breakdown of bonding with others. The breakdowns owe their force to a vicious circle of misconstrual and faulty dialogue about the nature of reality. With a 'derailment of dialogue', ordinary processes of interaction with others become mere dialogue with oneself. A reliable differentiation between the internal reality of the self and the external reality of others fails to be established. The dialogue with oneself is basically about the special narcissistic fear of 'death' that is mentioned throughout this paper. Experiences of the uncanny are counterpoints to such 'dying'. If these counterpoints are managed out of fear and with the defensive regression alone, the uncanny appears to be malevolent, 'spooky' or 'evil'. However, management of the uncanny according to a more mature, resilient narcissism shifts the dynamics of regression into means by which ego-mastery is enhanced. In this latter case, the uncanny takes a benevolent form, with 'heightened' or 'creative' experiences over-riding the un-conscious structure of narcissistic 'death'. Therefore, the uncanny can be evoked, not as a defensive strategy against personal developmental snags from our pasts, but as a point of embarcation for exploring the human potential to engage new frontiers of consciousness and creative new ways of being in the world.

References

Bach, S. (1975), 'Narcissism, continuity and the uncanny', *International Journal of Psychoanalysis* 35, 77–86.

Bach, S. (1971), 'Notes on some imaginary companions', *Psychoanalytic Study of the Child* 26, 159–171.

Bach, S. & Schwartz, L. (1972), 'A dream of the Marquis de Sade: psychoanalytic reflections on narcissistic trauma, decompensation, and the reconstitution of the delusional self', *Journal of the American Psychoanalytic Association*, 20, 451–475.

Bakan, D. (1958), *Sigmund Freud and the Jewish Mystical Tradition*, Boston, Beacon.

Bergler, E. (1934), 'The psychoanalysis of the uncanny', *International Journal of Psychoanalysis*, 15, 215–244.

Edel, L., ed. (1971), *Henry James: Stories of the Supernatural*, London, Barrie & Jenkins.

Edel, L. (1982), *The Stuff of Sleep and Dreams: Experiments in Literary Psychology*, London, Chatto & Windus.

Homans, P. (1979), *Jung in Context; Modernity and the Making of a Psychology*, Chicago, University of Chicago Press.

James, W. (1961), *The Varieties of Religious Experience*, London, Collier-Macmillan.

Kohut, H. (1966), 'Forms and transformations of narcissism', *Journal of the American Psychoanalytic Association* 14, 243–272.

Kohut, H. (1971), *The Analysis of the Self*, New York, International Universities Press.

Kohut, H. (1972), 'Thoughts on narcissism and narcissistic rage', *Psychoanalytic Study of the Child* 27, 360–400.

Sachs, H. (1933), 'The delay of the machine age', *Psychoanalytic Quarterly*, 2, 404–424.

Spitz, R.A. (1964), 'The derailment of dialogue', *Journal of the American Psychoanalytic Association* 12, 752–775.

Spitz, R.A. (1963), 'Life and the dialogue' *in* H.S. Gaskill, ed., *Counterpoint: Libidinal Object and Subject*, New York, International Universities Press.

Tausk, V. (1933), 'On the origin of the "influencing machine" in schizophrenia', *Psychoanalytic Quarterly* 2, 519–556.

SECTION III

RESEARCHING THE PARANORMAL

What is the objective evidence for paranormal belief and experience? What is a proper procedure for establishing the validity of a paranormal claim? Why do some people believe in the paranormal, while others do not? These are some of the issues taken up in the chapters of this section. The section is devoted to research methods and findings in both the social and the natural sciences.

Chapter 11 by Stanley Krippner takes the position that established and generally recognized research techniques are adequate for studying the paranormal. This point of view is questioned by many other contributors in the volume. In particular, Krippner discusses the uses and abuses of survey techniques for determining the extent and objective validity of paranormal experience. Krippner's chapter, which is addressed to the field of parapsychology, stresses the need for researchers to recognize the speculative nature of the field; to be candid about its controversial status; not go beyond what is warranted by evidence; and, finally, to be devoted to basic standards of scientific method.

Peter Nelson, in Chapter 12, places emphasis on the need to operationalize the definition of a class of paranormal experiences or events prior to the collection of data, rather than making a *post hoc* assignment of categories. Eleven categories of paranormal experience are devised by Nelson in order to formulate a questionnaire which he uses in a survey of a selected population of staff and students at an academic institution. Even more than previous surveys, Nelson's study reveals widespread experience of paranormal phenomena. Of particular interest is the fact that Nelson's study is based on theoretical and philosophical considerations of considerable depth and originality. Essentially, Nelson's eleven categories are conceptualized by him as being equivalent to fundamental orientations towards the real. On adoption, these orientations re-organize the responses of the experiencing person to the world. Thus Nelson's survey goes considerably beyond a mere assemblage of responses pertaining to just another questionnaire.

The next two chapters are less concerned with the objective evidence for paranormal experience than with identifying underlying personality or environmental factors which influence a person to believe or disbelieve in the existence of paranormal phenomena. Michael Thalbourne, a psychologist, investigates in Chapter 13 the association of factors such as religiosity, conservatism, intelligence, gender, and fear of death, with paranormal beliefs. In Chapter 14 William Sims Bainbridge, a sociologist, reports survey findings which point to the importance of geographic and other types of social mobility as factors associated with paranormal beliefs. Bainbridge points out that in modern social conditions mobility is vastly increased and consequently paranormal experiences are a natural result of contemporary social change.

The experimental work of the late British Psychologist, Robert Thouless, particularly in the area of psychical research early this century, is the subject of the next chapter by L.B. Brown. Brown points out that while Thouless and other early researchers were aware of fraud and delusion in reports of the paranormal, they did not, at least until the 1930s, recognize the importance of social psychological processes in maintaining belief patterns. One extraordinarily interesting fact to which Brown's discursive contribution attracts attention is that believers will obtain scientific results supporting claims for the existence of paranormal phenomena, while disbelievers will obtain opposite results. This itself casts light on science as a social enterprise.

As Krippner points out in the opening chapter of this section, the study of the paranormal reports on phenomena which are in some sense regarded as 'anomalous' because they contravene conceptions of what is possible scientifically regarded. In other words, research into the paranormal raises questions not only about human perception and belief, but also about the workings of the natural world. We are fortunate in being able to include in this section a contribution from a natural scientist. In the final chapter of this section Bevan L. Reid discusses results of experiments conducted as part of cancer research. Reid concludes that these experiments indicate the existence of a previously unrecognized force in space which originates and creates matter in a living state. Furthermore, Reid suggests that the study of this and other related forces in the biosystem is likely to shed light on more typically recognized paranormal phenomena such as extrasensory perception, clairvoyance, and psychokinesis.

CHAPTER 11
SOME TOUCHSTONES FOR PARAPSYCHOLOGICAL RESEARCH

Stanley Krippner

For as long as human beings have kept records of their experiences, they have described reveries that appeared to transmit thoughts of another person, dreams in which they seemed to become aware of faraway events, rituals in which future happenings supposedly were predicted, and mental procedures that were said to produce direct action on distant physical objects. These purported occurrences may have been instances of phenomena that parapsychologists now call telepathy, clairvoyance, precognition, and psychokinesis. Collectively, they are referred to as 'psi' — reported interactions between organisms and their environment (including other organisms) in which information or influence has occurred that can not be explained through modern science's understanding of sensory-motor channels. In other words, these reports are anomalous because they appear to preclude the constraints of time, space, and force.

Psychology is the scientific study of behaviour and experience; parapsychology studies those reported anomalies of behaviour and experience that appear to stand outside of the currently known explanatory mechanisms which account for organism-environment and organism-organism information and influence flow. Over the past century, considerable research has been conducted in an attempt to understand these reports and to determine whether they are worthy of combined attention and investigation (Edge, Morris, Palmer & Rush 1986).

Questionnaires, Surveys and Case Studies

Parapsychology began in the late 1800s with the collection and analysis of reported psi experiences as recorded by participants and witnesses. However, many ancient and classical traditions incorporated psi into their worldviews, their mythologies, and their daily practices. The first reported parapsychological experiment allegedly was designed by King Croesus of Lydia about 50 B.C. Attempting to determine which of several oracles was the most trustworthy, Croesus had his messengers ask them what he was doing on a certain date. Only the oracle at Delphi answered correctly, telling the messenger that his king was boiling a tortoise and a lamb in a cauldron. Croesus then confidently submitted a critical question: What would occur if he invaded Persia? The oracle is said to have replied that, following the invasion, a great empire would be destroyed. Croesus launched the attack; however, Persia was victorious and the doomed empire was Lydia. The ambiguity of the Delphic oracle's second response continues to characterize purported oracles and 'psychic sensitives'. Even though these statements may satisfy their gullible clients, the enigmas frustrate sincere researchers. However, the specificity of the oracle's first response is the hallmark of those experiments that produce clear-cut results and reinforce serious interest in the field.

The Society for Psychical Research, founded in Great Britain in 1882, was the first major organization to attempt to assess psi scientifically, beginning with surveys that would later evolve into controlled experiments. The 'Report on the Census of Hallucinations', organized by members of the society, analyzed and categorized some 17,000 responses to the question, 'Have you ever . . . had a vivid impression of seeing, or being touched . . ., or of hearing a voice; which impression, so far as you could discover, was not due to any external cause?' Affirmative answers were obtained from about one in ten of the respondents, with more visual hallucinations reported than auditory or tactile hallucinations (Sidgwick, Sidgwick & Johnson 1894). Marks and McKellar (1982) refer to this collection as a 'veritable mine of data', noting that the investigators attempted a pioneering effort to categorize the reports into sensory hallucinations, ordinary sense perceptions, dreams, and what today would be considered eidetic imagery.

This early survey did not claim to be a random sample of subjects, nor did it claim that the reports were necessarily accurate or anomalous. However, there were a number of provocative findings. For example, one in 43 of the death hallucinations occurred within 12 hours either preceding or following the death of the person who was seen in the hallucination. On the basis of the death rate in England and Wales at the time, only about one in 19,000 individuals died in a given 24-hour period. It would be expected, therefore, on the basis of chance if no other factor were involved, that only about 1 in 19,000 hallucinations would be within 12 hours of the person's death instead of the one in 43 that was reported. Because reports of this nature can be consciously or unconsciously distorted, they are not necessarily anomalous; nevertheless, they often offer leads that can be subjected to more rigorous inquiry.

A more recent questionnaire survey involved 375 college students focusing upon auditory hallucinations. Overall, 71% of the sample reported some experience with vocal hallucinations in wakeful situations. Also reported were hypnagogic hallucinations (which took place as people were dropping off to sleep) (30%) and hypnopompic hallucinations (which took place as people were waking up) (14%). Nearly 40% reported hearing their name being called when out-of-doors; 36% reported a similar experience indoors. Eleven percent claimed to have heard their own voice come from the back seat of their car, while a similar proportion stated that they had heard God 'as a real voice' (Posey & Losch 1983–1984).

Sometimes, surveys are conducted through the mail. One of them, published in 1979, obtained 354 completed questionnaires from residents of the Charlottesville, Virginia area and 268 University of Virginia students. One question read, 'Have you ever had, *while awake*, a vivid impression of seeing, hearing, or being touched by another being, which impression, as far as you could discover, was not due to any external physical or 'natural' cause?' This was essentially the same question asked by the British society a century earlier. It was answered affirmatively by 17% of the residential as well as the student respondents, about the same as the 13% giving positive responses in the earlier survey. However, the majority of hallucinations in the British group was visual while the American group's reports were predominantly auditory or tactile (Palmer 1979).

A question from the same survey read, 'Have you ever seen light . . . around or about a person's head, shoulders, hands or body, which, as far as you could tell, was not due to 'normal' or 'natural' causes . . .?' Five percent of the townspeople and 6% of the students answered this question affirmatively. Another question asked, 'Have you ever had, *while awake*, a strong feeling, impression, or "vision" that a previously unexpected event had happened, was happening, or was going to happen, and [learned] later that you were right?' At least one such experience was reported by 38% of the townspeople and 39% of the student sample. In the majority of the cases, the event was said to have occurred within 24 hours before or after the experience, and in over a quarter of the cases the respondents claimed that they had told someone of their experience before learning of the event. Therefore, a number of claims of this type are open to some type of veridical verification.

One question was phrased, 'Have you ever had a rather clear and specific *dream* which matched in detail an event which occurred before, during, or after your dream, and which you did not know about or did not expect at the time of the dream?' At least one dream of this type was reported by 36% of the town sample and 38% of the students. About two out of three of these dreams were reported to be 'more vivid' than respondents' ordinary dreams. In about one-third of the cases, the verifying event was said to have taken place within a 24-hour span. In about 20% of the cases, the dreamer claimed to have told someone about the dream before learning of the verifying event.

Another question was worded, 'Have you ever seen an object move with no "natural" or physical means of motion that you could discover?' Such an experience was claimed by 8% of the towns-people and 6% of the students. Fourteen percent of the town sample and 25% of the student sample answered affirmatively to the question, 'Have you ever had an experience in which you felt that "you" were located "outside" or "away from" your physical body . . .?' The difference between the two samples on this question was significant (or beyond chance) when evaluated by statistical means.

There was also a statistically significant difference between townspeople (68%) and students(88%) in response to a question about 'dèja vu': 'Have you ever had the strong feeling or impression that you had been some place or in the same situation before, even though you had never actually been there before or were experiencing the event for the first time in "real life"?'

A 1982 nation-wide survey in the U.S. discerned other group differences regarding opinions on life after death. A belief in reincarnation was held by 23% of the respondents and was spread fairly evenly among educational, economic, and racial groups. But the belief in contact with the dead was held by 28% of the college educated respondents versus 9% of those who only attended grade school. Of the generation under 30, 38% held this belief to be true versus 12% of those over 50. When a sample of scientists was drawn from *Who's Who in America*, one out of ten claimed to have had a 'verge of death' or 'near death' experience, compared to 15% of the general population (Gallup 1982).

A comprehensive survey by the National Opinion Center of the University of Chicago revealed that, in 1973, 35% of Americans claimed to have had a 'mystical experience'. When given standard psychological tests, members of this group did not manifest pathology; instead, they made rather high scores in mental health. In the same survey, 58% of Americans thought that they had experienced one or more purported psi events in their lives (McCready & Greeley

1976). The same group reported a follow-up poll in 1987, observing that the proportion was now 67%. In addition, the number of Americans claiming to have had contact with the dead had increased from 27% to 42% (Greeley, 1987). A poll of 2,000 randomly selected adults conducted by the Public Opinion Laboratory at Northern Illinois University in 1985 discovered that 75% agreed that 'there are good ways of treating sickness that medical science does not recognize' (Furlow 1986).

Studies of other cultures often yield high percentages of psi-related experiences as well. A survey of 2,494 school children in India identified 36% who reported an inexplicable experience (Prasad & Stevenson 1968) while 49% of a student sample in Iceland claimed to have had dreams that later came true in their waking life (Haraldsson 1975). In a 1977 survey in the USSR, 35% of the respondents claimed to have had at least one psi experience (Vilenskaya 1978). Similar surveys in Hong Kong, Italy, and Japan also yielded large percentages (MacKenzie 1987).

The use of case studies has allowed the examination of accounts described in greater depth than those solicited by surveys and questionnaires. The best known of these collections is that of L.E. Rhine (1977); by 1973, her collection of spontaneous cases of alleged psi numbered 12,837. The overall objective of Rhine's studies was to study the basic psi process; for example, she identified the main form in which psi is expressed as hallucinations, intuitions, realistic dreams, and non-realistic dreams (marked by symbolism and fantasy). A Study of 1,000 cases of reported psi phenomena in West Germany demonstrated that 47% emerged in realistic dreams, 15% in non-realistic dreams, 25% in intuition, and 15% in hallucinations (Sannwald 1963). These anecdotal reports stimulated Ullman and me (Ullman, Krippner & Vaughan 1989) to investigate anomalous dreams in a laboratory setting; we obtained results suggesting that some subjects could incorporate distant pictorial material (that had been randomly selected once the subjects had gone to bed) into their dreams at above-chance levels.

Stevenson (1970, p. 178) has presented an intensive study of 35 cases of 'telepathic impressions', concluding that they shared the same characteristics as did those in earlier decades. For example, '*a relationship*, not just an individual, is necessary for such experiences to occur'. In one instance, a woman recalled:

> When my five-year-old daughter came home from a birthday party, she was disappointed to find that her father and brother had gone to the Walt Disney movie without her . . . I told Joicey that her father expected her to join them there, so she waved goodbye and skipped towards the

corner . . . Suddenly, while I held a plate in my hand an awesome feeling came over me. I dropped the plate, turned my eyes toward heaven and prayed aloud, 'Oh, God, don't let her get killed!' . . . I immediately went to the telephone, looked up a number, and shakily dialed the theater. I gave my name and said, 'My little girl was on her way to the theater. She has had an accident. Is she badly hurt?' The girl answering the telephone stammered, 'How did you know? It — the accident — just happened. Hold the phone please!' . . . Soon a very calm voice, that of the manager . . . spoke, 'Mrs. Hurth, your little girl was struck by a car, but she is all right. Your husband is with her now. She appears to be in good shape, only stunned . . .' Joicey remembers that at the time she was hit she called, 'Mama.' She remembers sitting on the curb crying and calling 'Mama, Mama, I want my Mama.' (Stevenson 1970, pp. 61-62)

Contemporary parapsychologists would agree that survey responses, questionnaire responses, and case studies are subject to such confounding variables as coincidence, unconscious inference, sensory leakage, exaggeration after the fact, falsification of memory, and outright fabrication. However, several ingenious uses have been made of the data. Irwin (1979) administered college students a questionnaire inquiring into purported psi experiences as well as Paivio's Individual Differences Questionnaire which attempts to assess the extent to which a person relies on verbal processing or imagery processing in everyday life. Using statistical techniques, Irwin found a significant interaction between whether the processing style was visual or verbal and whether the reported psi experience involved imagery or intuition. Psi reports involving imagery tended to occur among people who habitually tended to rely more strongly on visual processing.

Wilson and Barber (1982) studied 26 individuals with vivid mental imagery. In comparison with 25 control subjects, the 'eidetikers' not only were better hypnotic subjects and engaged in more fantasy both as children and adults, but claimed to have had more clairvoyant, precognitive, and telepathic experiences. In addition, they reported more "out-of-body" experiences, lucid dreams, experiencing of apparitions, seeing "auras", and having mystical visions.

Persinger (1974a) has urged using reported psi phenomena in new and ingenious ways, observing that:

Across cultures and throughout history people have been reporting psi-experiences. Let us find out *what they are saying* . . . It is by looking at the similarities of the verbal behaviour that we may find enough consistencies to understand the factors responsible for the *reports*. (Persinger 1974a, p. 13)

Persinger (Schaut & Persinger, 1985) has examined several collections of spontaneous cases, including the 35 gathered by Stevenson (1970), reporting that they seem to occur most frequently when geomagnetic activity is calmer than the days before or after the experience — and lower than the month's average activity. Persinger (1974b) has also tallied the hour, weekday, and month of reported psi experiences, as well the respondents' health and state of mind. This approach can be applied to any collection of cases where the date of the alleged experience has been recorded; if repeatable, these effects may help to provide an understanding of the mechanisms underlying psi phenomena.

Controlled Observations and Experimental Studies

Valuable as these approaches may be, they do not address the potentially anomalous nature of psi phenomena. For this task, parapsychologists have turned to controlled observations and to experimental research. For example, a hospital technician was observed by Honorton (1974) to demonstrate, at a distance, movements of a small bottle in her home. She also produced compass needle deflections in the laboratory, but could not repeat her effect on the bottle. Honorton observed that these demonstrations were strongly suggestive of psi but did not reach the point where the conditions could be considered to have been controlled adequately.

The purported effect with the compass stimulated a controlled observation of the same subject at a different laboratory. Watkins and Watkins (1974) mounted a magnetic compass inside the sensitive coil of an electronic metal detector with sealed packets of photographic film underneath and at distances up to 3 metres from the detector. While the subject sat near this apparatus, the compass needle slowly turned 15 degrees and stopped while the signal from the metal detector changed in a way that normally would have indicated the presence of several pounds of metal in the surrounding coil. The subject then moved to a far corner of the room, but the compass needle's deflections did not change, nor was the needle responsive to a magnet brought near it. When removed to the distance of 1.2 meters, the needle slowly resumed its normal behaviour. When it was returned to its original location, the compass needle again was deflected 15 degrees and became insensitive to the magnet. After about 25 minutes, the compass gradually returned to normal functioning.

In formulating the controls for these types of observations, investigators must guard against the possibilities of technical artifacts, equipment malfunctioning, optical effects, mistaken sensory cues, and sleight of hand. Watkins and Watkins did not employ a magician; this omission can be interpreted as a flaw in otherwise well-controlled procedures. Indeed, at the 1983 convention of the Parapsychological

Association, an international body composed of some 300 psi researchers, the organization's governing council adopted a resolution stating, in part, that the association 'welcomes collaboration with magicians who . . ., regardless of their opinion on the existence of psi, would be willing to consult [with parapsychologists] . . . regarding adequate controls against fraud.'

Earlier that year, it had been discovered that two young men who had become well known for their purported 'metal-bending' feats were, in fact, magicians (Krippner, 1984). Despite the fact that the work with these alleged 'metal-benders' was not generally acclaimed within the field, none of the parapsychologists, or the other investigators who had worked with these two subjects, had taken the precaution of having a conjurer nearby. A few years before this incident, Pamplin and Collins (1985) had reported testing six children for supposed 'metal-bending' skills. In five instances, the children were observed using sleight of hand; in the sixth instance, no metal was bent.

No matter which experimental design is used to investigate psi phenomena, the process needs to adhere to several basic standards of the scientific method:

1. *The procedures must be public*. The design and results need to be communicated professionally in refereed journals. The report should contain a detailed description of what was done and how it was done, so that another scientist can repeat the procedure, at least in principle.

2. *The definitions must be precise*. Even allowing for the growing body of empirical data, each variable needs to be well defined and the techniques by which it was measured should be specific.

3. *The data collection must be as objective as possible*. Once the investigation is under way, the researcher needs to respect and follow the data, even if they challenge a cherished hypothesis.

4. *The findings must be replicable, at least to some degree*. Another scholar may want to test the findings by reproducing the study. If the data were collected incorrectly, if the variables were inadequately measured, or if the procedures were adversely influenced by experimenter bias, the findings obviously will fail to be repeated. The conclusions drawn should be weighed according to the replicability of the accumulated data on a given topic.

5. *The approach must be cumulative and systematic*. Scientists strive to unify entire bodies of knowledge through the use of theory and by building up an organized system of propositions (Tart 1975).

Psi researchers must keep all these standards in mind when investigating parapsychological phenomena. The unpredictability and variability of living subjects makes research in the life sciences an especially difficult task. When it comes to psi research the difficulty is compounded because the topics under investigation are complex and elusive. As a result, the lack of a strictly repeatable experiment may be understandable, but it has allowed critics such as Neher to label parapsychology an 'unsuccessful science' (Neher 1980, p. 148).

However, one set of experiments that fulfills most scientific standards is the body of work by Helmut Schmidt who developed a random event generator (REG) in which electrons emitted by strontium-90 decay triggered a two-position switch. Careful pretesting showed that under controlled conditions the output of the two positions was random. The subject was instructed to try to make the output register what seemed to be equivalent to faster (or slower) electron emission; automatic recording displayed the scores. Once Schmidt obtained significant results which he interpreted as supporting the psi hypothesis (Schmidt 1970, 1981), he made the equipment available to other investigators, some of whom also obtained significant results (e.g., Houtkooper 1977). Neher (1980, p. 146), in his critical evaluation, finds the REG replication count 'encouraging' enough 'to provide some of the strongest support for psi.'

Schmidt's REG experiments have produced some of para-psychology's most widely-cited results and some of its most robust laboratory data. An analysis of 56 reports of REG research published or presented from 1969 to 1984 indicates that a total of 332 individual experiments were conducted, 71 of which yielded statistically significant results (Radin, May, & Thompson 1985). Nevertheless, the REG data have been criticized by Hansel (1980) on several grounds:

1. Hansel claims that Schmidt's work has not been replicated. However, there have been several instances where significant results with REGs have been obtained in other laboratories (e.g., Jahn 1982).

2. Hansel asserts that Schmidt's experimental design fails to specify in advance the exact numbers and types of trials to be undertaken by each subject. In response to Hansel, it should be admitted that the initial REG experiment did not specify the total number of trials in advance, a problem that was corrected in later experiments. In addition, some REG experiments did not specify in advance the number of trials each particular subject would attempt because the purpose was not to determine whether a given subject demonstrated psi, but whether the experiment as a whole provided evidence for psi. However, the total number of trials for these experiments was preset in advance.

3. Hansel charges that the allocation of trials, in some experiments,

into high-scoring and low-scoring conditions is misleading because the designations could be changed once the data are collected. In response, it should be observed that the high and low conditions are recorded automatically on paper punch tape in difference codes. However, Hyman (1981) adds another criticism; conceding that Schmidt's randomizing tests control against 'long-term or even temporary' machine bias, Hyman does not think that they control adequately against 'possible short-run biases in the generator output.' Although Schmidt's control runs have demonstrated no long-run bias, the possibility of short-run bias has not been decided by either Schmidt or his critics. At the same time, it should be noted that some of Schmidt's studies have compared experimental runs against control runs with the statistical results favoring the experimental runs.

4. Concerning possible fraud, Hansel (1981) suggests that a subject could have shorted the input in the display panel. However, the REG outputs are completely buffered, and the design of the machine precludes the type of tampering Hansel suggests. Hansel also claims that there is little control of the experimenter, proposing that (1) at least one other experimenter should be present, (2) the forms and data tapes should be serially numbered, (3) separate machines giving distinguishable printouts should be employed for each type of test, (4) one set of counters should be non-resettable, and (5) one set should have been wired permanently in circuit to record trials, hits, and misses. In response, it needs to be pointed out that data have been recorded by non-resettable counters in some of Schmidt's work, with punched paper providing a permanent objective recording of the data (Schmidt 1969). Further refinements have made it virtually impossible for the REG data to be falsified. In one study, each of three experimenters knew different aspects of the research design unknown to the other two until the data were collected. Indeed, the results were prerecorded before the experiment had even started in order to determine if apparent psi influence on a 'past' event could occur (Schmidt, Morris, & Rudolph 1984). Rao and Palmer (1988) have suggested that a critic who is knowledgeable concerning these alleged shortcomings serve as a co-experimenter with Schmidt in some future experiments.

Some of Hansel's suggestions are thoughtful and well-considered. Those which have not been implemented could certainly be adopted because Schmidt's research represents an approach in which fraud can be virtually eliminated.

Another line of research that provides evidence for at least some degree of replicability is the use of a homogeneous visual field (or 'ganzfeld') to evoke imagery that is later compared to a hidden target.

A proponent and a critic (Hyman & Honorton 1986) examined 36 studies using this design; although they differed on the quality of the research, they agreed that 'there is an overall significant effect in this data base which cannot reasonably be explained by selective reporting or multiple analysis.'

Can fraud be completely eliminated in psi research? Hyman (1981, p. 39) states that 'there is no . . . experiment immune from trickery.' However, there are certain precautions that need to be taken by parapsychologists:

1. Isolating the subject from the psi target in ways that eliminate sensory cueing or muscular activity.

2. Taking precautions to insure that the person who records the responses is blind to the nature or identity of the target material.

3. Using a randomization method to select target material.

4. Deciding how many trials will be attempted before an experiment begins.

5. Testing high-scoring subjects (or repeating promising experiments) in different laboratories in an attempt to replicate findings.

6. Imposing proper security measures that would prevent the alteration of experimental data.

7. Writing an adequate description of the experimental procedure beforehand, one that can be distributed to interested parties both inside and outside the parapsychological community. This description should state the purpose of the experiment and, when possible, construct a hypothesis that is clearly falsifiable (Krippner 1974, 1977).

It is apparent that some parapsychological research does not attain these standards. A committee of the U.S. National Research Council has concluded that there is 'no scientific justification from research conducted over a period of 130 years for the existence of parapsychological phenomena' (Holden, 1988). Even though the report extended the history of psi research by several decades, its conclusions are still severe.

One parapsychologist (Akers 1984), after scrutinizing 55 well-known psi experiments, reported that about 90% suffered from one or more methodological flaws; he concluded that parapsychology should be regarded as still in its 'preliminary stages'. It is crucial that psi researchers be vigilant because the accumulation of human knowledge depends upon research methods that are well conceptualized and carefully executed. If similar psi data begin to emerge from a variety of laboratories, and if they begin to fit into some pattern that yields explanations of their nature, the fraud hypothesis will not be parsimonious and will cease to be taken seriously.

Parapsychology as a Science

Some writers take the position that parapsychology does not qualify as a science, but this evaluation depends on the assumptions that one makes about scientific enterprises. Science emerged from philosophy and originally proclaimed itself as the search for the understanding of nature. As this quest became more disciplined, greater demands were placed upon scientific undertakings. Today there is a demand by some critics that parapsychology produce 'replicable' psi experiments and 'battle-tested' results before it can be considered a science.

At one level of investigation, there already are 'replications' and 'battle-tested' results, specifically the findings that about 50% of an unselected group will report having had a 'psychic experience'. This percentage may vary from one culture, age group, and educational level to the next, but it has been repeated, in one study after another, for the last several decades. Further, these experiences have been ignored or ridiculed by far too many behavioural and social scientists despite the recent findings indicating that this type of experience 'is not only potentially significant for our personal lives, but that it also serves important functions in our society as a whole' (Neher 1980, p. 292). Subjective psi experiences interface with heightened sensitivities, creative imagery, self-regulation of body processes, and increased memory, allowing science an expanded vision of human capacities (Neher 1980, p. 288). Therefore, the case for parapsychology is simply that an understanding of these reported experiences is worthy of significant research efforts (Neher 1980, p. 292).

Parapsychology has pioneered research into several aspects of human behaviour and experience that are now a part of mainstream psychology, e.g., hypnosis, multiple personalities, anomalous healing. Other parapsychological topics, i.e., lucid dreaming, near-death experiences, out-of-body experiences, are slowly beginning to enter the psychological mainstream (e.g., Irwin 1985; LaBerge 1985; Osis & Haraldsson 1977) and the mechanisms for these phenomena are on their way to becoming understood. Perhaps telepathy, clairvoyance, precognition, and psychokinesis will travel the same road.

Part of parapsychology's research direction has been to take as a starting point the subjective reports that have accumulated over the years and ask what ordinary psychological processes could account for them. This direction in contemporary parapsychology needs to be reinforced and extended. I would agree with Neher (1980, p. 295) that psi research should commit itself 'to following up all leads — even if they result in "physical" or "nonmysterious" explanations — that might be helpful in understanding extraordinary and seemingly inexplicable experience.' Certainly there is nothing in the prefix 'para' that excludes physical phenomena or mechanisms that are understandable. 'Parapsychology' simply means 'alongside of' the mainstream of psychology (Neher 1980, p. 295).

After reviewing the two fields, Collins and Pinch (1982, p. 57) conclude that 'there is . . . nothing in psychology that definitely makes parapsychology unscientific. They also claim that 'it has not been demonstrated decisively that there are any specific physical principles that conflict with parapsychology.' Truzzi (1980) would consider parapsychology to be a 'legitimate scientific enterprise' whether or not psi actually exists because parapsychologists employ such scientific methods as target randomization, double-blind judging, control groups, and statistical tests. For Leahy and Leahy (1983), 'methodologically, parapsychology is a science; substantially, the verdict is still out.'

In its 1985 report, the Parapsychological Association made it clear that 'labelling an event as a psi phenomenon does not constitute an explanation for an event, but only indicates an event for which a scientific explanation needs to be sought.[1] Furthermore, 'Regardless of what form the final explanation may take . . ., the study of these phenomena is likely to expand our understanding of the processes often referred to as 'consciousness' and 'mind' and of the nature of disciplined inquiry . . .'

Agreeing with this basic position, Hovelmann (another parapsychologist) and I (1986) have presented 11 recommendations for the future of parapsychology:

1. As long as we use orthodox scientific methodology in parapsychology, our findings are, by definition, non-revolutionary, even if they do provide data that require paradigm revision.

2. The data on the topic of life after death are even more ambiguous and unreliable than those obtained in laboratory research. Therefore, we should not express ourselves with certainty on this topic.

3. We should not base conclusions on evidence from spontaneous cases as this material is open to various kinds of flaws and overinterpretations.

4. We should not assume that we are able to explain psi phenomena by means of the present terminology (e.g., 'extrasensory' perception). These terms are merely descriptive and will probably change as a standardized, empirically constructed terminology emerges.

5. In view of the frequent non-uniform nature of our experimental findings, we should not resort to the claim that these inconsistencies are necessarily constituents of psi phenomena.

6. We should carefully consider the arguments of our critics and collaborate with the scientifically-minded among them whenever

possible. Perhaps the day will come when the distinction between psi proponents and psi critics will vanish as both join in common scientific endeavours.

7. We should separate ourselves from those claimants who put forward untestable, unfalsifiable notions permeated with super-naturalism and metaphysics. Instead, parapsychology needs to commit itself to intellectual self-discipline and critical judgment.

8. We should provide complete data when publishing an experiment. This procedure will encourage others to attempt replications and will help prevent critics of the field from making unjustified accusations.

9. We should devote more of our effort to replicating each others' work. There are theoretical reasons why strict replicability of psi experiments is unlikely, but this does not excuse researchers from attempting to repeat important studies or from examining the data for trends, patterns, and promising leads.

10. We should devote ourselves to more long-range planning and inter-laboratory communication. This is difficult given the limited financial resources in the field, but parapsychology will not move forward if its research efforts are fragmented and haphazardly planned.

11. We need to study the whole range of alleged psi phenomena no matter which explanation turns out to be useful. 'Psi' may turn out to be hitherto misunderstood interpersonal expectancy effects, over-looked statistical artifacts, or undetected field interactions. Any of these interpretations of psi would make a genuine and significant contribution to scientific knowledge.

In other words, the essential touchstones for parapsychologists include the need to stress the speculative nature of the field, to be candid about its controversial status, and not to go beyond what is warranted by the evidence. However, this modesty should be combined with a devotion to scientific procedures and a commitment to the search for discovery and understanding. As the Parapsychological Association report concluded, 'Parapsychology has a century-old tradition of bringing scientific imagination and rigor to the study of phenomena typically ignored by other investigators. Whatever the eventual outcome of this search may be, it cannot help but add to the sum of knowledge about humanity and the human condition.'

References

Akers, C. (1984), 'Methodological criticisms of parapsychology' in S. Krippner, ed., *Advances in Parapsychological Research*, vol. 4, Jefferson NC, McFarland.

Collins, H.M., & Pinch, T.J. (1982), *Frames of Meaning: The Social Construction of Extraordinary Science*, London, Routledge & Kegan Paul.

Edge, H.L., Morris, R.L., Palmer, J., & Rush, J.H. (1986), *Foundations of Parapsychology*, London, Routledge & Kegan Paul.

Furlow, R. (1986), 'UFOs for real? Many say "yes"', *Racine Journal Times*, February 14, p. 12.

Gallup, G., Jr., with Proctor, W. (1982), *Adventures in Immortality: A Look Beyond the Threshold of Death*, New York, McGraw-Hill.

Greeley, A.M. (1987), 'The impossible: It's happening', *American Health*, January–February, 32–33.

Hansel, C.E.M. (1980), *ESP and Parapsychology: A Critical Re-Evaluation*, Buffalo NY, Prometheus Books.

Hansel, C.E.M. (1981), 'A critical analysis of H. Schmidt's psychokinesis experiments', *Skeptical Inquirer*, Fall, 26–33.

Haraldsson, E. (1975), 'Reported dream recall, precognitive dreams, and ESP' in J.D. Morris, W.G. Roll, and R.L. Morris, eds., *Research in Parapsychology 1974*, Metuchen NJ, Scarecrow Press.

Holden, C. (1988), 'Academy helps army be all that it can be', *Science*, *238*, 1501–1502.

Honorton, C. (1974), 'Apparent psychokinesis on static objects by a "gifted" subject' in W.G. Roll, R.L. Morris, and J.D. Morris, eds., *Research in Parapsychology 1973*. Metuchen NJ, Scarecrow Press.

Houtkooper, J.M. (1977), 'A study of repeated retroactive psychokinesis in relation to direct and random PK effects', *European Journal of Parapsychology*, *1*, 1–20.

Hovelmann, G., & Krippner, S. (1986), 'Charting the future of parapsychology', *Parapsychology Review*, *17* (6), 1–5.

Hyman, R. (1981), 'Further comments on Schmidt's PK experiments', *Skeptical Inquirer*, Fall, 34–40.

Hyman, R., & Honorton, C. (1986), 'A joint communique: The psi ganzfeld controversy', *Journal of Parapsychology*, *50*, 351–364.

Irwin, H.J. (1979), 'Coding preferences and the form of spontaneous extrasensory experiences', *Journal of Parapsychology*, *43*, 205–220.

Irwin, H.J. (1985), *Flight of the Mind: A Psychological Study of the Out-of-Body Experience*, Metuchen NJ, Scarecrow Press.

Jahn, R. (1982), 'The persistent paradox of psychic phenomena: an engineering perspective', *Proceedings of the IEEE*, *70*, 136–170.

Krippner, S. (1974), 'Telepathy' in E.D. Mitchell & J. White, eds., *Psychic Exploration: A Challenge for Science*, New York, J.P. Putnam's Sons.

Krippner, S. (1977), 'Editorial', *Psychoenergetic Systems*, *2*, 5–11.

Krippner, S. (1984), 'The Randi caper', *Association for Humanistic Psychology Newsletter*, July, 20–21.

LaBerge, S. (1985), *Lucid Dreaming: The Power of Being Awake and Aware in Your Dreams*, Los Angeles, J.P. Tarcher.

Leahy, T.H. & Leahy, G.E. (1983), *Psychology's Occult Doubles: Psychology and the Problem of Pseudoscience*, Chicago, Nelson-Hall.

Mackenzie, A. (1987), 'How common are psychic experiences?' *Fate*, November, 42–50.

Marks, D., & McKellar, P. (1982), 'The nature and function of eidetic imagery', *Journal of Mental Imagery 6*, 1–124.

McCready, W.C., & Greeley, A.M. (1976), *The Ultimate Values of the American Population*, Beverly Hills CA, Sage.

Meadow, M.J., & Kanoe, R.D. (1984), *Psychology of Religion: Religion in Individual Lives*, San Francisco, Harper & Row.

Neher, A. (1980), *The Psychology of Transcendence*, Englewood Cliffs NJ, Prentice-Hall.

Osis, K., & Haraldsson, E. (1977), *At the Hour of Death*, New York, Avon.

Palmer, J. (1979), 'A community mail survey of psychic experiences', *Journal of the American Society for Psychical Research 73*, 221-251.

Pamplin, B., & Collins, H.M. (1985), 'Correspondence. Spoon-bending: An experimental approach', *Nature 257*, 8.

Persinger, M.A. (1974a), *The Paranormal. Part I. Patterns*, New York, MSS Information Corporation.

Persinger, M.A. (1974b), *The Paranormal. Part II. Mechanisms and Models*, New York, MSS Information Corporation.

Prasad, J., & Stevenson, I. (1968), 'A survey of spontaneous psychical experiences in school children of Uttar Pradesh, India', *International Journal of Parapsychology 10*, 241-261.

Posey, T.B., & Losch, M.E. (1983-1984), 'Auditory hallucinations of hearing voices in 375 normal subjects,' *Imagination, Cognition and Personality 3*, 99-113.

Radin, D.I., May, E.C., & Thompson, M.J. (1985), 'Psi experiments with random number generators: Meta-analysis. Part I', *Proceedings of the Parapsychological Association 28th Annual Convention*. vol. 1, Alexandria VA, Parapsychological Association.

Rao, K.R., & Palmer, J. (1988), 'The anomaly called psi: Recent research and criticism', *Behavioural and Brain Sciences*, 10, 538-551.

Rhine, L.E. (1977), 'Research methods with spontaneous cases' in B.B. Wolman, ed., *Handbook of Parapsychology*, New York, Van Nostrand Reinhold.

Sannwald, G. (1963), 'On the psychology of spontaneous paranormal phenomena', *International Journal of Parapsychology 5*, 274-292.

Schaut, G.B., & Persinger, M.A. (1985). 'Subjective telepathic experiences, geomagnetic activity and the ELF hypothesis. Part I. Data analysis', *Psi Research 4*(1), 4-20.

Schmidt, H. (1969), 'Precognition of a quantum process', *Journal of Parapsychology, 33*, 99-108.

Schmidt, H. (1970), 'A PK test with electronic equipment', *Journal of Parapsychology, 34*, 5-181.

Schmidt, H. (1981), 'PK tests with pre-recorded and pre-inspected seed numbers', *Journal of Parapsychology, 45*, 87-98.

Schmidt, H., Morris, R.L., & Rudolph, L. (1984), 'Channeling evidence for a psychokinetic effect to critical observers' in R.A. White & R. Broughton, eds., *Research in Parapsychology 1983*, Metuchen NJ, Scarecrow Press.

Sidgwick, H., Sidgwick, E., & Johnson, A. (1894). 'Report on the Census of Hallucinations', *Proceedings of the Society for Psychic Research 10*, 25-422.

Stevenson, I. (1970), *Telepathic Impressions*, Charlottesville VA, University of Virginia.

Tart, C.T. (1975), *States of Consciousness*, New York, E.P. Dutton.

Truzzi, M. (1985), 'A skeptical look at Paul Kurtz' analysis of the scientific status of parapsychology', *Journal of Parapsychology, 44*, 35-55.

Ullman, M., Krippner, S., & Vaughan, H. (1989), *Dream Telepathy* (2nd ed.), Jefferson NC, McFarland.

Vilenskaya, L. (1978). 'Clarification of factors which facilitate production of parapsychological abilities', *International Journal of Paraphysics 12*, 110.

Watkins, G.K., & Watkins, A.M. (1974), 'Apparent psychokinesis on static objects by a "gifted" subject: A laboratory demonstration' in W.G. Roll, R.L. Morris, and J.D. Morris, eds., *Research in Parapsychology 1973*, Metuchen NJ, Scarecrow Press.

Wilson, S.C., & Barber, T.X. (1982), 'The fantasy-prone personality: Implications for understanding imagery, hypnosis, and parapsychological phenomena', *Psi Research 1* (3), 944–1116.

CHAPTER 12
A SURVEY OF MYSTICAL, VISIONARY AND REMOTE PERCEPTION EXPERIENCES

Peter L. Nelson

Introduction

Looking back as far as the late Nineteenth Century, there have been a number of attempts to survey and classify the occurrence of mystical and religious experiences. Starbuck's survey of conversion (1899), which led to James' classic study (1936), was followed later on by Bucke's *Cosmic Consciousness* (1923), and then by Laski's informal inquiry into ecstatic experience (1961) and, more recently, by Hardy's media survey which provided an overwhelming quantity of anecdotal material (Hardy, 1979). Although these informal studies have always revealed a surprisingly widespread occurrence of these experiences, the myth of the rarity and exclusiveness of these encounters has tended to persist until the recent more rigorous surveys of Back and Bourque (1970), Thomas and Cooper in America (1978), Macleod-Morgan in Australia (1985) and Hay and Morisy in Great Britain (Hay and Morisy, 1978). These surveys have revealed that a consistent 20–40% of the population claim to have had at least one encounter of this type in a lifetime.

The survey of Back and Bourque was more a technical exercise in order to determine whether or not 'very private' experiences could be investigated through the employment of regular survey and interview techniques. They found this to be possible but concluded by stating:

> The greatest difficulty which we found was the definition of an absolute minimum level of the experiences to be reported. It seems reasonable that there is no standard against which to measure the strength of transcendental experiences, and consequently there is variability in defining when an experience is sufficiently strong to be reported in an interview . . . We have also seen that the attitude of the interviewer toward questions of this kind and the proportion of the whole interview devoted to such questions probably has a further, complicating effect on the threshold definition of the experiences reported. (K. Back and L. Bourque, 1970, p. 495)

Over the course of their three sample periods of 1962, 1966 and 1967, the question they employed ('Have you ever had a "religious or mystical experience" that is, a moment of sudden religious insight or awakening?') brought increasing positive response rates of 20.5, 31.8 and 41.2 percent, respectively. They concluded that it was not a function of cultural change which caused the progressive increase over the three Gallup polls, but rather the interview technique which affected the threshold of what an experient would consider reportable (K. Back and L. Bourque, 1970, p. 493).

Thomas and Cooper found that one third of their respondents had had intense experiences which they described as spiritual in nature. They, too, concluded that these apparently subjective encounters could be studied through the application of standard social science techniques. They employed Greeley's general question ('Have you ever had the feeling of being close to a powerful spiritual force that seemed to lift you out of yourself?') and categorized the responses into four types which included 1) Uncodable (8%); 2) Mystical (2%); 3) Psychic (12%); 4) Faith and Consolation (12%) (Greeley, 1974).

Hay's qualitative study also used a single, catch-all question ('Do you feel that you have ever been aware of or influenced by a presence or a power, whether you call it God or not, which is different from your everyday self?') and produced a 65% positive response rate amongst postgraduate students in a department of education (1979). This sample revealed a statistically non-significant higher proportion of men claiming to have had these experiences, although in a larger-scale national study conducted together with Ann Morisy, the proportion of women to men was a significant 4:3 (1978). Most of Hay's sample reported that their encounters first occurred during mid-adolescence, a fact which concurs with Starbuck. Hay feels this fact points to a 'deep structure', which for him, as for Hardy, is biological (Hay, 1979; Hardy, 1966).

Hay's classification of experience types contained a more detailed breakdown and included 1) Awareness of a power controlling and guiding me; 2) Awareness of the presence of God; 3) Awareness of a presence in nature; 4) Answered prayer; 5) Experience of a unity with nature; 6) ESP, Out-of-the-body, visions, etc.; 7) Awareness of an evil power; 8) Conversion. These categories apparently were drawn from the subject's descriptions. Hay (1979) concludes that with the increasing acceptance of the phenomenological approach in the study of 'private' experience, as witnessed in cognitive anthropology, for example, it is now possible to provide increasingly accurate descriptions of religious experience from a position of ontological neutrality. He feels that although these experiences do not fit our usual definitions of reality, viz., by being repeatable and distinct, they are often believed by experients to be more 'real' than ordinary events. He further argues that although there is a great deal of paradox surrounding the occurrence and reportage of these experiences, their recurrence and apparent uniformity and consistency fits the requirements underlying all objective science.

The variety of experience types that have been reported in response to the single, catch-all questions quoted above open the possibility that we are looking at a broader phenomenon than the previous studies would indicate. Questions couched in religious and/or spiritual terms will obviously miss potential respondents who do not conceptualize their experiences in this way, and those who do may be dismissive of those experiences which do not appear to include an existential shift in ontological perspective in which a 'higher' being or reality appears to be perceived. The previous studies also have been lacking in a clear conceptualization of what they are exploring. This might account for the significant number of 'uncodable' responses in the Thomas and Cooper study and for the mixture of rational processes (for example, as in the case of 'conversion') coupled with encounters of 'other worldly' powers such as an 'awareness of a power controlling and guiding me'. From the results of these surveys it is apparent there is a need to operationalize the definition of this class of events *prior to* the collection of data, rather than making a *post hoc* assignment of categories. This present study attempts to do just this. The class of events was first conceptually operationalized and then a questionnaire was developed which specified the subclasses as specific questions about specific types of experiences. This method is described in the section which follows.

Methodology

In this chapter we will present the results of a non-random survey conducted in selected departments and schools at the University of Queensland and Griffith University in South East Queensland. As in the previous surveys cited above, we will accept, in this study, the use of phenomenological report of private experience, even though we feel that the questions of Hay and others were both too vague and conceptually loaded with a religious bias. As already indicated the potpourri of responses obtained in the earlier studies, some classically religious in quality and others not, indicate a possible relationship amongst a fairly broad range of experience types. For heuristic purposes we shall call this class of phenomena *praeternatural* experience.[2] Like the conceptualization of Hultkrantz (1983), we must look to the intended quality of 'supernaturalness' but, similar to Hay's position, this usage does not imply any final ontological position. Such a definition operationalizes the events in question as being members of the class of the præternatural in that they appear to derive from a 'supernatural' source or somehow stand apart from everyday sensate experience and, in addition, they are recalled in response to the eleven specific categories given in the questionnaire.

Based on the work cited above and information gathered in a preliminary survey,[3] eleven categories of experience were devised and appropriate questions formulated as part of the questionnaire used in this survey. These categories were: 1) conversion (changing or adopting religious worldview); 2) presence of God or other spiritual power; 3) mystical experience (sense of unity and/or merger with cosmic or ultimate ground of being); 4) the sacred (Otto's Numinous Experience [1958] or Zaehner's panenhenic experience [1980]; 5) near-death-experience (trauma and accident involving visions and/or 'other worldly' experiences); 6) visionary experience (all extra-sense modality veridical-like perceptions); 7) contact with the spirit realm (sensing presences that are not there in a physical way); 8) out-of-the-body-experience (perceptions of flying without extra physical means and perceptions which involve awareness of 'self' as separate from 'body'); 9) remote perception (pre-, post-cognition and telepathy); 10) the existential void (loss of sense of self and existential certainty); and 11) other-world experience (shamanic-like journeys or encounters).

These questions comprised part 2 of the questionnaire. Part 1 requested details of name, address, sex, age, nationality, marital status, education, qualifications and religious affiliation and attendance. Part 3 sought details on attempts made to induce these experiences (if any), self-perception of religiosity and/or spirituality, religious practice (prayer or meditation), drugs usage and mental illness.

A total of 1160 questionnaires were distributed to both staff and students in the departments of Studies in Religion, Social Work, Classics and Ancient History, Education and Philosophy, as well as in the counselling service at the University of Queensland and in the schools of Science, Social and Industrial Administration and Modern Asian Studies at Griffith University. From this canvassing, 316 usable questionnaires were returned and formed the data base for the following discussion. The following section presents the statistical breakdown for the collected data and can be skipped if desired. Section 4, Discussion of Results, presents the qualitative findings of the survey with examples of the types of experiences and a discussion of these results. However, tables 1–3 give breakdowns of the experience types and their frequencies which would also be of interest to the non-statistical reader.

Statistical Findings

The survey sample contained an equal number of men and women (Total N = 316) with a mean age of 29.5 years (min. = 16; max = 65). About 90% of the sample claimed some Christian denomination as their religion at birth with slightly more than 8% claiming no religious affiliation and the remaining 2% accounted for by two Jews, one Moslem and three Buddhists. A Student's t-Test of means for education across sex revealed a significant difference in total years of education between men and women ($p < 0.01$), with men showing a mean of 15.1 years and women 14.2 years. Although men showed a higher average number of qualifications, this difference was not significant ($p > 0.05$). Differences in church attendance between men and women were insignificant as well as those between the sexes on self-perceived religiosity/spirituality. As one would expect, there was a significant dependent relationship between self-perceived religiosity and rank order of rate of church attendance (Chi-Square = 53.6, $p < 0.001$) (Ott, Larson and Mendenhall, 1983).

Respondents were asked to rank the frequency of each of their præternatural experiences on a five point scale, indicating the total occurrence of each event in a life-time. The ranges were roughly logarithmic and were: 'never'; '1–5 times'; '6–20 times'; '21–99 times'; and '100+ times'. From these responses each experience was placed on a rank ranging from 0–4 and a total summary rank was calculated across all experiences for each experient and, in addition, the total number of different experience types was scored for each subject. The distribution of experients and non-experients for all types of præternatural experiences in this survey can be seen in Table 1. The sample obtained contained an overall positive response rate of 82.59% with women showing a higher, but non-significant average total ranking (women = 2.27, men = 1.97; $p > 0.05$; See Table 2). Women also showed a greater average variety of experience types (maximum of 10; women = 3.11, men = 2.59) which was not statistically significant, however (Table 3).

Question 14 of the survey asked if the respondent saw him/herself as a 'religious' or 'spiritual' person. This question did not attempt to differentiate Allport's and Ross's *extrinsic/intrinsic* dimension (1977) but some respondents tended to cross out the word 'religious' in the question and then answer it positively. However, the Chi-Square of religiosity versus rank order of total experience frequency yielded a highly significant result ($X^2 = 27.86$, $p < .001$, Cramer's V = .298). The mean rank of total præternatural experience for those identifying themselves as religious or spiritual was 2.43 as opposed to 1.73 for those not. A Kruskal-Wallis ANOVA of ranks performed on total experience rank on the factor of religiosity also yielded a highly significant result ($H = 18.877$, $p < .001$) (Ott, Larson and Mendenhall, 1983). When the responses to questions 2-4 of the questionnaire (presence of God, mystical experience and experience of the sacred) were separated from the others, it was found that most of the significance on the factor of religiosity was attributable to questions 2-4. This seems logical because anyone who ascribes labels and meanings such as God and the sacred to the experiences will, in all likelihood, see themselves as religious and/or spiritual. Whether or not it would be useful to separate the concepts of religiosity and spirituality remains to be ascertained in future research. However, these terms are vague in most minds and a clear operational definition would have to be established first.

Responses to questions 12 and 13 were combined so that any attempt or not to induce præternatural experience could be assigned to one of four categories: never tried (No Try); tried but never succeeded (Negative Try); tried and sometimes succeeded (Sometimes); and whenever tried always succeeded (Always). The Chi-Square of this variable against rank order of total experience yielded a highly significant result ($X^2 = 53.87$, $p < .001$, Cramer's V = .238), as did a Kruskal-Wallis ANOVA of frequency rank across the above factor of directed (Active) effort ($H = 41.761$, $p < .001$).

It must be noted that of those respondents reporting some experience, more than half (149) never made any active induction attempt. However, for those who did, there was a clear trend of increasing direct conscious involvement with the occurrence of præternatural experiences as subjects had increasing numbers of them. Whether this was cause or effect remains to be seen in further studies.

Respondents were asked to rank their level of religious practice ('meditation, prayer or any similar activity') into one of five levels: Never; 1-4 times/month; 5-10 times/month; 11-29 times/month; and 30+ times/month. Again, a Chi-Square against total experience rank orders revealed a significant dependency relationship ($X^2 = 50.20$, $p < .001$, Cramer's V = .1999) and a Kruskal-Wallis ANOVA of total experience rank across the factor of religious practice yielded a highly significant statistic ($H = 22.649$, $p < .001$). Of course, it is not possible to assign a causal direction (if in fact there is one), but the numbers of those who practised more frequently increased as the rank order of præternatural experience frequency increased and the mean rank of experience rate appeared to increase with increasing religious practice (Mean ranks of religious practice = 1.78; 2.14; 2.48; 2.38; 2.69). Although more than half (164) claimed that they did not engage in any

Survey of Mystical, Visionary and Remote Perception Experience

Table 1
Distribution of Experience Types vs Sex

Experience Type	Total	Male	Female	% Total	% Male*	% Female*
NONE	55	34	21	17.4	61.8	38.2
GOD	146	66	80	46.2	45.2	54.8
MYSTICAL	84	44	40	26.6	52.4	47.6
NUMINOUS	115	47	68	36.4	40.9	59.1
NDE	27	10	17	8.5	37.0	63.0
VISIONARY	62	29	33	19.6	46.8	53.2
PRESENCE	113	48	65	35.8	42.5	57.5
OBE	103	49	54	32.6	47.6	52.4
REMOTE PERCEPTION	176	77	99	55.7	43.8	56.2
EXISTENTIAL LOSS	57	31	26	18.0	54.4	45.6
SHAMANIC	24	15	9	7.6	62.5	37.5

* These percentages indicate the proportion of men and women represented in each category.

Table 2
Distribution of Experience Frequency Rank vs Sex

Frequency Rank	Total	Male	Female	% Total	% Male*	% Female*
0 (Never)	55	34	21	17.4	61.8	38.2
1–5 (Low)	65	34	31	20.6	52.3	47.7
6–20 (Medium)	65	29	36	20.6	44.6	55.4
21–99 (Med-High)	49	25	24	15.5	51.0	49.0
100+ (High)	82	36	46	26.0	43.9	56.1

* These percentages indicate the proportion of men and women represented in each category.

Table 3
Distribution of Præternatural Experience Type Totals vs Sex

Number of types	Total	Male	Female	% Total	% Male*	% Female*
0	55	34	21	17.4	61.8	38.2
1	51	26	25	16.1	51.0	49.0
2	54	26	28	17.1	48.1	51.9
3	47	20	27	14.9	42.6	57.4
4	42	21	21	13.3	50.0	50.0
5	20	11	9	6.3	55.0	45.0
6	18	11	7	5.7	61.1	38.9
7	11	2	9	3.5	18.2	81.8
8	10	4	6	3.2	40.0	60.0
9	5	3	2	1.6	60.0	40.0
10	3	0	3	1.0	0.0	100.0

* These percentages indicate the proportion of men and women represented in each category.

religious practice, it would be an interesting empirical investigation to determine whether experience leads one into practice or vice versa. From causal observation, one is tempted to conclude that increasing occurrences of præternatural events lead to increased overall interest and involvement in their meaning and occurrence and hence the adoption of activities, such as meditation, believed to be germinal to experience induction.

Finally, Figures 1 and 2 graphically display the mean rank of experience rate for the factors of 'religiosity' and 'practice' of those experience types which show a statistically significant difference. Numerical values of mean rank are displayed at the top of each column, thereby depicting the relationship of these factors to the average rate of occurrence of præternatural experience for all subjects.[4]

Figure 1

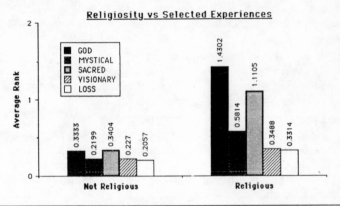

Religiosity vs Selected Experiences

Figure 2

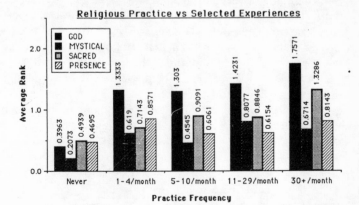

Religious Practice vs Selected Experiences

Discussion of Results

The positive response rate of 82.59% is higher than in any other previously reported studies. This could be due to the voluntary and hence self-selecting nature of the survey. If all those questionnaires not returned or returned but not properly completed were counted as non-experients, then the response rate would be 22.50%, which still falls well within the range of these other studies. No doubt unwillingness to take the time to fill in such a lengthy questionnaire would account for many who failed to return them. Meanwhile, the high positive response rate also may be due in part to the fact that subjects who have had experiences (like those described in the questionnaire) would be more likely to complete it because of personal interest in the material, although this certainly would not be their only reason for compliance. In addition, and germinal to the position of this chapter, the high positive response rate may be due to operationalising this class of experience as well as increasing the number and degree of specificity of the questions asked, thus effectively lowering the threshold for subjects of what they would consider a reportable event. This seems to confirm the position taken by Back and Bourque when rationalizing the progressive increase in response rates in their studies. In this case, however, it is the questionnaire which provides a broader and more 'sympathetic' field of enquiry rather than the interviewer.

Hay, when reporting his qualitative survey of postgraduate education students, explained his higher than average (65%) response rate as due to the quasi-religious nature of an educational vocation (1979, p. 166). This fact (if it is so), in conjunction with the possibility that professional educators may give wider and more varied interpretations to Hay's catch-all question will, in effect, generate results more in line with our hypothesized position, viz., this class of events will be better tapped by subdividing it into several types and asking a variety of questions of the survey sample. It is possible that the converse of the usual 'minority' hypothesis for these events is true. In other words, it may be a minority of the population which does not have or is incapable of remembering having had some sort of præternatural experience. The solution, as being suggested here, may be one of ascertaining the appropriate questions to ask and then surveying broadly enough, as well as setting the threshold at a sufficiently low level vis-à-vis Back and Bourque.

For example, as revealed in the interviews conducted as part of this study, a supposed *non-experient* was asked to relate an episode from her life which stood out clearly in her memory. She responded by relating an event which was unmistakably a 'pre-cognitive' type remote perception. She had failed to relate this occurrence to question 9 in the survey, even though she had understood the question. When asked about her failure to recognize the event as pertinent to the survey, she replied that she did not think that it was the type of event to which the questionnaire referred. It was revealed also in subsequent interviews that several others had failed to record all relevant events. The most common reason given for these omissions was that respondents believed that the events in question were not significant enough or they were not 'religious'. It seems that for some subjects the mere fact that the questionnaire was distributed from the department of Studies in Religion meant, ipso facto, that their experiences must have religious significance to be of interest.

In this section each of the eleven questions and their associated præternatural experience types will be further delineated and discussed drawing from specific examples of experient responses. Although 'conversion' was considered to be a possible result of a præternatural experience but not an occurrence itself, it is still included to illustrate the type of responses to this question. Following each præternatural experience category heading are the significance levels (if any) for the Kruskal–Wallis ANOVA for the experience rank (rate) across the factors of 'religiosity' and 'practice'. These statistics are then followed by the question used to evoke the response in each category together with response examples and discussion of the responses.

1. Conversion

> 'Have you ever encountered a time in your life, either precipitated by crisis or good times, which led to a relatively sudden revision of values and a desire to join a religion?'

This category is *not* counted as a præternatural experience in the final tally of responses because while it may be the end result of a præternatural encounter, it does not meet the operational definition of 'supernatural' giveness. Wainwright separates what he calls ordinary religious experiences, which are bound up with devotional life, from the mystical and numinous ones.

> Nevertheless these more ordinary experiences should, I think, be distinguished both from numinous experiences and from mystical experiences, for they do not appear to involve the sense of immediate presence which characterizes the latter. For the same reason, there is no *prima facie* case for the supposition that these experiences provide an independent source of knowledge, that they involve a glimpse of reality or some aspect of reality which is normally hidden from us. (Wainwright, 1975)

It is for this reason as well that the question on conversion is asked but not counted in the total score of præternatural experiences. This question can help us to evaluate questions 2, 3 and 4 which are sometimes answered affirmatively when, in fact, they refer to Wainwright's ordinary, devotional experience. An example of a typical conversion is given by a 33 year old woman:

> The first time (was when) I was 25, I had had a series of terrifying nightmares and a number of other experiences including feeling a 'presence' which seemed very hostile. The second, I was 32, (an experience) at the other end of the spectrum ... there is beauty, worthwhileness in life (which) encouraged me to take up yoga and learn about meditation.

The conversion was instigated by the experiences, but was not the experience itself. Another typical example is illustrative of the role of emotional upheaval and loss in the conversion process. An 18 year old male reported:

> During early weeks at the University I became very depressed and everything went down hill. Meanwhile my elder brother and sister appeared to have everything go right. They were both members of the Way International Research Group. Hence my affiliation with the group.

No doubt præternatural experience often plays a role in the process that leads to conversion, but in terms of the above operational definition, we cannot include this type of behaviour as an experience relevant to this study.

2. Presence of God or other spiritual power

Religiosity: H = 73.8, p < 0.001; Practice: H = 82.3, p < 0.001][5]

> 'Do you feel that you have ever been directly aware of or influenced by the presence of God; or, have you ever felt as though you were very close to a powerful spiritual force that seemed to lift you out of yourself?'

This was an adaptation of Hay's more general question combined with Greeley's. By using the combination, it was hoped that the intent of the question would indicate a perspective broader than standard theological conceptualizations of God, whilst including an experience of divinity as a subset of the general class. A typical example of a response to this question was that of a 55 year old female:

> Around age 35. Facing surgery — terrified — prayed — an inexplicable calm followed. I felt 'outside myself'.

Many responses did, however, indicate that the subject's experience was very shaped by religious beliefs as in the case of this 29 year old female:

I think I have become aware of the presence of 'God', since in certain stressful times I may close my eyes and feel myself going deep within and everything is dark and quiet. Twice when I have done this, outward circumstances have changed, as if someone understood and intervened.

But some who had this kind of experience did not find it 'protective' or re-assuring, such as this 20 year old female:

Went to a bible study class with a friend — to find out what bible study is. I was 19+ and it was 3:30 pm in the afternoon . . . sitting around a dining table and discussing the bible. I questioned the truth of the bible and God at that time. The lesson ended at 5:30 pm, we prayed and I felt something strange happening — as if my soul or body was going to leave my chair. I was going to fly, lifted up by some power. I got scared, so I opened my eyes and everything was normal again.

In quite a few instances, across several of the experience types, one can place a number of the experiences in more than one category. The one chosen by the experient, however, seems to be dependent on which characteristics or experiential qualities are emphasized in the recall. This, of course, will be influenced by the religious and cultural backgrounds of the experients, operating on the three levels of interpretation as suggested by Moore (1978).[6] The following encounter by a 39 year old female could be interpreted as the 'sensing of a presence' (question 7), but in this case the ontology was understood as divine by the recipient and hence placed in answer to this question.

I was aged 31 at the time of my 2nd daughter's birth. When told of her chances of survival (premature baby) and during the following crucial 48 hours I constantly felt 'someone' was with me, and encouraging me to keep faith. This, I did, and she pulled through.

It is possible that præternatural experience may take on religious significance and meaning as a result of what might be labelled 'ontic shift'. For example, two subjects can each have a pre-cognitive experience and whereas one will interpret the episode as an extension of perception beyond ordinary sensate experience, the other will attribute to it a divine, 'cosmic' or ontologically 'other' source. The research currently being undertaken here appears to indicate that this ascription is a result of an experient feeling 'as if' there has been an ontological 'shift', viz., a sudden change into another 'reality' or 'plane' and/or making contact with other-worldly 'beings'. For others, on the other hand, a similar phenomenological occurrence does not appear to have the same degree of existential impact and thus does not engender such beliefs. This, of course, is not an attempt to 'reduce' the ultimate ontology of these events to mere psychological factors, but rather to suggest how the assignment of category might be made by the experient. In positing this notion of 'ontic shift', we are attempting to follow Smart's advice and separate that which is believed to be 'real', from that which may or may not 'exist' (1973, p. 54). Reality in this definition seems to be what is personally and culturally acceptable as 'sensate experience' and 'knowledge', whereas the ultimate ontology of the events (once 'bracketed')[7] in question remains, like the hidden variables of quantum physics, unknown directly and most likely unknowable (Bohm, 1985). However, 'ontic shift' results when we attempt to re-assign the experience of reality as coming from a new or wholly 'other' source.

3. Mystical experience

Religious: $H = 13.5$, $p < 0.001$; Practice: $H = 26.6$, $p < 0.001$]

> 'Would you say that you have had a "mystical experience"; that is, an *intense* sense of union with the cosmic, divine or ultimate ground of being?'

This category was intended to coincide with Stace's 'introvertive' mysticism (1960, pp. 110–111) but did not try to make discriminations like those of Zaehner, comparing Christian with other types of mysticism (1980). This question did, however, bring forth a variety of experiences, some of which fit the classic definitions of mystical experience. Take this report by a 21 year old male:

> I had a particular experience once, while in the privacy of my own room. I felt and had such an intense union with God that I blacked out.

On the other hand, some responses in this category seemed to be more like Laski's description of ecstasy, as in this case of a 50 year old male whose experience was triggered by an intense aesthetic awareness:

> At a concert in the City Hall when (I was) around 18 years old. In the middle of Schumann's piano concerto I had a mind blowing awareness of PURE BEAUTY. Time seemed to stop and I was lifted to a state of bliss.

Other episodes, such as the following one reported by a 20 year old female, were less specific and somewhat vague about the phenomenological content.

> My 'mystical' experience happened when I was in Indonesia on a student exchange — I was 18 at the time. Thirty of us had climbed up to a temple (Imogiri) in the mountains of Java. After waiting an hour, we were sent into the shrine one by one, made to crouch prostrate in front of the shamans and a blessing was given over our heads. I did feel something, as if I was a part of a whole universal entity or something 'whole'.

Still others contained a number of James' classic elements such as transience and passivity (1936, p. 372) and, in this case of a 28 year old male, photism or the experience of the 'light' as described by Bucke (1923, pp. 72–73):

> ... whilst receiving a meditation technique, fully conscious, I saw a hand, palm forward, in front of me which moved aside to reveal a brilliant light ... it was very momentary — as soon as I noted to myself what I was experiencing it disappeared and everything was normal.

A few respondents indicated that they wanted to reply affirmatively to this question, but felt that their experiences were not intense enough to fulfil the requirements. However, others described a continuous background awareness as being mystical in quality. As in some of the other categories, these descriptions could be placed with the 'sacred' as well. Again, this may be a function of setting the threshold to a lower level and increasing the number and variety of questions in order to attain a higher degree of specificity.

4. The sacred (Numinous)

[Religious: $H = 35.8$, $p < 0.001$; Practice: $H = 30.4$, $p < 0.001$]

> 'Have you ever experienced a sense of the sacred in everything around you in which you perceived that all was connected as one?'

This roughly corresponds to Stace's 'extrovertive' mysticism (1960, pp. 61–62) as well as Otto's 'numinous' experience but does not necessarily include the sense of the 'Tremendum' (1958). Typical of this category is Zaehner's *panenhenic* or nature mysticism (1980, p. 28) as reported, for example, by a 42 year old female respondent:

> After an exhausting personal-growth course weekend I stretched out on the grass in a park and suddenly felt I was not 'on' the grass, but 'of' the grass, (and the trees, and the sky, and the river).

The majority of the responses to this question fell into this category, but the experience was not confined to beautiful natural surroundings as exemplified by this 36 year old female:

> The feeling of 'oneness' and incredible order in the universe and euphoria with it has happened just out of the blue with no wanting many times. I remember one incident when I was washing up! Suddenly, every action took on a special meaning and somehow fitted into a higher order of unity.

However, the experience was not always blissful and it is in these instances that we may be seeing the 'Tremendum' come into play in its negative aspect. A 20 year old female related:

> The most recent experience was about 2 months ago. I was studying late

for mid-semester exams. Round about midnight, I was alone and I suddenly felt frightened of everything — of everything around me, except my books.

For a minority, on the other hand, the experience of unity and sacredness stems from a rational source, as in the case of this 38 year old male:

> As a practising scientist I have often perceived the oneness of our world, our natural relationship with it, and the remarkable synthesis of fundamental laws which govern its behaviour. The unfolding truth about the nature of this universe presents us with a story far more remarkable and fascinating than imagination could create.

One is not sure, however, from such descriptions whether this rational entry has the same existential power and impact on awareness and perception that is reported by the majority of experients in this category who experience the 'numinous' or the *panenhenic*.

5. Near death experience (trauma)

[Religious: NS; Practice: NS]

'Have you ever had an accident or major surgery after which you remember having had a intense vision or awareness?'

This question overlaps somewhat with questions 6, 7 and 8 in that it evokes experiences of those types but within the context of trauma. It encompasses what has come to be called 'near death experience' (Moody, 1975). However, it is somewhat broader, including 'visionary', 'out-of-the-body' and 'presence' experiences. The classic 'near death experience' as described by Moody appears to show a phenomenological similarity over a broad range of reports. In this survey, on the other hand, very few responded positively to this question (8.7%) and still fewer from the sample fitted Moody's description. One that approached the standard scenario was reported by a 58 year old female:

> I had lost a lot of blood, and was virtually bleeding to death (unknown to me at that time). I had sunk down into a lovely cool cave outside of which greenery grew and water ran. I seemed to understand that I was dying, but had no fear — this place was where I wanted to be. I felt safe and secure. Fortunately (??), doctors and nurses rushing around brought me back to a slight measure of consciousness — I was being given blood transfusions.

The common element of the 'light' is missing, as are the 'guides' who so often appear in these recollections, but the elements of a sense of peace and 'going home' are illustrated by the contentment with her surroundings.

Another commonly reported aspect of traumatic or life-threatening episodes, often portrayed in fiction, is the instant replay of events and the flashing past of one's whole life, as illustrated in this example of a 36 year old female:

> During a car accident where I was the driver and only vehicle involved, I experienced a slowing down of the events and a sort of flashing past of my whole life. I thought of an old woman with whom I had had professional contact. She had advanced cancer and I was involved in getting her to hospital. I later learned she had died at the same time I had the accident.

This experience also contains an element of unconscious 'remote perception' (question 9) or what Jung would have called 'synchronicity' (1969, Vol. 8). The separation of these classes of experience has primarily a heuristic value and their overlap can be seen as further evidence for the need to place them in the single operational class of the præternatural, yet maintaining the distinctions which differentiate them. NDE's, in particular, appear to be defined primarily by the traumatic method of induction but contain phenomenology and existential qualities from a number of the other categories.

Another example of an obvious crossing over of 'types' is seen in this experience of a 54 year old male:

> Sitting in a chair and having the feeling of drifting/sinking slowly backwards — (jumped up abruptly) and saying as I was standing up — I'm not ready to die yet.

The 'sinking' sensation might be understood as the early stages of a 'merger' with some other 'reality' but for this subject the experience was of falling and dying. For others it might herald the beginning of an out-of-body experience (question 8) or a mystical experience (question 3), depending on the ontological status and meaning given to it by the experient.

The traumatic type of experience often leads to a revamping of personal values, as in the case of a 48 year old female:

> At age 46 I suffered a post operative pulmonary clot and I realized I could have very easily died. The awareness I experienced was a clear understanding of who were the givers and the takers in my life. It was the first time I understood why I did not want certain people near me as I had nothing left to give. I also experienced a need to live for myself and not for my children. It led me to a determination to get on with my life.

This sort of change in existential perspective has often been heralded as one of the typical end results of mystical experience. Bharati argues against this when he asserts, for example, that if one was a 'stinker' before a mystical encounter, one will probably remain so afterwards unless one makes particular efforts in an ethical direction (1976, p. 53). The mystical experience, itself, will not necessarily alter an experient in this dimension. This may be the case, but when præternatural experiences engender a radical 'ontic shift', the likelihood of efforts towards ethical transformation seem to increase. Perhaps it is this sudden change of perspective in which one finds oneself cast in a new image in relation to the world which provides a radically different awareness of self and thus a need to revamp one's ethics to match the newly experienced ontological relationship.

6. Visionary experience

[Religious: NS; Practice: NS]

'Have you ever seen or heard something which you realized in retrospect was not really there in the same way as ordinary everyday objects, people and events?'

This category included the 'seeing' of spectres, people and events which appeared to be occurring contemporaneously and co-spatially but were not presented in the normal sensate manner. Hearing voices and music that did not come from the usual physical sources were also included. Something during the event or immediately after it made the recipient of the vision aware that it was not happening in the usual physical way. As stated previously, there has been a considerable overlap of types and although the following experience of a 40 year old female was initiated by a car accident (trauma), its visionary qualities were dominant and so she responded with it to question 6.

The day before my 21st birthday — in the middle of crashing a car which had gone out of control, with no control in the wheel, flying through the air, I saw, and felt two hands placed over mine on the wheel, and the wheel was WRENCHED around to the other direction. The hands were greenish white, very strong, old Man's hands, with gnarled knuckles and raised semi-lunar valves. The sleeves were caftan-like, and disappeared into nothingness. The other occupant of the car also had his hands on the wheel, and felt the strength of the wrench, but did not see the hands. A car coming the other way, stopped, expecting to see us killed as the car was flying through the air; when suddenly, it veered in mid air and went the other way. Neither of us in the car were hurt. I had the mental message at the time it happened; 'Not yet. You have much more to learn.' I have been doing my best to learn ever since.

The sense of being 'guided' and 'protected' by a higher power, and hence an engendered 'ontic shift', was present here with attendant changes in life meaning and values.

Less dramatic and more typical was the following encounter of a 33 year old female:

> I awoke to find someone beside my bed, who beckoned me to go with
> them. I started to get up, but became very frightened and panicky. The
> person slowly vanished.

This night-time encounter of an unexplained 'guest' who then 'fades
way' is by far the most typical. Experients often reported being
awakened to find the spectre standing at the end of the bed trying to
attract attention. Here, too, there is a cross-over between what is
generally believed to be religious experience and a 'psychic' one, as
illustrated in this example from a 45 year old male:

> The only experience I would equate with my understanding of a 'vision'
> occurred one Christmas Eve about 6–7 years ago. I was in bed (but not
> asleep), very stimulated by a moving Christmas Eve service. I can only
> describe what happened as a sense of being surrounded by light and
> hearing exultant singing that I did not recognize. It left me with a feeling
> of elation.

Here the visionary and auditory event has a definite religious form and
possesses the quality of having emanated from some spiritual, other-
worldly source.

7. Contact with the spirit realm (presences)

[Religious: NS; Practice: NS]

> 'Have you ever felt a presence of someone who was not there in a
> physical way?'

This category was primarily concerned with the sudden feeling that
someone or something was present when there was no outward
physical or usual sense modality experience. Perhaps the most often
reported episode of this type was the feeling of a weight on the chest —
as if another body was pinning the experient down when there was
nobody apparently there in the usual way. A 42 year old female related
a typical instance:

> I was asleep. It was my first day in London so I had gone to bed fairly
> early. I became conscious of a weight on my body that felt like the
> weight of a man. I was startled and reached for my money belt even
> though half asleep. Next I was aware of a shiny blue coat moving
> through the light from the street. During my stay in this house I was
> often aware of other presences.

A variant on the above encounter was that of being physically
touched by a disincarnate 'hand' as reported by this 28 year old
female:

> I awoke one night with the awareness that 'someone' had laid a hand
> 'gently' across my forehead. I really felt this physical force and awoke
> with a scream. Although the presence was momentarily still there —

there was in fact no one else in the room or house.

In response to this question several experients claimed that the presence they sensed was God or Jesus Christ. In all such cases the subjects were committed Christians and tended to actively and apparently consciously filter all their experiences through this worldview in the manner of Moore's retrospective interpretation. Occasionally, however, as in the case of this 18 year old committed Christian male, the presence was oppositely interpreted:

> When sleeping or near awakening I felt the presence of some*thing* very powerful and highly evil which appeared in the roof corner of my room and seemed to spread throughout the room and crush me.
> When awakening I felt the presence of something or someone lying across or on top of my body and crushing me in its embrace. I could not open my eyes and when I screamed no sound emerged. The experience only halted after I began to mentally pray to God to help me.

By far the most common experience was 'feeling' the active presence of a dead relative or friend. This appeared to be particularly noticeable for experients immediately after such a death, with the 'presence' gradually becoming less distinct and finally fading away over a period of time ranging from days to years. In some cases, there even may have been physical sensations, like being caressed or touched by the presence, but in most of these episodes the encounter was experienced as reassuring as, for example, with this 40 year old female:

> (The) events (took place) during (my) mid-thirties, but occurred separately, over a period of some few days immediately after the deaths of two people who were both close to me and whose deaths saddened me greatly. The feeling of their presence was diffused rather than . . . being any sort of life-like apparition. The effect was a reassuring one and not frightening in any way.

Again, in the above episodes, we see the crossing over of phenomenological types such as visionary experience (question 6) and the experience of 'presences' in which one either 'feels' the 'presence' and then sees the apparition or vice versa. As noted above, the 'presence' sensed can be religiously interpreted in either its positive or negative aspect and thus phenomenologically also crosses over into question 2 (God or spiritual force) as well.

8. Out-of-the-body-experience

[Religious: NS; Practice: NS]

'Have you ever had a vivid experience, *while either awake or dreaming*, of suddenly finding yourself in a new location apart from where you recall yourself last being physically; and/or, have you had the sensation of 'flying' to a new location without any physical means; and/or, have you had the experience of seeing yourself from a perspective 'outside' of yourself?'

Although there were occasional problems of misinterpretation of this question, most participants seemed to grasp its intent. A small minority, however, answered positively when referring to the sudden location changes that are often experienced in 'normal' dreaming and were therefore eliminated from this category. A common response from those who understood the intent of the question was typified by this report of a 23 year old female:

> I sometimes see myself lying in bed at night from the top of the room (when I'm awake, but with my eyes closed).
> I sometimes get the feeling I'm 'flying' out of myself and end up somewhere I'm not at all familiar with.

This report contains the two most common phenomenological features of this category; 1) visualizing oneself (one's body, presumably) from a perspective physically removed from one's body and 2) 'flying' to a new location. This alteration of perspective can be caused by mind-altering substances, such as nitrous oxide at the dentist, or by the impact of an accident, as in the case of this 18 year old female:

> Whilst playing in a neighbour's cubby-house when I was about 8 or 9, I grabbed at a loose board which came off the cubby-house and I fell backwards onto the ground. A friend who was with me at the time stopped the board from hitting me, by catching it before it fell. I remember seeing my body lying on the ground and my friend catching the board, from a 'flying' or 'out of the body' position.

While some find the experience of floating upward pleasant, others panic and it seems that the sudden onrush of fear terminates the experience, as for this 31 year old female:

> I was resting one afternoon, when I felt myself leaving my body. I only seemed to rise about 5 feet or so, but panicked and returned.

A less common variety of this experience is to find oneself 'inside' another person, seeing oneself from the other's vantage point, as reported by this 20 year old female subject:

> When I was in primary school, I think I was 10 or 11, one day when the lesson was on, a student from another class brought in some books for the teacher. I was sitting on the last row in the classroom looking at her, then suddenly I was the teacher. I was in the teacher and was looking at myself. I even saw the books she had on her desk. Later when I was me again, I made an excuse to go up to her, just to see if the book I saw was actually there and, amazingly, it was!

The out-of-body experience has at least three of James' defining characteristics for mystical experience, viz., transience, passivity, and noeticity, as well as a transcendent quality in which events are often perceived as being more real than reality itself. Again, as in previous categories, the degree of 'ontic shift' engendered in an OBE, combined with the experient's worldview, determines whether it will be perceived as religious experience or not. One subject reported that 'flying' above the world and 'seeing' everything from this broadened perspective induced in her the phenomenology of the 'numinous' and a sense of the 'sacredness' of everything.

9. Remote perception (pre-, post-cognition and telepathy)

[Religious: NS; Practice: NS]

'Do you ever feel that at times you know about events before they happen; and/or you know people's thoughts or feelings without being told; and/or you know about past events without having heard or read of them?'

This category is the general class of experience the subset of which Targ and Harary have called 'remote viewing' (clairvoyance) (1983). Using a well controlled double-blind technique, they have conducted some convincing experiments to demonstrate this cognitive capacity in a laboratory at the Stanford Research Centre. 'Remote perception' can be taken as the general rubric for this type of occurrence which is experienced as if it is in one of the sensory modalities but yet operates across time as well as space. In other words, this type of perception appears to involve the conveyance of information across time and/or space without the apparent transfer of momenta (photons, mechanical vibration, etc.) characteristic of normal sensate perception but is experienced in a quasi-sensate and predominantly cognate fashion. This experience often takes the form of 'externalized' visualizations or 'internalized' mental 'pictures' (or sounds, smells and tactile sensations), as well as feelings of 'certainty' and 'knowledge' which have no visual or auditory components.

Many of the subjects' reports described the occurrence of this type of experience as a déjà-vu phenomena and, although many could not identify where they experienced the scene before, they were often able to accurately predict to themselves what would happen or be said next. A minority claimed that the déjà-vu experience resulted from encountering a situation in 'real life' which had previously occurred in a dream. Almost as common as déjà-vu was the experience of suddenly 'knowing' (again we see the characteristics of passivity, transience, noeticity) as reported by this 58 year old woman:

I had been very concerned about a friend of mine who was having marital problems, but didn't understand why. I woke one morning and *instantly* on waking knew that her husband was having a relationship with another woman we both knew. Although she had wondered if he was, she had no real proof, nor did I, if this was so (and if so who it might be). I did not tell her about my own enlightenment (whilst awake but no doubt coming out of a dreamtime). However, some months later it proved to be true when he left her for the other woman.

Precognitions and contemporaneous remote perceptions often occur as a dream whilst asleep, as in this episode reported by a 33 year old female:

I dreamt my father was fighting a huge fire, I felt it was a place where he was working although it was unfamiliar to me. I could hear him shout 'let it burn, just save that cooker!' and I saw a huge stainless steel cooker in the midst of the fire. I awoke in a cold sweat and couldn't go back to sleep. It wasn't until approximately 5.20 am that I suddenly felt calm and could sleep. The next morning I discovered my father's office that backed onto a store had burned down during the fire. Dad had been fighting the fire and he told the firemen to let it burn but to save a cooker that had only just arrived at the store and was worth $22,000. They had the fire under control by 5.20 am.

Although many of these episodes relate to people known to the experient, some relate to impersonal world events, as exemplified by this report of a 29 year old female:

... when I was really young I had visions of a man being shot — either someone important or famous and (in the vision) my parents were fishing at the time of the shooting. (Later) my parents were fishing when President Kennedy was shot.

Again, the cross over of types is evident in that this episode is reported as a 'vision', but what is emphasized, phenomenologically, for this subject is the precognitive remote perceiving. Also, as in all these categories of the præternatural, *the experience seems to descend on the recipient from some source outside the usual, natural world of ordinary events and perceptions.*

10. The existential void (loss of self)

[Religious: H = 3.9, $p < 0.05$; Practice: NS]

'Have you ever experienced, *without any obvious external cause*, a loss of certainty and security so great as to leave you with a long-term fear and insecurity?'

This is a category derived from Laski's work and confirmed by my own interviews with individuals who came for psychological counselling because of feelings left over from similar experiences. It appears to represent a radical ontological state change in the perceived structure of 'self', but unlike mystical or numinous episodes, fear seems to dominate and there is no definite conclusion, viz., the realization of God, the void, etc. Instead, the experient's sense of egological certainty appears to deconstruct causing fear and uncertainty which is followed by only a partial reintegration of the 'self'. It is included in the overall category of the præternatural because of the profound existential state shift which characterizes this encounter and gives the recipient the impression of it having descended from a source beyond immediate sensate reality. A classic example of this experience type is given in this episode reported by an 18 year old male:

> . . . when I was in first year (of university) I came across a couple of days where out of the blue I couldn't do anything or fare any more. People terrified me, bright light made me feel sick. I hid in my room (and at college that's a difficult thing) for those two days, but even when I worked up the courage to go outside to Uni I still avoided people by going out of my way, and couldn't for the life of me walk across the Great Court in daylight for months afterwards. All pretty minor I suppose, but it's only now I've recovered completely from it. And there never was any reason for it. I just woke up that day feeling half jolted out of my body, utterly awkward.

Whether or not there was a reason for this episode remains to be determined through a more in-depth psychological investigation. But in either case, the experience appears to descend from 'nowhere' and it profoundly uproots the experient's self-concept.

This class of præternatural event may be the prototype of the introvertive mystical experience but one that never culminates, leaving the experient in an infinite regress of fear and distorted perceptions which generally are regarded as pathological and schizophreniform. Hunt suggests that there is a biological basis for such cognitive behavioural state changes in the capacity for 'tonic immobility', as seen in lower animals (1984). When operating in conjunction with the 'recombinatory capability' of human cognitive 'microgenic structures', this capacity generates the experience of voidness and ontological shift, characteristic of this state and of mystical experience.[8] He states that this 'negative capability' is triggered by a sense of being overpowered and this is in line with the majority of reports, which attribute the onset to contemplating death or the vastness of the universe leading to feelings of personal fragility and significance that no amount of self-bolstering can overcome. However, such reductionist explanations ultimately fail on the grounds of their inability to account for the devastating existential impact which often follows these occurrences. Chickens certainly do not appear to have prolonged existential crises following 'tonic immobility' and Hunt's mapping of this behaviour unto human mystico–religious responses would appear to be a bit too simplistic and naive.

11. Other world experience (shamanic journey)

[Religious: NS; Practice: NS]

'*While awake*, have you ever suddenly been cast into a strange new world or reality which had a vividness that made the whole experience appear to be absolutely real although in retrospect you realized that the entire episode may not have physically happened?'

Although shamanic visionary experience contains many elements from previous categories (questions 6, 7, 8 and 9), it is given a separate class because of the totality of the experience. It appears from the writings of Eliade (1964), Elkin (1977), Harner (1980), Castaneda (1972, 1974) and others that shamanic journeys to the 'upper' and lower' worlds are the prototypes of ecstatic, mystical and visionary experiences, as well as containing elements of visionary experience, remote perception, OBE and, in some cases, NDE. In this survey only one 40 year old male subject reported what can be described as a classical initiatory experience of travelling to another 'realm' to experience discorporation and then rebirth:

I was lying on my bed listening to the radio when the news of Martin Luther King Junior's assassination came on. I experienced a great sense of loss and shock and as I lay there I became aware of a green luminous glow emanating from my chest which spread out to envelop the entire room. While absorbed in watching this phenomenon I suddenly found myself in an entirely new location — a landscape with mountains. I looked down and saw my body start to unravel. The flesh was stripped away and then the muscles and sinews until only a skeleton was left. After some time I witnessed my body re-assembled and I moved out across this strange new landscape. After some time I 'returned' to my room and could still see the glowing, green luminosity which then gradually faded away.

A more typical account is given by this 42 year old female:

After my infant son's funeral, I was lying on a bed in my mother's house and suddenly I was standing on a long, winding, white road. I knew if I walked on I would come on to where my son was but I looked back and could clearly see into the kitchen in my mother's house, where my husband and other son were, and I knew I couldn't leave them, so I turned and went back.

Sudden shock and stress seem to play a major role in the onset of most of these encounters. Harner suggests that the drumming characteristic of shamanic trance journeys of so many pre-literate societies produces a sonic driving of the electrical activity of the brain into a synchronous state which he believes is part of the necessary and sufficient conditions for the induction of 'shamanic consciousness'. Additionally, the austerities and mortifications practiced so widely by shamans may, in combination with incessant drumming, be a way of artificially inducing the same conditions of stress as seen in the onset of the spontaneous cases.

In the case of the shamanic journey, as in all of the above categories of experience, the onset of the episode seems to require a switching of conscious 'state'. Krippner has attempted to classify what he believes are the possible states of consciousness experienced by human beings (1972), but such a list fails because it represents the experiences of a Western psychologist only and hence is not exhaustive. On closer scrutiny, it seems to typify only different modes of what appear to be three primary states: sensate waking, sleeping and what he labels 'expanded' consciousness (trans-sensate waking), which would subsume a number of his other categories such as 'trance', meditation, hypnopompic, hypnagogic, etc. There are, no doubt, differing depths and intensities of all three primary states and it would seem that Krippner's classification might result from both a lack of an appropriate descriptive language as well as an incomplete empirical (experiential) data base from which to make his comparisons.

Tart urges that we develop 'state specific sciences' and he provides us with a general paradigm for such an approach (1975). He argues that we cannot understand reports of experiences which take place in one state while listening to them in another. From this position one can go further and assert that different languages are more appropriate for different states and, as Whorf believes, the European languages have severe limitations when confronting notions such as timelessness, force and intensity (Carroll, 1956). Therefore, our attempts to describe præternatural experiences are forced into the mould of both the constraints of our Western cultural framework and an inadequate language resulting in what Tart rightly asserts to be the considerable difficulty we experience in our attempts to describe one state or its events while in another.

In the case of the præternatural experiences described in this chapter, we can identify two general types: 'Ontic' and 'Perceptual'. When, as in the case of OBE, visionary or remote perception experiences, the phenomenology includes sensate-like phenomena, we are able to report this aspect of their phenomenology without too much difficulty provided the 'contents' of the experience are somewhat similar to that of ordinary waking sensate experience, viz., objects, people and events that fit our linguistic framework. These experiences generally can be classified as the 'Perceptual' types. However, when the focus, or primary awareness of the experience, is centred on an intense state shift in which there is a significant degree of ontological 'deconstruction' and subsequent ontological reassignment with sensate content becoming secondary, such as in the case of introvertive mysticism, then the experience can be considered to be of the 'Ontic' type.[9] It is as a result of this latter type that experients seem to feel that words fail in any attempt to convey what happened.

In the 'Ontic' case, the base state change, or the sudden descent of the experience as if from a præternatural source, appears to be inaccessible to language (and even prior to language) so that *the state itself becomes the existential operational definition of reality*. All other consequent changes in state, which are accompanied by a profound sense of 'ontic shift', further reinforce our sense that we are moving in and out of differing realities. Indeed, most of our lives are spent primarily in either the waking sensate or sleep states and hence any major conscious shift out of them, of which we are consciously aware, is experienced as highly unusual and, *ex nihilo*, a descent of the præternatural.[10]

Being conscious of the 'shift' itself is essential for one to experience the change as having its origins in an 'other reality'. Many of these experiences, such as remote perception, are so fleeting, and to some experients so common, that the shift is never consciously experienced. Instead, only the sensate-like phenomenological content is remembered and appears to the experient as if it dropped in from 'nowhere' like an unbidden thought or memory but without an awareness of state change and/or ontological ground. The 'shift' is more apt to be noticed when the experiences are rare and unusual, and therefore novel, and one finds that experients who have had very few such encounters more often tend to assign other-worldly sources and/or religious meanings (divine or demonic) to the resultant phenomenology.[11] These ascriptions of religious import are, in most cases, in line with current worldviews held by the experients or, in some cases, with worldviews soon to be found, which 'fit' the 'facts'.

From the above discussion it would seem that mystical encounters and experiences of the divine by definition must always have a fairly high degree of 'existential impact', and hence resultant sense of 'ontic shift'. In the case of mystical experience, there may be sensate-like content, as in Otto's numinous or Stace's extrovertive mysticism, or it may be phenomenologically 'empty', as in the instances of Buddhist Shunyata or introvertive mysticism (Stace, 1960). However, the *apparent shift* of ontological ground must be prominent and noticeable for the experient, such that it is capable of disturbing the ontological foundations of his existential worldview in order to qualify as 'Ontic'.[12] As we have noted, on the other hand, this sense of ontological shift is not always present, as, for example, in 'remote perception'. In these 'Perceptual' experiences the recipient still feels, nonetheless, that his/her experience has 'descended' as if from some trans-sensate (præternatural) source but *without great existential impact*, and thus without the need for ontological reassignment. It is, therefore, the degree of existential impact which appears to determine whether or not a given præternatural event is regarded as having mystical, cosmic or religious import, and, in turn, this seems to be determined by the degree of familiarity the experient has with any given type of encounter as well as by previous personality factors and worldview.

Conclusions

This survey, although not a random representative sample of the population studied, nonetheless reveals a general consistency with previous surveys in that it demonstrates a widespread occurrence of præternatural phenomena in a selected, educated population. Respondents often have remarked in follow-up interviews that they have never related their experiences to others before this survey. This is consistent with the pattern that is emerging vis-à-vis the widespread occurrence of mystical, visionary and remote perception experiences in the general population in the context of a pronounced cultural silence about such experiences.

By operationalizing the præternatural as a class of related phenomenological and psychological events and by producing separate questions which emphasize differing salient features of this general class, we have demonstrated that the percentage of experients in the population might be even greater than other studies have led us to believe. The anecdotal data further suggests that the divisions between classes of events is somewhat arbitrary with most of the features characterizing either the 'Ontic' or the 'Perceptual' experiences as being widely distributed throughout both classes. However, separating the experiences into a variety of questions is a useful technique because it lowers the 'threshold' for the respondent, thereby encompassing events otherwise missed by the single catch-all questions of other studies.

As we continue to explore phenomenological (consciousness) events, it is apparent that we may be looking at a fundamental capacity in human cognitive behaviour whether this capacity originates from a 'deep' biological structure as suggested by Hardy and Hay, from the cognitive 'negative capability' as hypothesized by Hunt, or from some other innate aspect of our psychology. Whatever the origins of this function, it is inextricably connected to and part of the processes of consciousness. By recognizing that these experiences can be understood as operations (functional formations) of consciousness and overt behaviour and, further, by recognizing that the apparent ontological shift which sometimes accompanies these state changes is the result of achieving a particular intensity and formation of perceived consciousness alteration, we may not only shed some light on the epistemological paradox of the mystical state, but on normal, sensate experience as well.

This conceptualization of mystical and related experiences may go some way to resolving the differences between scholars such as Almond (1982), who posits 'contentless' mystical experience, and Katz (1978), who in following on from Garside's position (1972), suggests that all mystical experience is shaped and interpreted by and through the religious and cultural context in which it arises. The 'contentless' experience would appear to be the sense of 'ontic shift' but, of course, all reportage must take place through language and context which give form to the phenomena of the experience. Hence the experience can be understood as both 'contentless' and contextually determined.

It would seem, therefore, that this sort of 'operationalized' empirical research into the nature of præternatural experience is not only a very useful way of studying the distribution of its occurrence, but it can contribute to an explication of the possible psychological mechanisms of induction, as well as aiding in the resolution of the ontological debate surrounding mystical, visionary and remote perception experiences.

Notes:

1 This survey was conducted as part of a research project conducted in fulfilment of the requirements for a Ph.D. degree at the department of studies in Religion at the University of Queensland, Australia.

2 We are employing the older spelling to signify our particular operational/ intentional definition as opposed to the 'supernatural' as ontological fact.

3 This was the informal collection of anecdotal data over a ten year period from counselling clients who reported præternatural encounters.

4 'Religiosity' (question 14) is answered either 'yes' or 'no' and 'Practice' (question 15) is ranked from 0–4 based on frequency of engagement.

5 Alpha was set at 0.05.

6 These are: 'Retrospective' interpretation or 'References to doctrinal interpretations formulated after the experience is over.' 'Reflexive' interpretation or 'References to interpretation spontaneously formulated either during the experience itself or immediately afterwards.' 'Incorporated' interpretation or 'References to features or experience which

have been caused or conditioned by a mystic's prior beliefs, expectations and intentions.'

7 'Bracketing' here refers to Husserl's *epoche* — a suspension in the belief in the existence of objects.

8 Hunt uses the term 'tonic immobility' to describe what is commonly called 'animal hypnosis'. For example, when one holds a chicken firmly without letting it move, it will remain in that position when released until such a time as another significant stimulus occurs. This is believed to be a biologically evolved survival mechanism in the face of totally over-whelming odds. By 'freezing' the chicken can possibly 'fool' its predator into thinking that it is not alive and of no interest. Hunt sees the 'negative capability' (the entry into the void of an 'introvertive mystical state in the case of Homo Sapiens) as a similar response to an overwhelming affective/cognitive event, viz., a cascading into an affective/cognitive tonic immobility in order to escape overpowering circumstances.

9 Ontological 'deconstruction' derives from the movement of literary critique known as 'deconstructionism'. This viewpoint asserts that the 'reading' of the text is the 'writing' of the text. In other words, the reader's perception of the meaning of the text, in a sense, creates the actual intent of the text. In the current context, some experients 'rewrite' the ontology assigned to their experiences by 'discovering' some 'ultimate' or 'underlying' source and thus 'rewrite' meaning through a re-assignment of the ontological roots of their experience.

10 An intense state change, with its totality of 'psychological' and 'physical' causes and attributes, *is* the operational matrix which defines (creates) the existential sense of what is 'real' and hence the beliefs about what ultimately 'exists'.

11 This appears to be the case when one compares the statements made by 'high' and 'low' occurrence experients in follow-up interviews.

12 Here, 'existential worldview' means the belief system which is operative at the perceptual, affective and behavioural levels without necessarily having a cognitive component. The experient acts 'as if' something is 'real', and this implies the ultimate form and quality of what is 'out there'. Ontological foundations, or 'what is', are thus those perceptual, be-havioural and affective activities from which we derive our sense of the 'real' no matter what we may believe conceptually or express linguistically. From this lived activity (existential worldview) the experient derives an ontological conception as a second order process. However, if the perceptual-affective-behavioural matrix undergoes a radical enough shift (state change), then the existential boundaries surrounding and defining the 'real' change accordingly. This change leads to a re-assignment of ontological beliefs referred to as 'ontic shift'.

References

Allport, G.W. and Ross, J.M. (1977), 'Personal religious orientation and prejudice', in Malony, H.N., *Current Perspectives in the Psychology of Religion*, Michigan: William B. Eerdmans, pp 117–137.

Almond, P.C. (1982), *Mystical Experience and Religious Doctrine: An Investigation of the Study of Mysticism in World Religions*, Berlin: Mouton.

Back, K. and Bourque, L. (1970), 'Can feelings be enumerated?' *Behavioral Science*, Vol. 5, pp 228–239.

Bharati, A. (1976), *The Light at the Centre: Context and Pretext of Modern Mysticism*, London: East–West Publications.

Bohm, D. (1985), 'Hidden variables and the implicate order', *Zygon* Vol. 20, pp 111–124.

Bucke, R.M. (1923), *Cosmic Consciousness*, New York: E.P. Dutton.

Carroll, J.B., ed. (1956) *Language, Thought and Reality: Selected Writings of Benjamin Lee Whorf*, Cambridge, Mass.: The MIT Press.

Castaneda, C. (1972), *Journey to Ixtlan: The Lessons of Don Juan* New York: Simon and Schuster.

Castaneda, C. (1974), *Tales of Power* New York: Simon and Schuster.

Eliade, M. (1964), *Shamanism: Archaic Techniques of Ecstasy*, translated by W.R. Trask, Princeton: Bollingen Series LXXVI, Princeton University Press.

Elkin, A.P. (1977), *Aboriginal Men of High Degree*, 2nd Edition, St. Lucia: University of Queensland Press.

Garside, B. (1972), 'Language and the interpretation of mystical experience', *International Journal for the Philosophy of Religion* Vol. 3, pp 93–102.

Greeley, A.M. (1974), *Ecstasy: A Way of Knowing*, Englewood Cliffs, N.J.: Prentice-Hall.

Hardy, A.C. (1966), *The Divine Flame*, London: Collins.

Hardy, A.C. (1979), *The Spiritual Nature of Man*, Clarendon Press.

Harner, M. (1980), *The Way of the Shaman: A Guide to Power and Healing*, San Francisco: Harper & Row.

Hay, D. (1979), 'Religious experience amongst a group of postgraduate students: a qualitative study', *Journal for the Scientific Study of Religion*, Vol. 18, pp 164–182.

Hay, D. and Morisy, A. (1978), 'Reports of estatic, paranormal or religious experience in Great Britain and the United States — a comparison of trends', *Journal for the Scientific Study of Religion*, Vol. 17, pp 255–268.

Hultkrantz, A. (1983), 'The concept of the supernatural in primal religion', *History of Religions*, Vol. 22, pp 231–253.

Hunt, H.T. (1984), 'A cognitive psychology of mystical and altered-state experience', *Perceptual and Motor Skills*, Vol. 58, pp 467–513.

James, W. (1936), *The Varieties of Religious Experience*, New York: The Modern Library.

Jung, C.G. (1969), 'Synchronicity: an acausal connecting principle', in *C.G. Jung: The Collected Works. The Structure and Dynamics of the Psyche*, Vol. 8, 2nd Edition, translated by R.F.C. Hull, London: Routledge & Kegan Paul.

Katz, S.T. (1978), 'Language, epistemology, and mysticism', in Katz, S.T., *Mysticism and Philosophical Analysis*, London: Sheldon Press.

Krippner, S. (1972), 'Altered states of consciousness', in White, J., *The Highest State of Consciousness*, Garden City, New York: Anchor Books, pp 1–13.

Laski, M. (1961), *Ecstasy*, London: Cresset Press.

Macleod-Morgan, C.M. (1985), 'Quantifying the unspeakable: the incidence of numinous experience in an Australian university sample', Paper presented at the XVth International Association for the History of Religions Congress, Sydney, Australia.

Monroe, R. (1971), *Journeys Out of the Body*, Garden City: Doubleday.

Moody, R. (1975), *Life After Life*, New York: Bantam Books.

Moore, P. (1978), 'Mystical experience, mystical doctrine, mystical technique', in Katz, S.T., *Mysticism and Philosophical Analysis*, London: Sheldon Press, pp 101–131.

Otto, R. (1958), *The Idea of the Holy*, London, Oxford University Press.

Ott, L., Larson, R.F. and Mendenhall, W. (1983), *Statistics: A Tool for the Social Sciences*, Boston: Duxbury Press.

Smart, N. (1973), *The Science of Religion and the Sociology of Knowledge*, Princeton: Princeton University Press.

Stace, W.T. (1960), *Philosophy and Mysticism*, Philadelphia: Lippincot.

Starbuck, E.D. (1899), *The Psychology of Religion*, New York: Walter Scott.

Targ, R. and Harary, K. (1983), *The Mind Race: Understanding and Using Psychic Abilities*, New York: Villard.

Tart, C.T. (1975), 'Science, states of consciousness, and spiritual experiences: the need for state-specific sciences', in Tart, C.T., *Transpersonal Psychologies*, New York: Harper and Row.

Thomas, L.E. and Cooper, P.E. (1978), 'Measurement and incidence of mystical experiences: an exploratory study', *Journal for the Scientific Study of Religion*, Vol. 17, pp 433–437.

Wainwright, W.J. (1975), 'Mysticism and sense perception', *Religious Studies*, Vol. 9, pp 257–278.

Zaehner, R.C. (1980), *Mysticism:: Sacred and Profane*, New York: Oxford University Press.

CHAPTER 13
ON THE PSYCHOLOGY OF BELIEF IN LIFE AFTER DEATH

Michael A. Thalbourne[1]

The essential idea intended by the expression 'life after death' (or by the synonymous phrase '*post mortem* survival') appears to be the

> Continued existence of the consciousness of the individual person in some form and for at least some time after the destruction of their physical body. (Thalbourne, 1982, p. 79)

There are of course a number of views as to the *details* of such a *post mortem* existence, differing on such questions as whether the surviving component is itself subject to a death of its own or whether it is immortal, whether reincarnation occurs or not, and so on (Thouless, 1979; Grosso, 1979; Thalbourne & Williams, 1984). Nevertheless, these variations all have in common the assumption that death does *not* necessarily cause the permanent cessation of consciousness and/or personality.

But is this assumption correct? For more than a century now, research has been conducted in an effort to investigate scientifically various types of evidence thought to be suggestive of survival. This evidence comes from such phenomena as apparitions and hauntings, the physical and verbal productions of mediums, claims to have lived previous lives, death-bed visions and near-death experiences, and others. Important and interesting though such data are, it is not the purpose of this chapter to review them. For that, the reader is referred to the excellent treatments of the topic by Gauld (1977, 1982), Stevenson (1977), and Thouless (1971). A summary of some of the skeptical responses to such claims can be found in Siegel (1980; see also a reply to Siegel by Stevenson, 1981). Suffice it to say that the evidence has not yet led to a consensus as to whether there is an afterlife of any form.

Rather than focusing upon the *evidential* issue, the question I have chosen to discuss in this essay is a *psychological* one, namely, *Whether or not there is an afterlife, what are the factors which influence a person to believe or disbelieve in one?* One *might* suppose that a rational human being would base their belief or disbelief so far as possible on the objective evidence available to them. But my underlying assumption will be that the degree of belief or disbelief in life after death expressed by many people is determined to a large extent — some would say it is determined completely! — by factors *other* than consideration of the objective evidence. My aim in this chapter is to review the evidence for these 'non-rational' factors. But first, let us consider the question *what proportion of the population actually believes in life after death?*

The Extent of Belief in Life After Death

It seems to be a well-accepted anthropological fact that in virtually every culture and in every period of history there can be found the belief in some sort of afterlife. The present age is no exception. According to a Gallup Poll conducted in the United States during 1980–81, 67% of Americans interviewed said they believed in survival of death (Gallup, 1982, p. 183). Though there has been 'an erosion of belief during the post-war era in every nation for which temporal comparisons could be made — except the United States', (Sigelman, 1977, p. 292; see also Hynson, 1975), it is nevertheless the case that belief in survival is not confined to an insignificant proportion of humanity.

But equally, the number of disbelievers is not by any means small. There have always been doubters, disbelievers and scoffers, since the time of the ancient philosophers Democritus, Lucretius, and (at least until the death of his daughter Tullia), Cicero. In the 1980–81 Gallup Poll (Gallup, 1982), the percentage of disbelievers in the USA was 27%. Skepticism has in fact been on the rise in most countries since the end of World War II (Sigelman, 1977).

The prevalence of belief in an afterlife varies quite markedly from one country to another. The USA and India each have a large percentage of believers — about 70% — while Japan has what is probably the lowest, namely, 18% (Gallup Opinion Index, 1976). Again, while the figure for Australia is reported to have been 48% in 1975 (Sigelman, 1977, p. 292), the percentage of believers in Iceland is between 68 and 88% (Haraldsson, 1978, p. 20). Later in this essay I shall suggest a rather simple explanation for these striking international differences.

We may now begin to tackle the question which forms our central theme: *What factors are associated with belief in survival? Why does one person believe that there is an afterlife, while another person does not?'* Information relevant to this question is scattered about in a large number of experiments and surveys, but few attempts have been made to assemble that evidence into a coherent whole. The aim of this essay, therefore, is to effect such a synthesis. Research has suggested that there is not just one but a *number* of factors which are associated with afterlife-belief. I shall summarize the evidence for each factor separately, in order of the *contribution* apparently made by each to afterlife-belief. But I shall then go on to argue that most of these factors are not actually independent but are instead *related* to each other, in a way that allows us to discern a *pattern* underlying the phenomenon of afterlife-belief.

While I have attempted in this essay to avoid reference to terms and concepts unfamiliar to those without a background in research methodology, one such concept which I cannot do without and which I must therefore explain is that known as 'accounting for the variance'. Now it is obvious that opinion as to the existence of an afterlife differs — it varies from individual to individual. Afterlife-belief is thus said to exhibit 'variability', or 'variance'. The extent of this variance can be thought of as a quantity, and *the total quantity of variance exhibited by a given factor — in this case, afterlife belief — can be expressed as being equivalent to 100%.* Any outside factor which is *connected* with our factor of interest can then be said to *'account for a certain percentage of the variance'* in that factor; if the connection is strong, then a larger percentage of variance is accounted for than if the connection is weak. It follows, then, that if we know *all* the factors which are connected with our factor of interest, then the *total* quantity of variance accounted for should add up to 100%. A total *less* than 100% usually indicates that some relevant factors remain to be discovered.

With that in mind, therefore, let us proceed to our first and most important factor connected with belief in an afterlife.

Religiosity

Belief in an afterlife is of course part of many religious traditions. Obviously, then, if a person is raised in a religious environment they are more likely to adopt the belief that there is an existence beyond the grave. On the other hand, it might be expected that persons brought up in an essentially *non*-religious setting would be rather less prone to imbibe the belief.

Somewhat surprisingly, I have not been able to locate any studies relating afterlife-belief and, specifically, *religion of upbringing*. Linda Williams and I attempted to do this in a survey of 52 American members of the high-IQ club MENSA (Thalbourne & Williams, 1984). However, only two persons had a non-religious background, which made it impossible to compare them validly with the others who *did* grow up in a religious context. I have recently conducted a large-scale survey of psychology students at the University of Adelaide, South Australia, and I am hopeful that one of the questions on which the data will throw some light is the extent to which religion of upbringing is related to belief in survival of death.

By contrast, quite a few surveys have been reported concerning the relationship of afterlife-belief and *present religious affiliation or preference*. Hynson (1975) presents a useful summary of the results from four large surveys conducted in the USA. Indications were in line with what we might have expected: in general, at least 70% of Christians subscribe to belief in an afterlife, while the belief is endorsed by only 39% of persons who have *no* religious affiliation. Intriguingly, the level of belief is even *lower* than that — a mere 20% — for people who are Jewish.[2] Gorer (1955), Kalish (1963), and Osarchuk and Tatz (1973) report a similar pattern of results, (as did Linda Williams and myself (1984) in our MENSA study, though again, there were too few participants to permit statistical analysis). Unfortunately, for technical reasons, I have not been able to estimate the amount of variance accounted for by this particular factor, but it is evidently considerable.

It may be added that while some of Hynson's surveys revealed large *differences* between various Christian denominations in prevalence of afterlife-belief (see also Glock & Stark, 1965, pp. 97–98), other surveys suggested that there is a good deal of *similarity* (e.g., Gallup, 1982, p. 184), so in this respect the picture is unclear.

Do similar findings appear if, instead of present religious affiliation, we consider various *other* aspects of religious behaviour and belief? The answer is quite clearly yes. For example, in one of the studies discussed by Hynson the participants were also asked how often they attended religious services. It was found that afterlife-believers who were Christian said that they attended such services more frequently than did those who were afterlife-disbelievers, and that this was especially true in the case of Episcopalians and Lutherans.

A similar question was put to two groups of students at the University of Iceland (Thalbourne & Haraldsson, 1984, studies II and IV), and in both groups afterlife-believers more often said that they attended religious gatherings. In this same series of studies — which comprised a total of four different groups, one of them a large group of 900 people selected at random from the Icelandic population — it was found that afterlife-believers more often described themselves as being religious in a general sense,[3] as thinking about religious matters, as reading about religion in general and, to a lesser extent, as reading the Bible, as having had a vivid religious or spiritual experience,[4] as believing in some sort of God, as having experienced divine guidance, as having felt the presence of God, and as praying. When one combines these questions to produce a Religiosity Questionnaire, it is quite clear that afterlife-believers are, overall, much more religious than are disbelievers.[5]

But religious in what sense? In the Christian sense? Or, as Haraldsson (1981, p. 300) seems to suggest, in a non-sectarian sense which is equally valid for persons of *other* religious persuasions (or even for people with *no* official persuasion)? The answer to this question will probably not emerge clearly until the Religiosity Questionnaire is given to large groups of devout Hindus and Buddhists: if the Questionnaire rates such people as being 'not religious', then that would strongly suggest that it was measuring specifically *Christian* religiosity.

In the meantime, we have a few pieces of information which are relevant to the question but whose interpretation is somewhat ambiguous. For example, in 1983, my student John Hensley gave the Questionnaire to 72 students at Washington University in St. Louis. He found that those rated most religious were, in order, the Roman Catholics, Protestants, and 'Other's, followed closely by the 23 Jewish people; those claiming no affiliation, however, were rated as being far *less* religious. Thus, whatever is the sense of 'religiosity' being measured by the Questionnaire, Jewish people come out almost as religious as Christians, while the non-affiliated trail way behind. Whether the non-affiliated tend to be less religious in *every* sense, or just in the *Judeo–Christian* sense, remains to be clarified by future research.

The second piece of information comes from a recently conducted study (as yet unpublished) in which I gave the Wilson–Patterson Attitude Inventory (Wilson, 1975) to six small groups of persons of quite diverse backgrounds in St. Louis, USA. This Inventory provides several ratings, one of which is the extent to which a person is 'religious/puritanical'. The rating seems in fact to describe the degree to which a person displays attitudes characteristic of Christian Fundamentalism. Though I have no information as to how the Inventory would rate adherents of *Eastern* religion on this aspect, I would doubt that it would classify them as being highly 'religious-puritanical'. The point of all this is that I found this rating to be strongly related to belief in the afterlife: there is little doubt that believers are *considerably* more 'religious-puritanical' than are disbelievers. Once again, the large-scale survey which I am presently conducting in Adelaide has been designed to allow some clearer conclusions to be drawn about the difficult question of what sort of religiosity is related to belief in an afterlife.

In conclusion, I would estimate that religiousness accounts for approximately 36% of the variance in afterlife-belief. Thus, religiosity appears to be a large part of the explanation.[6] At the same time, it does not provide the *complete* explanation. So what other factors may be responsible for belief in life after death?

Conservatism

What exactly are we to understand by the term 'conservative'? Glenn Wilson, who devised the Wilson–Patterson Attitude Inventory — a widely-used questionnaire to measure the extent to which a person is conservative — intends the term to imply 'resistance to change and the tendency to prefer safe, traditional and conventional forms of institutions and behaviour' (Wilson, p. 10). Again, conservatism is one of the personality dimensions assessed using the Cattell Sixteen Personality Factor Questionnaire (Cattell, Eber, & Tatsuoka, 1970): conservative people are

> confident in what they have been taught to believe, and accept the 'tried and true', despite inconsistencies, when something else might be better. They are cautious and compromising in regard to new ideas. Thus, they tend to oppose and postpone change, are inclined to go along with tradition, are more conservative in religion and politics, and tend not to be interested in analytical 'intellectual' thought. (Institute for Personality and Ability Testing, 1972, p. 25)

It is thus clear that different researchers have defined conservatism in much the same way.

The relevance of conservatism becomes apparent if we note that in *most* cultures, belief in an afterlife is a *traditional* one. Moreover, not only has the belief been around since time immemorial, but in a good many cases it is held by the *greater proportion* of the population (as can be deduced from the national surveys cited earlier). If this is so, then a child born into such a social group is likely early in life to adopt the belief in the afterlife simply by 'osmosis', as it were, that is, as a result of being surrounded by believers and imbibing so many of the attitudes that are part and parcel of the 'received wisdom'. (If this 'social learning' process is indeed operating, then we might make the following two predictions for future research: (1) children, provided they have reached an understanding of what death is, might display a level of afterlife-belief which is not only high but perhaps even *higher* than that in the general population; and (2) *children* who believe in life after death might be expected to have *parents* who believe (see Argyle & Beit-Hallahmi, 1975, pp. 30–34).

Of course, as children become adults many of them question and even reject the beliefs they learned during their upbringing. It is at this point, I suggest, that the influence of the personality trait of conservatism may become apparent: faced with a preponderance of believers around a person, an individual respectful of tradition and convention and disinclined to deviate from established ways of thinking, might be more likely to retain the popular belief in life after death. Other individuals, by nature less likely to be impressed by the received wisdom, more willing to experiment, and preferring to be free-thinking individualists, might be expected to *question* assumptions that others take for granted, and thus would perhaps be more likely to *reject* the afterlife-belief, and without caring about adverse social consequences that might ensue. Two suggestions for future research: (1) look at the level of conservatism and afterlife-belief in young adolescents, and ascertain their afterlife-belief ten years later, to see whether those who end up rejecting belief in life after death are the ones who as young teenagers tended also to have been rather liberal; (2) In Japan, belief in an afterlife is comparatively *unpopular*, only 18% of the nation subscribing to it; it might therefore turn out to be the case that in Japanese society it is the *disbelievers* who are the conservatives and the believers who are the rebels!

So much for theory. What about the evidence? There is in fact ample evidence that, at least among adults in Western countries, believers in life after death *do* tend to be more conservative. One of the earliest studies to suggest that this might be so was reported by Glock and Stark (1965). Their group consisted of 1690 British adults polled in 1957 by Social Surveys Ltd — the British Gallup organization. They examined the level of afterlife-belief in those persons who voted Tory and in those who voted Labour. Labour-voters were considerably *less* likely to believe in life after death than were those who voted conservative or who had other party-preferences. Glock and Stark interpreted this difference in terms of the different ideologies of the two parties: a person who believed that all the deficiencies of their present life-situation would be righted after death as a Heavenly reward *might* be more reconciled to an unsatisfying life here and now, and thus might be less motivated to agitate for social change; on the other hand, a person experiencing an unfulfilling life but who did *not* believe in '*post mortem* worker's compensation' as it were, might be more inclined to support radical political moves to create Paradise here on Earth instead. Thus, disbelievers in life after death might be expected to be more radical politically.

It may be of interest to note that Glock and Stark (1965, pp. 198–199) uncovered what *appeared* to be a relationship between afterlife-belief and *social class*, namely, a progressive decline in percentage of believers from 85% in the upper class to 49% in the working class. However, they were able to demonstrate that this difference was largely due to the factor of political radicalism, since the upper classes tended to be conservative (hence believers) and the working class radical (hence disbelievers). So much for religion being the opiate of the masses! On the contrary, the working classes in Britain are known for their religious apathy.

Over the last 20 years or so, additional evidence has been obtained in support of the notion that conservatism and afterlife-belief tend to go together. In Reykjavik, my colleague Erlendur Haraldsson and I analyzed the results obtained from administering the Cattell Sixteen Personality Factor Questionnaire to two groups of Icelanders. We found that, in one of these groups, people who believed in survival of death were indeed more conservative (Thalbourne & Haraldsson, 1984, study III). (Along these same lines, we also found some suggestion that believers might be more conventional, conscientious, group-oriented and subdued.) More recently still, in the study where I gave the Wilson–Patterson Attitude Inventory to six small groups of people in St. Louis, USA, I discovered a strong and consistent tendency for afterlife-believers to be more conservative. Conservatism would appear to account for about 27% of the variance in afterlife-belief.

It is of interest to note that use of the Wilson–Patterson Inventory also permitted the conclusion that afterlife-believers tend to be more militaristic as well as more anti-hedonistic: that is, they favor the use of authority and military force to control social behaviour, and they frown upon what they see as frivolous pleasure-seeking activities; conversely, disbelievers oppose such authoritarianism, and appear in effect to subscribe to the dictum, 'Eat, drink, and be merry, for tomorrow we die!' However, it should also be pointed out that Wilson considers both militarism-punitivism and anti-hedonism to be specific *aspects* of the general concept of conservatism.

Abstract Belief That Mind Can Behave Paranormally

Brian and Lynne Mackenzie, currently at the University of Tasmania, have given what is to my mind the most insightful analysis of what it is that makes something paranormal (Mackenzie & Mackenzie, 1980). They point out that, for several hundred years now — ever since the time of Galileo — orthodox science has held several deeply-engrained beliefs about the nature of mental activity: it believes that mind cannot exist independently of a brain and nervous system (thus ruling out the possibility of life after death); and it believes that mind can influence the external world and obtain information about it only through the recognized bodily organs of movement and sensation (thus ruling out the possibility of psychokinesis and extrasensory perception); thus, the scope of mind's operation has long been assumed to be restricted to the familiar and well-understood functions of the nervous system.

On the other hand, reports of such 'paranormal' phenomena as levitation and materialization appear to suggest that the mental apparatus can behave not only in a way that *exceeds* the limits which science has assumed are known and fixed, but in such a powerful way that it is no longer at all clear *what* limits can be placed on its operation! From the point of view of many orthodox scientists, the existence of the paranormal *seems* to suggest that mind can behave in an outrageously *unlimited* way, like a genie released from its bottle, or in an annoyingly *unpredictable* way, like a naughty child which, as soon as you have tidied up a room, succeeds in turning it into a mess again! Such *apparent* implications[7] cause the orthodox scientist to feel that the paranormal poses a considerable threat to his ability to predict the workings of the physical universe. Mind cannot be permitted to intrude into nature in this radical, untameable way, and advocates of the paranormal must be treated as dangerous subversives who are trying to render the practice of science impossible by destroying long-standing confidence in our ability to understand the world.

The same Icelandic research-program which I have mentioned in regard to religiosity and conservatism also permitted us to examine the question *is belief in an afterlife connected in any way with acceptance or rejection of psychic phenomena in general and of ESP in particular?* Erlendur Haraldsson and I (1984; Haraldsson, 1981) in fact asked four different groups of Icelanders about the extent of their belief in telepathy, clairvoyance and precognition, as well as how often they *read* about psychic phenomena. The answers to these questions were combined to form an overall rating of attitude. It was quite clear that afterlife-believers in each of the four groups tended to be *much* more accepting of ESP phenomena than are afterlife-disbelievers.[8] The amount of variance accounted for appears to be at least 22%.

It might be objected that this result is rather obvious and therefore trivial. But it is not. Believing in life after death does not *necessarily* entail accepting the existence of this-worldly psychic phenomena; for example, I have observed informally that, for some reason, many Roman Catholics believe in an afterlife but not in ESP. Likewise, one can be favorably disposed to accept the existence of ESP and psychokinesis without at the same time being convinced that there is an afterlife — I myself hold this viewpoint. It is simply the case that there is a statistical *tendency* for belief in the psychic and in the afterlife to be found in the same people, and likewise for disbelief. Thus, those people who believe that mind can *occur* paranormally — that is to say, independently of the nervous system (most notably, following death) — also more often than not believe that the mind of a living person can *interact with this world* paranormally.

Ostensible Experience of Mind Behaving Paranormally

In addition to the factor of *abstract belief* in the existence of paranormal processes is the factor of whether a person believes they have actually *witnessed or experienced* a paranormal event, either of a 'this-worldly' nature (such as a premonition, psychic dream, or psychokinetic event), or of an 'other-worldly' nature (such as an apparition). Obviously, these two factors are closely related: while a person can intellectually believe that mind can behave in a paranormal fashion without their ever having personally witnessed or experienced such behaviour, the converse would appear to be logically impossible: it would seem inconsistent to assert that you had *experienced* a psychic phenomenon without at the same time being prepared to admit that you *believed* in it! Indeed, as Irwin (1985) found, having an ostensible psychic experience is the most frequently reported reason for many people coming to believe in the paranormal.

Thus, given that we know already that those who believe in the afterlife also tend to give *credence* to the paranormal hypothesis, it would not be altogether surprising to find that these same persons also tend to report having ostensible psychic *experiences*. Some support for this notion was obtained in a large national survey in Iceland (Thalbourne & Haraldsson, 1984, Study I). Yet Palmer (1979, p. 236) carefully surveyed over 600 students and townspeople in the university-town of Charlottesville, Virginia, in the United States and was unable to detect a connection between afterlife-belief and ostensible ESP experiences. The probable cause for these apparently inconsistent results is that, while there *is* a relationship between afterlife-belief and ESP experiences, it is exceptionally slight, accounting for only a very few percent of the variance. In such situations, the results of a given experiment may not be strong enough for a researcher to be able to conclude with confidence that two factors are definitely related.

Education and Intelligence?

Given that antagonism towards the paranormal hypothesis is characteristic of orthodox science, it *might* be expected that the more education a person has received the less they would believe in an afterlife. Yet the results obtained both by Gallup (1982, pp. 183) and by Thalbourne and Haraldsson (1984, Study I) suggested, if anything, the opposite, with belief slightly *higher* in the university-educated!

It could be argued that the sort of education required to erode belief in the paranormal must be more specific, in particular, in physics or medicine (e.g. Poppleton & Pilkington, 1963; Rogers, 1966). Gallup

(1982) noted that while 67% of the general US population expressed belief in an afterlife only 32% of eminent physicians and a mere 16% of scientists did so. It is of interest that when my colleague Michael McBeath and I surveyed a large group of students taking General Physics at Washington University in St. Louis we found 53% to be survival-believers — less than the national average yet higher than in a class on Controversial Issues in Psychology, where it was 44%. (These figures are consistent with the finding of Leuba (1934) that psychologists and social scientists tend to believe in immortality to a lesser degree than do physical scientists.) A researcher interested in pursuing this hypothesis could perhaps ask adults *how many years of science* they had taken (and in what area), to see if there is a relationship with level of afterlife-belief. Better, however, would be a longitudinal study looking at whether belief in survival declines between the time when youngsters enter high-school and when they graduate years later from university.

A somewhat similar idea is the one that has been put to me by several psychologists to the effect that believers in survival of death must be less intelligent. In the two studies of which I know where there was a rating of intelligence (Thalbourne and Haraldsson, 1984, studies II and III), no support was obtained for this conjecture. Moreover, the percentage of afterlife-belief studied in the high-IQ group MENSA (Thalbourne & Williams, 1984) was, at 62%, not appreciably lower than the national average of 67%. Nevertheless, members of MENSA may not be typical of highly intelligent persons, and the intelligence rating used by Thalbourne and Haraldsson (namely, Factor B of the Cattell 16PF Questionnaire) is considered inferior. It is thus conceivable, though I think it unlikely, that better intelligence tests would yield a non-trivial difference between believers and disbelievers.

Gender

The possibility of a connection between gender and afterlife-belief has been examined in a large number of studies (e.g. Argyle & Beit-Hallahmi, 1975, who cite two surveys (p. 73); Blackmore, 1984; Cavan et al., 1949; Gallup, 1982; Gorer, 1955, who reports two surveys; Irwin, 1985; Thalbourne & Haraldsson, 1984, studies 1, III and IV; and Thalbourne & Williams, 1984). In each and every study where the difference between the sexes has been statistically significant, belief in an afterlife was somewhat more prevalent amongst women than it was amongst men. With one possible exception which I shall discuss below, the prevalence of afterlife-belief has *never* been found to be significantly higher in men than in women. However, I estimate that gender accounts for only about 6% of the variance in afterlife-belief.

The relationship between gender and belief in survival is so slight — there are so *many* male believers and female disbelievers — that a sizeable percentage of studies fail to detect any sex-difference at all.

In this connection it is of interest to note that there is an item about belief in life after death (namely, #115) in the widely-used questionnaire known as the Minnesota Multiphasic Personality Inventory (MMPI), devised by Hathaway and McKinley (Dahlstrom, Welsh, & Dahlstrom, 1972). The reason why this item is included is that one of the several ratings obtained from the MMPI is the degree to which a person supposedly has stereotypically 'feminine' interests. For some reason, expressing belief in an afterlife was considered by Hathaway and McKinley to be an indicator of *masculine* attitudes! However, in an investigation of masculinity–femininity conducted at Adelaide University, Andrew Livingstone (1973) found that, while virtually all of 40 teachers college students considered afterlife-belief to be stereotypically feminine, there was no significant difference between the male and female university students he tested as regards their *actual* level of belief.[9] The differences between male and female are real but very minimal.

Fear of Death

As Collett and Lester (1969) have pointed out, fear of death may comprise not one factor but several: we may be talking about fear of *the actual process of dying* or *the fact of being dead*, or we may be referring to fear of *our own death* or *the death of someone else*. But no matter how we interpret the phrase 'fear of death', it would certainly seem a natural human reaction to experience a degree of thoughtfulness, apprehension, dread or even fear when the subject is raised: a person may fear experiencing (or witnessing in another) the *pain and wasting* often involved in the process of dying; they may be apprehensive about *the possibility of the conscious personality — their own or that of a loved one — undergoing annihilation*; they may fear the unknown; or they may be filled with dread at the thought that *death can strike suddenly, unpredictably, and apparently unfairly*, threatening to thwart their need to have at least *some* 'cognitive control' over significant events.

A good deal of recent research has been conducted on fear of death (see Kurlychek, 1978–79), as well as on the different strategies which people may use to deal with such fear: for example, a person may *evade* the fear by denying the fact of death or its importance; they may *acknowledge* their fear and try to come to terms with death; or they may *acknowledge* their fear of death but be unable to reduce that fear. As pointed out by Ray and Najman (1974) of the University of New South Wales, the same people may, over time, make use of more than one of these different strategies.

There has been considerable speculation about the relationship between afterlife-belief and attitude to death. One hypothesis is that a way of reducing fear of death is to believe that there is a life *after* death. Certainly, Jeffers, Nichols, and Eisdorfer (1961) found that, amongst the elderly persons they interviewed, those who feared death least expressed strongest belief in an afterlife. However, this does not demonstrate that initial fear of death was *instrumental* in the adoption of afterlife-belief. Thus, Osarchuk and Tatz (1973) exposed afterlife-believers and disbelievers to either an audio-visual presentation designed to arouse fear of death, to the threat of electric shock, or to a non-threatening task. Afterlife-believers whose fear of death was aroused, afterwards expressed significantly *stronger* belief in life after death. (Whether this was a temporary or a permanent change was not ascertained; nor was it clear that the attitude–change actually reduced the anxiety about death.) The disbelievers, on the other hand, remained at the same low level of afterlife-belief. Presumably, disbelievers either felt less fear of death, or dealt with their fear in some way *other* than adopting a stronger belief in the afterlife.

Another hypothesis is that afterlife-belief is adopted as a result of *a human need for immortality*, which leads a person to deny the reality of death. A variant of this idea goes on to suppose that the need for immortality is either caused or intensified by a person's fear of death, and that therefore, once again, afterlife-belief has the psychological function of reducing fear of death. Such a need might also give rise to certain experiences which, on the surface at least, *suggest* that consciousness may be able to exist independently of the physical body: these include out-of-the-body experiences (OBEs), hauntings, poltergeists, near-death or verge-of-death experiences, and apparitions and other ostensible communications with the dead experienced either by the healthy or by those on their death-bed.

Irwin (1981) provides an excellent discussion of the 'need for immortality' hypothesis in relation to OBEs, and finds it appealing but not well-supported by research. Evidence that OBEs are reported more often by persons who believe in survival was obtained by Blackmore (1984) in her Bristol study but not by Thalbourne and Haraldsson (1984, Study I) in Iceland nor by Palmer (1979) in the USA. These two American and Icelandic studies likewise failed to turn up evidence that afterlife-believers were any more likely to have lived in a house reputedly haunted or beset by poltergeist disturbances, or to have experienced an apparition or communication with the dead, or a 'memory' of a previous lifetime. On the other hand Sabom (1982) was able to verify the impression gained from anecdotes that having a near-death experience brings about a reduction in fear of death and an increase in belief in an afterlife. Greyson (1981a. 1981b), however, found that among persons who had attempted suicide there was no tendency for those who believed in life after death *prior* to their suicide-attempt to have had a near-death experience *during* that attempt. Thus, while a person's belief in survival of death may be strengthened as a *result* of experiences such as these, there seems little evidence that afterlife-belief *causes* such experiences in the first place.

Again, some psychologists have suggested to me (and in a rather confident manner!) that believers in life after death must be more *neurotic* — constitutionally more liable to react emotionally under stress — than are persons who do not believe. However, while evidence has been sought in one British and two Icelandic groups (Thalbourne, 1981; Thalbourne & Haraldsson, 1984), no support has as yet been obtained for the conjecture. Nor does afterlife-belief appear to be related to the tendency to develop schizophrenia (further analysis of Thalbourne, 1985).

A more profitable line of reasoning might be to suppose that fear of death is stronger in people who are in some sense '*closer*' to death. This *might* be a possible explanation for the fact that *older* persons are often found to have a higher level of belief in survival (e.g., Argyle & Beit-Hallahmi, 1975; Cavan et al., 1949; Gorer, 1955; Thalbourne & Haraldsson, 1984, Study I). As Thouless (1971) points out, however, we have no evidence that fear of death increases with age and there is some suggestion that it in fact *decreases*; what *does* come with age is the 'immediacy of the problem of death and the mental necessity to come to terms with it' (Thouless, 1971, pp. 63–64). Another possibility is that the increasing infirmity of the body in old age may lead to an attitude of regarding the body as an object, and a feeling that one is an *observer* looking on at the affliction of the body. Finally, we cannot exclude the possibility that the explanation of why our elderly tend to be believers is a generational one: all over the world, afterlife-belief appears to be becoming less prevalent than it was years ago; thus, people born in 1900 tend to believe to a greater extent than do those born in 1950, and so on. Only a proper longitudinal study would allow us to say. But in any case, a person's age appears to account for even *less* variance in afterlife-belief than does their gender, and it is thus a relatively minor factor. Consequently, a fair number of studies (e.g. Blackmore, 1984; Thalbourne & Haraldsson, 1984, Study III) have failed to detect a difference between the degree of belief in young and in old.

Other people are close to death in a different way: they are the bereaved. Especially if the deceased has been a life-long companion, the bereaved person may find consolation in believing that their loved one still exists, can perhaps be communicated with, and will be re-united with them in the next world (Argyle & Beit-Hallahmi, 1975, p. 57). Thus, one might predict a higher level of afterlife-belief in people who are widowed, and Gorer (1955) has reported exactly this in England (though it must be remembered that widowed persons tend to be older as well). Again, Palmer (1979) has reported that the widowed people in his Charlottesville study had a higher incidence of apparitions and hauntings than did single and married persons. It might also be possible to gauge the level of belief in people *before and after* they are widowed — and to compare that level with the level in people who are living alone following divorce. If such comparisons suggest that the death of a *marriage-partner* is associated with an increase in belief, a researcher might also expect to find stronger afterlife-belief in persons grieving from the death of *other* types of relationship, and if this were found, it would be interesting to learn if this increase persisted *beyond* their recovery from grief. Similarly, higher levels of survival-belief might be anticipated in nations engaged in war, and in particular, in soldiers as they graduate from being trainees into becoming engaged in actual combat (see Argyle & Beit-Hallahmi, 1975, pp. 52–54). There is obviously ample scope for research!

In summary, however, it seems most reasonable to conclude that while a person's emotional response to death or the threat of death *might* plausibly be expected to play a rôle in the development of afterlife-belief, the nature and extent of that rôle have received more speculaton than research.

Belief in a Just World

Finally, mention should be made of a factor which is not so much an emotional reaction towards death but a *belief* — the belief that the world is a *just* world. The 'Just World Hypothesis' is well-described in Sigmund Freud's essay *The Future of an Illusion:*

> Death itself is not extinction, is not a return to inorganic lifelessness, but the beginning of a new kind of existence which lies on the path of development to something higher. And, looking in the other direction, this view announces that the same moral laws which our civilizations have set up govern the whole universe as well, except that they are maintained by a supreme court of justice with incomparably more power and consistency. In the end all good is rewarded and all evil punished, if not actually in this form of life then in the later existences that begin after death. In this way all the terrors, the sufferings and the hardships of life are destined to be obliterated. Life after death, which continues life on earth just as the invisible part of the spectrum joins on

to the visible part, brings us all the perfection that we may perhaps have missed here.

(Freud, 1961, p. 19)

The 'Just World Hypothesis' — the belief that people reap what they sow and that life after death is the Great Equalizer — is common to many metaphysical outlooks: the enforcer of justice is, in the West, God, and in the East, karma. It may help to explain, for example, Gorer's (1955) finding that the very poor in England showed high levels of belief in an afterlife. But, so far as I know, no work has been done to examine the validity of Freud's hypothesis that *belief in the afterlife arises from the belief that the world is a just world*. It should not be difficult to devise questions by means of which we could study the influence of this factor and see how important it is by comparison (or in combination) with general religiosity.

Conclusions, and Suggestions for Future Research

Having now reviewed the evidence for various factors connected with belief in life after death it would be tempting to add up the *total* percentage of variance that they collectively accounted for, to see how nearly the sum approaches 100%. However, even if we had variance estimates for all our factors — which we do not — such an exercise would in this case turn out to be misleading, for the technical reasons that it assumes that the various factors are *independent* of each other. To the extent that two or more factors are related to each other rather than independent, to that extent they may have to be considered as being more like a single process being examined from different angles, just as facility at Latin and facility at Greek may each be manifestations of a general aptitude for language. Our interpretation of the overall pattern of belief or disbelief must therefore proceed with full knowledge of the relationships *between* our various factors.

For instance, it turns out that, compared with men, women tend to be more religious (Argyle & Beit-Hallahmi, 1975, Ch. 5), more conservative (Wilson, 1975, p. 37), more positive in attitude to the paranormal (Haraldsson, 1981, p. 305), and even more anxious about death (Ray & Najman, 1974, p. 314). Thus, the finding that afterlife-believers tend to be female should inform us *even without further research* that such believers are also likely to be more religious, more conservative, more pro-paranormal, and more anxious about death. Again, religiosity and conservatism tend to go together (Scobie, 1975, Ch. 5; Wilson, 1975). From one point of view, then, the factors I have discussed are perhaps less informative and explain less of the puzzle than they might have appeared to do at first sight. Statistical techniques of a much more sophisticated type than have usually been used in this area — multiple regression and discriminant analysis, for example — will be required to tease out those factors which are important for afterlife-belief and those which are merely piggy-backing on others without contributing anything in their own right.

Moreover, several assumptions have been made during this review, and it is now time to question them. First of all, it has been assumed that people can be neatly categorized into those who believe in an afterlife and those who do not. It is not yet clear whether this is the most useful approach, or whether a person's degree of afterlife-belief should be described as falling at some point on a graduated *scale*, ranging gradually from utter certainty that there *is* an afterlife, to complete conviction that there is *not* — an approach taken by Osarchuk and Tatz (1973), for example. In particular, it may be that persons who are *agnostic* on the issue cannot in all psychological respects be thought of as simply 'somewhere in between' believers and disbelievers. In my recent St. Louis study I discovered that, while afterlife-believers were the most conservative — and rather more so than were the disbelievers, the most *liberal* persons were those who said they were *uncertain* as to the existence of an afterlife. I will be looking to see whether this same result occurs in my recent Adelaide survey.

Secondly, at the beginning of this review I alluded to the fact that there is, among afterlife-believers, diverse opinion as to the *details* of the supposed afterlife: while Christianity posits immortal life with resurrection of the dead for all, non-Christian faiths often see the afterlife as involving a process of successive incarnations, and possibly for select souls only. Yet the assumption tacitly made in this essay is that nevertheless all afterlife-believers could be considered as being one homogeneous group, to be distinguished from 'the disbelievers'. Recent research (Thalbourne & Williams, 1984) suggests that this assumption might be wrong: for instance, only in the case of the *immortality* hypothesis did MENSA women demonstrate significantly higher levels of belief than did men; when it came to *other* theories of *post mortem* continuation — including reincarnation — men and women apparently believe to the same degree. This finding led me to hypothesize that immortality-believers and reincarnation-believers may, depending on the country of residence, have rather different psychological characteristics. I am currently following up this hypothesis in the Adelaide study. Preliminary results, using the Wilson–Patterson rating of conservatism, suggest that while im-mortalists are indeed more conservative than *non*-immortalists, believers in *reincarnation* are actually significantly more *liberal* than are non-reincarnationists. This would appear to confirm an earlier impression gained by Wuthnow and Glock (1974) that readers of *Psychology Today* who were 'experimenting with Eastern religion' not only showed a high level of belief in reincarnation but were also rather radical, socially and politically. Reincarnation is subscribed to by only 23% of the US population (Wuthnow & Glock, 1974; Gallup, 1982), and as a less popular, non-traditional belief one might *expect* it be adopted by fewer conservatives. In Asian countries, however, where reincarnation is widely believed, it might be the *disbelievers* who are the liberals.

Clearly, then, a number of interesting new research projects suggest themselves. Participants have been asked in a large number of surveys and experiments whether they believe in life after death or not. Yet researchers have not, in general, looked as closely as they could at the possibility that believers and disbelievers differ in psychologically interesting ways (e.g., Palmer, 1979; Tobacyk & Milford, 1983). It is to be hoped that the results of this review may encourage workers to deem it worth their while to undertake such analyses in their future studies, as well as to re-examine the wealth of data accumulated in the past.

But given the evidence reviewed in this essay, what can we say we have learned about the psychology of belief in life after death? The question 'why do people believe in an afterlife?' in fact turns out to be more complex than it appears: it may be interpreted as a request for information about the factors which *instill* such belief in a child, or about the social or psychological factors which *maintain* the belief over time, or about the psychological *functions* that it serves for the individual. It seems clear that no *single* factor can account for *every* case of belief or disbelief in the afterlife: some *combination* of factors is required, and it may be that different combinations operate in different people. We have seen that the answers seem to involve an ongoing interaction between the particular climate of metaphysical belief surrounding a person, their style of personality, and perhaps the extent to which life calls upon them to deal with death-related concerns.

This review, while hopefully of interest in its own right, may also provide some support for a more *general* thesis, namely, that our beliefs can be influenced not only by reason but also by non-rational factors connected with personality and environment. If such a thesis can be sustained, then it may have important implications for the question of the extent to which beliefs are responsive to evidence in general, and, in particular, for the question of the degree to which evidence which is *counter-attitudinal* can be evaluated with objectivity.

Footnotes

1. I would like to express my thanks to Drs Bruce Greyson and Erlendur Haraldsson for their assistance with various aspects of my research in this area.

2. Unlike in Christianity, the concept of an afterlife is of very little importance in Judaism. Says Freud (1964, p. 20), in his second essay on *Moses and Monotheism*, '. . . the ancient Jewish religion renounced immortality entirely; the possibility of existence continuing after death is nowhere and never mentioned.' Freud puts this down to what he thinks is influence on early Judaism from the religious ideas of the heretical Egyptian Pharoah Akhenaten, who, so fanatical was his monotheism, attempted to eliminate the whole polytheistic pantheon, including Osiris, god of the afterlife.

3. This finding has recently been confirmed by Irwin (1985) using Australian students. Moreover, it seems that the reason for the large *national* differences in afterlife-belief — mentioned earlier — is that belief is higher in those nations whose people report themselves to be very religious: for example, it can be seen from figures reported by Sigelman (1977) that in India, where the majority believe in an afterlife, 81% say they are 'very religious', while in disbelieving Japan only 12% describe themselves in this way. For the 16 countries I examined, this correlation was extremely strong.

4. This finding appears to have been confirmed by Gallup (1982) in the USA and by Blackmore (1984): Blackmore asked more than 300 people in Bristol, England, the question, 'Have you ever had a profound or moving religious or mystical experience?'

5. It is important to point out that in this case, as in all of the studies which I shall be discussing in this review, to say that afterlife-believers are '[significantly] more X' must *not* be taken to imply that *all* such believers possess the characteristic X. Thus, to say that there is a 'statistically significant' relationship between being an afterlife-believer and being religious means that, as a rule, the *majority* of believers are religious while the *majority* of disbelievers are not. At the same time, there do exist some afterlife-believers who are not religious, as well as a few afterlife-disbelievers who are religious; it is simply that such people are in the minority.

6. It is interesting in the light of this conclusion to note that in Blackmore's (1984) English survey the reason most commonly given by people for their belief in survival was religion.

7. '*Apparent*' implications, because I do not myself think that they necessarily follow. *I* believe that the existence of paranormal phenomena merely points to the fact that the scope of mental influence and human potential is *more extensive* than is currently recognized by orthodox science. Moreover, I am not yet persuaded that the scope of such powers is either unlimited or that their operation is capricious and unpredictable. On the contrary, I am impressed by the great *difficulty* of eliciting even the weakest manifestations of paranormal phenomena, either from oneself or from other persons under controlled laboratory conditions.

8. Blackmore (1984) obtained comparable findings in England.

9. I am grateful to Dr. Eric Rump for helpful discussions on this topic.

References

Argyle, M., & Beit-Hallahmi, B. (1975), *The Social Psychology of Religion*, London & Boston, Routledge & Kegan Paul.

Blackmore, S.J. (1984), 'A postal survey of OBEs and other experiences,' *Journal of the Society for Psychical Research*, 52, 225–244.

Cattell, R.B., Eber, H.W., & Tatsuoka, M.M. (1970), *Handbook for the Sixteen Personality Factor Questionnaire (16PF)*, Champaign, Ill., Institute for Personality and Ability Testing.

Cavan, R.S., Burgess, E.W., Havighurst, R.J., & Goldhammer, H. (1949), *Personal Adjustment in Old Age*, Chicago, Science Research Associates, Inc.

Collett, L.J., & Lester, D. (1969), 'The fear of death and the fear of dying,' *Journal of Psychology*, 72, 179–181.

Dahlstrom, W.G., Welsh, G.S., & Dahlstrom, L.E. (1972), *An MMPI Handbook, Volume 1: Clinical Interpretation*, :chlbrevised edition], Minneapolis, University of Minnesota Press.

Freud, S. (1961), *The Future of an Illusion*, New York and London, W.W. Norton & Co. [First published in 1927. English translation by J. Strachey.]

Freud, S. (1964), 'Moses and Monotheism: Three Essays,' in *The Standard Edition of the Complete Psychological Works of Sigmund Freud, Volume XXIII*, London, Hogarth Press. [First published in 1939. English translation by J. Strachey.]

Gallup, G. (Jr) [with W. Proctor] (1982), *Adventures in Immortality*, New York, McGraw-Hill.

Gallup Opinion Index (1976), 'Report No. 130'.

Gauld, A. (1977), 'Discarnate survival,' *in* B.B. Wolman, ed., *Handbook of parapsychology*, New York, Van Nostrand Reinhold.

Gauld, A. (1982), *Mediumship and Survival*, London, Heinemann.

Glock, C.Y., & Stark, R. (1965), *Religion and Society in Tension*, Chicago, Rand McNally & Co.

Gorer, G. (1955), *Exploring English Character*, New York, Criterion.

Greyson, B. (1981a), 'Attempted suicide and near-death experiences,' Paper presented at the Annual Meeting of the American Psychiatric Association, New Orleans.

Greyson, B. (1981b), 'Empirical evidence bearing on the interpretation of near-death experiences among suicide attempters,' Paper presented at the Annual Convention of the American Psychological Association, Los Angeles.

Grosso, M. (1979), 'The survival of personality in a mind-dependent world,' *Journal of the American Society for Psychical Research*, 73, 367–380.

Haraldsson, E. (1978), *Thessa Heims og Annars [Of This World and Another]*, Reykjavik, Bókaforlagid Saga.

Haraldsson, E. (1981), 'Some determinants of belief in psychical phenomena,' *Journal of the American Society for Psychical Research*, 75, 297–309.

Hynson, L.M. (Jr.) (1975), 'Religion, attendance, and belief in an afterlife,' *Journal for the Scientific Study of Religion*, 14 285–287.

Institute for Personality and Ability Testing (1979), *Administrator's Manual for the 16PF*, Champaign, Ill.

Irwin, H.J. (1981), 'The psychological function of out-of-body experiences. So who needs the out-of-body experience?' *The Journal of Nervous and Mental Disease*, 169, 244–248.

Irwin, H.J. (1985), 'A study of the measurement and the correlates of paranormal belief,' *Journal of the American Society for Psychical Research*, 79, 301–326.

Jeffers, F.C., Nichols, C.R., & Eisdorfer, C. (1961), 'Attitudes of older people towards death: A preliminary study', *Journal of Gerontology*, 16, 53–56.

Kalish, R.A. (1963), 'Some variables in death attitudes', *Journal of Social Psychology*, 59, 137–145.

Kurlychek, R. (1978–79), 'Assessment of attitudes toward death and dying: A critical review of some available methods', *Omega*, 9, 37–47.

Leuba, J.H. (1934), 'Religious beliefs of American scientists', *Harper's Magazine*, 169, 297.

Livingstone, A. (1973), 'A study of the relationship between creativity and masculinity–femininity in the First-Year College students', Unpublished B.A. (Honours) thesis, Department of Psychology, University of Adelaide, South Australia.

Mackenzie, B. & Mackenzie, S.L. (1980), 'Whence the enchanted boundary? Sources and significance of the parapsychological tradition,' *Journal of Parapsychology*, 44, 125-166.

Osarchuk, M., & Tatz, S.J. (1973), 'Effect of induced fear of death on belief in afterlife', *Journal of Personality and Social Psychology*, 27, 256–260.

Palmer, J. (1979), 'A community mail survey of psychic experiences', *Journal of the American Society for Psychical Research*, 73 221–251.

Poppleton, P.K., & Pilkington, G.W. (1963), 'The measurement of religious attitudes', *British Journal of Social and Clinical Psychology*, 2, 20–36.

Ray, J.J., & Najman, J. (1974), 'Death anxiety and death acceptance: A preliminary approach', *Omega*, 5 311–315.

Rogers, D.P. (1966), 'Some religious beliefs of scientists and the effect of the scientific method', *Review of Religious Research*, 7, 70–77.

Sabom, M.B. (1982), *Recollections of Death*, New York, Wallaby.

Scobie, G.E.W. (1975), *Psychology of Religion*, New York, Halsted Press.

Siegel, R.K. (1980), 'The psychology of life after death', *American Psychologist*, 35, 911–931.

Sigelman, L. (1977), 'Multi-nation surveys of religious beliefs', *Journal for the Scientific Study of Religion*, 16 289–294.

Stevenson, I. (1977), 'Research into the evidence of man's survival after death', *Journal of Nervous and Mental Disease*, 165, 152–170.

Stevenson, I. (1981), 'Comments on "The psychology of life after death".' *American Psychologist*, 35 1459–1461.

Thalbourne, M.A. (1981), 'Extraversion and the sheep-goat variable: A conceptual replication'. *Journal of the American Society for Psychical Research*, 75 105–119.

Thalbourne, M.A. (1982), *A Glossary of Terms Used In Parapsychology*, London, Heinemann.

Thalbourne, M.A. (1985), 'Are believers in psi more prone to schizophrenia?' in R.A. White & J. Solfvin eds., *Research In Parapsychology 1984*. Metuchen, N.J., & London: Scarecrow Press.

Thalbourne, M.A., & Haraldsson, E. (1984), 'A retrospective search for correlates of belief in life-after-death. I. Icelandic data', in R.A. White and R.S. Broughton, eds., *Research In Parapsychology 1983*. Metuchen, N.J., & London, Scarecrow Press.

Thalbourne, M.A., & Williams, L. (1984), 'Varieties of belief in survival: An exploratory study', *Theta*, 12 26–29.

Thouless, R.H. (1971), *An Introduction to the Psychology of Religion* [3rd edition], London, Cambridge University Press.

Thouless, R.H. (1979), 'Theories about survival', *Journal of the Society for Psychical Research*, **50** 1-8.

Tobacyk, J., & Milford, G. (1983), 'Belief in paranormal phenomena: Assessment instrument development and implications for personality functioning,' *Journal of Personality and Social Psychology*, **44** 1029-1037.

Wilson, G.D. (1975), *Manual for the Wilson–Patterson Attitude Inventory*, Windsor, England, NFER Publishing Co.

Wuthnow, R., & Glock, C.Y. (1974), 'God in the gut', *Psychology Today*, **8** 131-136.

CHAPTER 14

WANDERING SOULS: MOBILITY AND UNORTHODOXY

William Sims Bainbridge

Human experiences do not come with labels attached; everything we perceive must be interpreted to some extent before it is meaningful. Interpretation shapes memories, and recollections of unusual experiences are usually recast in terms of an ideology or a system of beliefs. People who are solidly integrated into the moral and social community which surrounds them will tend to interpret their experiences in conventional terms. But some individuals wander, both culturally and geographically, through the world. For them, glimpses of other worlds are a constant possibility.

To the sociologist, paranormal experiences are simply deviant experiences, the word *deviant* merely meaning that they diverge from the standards of the society. For purposes of this essay, I place paranormal experiences in the same cultural territory as the occult. While for other analytic purposes it would be quite reasonable to examine conventional religious experiences under the rubric of the paranormal, I shall not do so here. In societies where traditional religion retains substantial strength, religious experiences are normal, not paranormal.

Most people occasionally have unusual experiences that could be interpreted in many ways. Whether they define these experiences in an occult fashion or place more conventional religious labels upon them is greatly the result of how securely bound into standard religious traditions they are. Whether they dismiss the experiences as meaningless or interpret them in a spiritual light depends greatly on the degree of secular social control they are under, the freer their circumstances the more likely is a paranormal interpretation. Persons who are geographically mobile lack the stable social bonds which enforce conventionality in more immobile folk, and thus mobility across the map may also encourage beliefs and experiences (Faris & Dunham 1939).

Michael Carroll (1983; 1985) has studied the process by which apparitions of the Virgin Mary are created. First, a member of a strongly Catholic community has an unusual experience, perhaps a confused vision of some unidentified person. He shares the experience, somewhat incoherently, with members of the community who want it to be a vision of the Virgin. An implicit and even unconscious negotiation between him and the community reshapes the story until it conforms to standard religious expectations, and an apparition of the Virgin is announced. What the person really saw, if anything, has been lost in the social construction of a proof of faith.

A person who is poorly integrated into the community might resist this social reinterpretation of his experience. In a cosmopolitan society, like modern industrial nations, several quite different interpretations are culturally available to such an individual. From among them he can select the one personally most satisfying, or mere accident may present a particular interpretation at the right time. The influence of traditional religion varies across groups in the population, and therefore the prevalence of deviant spiritual experiences will also vary somewhat predictably from one group to another.

A considerable body of evidence has shown that geographic mobility reduces people's involvement in conventional religion (Wuthnow & Christiano 1979; Bainbridge & Stark 1981; K. Welch 1983; Stump 1984; M. Welch and Baltzell 1984; Stark & Bainbridge 1985). Involvement in religion means membership in a particular congregation, and mobility rips people away from their congregations without automatically providing new affiliation. Furthermore, in areas of high migration, the general social instability undercuts the capacity of congregations to maintain themselves. Although some individuals and families may remain strong in their faith despite lack of membership in a congregation, in general people drift away from orthodoxy of belief unless their social involvement in religion is high (Gaede 1976; K. Welch 1983; Stark & Bainbridge 1987). Some research has been done in Canada (Veevers & Cousineau 1980; Stark & Bainbridge 1985), but most studies are American, and thus it would be good to compare data from other countries.

Australian census reports contain a wealth of information about religion, and they permit several analyses of the connection between geographic mobility and religious deviance. For example, the 1886 census of the colony of Queensland reports the number with 'no religion' and the numbers with various birthplaces for 58 census districts, while the 1891 census does the same for 60 districts (Blackeney 1887; 1892). For both years, there is a strong correlation between the proportion of native-born men with no religion and the proportion who moved to Queensland from other parts of Australia or New Zealand.[1] In other words, high mobility districts were also high in deviance from the religious standard of the country.

The 1911 Australian census contains a set of tables giving religious affiliation by birthplace for each state (and the Capital Territory) for each sex (Knibbs, 1914). I have reanalyzed these data to compare the religious affiliations of people living in their states of birth with the affiliations of people who have moved from one state to another. Table 1 reports on 1,814,897 men and 1,800,782 women born in Australia. A slightly higher proportion of men are migrants from one state to another, 12.5 percent compared with 10.8 percent, and the rates of deviance are much higher for men in all categories except the Seventh-Day Adventist sect.

When most people profess a conventional religious affiliation, it is very deviant to assert that one is an Atheist. Perhaps several thousand Australians in 1911 privately rejected the existence of God, but only a few were willing to risk the censure of their communities by proclaiming Atheism. Agnosticism is a milder affront to the sentiments of the community, because it does not assert so confidently that the majority is wrong in its most basic beliefs. Freethinkers often believe in God, but they refuse to let orthodox churches speak for them, and they assert the right to develop their own, personal faiths. Such religious independence is certainly deviant with a predominantly religious society with strong churches. Persons who respond 'no religion' to the census taker are a mixture of persons hostile to religion and others only mildly indifferent to it. Thus, this category represents a range of deviance that on balance should be milder than the more self-assertive Atheists, Agnostics, and Freethinkers.

The 'Other' category was labelled 'Other (Indefinite)' in the census volume to distinguish it from the sects and minor denominations in the 'Other (Christian)' category and the Asian faiths in 'Other (Non-Christian)'. Spiritualism dominates, its 2,362 native-born members constituting 41.8 percent of the Other category. The second most populous subcategory was Socialists, representing only 294 persons, and there were also 186 Realists. Other subcategories with more than 50 members are a bewildering collection: Deist, Undecided, Cosmopolitan, Unknown, Reasonist, Any Religion or Anything, Calathumpian, Humanitarian, Metaphysician, Pantheist, Universalist, and Indefinite. There were also a few Monists, New Thought people, Spiritists, Freemasons, Communists, and Single Taxers. I suspect that the 32 Wowsers were described as such by members of their households, rather than by themselves, because 'wowser' is the Australian word for an obtrusively puritanical person. Despite the variegation of the Other category, half or more of its members are cultists, and the rest are such a miscellaneous lot that we can consider it a decent indicator of Australian cultism.

The Objectors were people who objected to stating what their religion was. Many of the Objectors may have been devout members of ethnic or minority religions, and in early twentieth-century American censuses of religion the largest group reluctant to provide information were Jews. Thus, although objecting to state one's religion was an act of mild deviance, it did not necessarily betoken religious radicalism. Seventh-Day Adventists were listed among the ordinary Protestant denominations, and we typically refer to this group as a sect. But it was so far from mainstream Christian traditions, and so emphatic in its assertion of unusual beliefs and practices, that we will not go wrong to call it a cult in the years when it was first being introduced into Australia.

The purpose of Table 1 is the comparison it offers between migrants and non-migrants. Consider the male Atheists, for example. The rate was 43 Atheists per 100,000 migrant males, compared with only 9 Atheists per 100,000 among those residing in their state of birth. The final column of the table compares these rates in terms of a ratio. Among males, migrants had 4.8 times the chance of being Atheists as did non-migrants. Among females, the Atheism ratio in favour of

Table 1: Geographic Mobility Increases Deviance from Religious Standards: Australia in 1911

Rate per 100,000 population

Religion	Number	Born in Same State	Born in Other State	Ratio of Other/Same
MALES:				
Atheist	238	9	43	4.8
Agnostic	1294	53	203	3.8
Freethinker	1451	59	226	3.8
No religion	4049	183	507	2.8
Other	1963	95	203	2.1
Objectors	39119	2009	3179	1.6
Adventists	2014	104	163	1.6
FEMALES:				
Atheist	47	2	6	3.0
Agnostic	394	18	53	2.9
Freethinker	330	16	39	2.4
No religion	1289	68	103	1.5
Other	1479	77	126	1.6
Objectors	22816	1252	1394	1.1
Adventists	2014	138	302	2.2

migration was 3.0. Some people still living in their state of birth may have moved a great distance within it, so many cases of deviant religion currently in the non-migrant category are in fact unrecognized migrants, and the ratios are all conservative estimates.

I arranged the table's categories in order of the ratios for men. This places them roughly in order of decreasing deviance. To be an Atheist is more deviant than to be an Agnostic or a Freethinker. All the groups are deviant, despite the fact that some are irreligious while others represent religious cults. Thus, geographic migration frees people from the constraints of standard religion, and they are then at liberty either to abandon the sacred or to experiment with novel faiths. Table 1 says little about paranormal experiences, although the Spiritualists who make up nearly half the Other category pursue contact with departed souls, but it establishes a connection between two ways in which a soul may wander in this life: geographically and spiritually.

We can examine empirically the thesis that paranormal experiences are most common for wandering souls, using statistics on 120 American metropolitan areas with populations over 300,000 in 1980. The Standard Metropolitan Statistical Area (SMSA) is a creation of the census bureau, a geographic unit that typically combines a central city with its suburbs, more valid for statistical studies than the city itself, because the governmental boundaries of cities are pure accidents of history. The largest SMSA is Greater New York City, with 9,120,000 residents, and the total population of all 120 SMSAs was about 133,056,000. A good measure of geographic migration is the percent who have moved to a new home in the past five years, data published in the 1980 census. This figure ranged from 30.4 percent of the population, up to 66.1 percent, across the 120 metropolitan areas.

For a measure of conventional religion, we can use the percent of residents who are formal members of churches or other standard religious groups. I was able to estimate this from a survey of 111 denominations comprising 231,708 congregations, carried out in 1980 (Quinn, Anderson, Bradley & Schriver 1982; cf. Stark 1980). The religion data were tabulated by county or similar unit, and for most of the country SMSAs are simply combinations of counties. But in New England, counties and SMSAs do not correspond, so I could not include New England in the following analysis. The church member rate ranged from a low of 28.8 percent, up to a high of 81.1 percent.

Data on the geographical distribution of paranormal experiences come from four sources: Scientology, *Fate* magazine, the *Spiritual Community Guide*, and Transcendental Meditation. These four provide very different measures, so that a wide segment of paranormal experience is included. Scientology is an authoritarian cult, while *Fate* is an open-minded clearing house for all kinds of personal, spiritual experience. The *Spiritual Community Guide* lists a great variety of organizations promoting consciousness expansion, while Transcendental Meditation was a consciousness-altering technique which touched a vast number of individuals. I am always on the lookout for other data, but we already have an excellent collection.

Scientology, originally called Dianetics, is one of the best-known enduring cults, now approaching its fortieth birthday (Gardner 1957; Wallis 1976; Stark & Bainbridge 1985; Bainbridge 1987). Founded by science fiction writer, L. Ron Hubbard, it promises members vastly increased mental and spiritual powers, achieved through a series of consciousness-altering techniques. The first I experienced, when I studied Scientology ethnographically in 1970, was TR-0 (Bainbridge 1978, p. 205). For up to two hours, I and another person would gaze unrelentingly into each other's eyes, our overtaxed vision providing us ever stranger pictures. Commonly, Scientologists report seeing the other person's aura and reflections of his previous incarnations. Several visualization techniques are used in group sessions, such as mocking up objects, 'havingness' procedures, spotting spots in space, and holding anchor points.

The most famous Scientology technique is E-Meter auditing, a psychoanalysis-like procedure in which an auditor (therapist) explores the memories of the preclear (patient) with the aid of a simple electronic lie detector device, the E-Meter. Indeed, preclears develop entirely new memories in the process, which they say are as real and vivid as ordinary recollections. For the first time in their current lives, they *remember* having lived before, often on other planets.

In his first Dianetics publications, Hubbard drew an analogy between the human mind and a mechanical calculator, saying that the way to get each to produce correct answers was to 'clear' its memory registers (Hubbard 1950a, 1950b). Scientology reprograms memory to make Scientologists believe they have had many experiences which outsiders find utterly incredible.

About halfway through the entire course, after investing thousands of dollars and years of effort, a person may become *clear* and individuals whose memory registers have been sufficiently adjusted are called *clears*. Above clear are several levels of OT or Operating Thetan. The central organization maintains good records of all Scientologists who have gone clear, and David Aden of the Boston church was kind enough to provide me with a computer printout, giving the numbers of clears in each of the 3-digit postal 'zip' code areas, as of November 1985. These are not identical to the standard census districts of the United States, but I was able to assign the zip code areas to metropolitan areas with high confidence. Altogether, 8,256 clears lived in the 120 SMSAs.

A second source of data on unusual experiences is the occult magazine, *Fate*. Since 1948, this publication has printed stories of ancient mysteries and modern encounters with the beyond. In addition to an ordinary column of letters to the editor, there are two sets of brief reports of paranormal experiences, 'True Mystic Experiences', and 'My Proof of Survival'. Take the February 1980 issue, for example, which reports six mystic experiences. The day a family discovers grandma has cancer, her spirit calls them telepathically from the hospital. Footprints in a snowy cemetery look like those of ghosts. A poltergeist saves a man from an accident at work. The pranks of a second poltergeist chase a family out of a rented home. The inexplicable crash of a picture from the wall warns a miner to stay home, and he thus avoids a cave-in. At the exact moment a man narrowly escapes death, his image appears to his family, three thousand miles away.

The seven proofs of survival are equally dramatic. A woman sees a robed apparition and feels the wagging tail of a ghost dog. Wisps of blue smoke from a dead man's pipe alert a family that their daughter must be rushed to the hospital. Two women are simultaneously visited in their dreams by a relative murdered by the Bulgarians. A husband's ghost returns to remind his wife to make the payment on his cemetery plot. Clairvoyance gives a man warning of his decapitation, twenty-five years before the event. Calmly, a man faces death from cancer, serene in his knowledge of the afterlife he glimpsed when he had briefly died, years before. The spirit of a dying man visits his granddaughter to say farewell.

The miscellaneous letters to the editors also include several about unusual experiences. In the distance, a skier sees children who leave no tracks on the snow. A writer thinks someone mentioned in a story is a reincarnation of his grandfather. A dream warns of a friend's death. A woman desperately seeking a job performs meditation on the colors pink and green, and soon she is working for a Mr. Pinkham at Greensberg Savings. Finally, without consulting each other, a woman and her niece submit stories to True Mystic Experiences, and they are printed on the same page of the same issue. This last story was printed just a year after the pair of mystic experiences, but many stories report events from decades past, and writers have had ample opportunity to reinterpret events and construct paranormal memories.

I obtained copies of all 120 *Fate* issues published from 1975 through 1984 and examined all the letters. Careful to discount multiple missives from the same person, I tabulated the number of people writing from each of the 120 SMSAs, a total of 1,334. This task required me to locate each of the addresses on maps of the country, to determine which should be counted in each area and which came from outside the major cities.

The third set of data is based on entries in the 1974 *Spiritual Community Guide* (Singh 1974), a book listing New Age enterprises around the United States. Half are described as *centers* 'devoted to the spiritual path, raising one's consciousness, transmitting higher knowledge or promoting universal love and unity.' The rest are communes, New Age book stores, natural food stores, and organic restaurants. Many listings are branches of national cults, such as Baha'i and 3HO (Healthy Happy Holy Organization), while others are local ashrams. Leaders of several esoteric movements contributed essays to the guide, including Swami Satchidananda (of the Integral Yoga Institute), Swami Kriyananda (of Ananda Cooperative Village), Alan Watts (proponent of Zen), Ram Dass (formerly named Richard Alpert, Timothy Leary's partner in psychedelics), Wernher Erhard (founder of *est*, a derivative of Scientology), and Elizabeth Clare Prophet (of the St. Germain cult, Summit Lighthouse).

As represented in the *Spiritual Community Guide*, the New Age subculture combines elements of Asian religion, Western occultism, and food faddism. Perhaps the common element is self-transformation, whether by raising one's consciousness or cleansing one's body. Many of the practices advertised in the guide are designed to produce paranormal experiences, and the subculture as a whole endorses them again. Again, working with detailed maps, I was able to locate the entries in their metropolitan areas, finding a total of 1,599 in the 120 SMSAs.

Our final measure of the geographic distribution of deviant consciousness is Transcendental Meditation, the movement founded by Maharishi Mahesh Yogi. In the 1970s, nearly a million Americans learned 'TM', a simple practice said to produce good physical, emotional, and mental health. The public was further told that TM produced a new state of consciousness, and members of the movement were able to publish this dogma in the journal *Science* and the popular science magazine, *Scientific American* (Wallace 1972; Wallace and Benson 1972). Only after TM had peaked in 1975, when 292,517 Americans were initiated into the practice, were these claims effectively challenged (Pagano et al. 1976; White 1976a, 1976b; Allen 1979).

By the late 1970s, inner members of the TM movement were reporting extremely strange experiences, notably physical levitation, but TM had always aimed to transform consciousness. Today, committed members believe that TM sessions conducted by hundreds or thousands of meditators project a telepathic force so powerful that it can reduce the crime rate or boost the stock market.

With the help of Daniel H. Jackson, I obtained a highly-accurate computer printout of the numbers of people initiated into TM in each of about 3,200 urban areas for the years 1967–1977. Urban areas are not the same as metropolitan areas. Typically, a metropolitan area consists of several urban areas, plus some rural areas that happen to be included in the counties which the census bureau combines to make the SMSA. These rural areas were left out of the TM data, so I had to remove the rural populations of the metropolitan areas before calculating rates for TM. Fully 506,475 TM meditators lived in the urban portions of the 120 SMSAs.

Now it is time to see if these four measures of paranormal experiences show high values where geographic mobility is high, and low values where the church member rate is high. Table 2 answers the question for geographic mobility, giving the cult rates per 100,000 for three groups of cities. I divided the 120 metropolitan areas into thirds, in terms of the percent of their populations that had moved to a new residence in the past five years, as reported in the 1980 census. For the 40 most stable cities, on average just 39.7 percent of the population had moved during the past five years, compared with 56.7 percent for the 40 most mobile cities. The pattern could not be more clear. For each of the four measures of paranormal experience, the rate is highest in the most mobile cities, and lowest in the most stable cities.

The data let us look again at the connection between migration and conventional religion. In the 40 most stable cities, on average 59.5 percent of people belong to a church or synagogue. In the 40 medium

Table 2: Geographic Stability Reduces Paranormal Experiences: 120 American Metropolitan Areas in 1980

Rate per 100,000 Population

Cities — in Terms of Mobility	Percent Moved in 5 years	Scientology Clears	Fate Letter Writers	Spiritual Guide Listings	T.M. Meditators
40 Stable	39.7%	0.99	0.69	0.52	377.32
40 Medium	48.1%	2.69	0.76	0.81	394.69
40 Mobile	56.7%	6.37	1.33	1.94	603.74
120 Total	48.2%	3.35	0.93	1.09	458.58

on geographic mobility, the rate is 56.9 percent. And in the 40 most mobile cities, only 43.7 percent are members of churches.

In Table 3, I have divided the 120 metropolitan areas into three groups in terms of their church member rate, rather than mobility. In the most highly churched 40 cities, 66.9 percent are members, compared with only 39.0 percent in the unchurched group of cities. The thesis that conventional religion inhibits paranormal experience is strongly supported; the four measures are highest in the unchurched cities and lowest in the churched cities. This is not a mere tautology, stemming from the ways conventional religion and cultism are defined. Of the four, only Scientology considers itself a religion in direct competition with standard denominations, and certainly it is

Table 3: Church Membership Reduces Paranormal Experiences: 120 American Metropolitan Areas in 1980

Rate per 100,000 Population

Cities — in Terms of Religiousness	Percent Church Members	Scientology Clears	Fate Letter Writers	Spiritual Guide Listings	T.M. Meditators
40 Churched	66.9%	1.13	0.67	0.68	349.26
40 Medium	54.1%	1.40	0.79	0.79	417.81
40 Unchurched	39.0%	7.53	1.32	1.79	608.68
120 Total	53.4%	3.35	0.93	1.09	458.58

easy to read *Fate* magazine while remaining a church member. But involvement in conventional religion reduces the likelihood of having paranormal experiences, because any unusual experiences the churched person does have can be reinterpreted in conventional religious terms, under the social influence of the local minister and congregation.

Using a statistical technique known as multiple regression, I have looked at the way migration and church membership fit together with other variables to determine our four cult rates. Three other variables were most important to the analysis: education, income, and marital status. Many people imagine that cults and paranormal experiences are marks of low education, but the opposite appears to be true. The higher the proportion of people in a city who have completed college or university studies, the higher is each of our paranormal rates. Except for *Fate* magazine, which is quite cheap, they require substantial monetary investments, so it is not surprising that cities with higher per capita incomes have higher paranormal rates. For two reasons, we might expect high cult rates where the divorce rate is high. First, married people possess strong social bonds that may tie them to conventionality, while a divorced person may be as free of stabilizing social influences as are many migrants. Second, divorce sends many people in search of a new way of life and fresh perspectives to replace the ones that were discredited when the marriage went sour.

When I combined all the explanatory variables, in a series of multiple regression analyses, a clear picture emerged. Church membership always matters, for all four paranormal rates, even taking account of all the other variables. Migration does not matter in and of itself, but primarily is the chief factor shaping the church member rate. That is: migration reduces church membership; low church membership increases paranormal experiences.

High levels of education increase the rates for the *Spiritual Community Guide* and Transcendental Meditation, but not for the other two. Per capita income doesn't matter; it merely appears to at first because income tends to be high where education and mobility are high, and where church membership is low. Divorce increases the *Spiritual Community Guide* and Scientology rates, but divorce rates are greatly determined by the church member rate. Thus conventional religion has an indirect effect by holding down the divorce rate, as well as its direct effect on these two cult rates.

Even in areas of high mobility, vigorous forms of traditional faith may still have the power to reduce paranormal experiences. In 1979, I administered a long questionnaire to 1,439 students at the University of Washington in Seattle (Stark & Bainbridge 1985). While 241 professed to have 'no religion', another 245 claimed to be 'born again' — to belong to the Protestant Evangelical movement which was then sweeping the campus. One item asked whether respondents agreed that 'Some Eastern practices such as Yoga, Zen, or Transcendental Meditation, are probably of great value.' While only 28.1 percent of the born agains agreed, fully 72.5 percent of those with no religion did so. Another item was: 'Some occult practices, such as Tarot reading, seances, or psychic healing, are probably of great value.' Only small minorities agreed with this one, but the born agains were far less enthusiastic than those with no religion, 5.5 percent compared with 16.4.

Souls that wander geographically loosen their bond to society, and in particular they may escape the controlling influence of a conventional church congregation. Souls that wander spiritually will lack the conventional frameworks for interpreting the unusual experiences which most humans occasionally have. Robert Angell (1949; 1974) has distinguished two ways in which an individual may be integrated into a community: social integration and moral integration. Social integration means the possession of stable social relationships with other individuals, something that geographic mobility disrupts. He says 'a high degree of moral integration involves a mutually consistent set of norms derived from common values, norms which members of the group, community, or society have internalized as guides to their behavior' (Angell 1974, p. 610). Many sociologists regard the church member rate to be the best measure of moral integration.

We have seen that social integration and moral integration are closely linked: where people live in the same home for many years, the church member rate is high. Thus, wandering souls tend to wander across both dimensions simultaneously, the geographic and the spiritual. Geographic mobility loosens the grip of conventional religion, liberating people to experience the paranormal. Thus, far from being the remnant of ancient superstition, as some critics of the occult might claim, paranormal experiences are a natural result of modern social conditions.

Footnote
[1] The proportions for women are too low for reliable statistical analysis. The correlations for men are large and significant: 0.48 for 1886 and 0.66 for 1891.

References

Allen, D. (1979), 'TM at Folsom Prison: A critique of Abrams and Siegel,' *Criminal Justice and Behavior*, **6**, 9–12.

Angell, R.C. (1949), 'Moral integration and interpersonal integration in American cities,' *American Sociological Review*, **14**, 245–251.

Angell, R.C. (1974), 'The moral integration of American cities — II,' *American Journal of Sociology*, **80**, 607–629.

Bainbridge, W.S. (1978), *Satan's Power: A Deviant Psychotherapy Cult*, Berkeley, Calif, University of California Press.

Bainbridge, W.S. (1987), 'Science and religion: The case of Scientology,' pp. 59–79 in D.G. Bromley and P.E. Hammond, eds., *The Future of New Religious Movements*, Macon, Georgia, Mercer University Press.

Bainbridge, W.S. & Stark, R. (1981), 'Suicide, homicide, and religion: Durkheim reassessed,' *Annual Review of the Social Sciences of Religion*, **5**, 33–56.

Blackeney, W.T. (1887), *Seventh Census of the Colony of Queensland*, Brisbane, James C. Beal, Government Printer.

Blackeney, W.T. (1892), *Eighth Census of the Colony of Queensland*, Brisbane, James C. Beal, Government Printer.

Carroll, M.P. (1983), 'Visions of the Virgin Mary: The effect of family structures on Marian apparitions,' *Journal for the Scientific Study of Religion*, **22**, 205–221.

Carroll, M.P. (1985), 'The Virgin Mary at LaSalette and Lourdes: Whom did the children see?' *Journal for the Scientific Study of Religion*, **24**, 56–74.

Faris, R.E.L. & Dunham, H.W. (1939), *Mental Disorders in Urban Areas*, Chicago: University of Chicago Press.

Gaede, S. (1976), 'A causal model of belief-orthodoxy: Proposal and empirical test,' *Sociological Analysis*, **37**, 205–217.

Gardner, M. (1957), *Fads and fallacies in the Name of Science*, New York, Dover.

Hubbard, L.R. (1950a), 'Dianetics: The evolution of a science,' *Astounding Science Fiction* **45** (May), 43–87.

Hubbard, L.R. (1950b), *Dianetics: The Modern Science of Mental Health*, New York, Paperback Library.

Knibbs, G.H. (1914), *Census of the Commonwealth of Australia — 1911*, Melbourne, McCarron, Bird & Company.

Pagano, R.R., Rose, R.M., Stivers, R.M., & Warrenburg, S. (1976), 'Sleep during Transcendental Meditation,' *Science*, **191**, 308–310.

Quinn, B., Anderson, H., Bradley, M., Goetting, P., & Schriver, P. (1982), *Churches and Church Membership in the United States, 1980*, Atlanta, Georgia, Glenmary Research Center.

Singh, P. (1974), *Spiritual Community Guide, 1975–76*, San Rafael, Calif, Spiritual Community Publications.

Stark, R. (1980), 'Estimating church-membership rates for ecological areas.' (National Institute of Juvenile Justice and Delinquency Prevention, LEAA, U.S. Department of Justice), Washington, D.C., U.S. Government Printing Office.

Stark, R. & Bainbridge, W.S. (1985), *The Future of Religion: Secularization, Revival, and Cult Formation*, Berkeley, Calif, University of California Press.

Stark, R. & Bainbridge, W.S. (1987), *A Theory of Religion*, New York, Peter Lang.

Stump, R.W. (1984), 'Regional migration and religious commitment in the United States,' *Journal for the Scientific Study of Religion*, **23**, 292–303.

Veevers, J.E. & Cousineau, D.F. (1980), 'The heathen Canadians,' *Pacific Sociological Review*, **23**, 199–216.

Wallace, R.K. (1970), 'Physiological effects of Transcendental Meditation,' *Science*, **167**, 1751–1754.

Wallace, R.K. & Benson, H. (1972), 'The physiology of meditation,' *Scientific American*, **226** (February), 84–90.

Wallis, R. (1976), *The Road to Total Freedom*, New York: Columbia University Press.

Welch, K.W. (1981), 'An interpersonal influence model of traditional religious commitment,' *Sociological Quarterly*, **22**, 81–92.

Welch, K.W. (1983), 'Community development and metropolitan religious commitment: A test of two competing models,' *Journal for the Scientific Study of Religion*, **22**, 167–181.

Welch, M.R. & Baltzell, J. (1984), 'Geographical mobility, social integration, and church attendance,' *Journal for the Scientific Study of Religion*, **23**, 75–91.

White, J. (1976a), 'A critical look at TM,' *New Age Journal*, January, 30–35.

White, J. (1976b), 'Second thoughts: What's behind TM?' *Human Behavior*, October, 70–71.

Wuthnow, R. & Christiano, K. (1979), 'The effects of residential migration on church attendance in the United States,' pp. 257–276 *in* R. Wuthnow ed., *The Religious Dimension*, New York, Academic Press.

CHAPTER 15
DR. THOULESS AND PSYCHICAL RESEARCH

Lawrence B. Brown

Robert Thouless, who lived from 1894 to 1984, was one of the early leaders of psychology in Britain. His work covered an unusually broad range: beginning as an experimental psychologist. Dr. Thouless later applied his experimental sophistication both to parapsychological and perceptual problems, at his death leaving the manuscript of a book on 'How the world looks'. After a degree in Natural Sciences at Cambridge, service in the First World War and a research degree, Thouless lectured at Manchester and at Glasgow. He became Reader in the Department of Education at Cambridge in 1938 and retired in 1961, to continue his writing and produced *Experimental Psychical Research* (1963) and *From Anecdote to Experiment in Psychical Research* (1972), which he said at the time was his 'main contribution to parapsychology'. Both books are systematic accounts of the proper procedures by which to establish the validity of parapsychological claims, although neither of them is referred to in Edge et al.'s (1986) *Foundations of Parapsychology*.

Thouless's first book was *An Introduction to the Psychology of Religion* (1922, and revised in 1971). His second was a textbook on *Social Psychology* (1925), republished in 1937 as *General and Social Psychology*. His most successful book concerned what he called 'psychological logic', published in Britain under the title *Straight and Crooked Thinking* in 1930, and in America as *How to think straight*. It was revised several times, most recently in 1953. His early papers related to 'Some observations on contrast effects in graded discs' (January, 1923), 'The psychology of the contemplative life' (July, 1923), 'Soul beliefs and hypotheses' (1924) and 'The psychogalvanic phenomenon in dream analysis' (July, 1924). They set a pattern of interests which turned increasingly towards establishing the validity of claims to paranormal phenomena.

Thouless said that he differed 'from most other experimental psychologists in being willing to try out alleged paranormal phenomena', although for a long time his 'scepticism was reinforced by the uniform failure of these attempts'. In the mid-twenties he was asked to observe experiments performed by the assistant of Alrutz from

Sweden, who believed that hypnosis was produced by 'a nervous effluence from the finger tips of the operator'. The other observers then included McDougall, Janet and Bartlett, all well-known psychologists. They concluded that the 'alleged paranormal effect was simply due to suggestion'. Thouless's first published work in parapsychology had been a review of Ostry's *Supernormal Faculties in Man* in 1924, requested by Dean Hewlett Johnson. He said this 'shook but did not destroy his scepticism' but that he was more challenged in 1935 by Rhine's *Extra-sensory Perception*, although he was not convinced even then that parapsychological effects were genuine because the experiments were not 'sufficiently safeguarded to an experimental psychologist'. When he replicated Rhine's experiments he got only chance results. His next study reworked Whately Carington's data on trance personalities, using analysis of variance, 'with which', he said, 'up to that time, I had not been familiar'. This may well be one of the first applications of Fisher's methods to psychological data (Thouless, 1937a), although that reanalysis showed only chance results which were, however, 'unequivocally accepted' by Carington.

Thouless continued to examine and replicate other studies and found evidence for a significant 'displacement' in 'telepathic transmission of drawings' when 'subjects seemed to be bearing on targets exposed on other nights than that on which the attempted reproduction was made' (Thouless, 1942). He had by then become convinced of the reality of ESP from the results of his own studies, but did not claim that they should convince anyone else. Becoming president of the Society for Psychical Research in 1942 may have further strengthened his convictions, although it did not lessen his concern for properly controlled experiments that would 'find out more about it'.

He also identified what has been called Thouless's law. This holds that questions of fact (for example, that 'hornets live in nests under the ground', which was given a mean certainty score of 1.21 on a 3 point scale) are held less strongly than belief statements (that for example, 'the spirit survives death', with a mean certainty score of 2.07) (Thouless, 1935, and Brown, 1987, pp. 31–32). In this context, a recent study in Australia found that 88 percent of Catholics and 55 percent of non-Catholics, but only 13 percent of those who said they had no religion, claimed the belief that the 'spirit survives death' (ibid. p. 31). In recent American study of 'elite scientists', 29.2 percent considered ESP an established test or a likely possibility and 69 percent thought that ESP was 'a legitimate scientific undertaking' (McClenon, 1982).

William James

In an unpublished autobiographical note, Thouless said that his interest in psychology was stimulated by reading William James's *Principles of Psychology* during his war service, 'when it was difficult to keep up interest in Chemistry and Physics'. On becoming a research student in Cambridge after the First War, Thouless was 'most influenced' by W.H. Rivers, who suggested that 'the sensible thing to do was to start research', also telling him that 'psychology was being transformed by an Austrian called Freud'. So Thouless began the work that resulted in his 1922 text-book on 'religion in the light of Freud, William James, Coe, and other influences of that time'.

Both Thouless and the American psychologist William James, who died in 1910, were fascinated by religion (James, 1985) and by psychical research (James, 1986). Both men served as Presidents of the Society for Psychical Research (Haynes, 1982). McDermott's (1986) Introduction to James's *Essays in psychical research* asserts that it was William James's primary motivation to 'reconcile science and religion . . . that renders his work in this area original and enduring', with its 'Fidelity to fact, avoidance of abstract categories, patient attention to ultimate questions and preference for complexities over the dogmatism of either the skeptic or the believer' (pp. xiii–xiv). That description also characterises Thouless's work, science provided the methods to test psychological claims on valid data.

On my last meeting with him, in Canberra in 1983, Thouless said he was keeping himself active, at least intellectually, by woking on another book. I asked what it was about, and he replied, 'The survival of death' (Thouless, 1984). This small book of 52 pages emphasises the incorrigibly empirical approach and the high standard that Thouless set (and hoped to maintain) for evidence, even of an after-life. The book outlines a test for the survival of bodily death that he had set up in July, 1948, and which he said, in a 1982 letter, was 'my most significant contribution to parapsychology. I don't think the introduction of the term 'psi' in my presidential address to the SPR (in 1944) can count as a significant contribution'. It might even seem that such a 'test' preoccupied Dr. Thouless (1924, 1948a and b, 1960, 1963, 1984).

Thouless's test

Thouless's 'test of survival' was devised in response to previous, but unsuccessful, attempts to communicate with those who have died. This has not only been a continuing religious question (Luke 16.31) but, as Edge et al. (1986, p. 325–360) stress, a central philosophical and empirical issue of relevance to dualism and scientific materialism.

Empirical questions about survival are, however, no simpler than perennial questions about what it is that survives, or the evidence that can support a trust in the New Testament's hope or promises and Christian doctrines about the 'resurrection of the dead and the life of the world to come'. Since Jesus is not reported to have said what it was like after his resurrection, many specific beliefs about that depend on an apocalyptic vision that must be set against the problems faced by those who had known Jesus, in recognising his 'risen form'. Their difficulties suggest that the 'eye of faith' might have been needed to recognise him. That the statement in the Apostle's Creed, 'I believe in . . . the resurrection of the body and the life everlasting', is controversial is evidenced by contemporary theological disputes (including J.A.T. Robinson's *Honest to God*, 1964, and the Church of England's recent Doctrine Commission Report, 1987). Thouless (1984) noted that Buddhists hope to avoid repeated reincarnations by devout meditation and a destruction of craving, and that medieval Christians' belief in an everlasting torment in hell, which apparently engendered such great fear, seemed to have declined.

While doctrines about an 'after-life' have often been identified as one of the origins of religion, Bowker (1987, p. 12) emphasises that religions are fundamentally 'a consequence of *this*-life, *this*-worldly discoveries, whatever further inferences may subsequently have been drawn'. Yet Spilka et al (1985, p. 127f) conclude from their survey-data on 'religion and death' that the more religious people within Christian traditions are, 'the greater the likelihood that they believe in an after life' (p. 128), although such beliefs are not only 'a function of religion, but of other demographic factors as well' (p. 129), with higher education and economic status going with less belief in a life beyond death. A study by Marty et al. (1968) found that 68 percent of Americans believe in Heaven and 54 percent believe in Hell, although only 7 percent thought there was 'any real possibility' that they would go there.

Belief and experience

Beyond any specifically religious doctrines or claims, the evidence that there must be 'something' beyond 'the weeping in this vale of tears' comes classically from apparitions, poltergeists, possessions, death-bed wishes, hallucinations, and other unanticipated or haphazard experiences, that may be interpreted in religious or aesthetic terms (Back & Bourque, 1976). The most current evidence for our survival mentions out-of-the-body and near-death experiences, described, for example, in the widely discussed television program on Britain's

Channel 4 in January, 1988, and in *The Australian* on 14 May, 1988. But Mrs Thouless, after having been resuscitated in the Manly Hospital following her swimming accident on a visit to Sydney, remarked that Robert *would* be disappointed to know that she had not been met by 'those people in white, coming to take me away'. She was confident that death brings complete oblivion.

In the hope of clarifying beliefs about paranormal experiences, William James (1986, pp. 56–63) made an exhaustive 'census of hallucinations' through the Society for Psychical Research (SPR) in 1889, by sending out questionnaires to find 'the correspondence between ghostly apparitions and events in the real world' (pp. 57–8). Of the 6,311 answers received, 10.97 percent of men and 17.14 percent of women gave 'affirmative answers'. In the same tradition, Sir Alister Hardy (who was also involved with the SPR) set up his 'Religious experience research unit' in Oxford in 1969, to collate answers to similar questions. When a question about 'religious or mystical experience' was asked in an opinion survey in Britain in 1976, 36 percent of adults said they had had such a 'sudden religious insight or awakening' (Hay, 1982, p. 116f).

It was to foster studies like these that the Society for Psychical Research was established in England in 1882, with one of its objects the 'Investigation of evidence suggesting (sic) survival after death and of evidence suggesting reincarnation'. The group of scientists and philosophers connected with Trinity College, Cambridge, who founded this Society, also wanted 'to examine without prejudice or prepossession and in scientific spirit those faculties of man, real or supposed, which appear to be inexplicable in terms of any generally recognised hypotheses' (Haynes, 1882, p. xiii). The Society's articles that were signed in 1895 declared that its functions also included the investigation of hypnotism (even now a live issue), somnambulism and thought transference. One stated aim was therefore 'To investigate that large body of debatable phenomena designated by such terms as mesmeric, psychical and spiritualistic . . . (in) the same spirit of exact and unimpassioned enquiry which has enabled science to solve so many problems, once not less obscure nor less hotly debated'. In his Presidential Address to the Society in 1944, on 'The present position of experimental research into telepathy and related phenomena', Thouless stressed the necessity for observation and experimental control to resolve those parapsychological questions.

Mediums

David Hays's (1981) survey found that experiences of being 'aware of or influenced by a presence or a power' were described as vague feelings, premonitions, answered prayer, or as the presence of God, of others, or of the dead (1982, Chapter 9). Clairvoyance and messages from specific individuals in the after-life that are received through mediums, cross a barrier (and some skepticism) between life and death. Accounts of the 'sittings' for such communications include William James's lengthy 'Report on Mrs Piper's Hodgson-Control' (1986, pp. 253–360), which extended over 75 occasions. F.W.H. Myers, a founder of the SPR who died in 1901, is purported to have been responsible for 'more than 3,000 scripts collected over a thirty-year period, involving eventually over a dozen mediums (Edge et al., 1986, p. 340) including Mrs Piper. His other communications were through Geraldine Cummins (1932, 1984), who also had communications from Mrs Coombe Tennant (known as Mrs Willett) who had herself been a medium (Cummins, 1965, Thouless, 1984, pp. 12–13). William James (1909/1986) had concluded that this 'literature, however, is not overwhelmingly positive', and he offered as alternative explanations information from 'this world' a 'super ESP hypothesis' and 'retrocognition' (p. 338), instead of directly rejecting the evidence from mediums.

Nevertheless, as Grace Adams, a psychology student of Titchener's, noted in 1932, 'James stated his faith in Mrs Piper's mediumistic revelations in his most serious psychological texts' and hoped that his conviction of her powers might 'draw a reader or two into a field which the *soi-disant* (or self-styled) "scientist" usually refuses to explore' (p. 70). Adams said that James considered a 'serious study of these trance-phenomena one of the greatest needs of psychology' and never denied his own private convictions about the reality of such experience while writing 'as sceptically and as mechanistically as the best of determinists' (ibid.). James, like so many of his contemporaries, said he 'yearned for some higher power' beyond crude experiences, although he was criticised for this hope by his contemporaries (including Ward and Munsterberg: see McDermott, 1986, p. iii and xxxiii).

Tests of survival

F.W.H. Myers, who thought that any messages through mediums should be focused, left a 'sealed package' as a formal test of his own survival. A similar test was also tried by Oliver Lodge ten years before his death in 1940, with the information or message to be sent back after death written, sealed, and deposited with those interested in the experiment. While Myer's message had referred to the garden of a lover, 'the interviewing committee concluded that the package contained a reference to Plato's Symposium' (according to one of Thouless's notes). This failure suggested to Thouless that the message's 'communicator' must have been unaware of it, because if he had known 'he could have given the message directly'. Oliver Lodge left a description of the habit he had of drumming his fingers, although that message was not discovered until the package had been opened. Such tests could not, of course, be repeated once the message-pack was opened, and they did not exclude a clairvoyant finding what was contained in it.

Other experimental tests of survival that were proposed include Whately Carington's (1967) suggestion that mental tests should be administered to known communicators, preferably both before and after their death. Although that does not seem to have been tried, Stevenson (1968, 1976), an American psychiatrist and President of the SPR, has set several numerical codes into locks that might be opened by ESP while he is alive, or by 'sending back the key after he dies'. Stevenson (1974, 1977), and Cook et al. (1983) also report evidence suggestive of reincarnation from hypnotic age-regression, and from children's recollections. These and other spontaneous reports of a previous life do, however, 'involve retrospective rather than concurrent information' (Edge et al., 1986, p. 347).

The method of 'cross-correspondences' was also used to test for survival in the early part of the century, by collating results from separate mediums at different seances (or from automatic writing) when in communication with the early figures in psychical research. Thouless, however, argued that this method does not exclude chance effects. He also questioned the validity of all the other methods, and seemed to dislike having to rely on mediums' messages, since their 'communicators' might themselves be fakes! He thought that their independence had to be carefully established. The notoriety of efforts to communicate from the dead was increased by Houdini's showman-like claim to prove that he lived after his death (in 1923) by sending his wife the message, 'Rosabelle, believe' in a code they had used in mind-reading: Arthur Ford, the medium who claimed to have received that message in 1926, was later exposed as a fraud (Spraggett & Rouscher, 1973).

That all these 'tests' require inductive conclusions about their validity further weakens them. Furthermore, Edge et al. (1986) note that E.S.P. is more like catching a disease than knowing (p. 350) and, like metaphysical theories about the self and its powers, reports of coincidences might simply involve 'implicit expressions of psychological needs'. While some people in our society do believe that they are themselves specific reincarnations, it is more parsimonious to regard such beliefs as illusory rather than as explicit delusions, since survey results show that they are not uncommon.

An experimental model

Thouless believed that to overcome the difficulties, and the spurious results from any test of survival, the information to be conveyed must only be in the communicator's mind, related to an act in this world, and able to support an indefinite number of attempts to capture it, but not so many that a large amount of material would accumulate, some of which would be true merely by chance. In 1948 he therefore published a test (having had at least four sittings that were taken down in shorthand, in 1947, in which Sir Oliver Lodge was 'contacted') that would

1. have no hidden object or writing as a possible target for clairvoyance,
2. allow the possibility of an indefinitely large number of checks of the attempted solutions,
3. allow any attempted solution to be definitely right or wrong,
4. and leave 'no uncertainty about whether the supposed communicator was giving the correct answer'.

In his test 'the communicator (Thouless) would prove his identity by communicating the key to a passage in cipher which he had prepared during this lifetime . . . The test of it being the right key would be the fact that it enabled the enciphered passage to be read', with 'each answer being unmistakably right or wrong'. Thouless encoded two messages from a Vigenere letter square in the form

ABC . . . YZ
BCD . . . ZA etc.

After writing the chosen 'key-word' repeatedly over the passage to be enciphered, the letters to be used in the cipher are 'found at the intersection of the row starting in the original message with the column headed by the letter of the keyword immediately above it. So if the key-word were *crab* and the message to be enciphered were *There is no death*, the process of encipherment would be,

CRABC RA BC RABCR (key)
THERE IS NO DEATH (message)
VYESG ZS VQ UEBVY (cipher) (from the letter square)
(Thouless, 1948a)

Those ciphers are, he said, usually written in five letter blocks, and are not easily decoded without reference both to the key and to an appropriate letter square.

Thouless made his cipher even more complicated by using a

random sequence of letters for the key, in which 'Each word in a continuous passage is replaced by a simple letter which is obtained by adding up the serial numbers of letters in the word (i.e. 1 for a, 2 for b, etc.), and then taking the letter whose serial number is this total or, if the total is greater than 26, taking the letter whose serial number is the remainder after division (sic) by 26.' So, to encode the word 'To', 'The serial number of t is 20, while that of o is 15. Since $20 + 15 = 35 = 26 + 9$, the first letter of the key is, therefore, the ninth letter of the alphabet which is I.' Using that routine Thouless showed how with Hamlet's soliloquy 'To be or not to be' as the key passage, IGGWW BG PI VNWNU is the key letter series for his earlier example 'There is no death', which then encodes as BNKNAJYCWYRWGB when referred back to the latter square.

Thouless claimed that this system is unbreakable if the key series of letters is random and if only one passage is enciphered by that series. He reiterated in 1963(b) that 'I think it should be regarded as strong evidence for my survival if I manage to communicate the key for either passage after my death, if attempts made by similar methods before my death have failed'. But in a supplementary note (1948b) Thouless had already withdrawn the first message he produced because its key, SURPRISE, which had been enciphered by the Playfair system, was uncovered after two weeks' work by a cipher expert. Since his continuous passage was still uncoded, Thouless prepared another with a two word key, using the method he had described, 'so that all that is to be communicated is the key in each case' (1948b). The first of these encoded passages began INXPH CJKGM JIRPR . . . (1972, p. 163).

Thouless (1984) referred to the short stories of Conan Doyle and Edgar Allan Poe to give a general idea of what a cipher is. He also produced a handout with the enciphered messages and the questions that mediums (or their contacts) should be asked when trying to obtain the keys which, he said, are 'easy to remember'. He said that if no message comes through after his death, 'it will not, of course, be a proof that I have not survived', because the key 'may be a difficult matter after one has lost the material brain which one has used for remembering during one's lifetime'. But even if remembering were still possible, he said it could be as difficult as it is 'when one loses the pocket diary used for making notes of things one wants to remember in this life'.

Data on Dr. Thouless's Test

Solutions to Thouless's cipher test are still being collated by the Society for Psychical Research in London (W8 6UQ). Despite an offer from the 'Survival Research Foundation' in the United States for a $US2,000 prize (with a 'deadline' that was set for the beginning of 1988), it has not yet been adequately solved. While some of the solutions are ingenious the enciphering method was complex and none of the messages reported even seems to be close to the target. They have all failed when tested on computer programs written for this purpose.

The Secretary of the Society for Psychical Research in London is now coordinating the messages and had himself had 'about 14 effective sittings with eight mediums' during 1986. He has written that, 'It seems to me that I have been able to obtain good contact with Dr Thouless through each of these mediums, but it seems that he cannot remember the keys. One medium reported him as saying that it is like trying to remember something from a dream and that he had not expected that . . . I have asked at a recent sitting whether it could possibly be helpful if he were to try to arrange for a group of friends to help him to recall and transmit the keys (a procedure used earlier with Oliver Lodge), but he says he prefers to handle it himself and expresses confidence that before too long he will succeed.

From direct experience at my first ever seance, in a sitting that was arranged for me at the College of Psychic Studies in London in February, 1988, while I was preparing this paper, it is obvious that one central problem is to diagnose the meaning of whatever was being conveyed, and to decide when the target message might have been given. But it seems to be accepted that interpreting what the medium produces is a critical feature of any seance, and that this is helped by descriptions of previously known incidents in the communicator's life or by recognising their linguistic style.

I was told to take something to the sitting that belonged to the person to be contacted, so I took one of Dr. Thouless's handwritten but unsigned letters. I also followed as closely as I could the questions Thouless wanted to be asked, which included 'I want to know about something that was left by a man in order to prove his survival. It is a passage in cipher, and the key to the cipher is only two words. Could you try to get for me what these two words are?'

I was not given two words, but the medium said 'He tells me that when they are put together the message will mean "I have arrived". I don't know if that's literally what it will say,' When I asked about the longer passage from literature, the medium said, 'He didn't say anything here, sir, he just nodded his head. (pause) And I don't know why, but I'm getting the name of Milton, or it sounded like Milton . . . He speaks as if the passage was unimportant in itself, but what underlies it is important.'

It has been suggested that I should have more sittings, adopting the attitude required to solve *The Times* Crossword for clues to the two passages. But that is clearly not the way Thouless expected anyone to solve the test he set up in 1948. Letters on the files of the SPR from others who have looked for the message report that in Thouless's 'world' now, he had hoped to 'refer to it as total recall but he does not have total recall', that his message is 'The day thou gav'st Lord, has ended. Thank God', and that he has forgotten the code.

Logical problems

To persevere in solving this problem demands a conviction that it can be done. I am unconvinced, although fascinated by the interest (pro and con) that the test has aroused, and the conjectures being used to distance failure or to process the information received. These include a suggestion that someone is standing in for Thouless, and that the test was set up as a Cambridge joke. Even if the keys have been communicated, it is not clear how any claims to survival that were substantiated in this way might be used. An interpretable message, even if it were recognised, would scarcely clarify whether 'a life is but a day, and death so much like the act of bidding an ordinary good-night', as William James wrote in a letter to his father, in his last illness. The difficulties in getting Thouless's code-words suggest that communication with the dead may not be as easy as is claimed by the advocates, with their own familar procedures.

Thouless's test could even be taken as a work of conceptual art, like the Australian Imants Tiller's *Secret painting* (1987) which, on a yellow ground simply says that 'The content of this painting is invisible, the character and dimension of the content are to be kept permanently secret, known only to the artist'.

Thouless supported the descriptions of his test by an analysis of the logical problems involved in understanding what 'survival' might involve. He wrote in 1984 that he was more concerned with whether there is a continuance of his own stream of consciousness, as in waking after sleep, than with 'whether the Robert Thouless others have known and met still exists'. Although he said that his test of survival is more relevant to the second question, a positive answer there implies 'yes' to the first. Even if his test of survival did not produce a conclusive answer, 'this does not mean that it (his test) has not been worthwhile' because of its scientific value for those with an open mind who want to know how things are. In that connection he cited C.D. Broad who, he said, hoped for the extinction of conscious life but feared that the early findings of psychical research made it unlikely that that hope would be fulfilled. There is obviously a polemical component to this work, although the scientists who set out to look for levitation, psychokinesis, telepathy, and communication with the dead, found little, while others were developing the steam engine, automobile and telephone, and 'pure' researchers found photography, relativity, x-rays and then transistors.

Thouless stressed the need to decide if communications through a medium were real, before drawing out their implications for consciousness or timelessness, although if the communicator were in a timeless mode there would be no time common to them and the sitter. Contact would then, he thought, be impossible. A communication that proved to be real would therefore provide evidence against timeless survival. While Thouless seemed to accept Cummins (1965) as a source of information about mediumship (and mediums are still being trained at the College of Psychic Studies in London), he doubted their claims to valid communication, since exaggerated claims might be deliberately inserted to test one's 'faith'. 'A purely imaginary communicator may contradict the expectations of those who imagined him' just as, 'The figures of our night dreams also may show such independence of our expectations', and the thought forms in novels and plays 'may show some signs of leading a relatively independent life'. Thouless's test was also a challenge for mediums, who now seem to align their role with 'a telephone', although it seems that they can not always be sure whether or not 'a caller is impersonating the identity they claim'.

Scientific evidence

There is a perennial conflict between acceptable evidence, scientific principles, and prior beliefs about the plausibility of whatever is being investigated. In ESP work between 1945 and 1951, Gertrude Schmeidler described the 'sheep–goat effect', and found that a total of 692 'sheep' (or believers in ESP) 'making 149,652 guesses, had 614 more hits than the mean chance expectation of 29,925. In the same experiments, 465 "goats" making 101,250 guesses had 301 fewer than the mean chance expectation of 20,250. In other words, those who believed in ESP succeeded in getting 0.4 percent excess of hits while those who did not believe in the possibility of ESP had a deficiency of 0.3 percent (where $p = 0.00003$)' (Thouless, 1972, p. 119). It is of passing interest that Edge et al.'s (1986, p. 201) account of that work refers to a mean of 5.10 hits per run for 'sheep' and 4.93 for 'goats'. In my sitting with the medium to try for Thouless's key, I was initially impressed by the hits she appeared to produce that were not in response to any specific questions I asked. But in retrospect the procedure itself looked like a placebo trial, with an effort being made on her side to find if the 'communications' might be correct. Susan Blackmore, now at the University of Bristol, faced a similar question when she asked if psychical research is in any 'technical' sense scientific, because of the hidden issues about where the limits of 'science' should be set.

Psi has been common property for a long time, moving from parlour games and magicianship to being a goal, if not a means for 'Aquarians; to unlock their (unrealised) potential. And the concept of independent right and left-brain functions has been a gift to those of a mystical cast who would refer their intuitive conclusions to the self validating nature of experiences based in their non-dominant hemisphere (cf., Jaynes, 1976). A recent NRC report on several performance-enhancement techniques that were considered by the U.S. Army concluded, however, that 'despite a 130-year record of scientific research on parapsychology, our committee could find no scientific justification for the existence of phenomena such as extra sensory perception, mental telepathy, or "mind over matter" exercises' (*APA Monitor*, January, 1988, p. 7). That such phenomena were seriously considered as possible ways to enhance performance gives astonishing evidence for the continuing power of poorly understood phenomena to attract belief, and support 'anti-matter', whether in holistic medicine, 'deeper' consciousness, or the exorcisms that are probably less 'religious' than '*sacrale*.

One analogy to a meaningful seance might be found in reactions to the different editions and readings (or readers) of novels, perfor-mances of plays, and even to one's inability to 'get into' particular novels (or scientific problems). Must one expect consistency in the messages received through those 'mediums', or in the rumours that Gordon Allport (another psychologist interested in religion) studied in 1945? Problems of the availability and readiness of a spirit medium to pass on any message that a 'communicator' might give, and the frustrations of those 'on the other side' who are trying to find a medium to communicate with a targeted person, are too easily managed. It is little wonder, however, that the discovery of electro-magnetism was an early stimulus to the search for 'extra-sensory' communications and the 'power' of mediums, and to allay the difficulties some people had in accepting any disproof of what is strongly believed about the power of 'non-scientific' phenomena, including for example the 'laying on of hands'. Quantum physics is now being (mis)used in a similar way (Capra, 1975).

Experimenter effects

Experiments are designed to reduce the likelihood that experimenters will be misled by their own wishes; yet no investigation is ever epistemologically 'neutral', since they all entail prior expectations about possible and plausible results. Parapsychology carries strong assumptions about links between body and mind, thought or action, and the logical or cosmological problems in 'knowing' about, let alone communicating with any future (or other) life. Although Thouless was aware of experimenter error, Pygmalion effects, and the social psychology of psychological experiments (Rosenthal, 1976), he persevered in the study of parapsychological phenomena. In his test of survival he disregarded James's Law, 'that the evidence of life after death shall always be strong enough to reassure the converted but never conclusive enough to have the slightest influence on unbelievers'. James himself called this 'over-belief', while Thouless identified it with the 'autonomy possible with a scientific discipline and its distrust of human descriptions'.

Thouless's work on psychical phenomena was empirical, and as far as possible experimental, as he looked at salience effects, precognition, spontaneous cases, the efficiency of ESP, factors favouring success in PK, and likely occasions for PSI in everyday life. His critiques of others' findings, and his quest for future prospects always looked at the data first. In 1948 he emphasised that some facts in parapsychology are less well-attested than others, and that 'only some have so far been demonstrated under laboratory conditions'. I have already noted his proposal that the Greek letter 'psi' might cover the separate processes in telepathy, clairvoyance and so on, and he carefully distinguished the receptive from the motor effects of psychokinesis, which he thought were 'supported by strong evidence'.

Thouless believed that the scientific rejection of psi was a product of 'malobservation, careless experimenting, chance coincidence or the selective accumulation of positive results while negative ones were ignored'. Yet, as he said, 'to ignore what is unexplained never challenges the existing principles of explanation, although unexpected observations are a starting point for new theoretical systems. Much of our thinking in current psychology has ignored the revolution in theoretical physics, and we are still content with the older view which regards the starting-point of our science as the physical organism interacting with a physical environment' (Thouless, 1948). In psi studies, where expectancies and beliefs can be shown to affect the success or outcome (Thouless, 1969), and in his argument for the need to move 'from anecdote to experiment' (1972) (which some now reject because of the 'unpredictable' nature of psi), Thouless recognised that anomalous findings could be social, because of 'the introduction of witnesses and by change of task, position effects, displacement, group differences (like the "sheep–goat" separation, and other psychological variations), as well as the differential effect, the variance effect, and the focusing effort' (p. 200). From that perspective, mediumship seems to imply that our social rules and relationships continue to bind those who would communicate their (necessarily) ambiguous messages to us, which can be a problem with our current neighbours as well as for the 'departed'. It is not surprising that Thouless gave advice to an Anglican Commission on Christian Doctrine examining 'Prayer and the departed' (1971).

While mediums appear to look for feed-back, it would be useful to look carefully at sitters' interpretations of any *'hits'* in their encounters with mediums and fortune tellers. The search for the messages that might be encoded in whatever material is produced could also be aligned with the messages that are left more concretely as wills, codicils and perhaps suicide notes in the hope of ensuring some continuing influence (cf. Leenaars, 1988) (although the messages transmitted by mediums typically seem to be understood as optimistic).

Religious psychology

That the literature even Dr. Thouless cited to support the findings in parapsychology was largely restricted to psychical research journals makes it seem rather sectarian. Despite the failure of William James, William McDougall, Gardner Murphy, and Robert Thouless to bring psychical research through a sceptical filter and into our paradigmatic psychology, they helped to change parapsychology through their tests of minority assumptions about the nature and capacities of mind. But parapsychology still looks more like a 'religious psychology' which builds on the truth of religious doctrines, than being like the psychology of religion which uses the theories and methods of psychology to understand religious beliefs, experience and behaviour.

In an introductory lecture on the psychology of religion in May, 1951, Thouless emphasised the independence of our beliefs, and distinguished questions about why we believe from the truth or falsity of what is believed. He noted that psychology 'warns us of the danger of being misled by our wishes, but it remains possible that what we hope for may be true'. Godin (1971) made a similar point when he stressed the necessity of decentering any religious beliefs that derive from a doctrinal system, 'purifying' the 'magical mentality' that focuses on satisfying our own needs.

DR THOULESS AND PSYCHICAL RESEARCH 265

William James expressed a parallel scepticism about psychical phenomena despite his own wishes, saying that they are 'so fragmentary, sporadic, and contextless that they weave themselves into no system' (p. 117). A more useful task might have been to account for the resilience of those beliefs, giving up direct attempts to establish their validity. As James went on to say, 'It almost seems as if it were intended in the nature of things that these events should be always present in sufficient measure to tempt belief, but always in insufficient measure to justify it . . . (Perhaps) what is needed to make the mind close upon telepathy, veridical apparitions, and ghosts, and embrace them, is a philosophical theory of some kind which has a use for such facts' (p. 117). James also noted that 'lovers all over the world are more or less unconsciously pressing in the direction of this experiment (making "his phantom appear to a friend situated at a distance") (1986, p. 117). But we get few reports of those successes, perhaps because the world is not construed in a way that turns such wishes into psi-type phenomena.

Science and religion

The importance for science or religion of parapsychological research since Thouless might be found less in what it shows about survival (or 'life after life' as some piously say) than what it says about what people can believe, the lengths to which they will go in upholding those beliefs, and the support they can find for any 'natural' or primary beliefs (Rokeach, 1960). The tenacity with which 'beliefs of the semi-supernatural order retain their hold upon the mind' (James, 1985/1986, p. 117) was an issue rejected by philosophy and the sciences at the end of last century, despite the commonsense view that there *must be* 'something out there'.

Yet James had confidence in Mrs Piper as a medium. He said her trances produced knowledge 'she has never gained by the ordinary waking use of her eyes and ears and wits. What the source of this knowledge may be I know not, and have not the glimmer of an explanatory suggestion to make; but from admitting the fact of such knowledge I can see no escape' (p. 131). He also acknowledged that he could not carry 'the irreversibly negative bias of the rigorously scientific mind', which is never committed to a 'scientific-perspective on all aspects of life or belief', and may 'easily over reach itself' (p. 132). Nevertheless, science no longer implies any general beliefs, but a dispassionate *method* — although that is confused by meta-theoretical implications and assumptions about the usefulness of particular procedures, like the classical and operant conditioning paradigms in psychology, for example.

Despite recent work showing that mental imagery *is* a real phenomenon, methods to tap the primary qualities of another's experiences directly are scarce, except perhaps in displays of the most fearsome or ecstatic reactions (Darwin, 1872), and in studies of the language by which emotions are conventionally described and experienced (Harre, 1985). For most people that language is received, although the Romantic poets successfully invented a new rhetoric for their experiences. A perceptual analogy to this can be found in the impressionist painters' discovery of how to mimic some of the visual system's procedures (Livingstone, 1988).

Beliefs and questions about the survival of death continue, even if they preoccupy only a minority of religiously or mystically inclined people. Those who, like parapsychologists, are researching these questions are largely resourced by private benefactions. While parapsychology stands on the shoulders of those who gave it scientific respectability, most psychologists are now sceptical about it, and distance themselves from it with reference to decision-making under conditions of uncertainty, and to sceptical or creative solutions. But as long as parapsychologists continue to accept psi (at least rhetorically), systematic tests of it are better than relying on naive overconfidence or politically motivated fraud as the evidence for it (Marks & Kammann, 1980, p. 200).

Conclusion

Explorers of mental processes in the 19th century used physical analogies to support conjectures about the (ephemeral) and hypnotic effects at a distance they believed they were investigating or discovering. While they were aware of the fraud and delusion that was practised, their paradigms could not recognise the social psychological processes that support wide-spread, and often erroneous beliefs, because of the priority they gave to biological or 'instinctual' processes or because social psychology had hardly established itself as a separate field then. The independent role of the social and interactive processes that support our beliefs and traditions were only recognised in the 1930s, as Thouless himself acknowledged in the later revisions of his book on social psychology. It might not even have been necessary to test those beliefs directly since, as Coe said, 'I do not believe in ghosts, but I am afraid of them' (p. 274).

When it comes to questions about death and survival, we might quietly accept the admonitions against empirical work on those topics, and look to our writers' judgements. James Joyce's story, *The Dead* (1914), which finishes with an embedded account of the earlier death of Gabriel's wife's youthful suitor, has Gabriel remarking that 'One by one, they were all becoming shades. Better pass boldly into that other world, in the full glory of some passion, than fade and wither dismally with age'. Perhaps it was something like this that grabbed Dr. Thouless into his late 80s.

Acknowledgements

I am most grateful to Dr. Thouless's son, David, for access to his father's papers, and to the Secretary of the Society for Psychical Research for advice, assistance and access to their records. The use that I have made of this material is, however, my own responsibility. And I am aware that 'spiritism' still flourishes in Brazil, for example, where many novels are published that have been dictated from the next world, or so it is claimed (Ryle, 1988, p. 448). This, like any concrete dependence on that 'other place', implies a baroque fantasy I had not intended to invoke when I began what I had hoped would be a biographical note on Dr. Thouless. Such a theme is reminiscent of what D.W. Harding (in *Experience into words*, 1974, p. 122) calls 'the pentecostal idea' in Eliot's 'Little Gidding', where Eliot says:

And what the dead had no speech for, when living,
They can tell you, being dead: the communication
Of the dead is tongued with fire beyond the language of the living.

References

Adams, G. (1932), *Psychology: science or superstition*. London: Rider and Co.

Allport, G.W. & Postman, L.J. (1945). The basic psychology of rumour. *Transactions of the New York Academy of Sciences, Series II, 8*, 61–81.

Back, C.W. & Bourque, L.B. (1970). Can feelings be enumerated? *Behavioral Science, 15*, 487–496.

Bowker, J. (1987), *Licensed Insanities: religion and belief in God in the contemporary world*. London: Darton, Longman & Todd.

Brown, L.B. (1987), *The psychology of religious belief*. London: Academic Press.

Capra, F. (1975), *Tao of physics: an exploration of the parallels between modern physics and Eastern mysticism*. London: Wildwood House.

Carington, W.W. (1967). Survival of death. In *Chambers's Encyclopedia* (New Revised Edition) London: Pergamon.

Cook, E.W. et al. (1983), A review and analysis of unsolved cases of the reincarnation type. *Journal of the American Society for Psychical Researchl, 77*, 115–135.

Cummins, 'G. (1965), *Swan on a black sea*. London: Routledge and Kegan Paul.

Cummins, G. (1984), *The road to immortality: being a description of the after-life purporting to be communicated by the late F.W.H. Myers through Geraldine Cummins*. Norwich: Pilgrims Book Services.

Darwin, C. (1872), *The expression of the emotions in man and animals*. London: J. Murray.

Doctrine Commission of the General Synod of the Church of England (1987). *We believe in God*. London: Church House Publishing.

Edge, H.L., Morris, R.L., Palmer, J. & Rush, J.H. (1986). *Foundations of parapsychology*. London: Routledge and Kegan Paul.

Godin, A. (1971). Some developmental tasks in Christian education. In M.P. Strommen (ed.), *Research on religious development: a comprehensive handbook*. New York: Hawthorn Books.

Harre, R. (1985), *The construction of emotion*. Oxford: Blackwell.

Hay, D. (1982), *Exploring inner space: scientists and religious experience*. Harmondsworth: Penguin Books.

Haynes, R. (1982), *The Society for Psychological Research: a history*. London; Macdonald.

James, W. (1902/1985), *The varieties of religious experience*. Harvard University Press.

James, W. (1986), *Essays in psychical research*. Harvard University Press.

Jaynes, J. (1976/1982). *The origin of consciousness in the breakdown of the bi-cameral mind*. Harmondsworth: Penguin Books.

Leenaars, A. (1988), *Suicide notes*. (in press).

Livingstone, M.S. (1988). Art, illusion and the visual system. *Scientific American*, *258*(1), 68–75.

Marks, D. & Kammann, R. (1980), *The psychology of the psychic*. Buffalo: Prometheus.

Marty, M.E. et al. (1968), *What do we believe?* New York: Meredith.

McClenon, J. (1982). A survey of elite scientists: their attitudes toward ESP and parapsychology. *Journal of Parapsychology*, *46*(2), 127–152.

Robinson, J.A.T. (1964), *Honest to God*. London: SCM. Press.

Rokeach, M. (1960), *The open and closed mind: investigations into the nature of belief and personality systems*. New York: Basic Books.

Rosenthal, R. (1966), *Experimenter effects in behavioural research*. New York: Appleton-Century-Crofts.

Rosenthal, R. & Rosnow, R. (1969), *Artifact in behavioural research*. New York: Academic Press.

Ryle, J. (1988). Dictation from the dead. *Times Literary Supplement*, April 22–28, p. 448.

Spilka, B., Hood, R.W. & Gorsuch, R.L. (1985). *The psychology of religion: an empirical approach*. Englewood Cliffs: Prentice-Hall.

Spraggett, A. & Rauscher, W.V. (1973). *Arthur Ford: the man who talked with the dead*. New York: New American Library.

Stevenson, I. (1968). The combination lock test for survival. *Journal of the American Society for Psychical Research*, 62. 246–254.

Stevenson, I. (1974), *Twenty cases suggestive of reincarnation*. Charlottesville: University Press of Virginia.

Stevenson, I. (1976). Further observations on the combination lock test for survival. *Journal of the American Society for Psychical Research*, 70, 219–229.

Stevenson, I. (1977). Reincarnation: field studies and theoretical issues. In B.B. Wolman (ed.), *Handbook of parapsychology*, pp. 631–663. New York: Van Nostrand.

Thouless, R.H. (1922/1971). *An introduction to the psychology of religion*. Cambridge: University Press.

Thouless, R.H. (1923a). Some observations on contrast effects in graded discs. *British Journal of Psychology*, *13*(3), 301–307.

Thouless, R.H. (1923b), The psychology of the contemplative life. *Proceedings and Papers of the VIIth International Congress of Psychology*.

Thouless, R.H. (1924a). Soul beliefs and hypotheses. *Mind: a quarterly review of psychology and philosophy*, *33*(131), 262–274.

Thouless, R.H. (1925), *Social psychology*. London: University Tutorial Press.

Thouless, R.H. (1935). The tendency to certainty in religious belief. *British Journal of Psychology*, *34*(1), 16–31.

Thouless, R.H. (1937a). Review of Mr. Whately Carington's work on trance personalities. *Proceedings of the Society for Psychical Research*, *44*, 223–275.

Thouless, R.H. (1937b/1958). *General and social psychology, 4th Edition*. London: University Tutorial Press.

Thouless, R.H. (1942). Experiments on paranormal guessing. *British Journal of Psychology*, *33*(1), 15–27.

Thouless, R.H. (1948a). A test of survival. *Proceedings of the Society for Psychical Research*, *48*(176), 253–263.

Thouless, R.H. (1948b). Additional notes on a test of Survival. *Procedures of the Society for Psychical Research*, *48*(176), 342–343.

Thouless, R.H. (1958), *Straight and crooked thinking*. Revised and enlarged edition. London: English Universities Press.

Thouless, R.H. (1960). The empirical evidence for survival. *Journal of the American Society for Psychical Research*, *60*, 24–23.

Thouless, R.H. (1963a). The cipher test of survival. *Theta*, No. 2, pp. 1–6.

Thouless, R.H. (1963b). *Experimental psychical research*. Harmondsworth: Penguin Books.

Thouless, R.H. (1972), From anecdote to experiment in psychical research. London: Routledge and Kegan Paul.

Thouless, R.H. (1984). Do we survive bodily death? *Proceedings of the Society for Psychical Research*, *57*(213), 1–52.

Thouless, R.H., Ikin, A. & Pear, T.H. (1924b). The psychogalvanic phenomenon in dream analysis. *British Journal of Psychology*, *15*(1), 23–43.

CHAPTER 16

BIOLOGICAL ACTION AT A DISTANCE : A CONTRIBUTION FROM BIOLOGY TO INVESTIGATIONS OF THE PARANORMAL

Bevan L. Reid

Some nine years ago as part of a continuing project on the nature of biological growth and cancer (or new growth) experiments were undertaken to test the idea that stimuli producing growth originate outside the living organism in its spatial environment. The results of these experiments indicated that there was a force in space which was able both to originate or create matter in a fashion which we could call biological growth and further to sustain this matter through time in what we call the living state. Many of the qualities of this force which can be shown to exist in the environment or space of the living organism are not apparent to the five senses. This and other attributes to be described mark it as a paranormal force, one that may underline many phenomena described elsewhere in this book.

The experiments which revealed these qualities are well within the compass of contemporary science as practiced in a non-specialised laboratory so that they give some inkling that the paranormal may be investigable in the same way as presently is the normal. Indeed having regard to the well known origins of existing normal phenomena in what was regarded as arcane some centuries ago, one senses that science history may be merely repeating itself, as normal methods together with the concepts they beget come to invade that which is considered in the contemporary reference as paranormal.

Synopsis of Laboratory Findings

Because of the notorious complexity of experimenting on the living matter, recourse was made early in the experimental plan to growth of crystals. Familiarity with crystal growth led to an adoption of the same approach to the complexities of living matter. The following synopsis is derived from results using both living and non-living matter.

1. Growth of crystals and cells is affected by reactions occurring from a distance measurable from millimetres to hundreds of metres. These astonishing distant reactions take the form either of 1) chemical reactions, some of which involve the construction or destruction of long-chain molecules termed polymers or 2) physical reactions elicited by the presence of matter, such as lead or ice, in spatial proximity. As a result of these stimuli, crystals or cells in a remote observation site take on new growth patterns or alter the rate of existing patterns (Anderson and Reid 1985, Reid 1986).

2. The space in which crystals or cells displayed this novelty, attendant on the distant stimulus, can remember and store its qualities and make the novel information available for display when fresh crystals or cells are grown in that space in the absence of the stimulus. In this chapter, such a property is termed memory. The storage of the memory of an event in space is measurable in days, weeks or months.

3. Contrasted with this memory property, space has an inability to support repetition of a particular experiment at a chosen time. In other words, the memory recall is evidently a property of space itself rather than of the experimenter or his materials. Recall is facilitated when the experimental arrangements provide for using paired rather than individual pieces of apparatus.

4. Although growth pattern was used as the effect under study of the long-range transmission of space properties in the early part of the experimental programme, other parameters were studied later. These included electromagnetic properties of solutions from which the crystals were grown and, further, fluctuations in local air pressure at the observation site. The electromagnetic capacitance, or ability to contain charge, of solutions at the experimental site was sometimes raised by several orders of magnitude.

5. It is possible to investigate structural properties of the space concurrent with the operation of the remote stimuli that are producing the local effects. One way is by exposing to this space a thin film of a plastic polymer such as polystyrene drying from solvent benzol on a glass slide. When unstimulated space is so examined one or two dots of a fraction of a millimetre size are seen by the naked eye as white opacities in an otherwise clear background of the thin film adherent to the slide. Placing the slide under the microscope, these dots can be resolved as spirals or vortices which form around specks of foreign matter in the air of the space concerned. When a stimulus such as a distant chemical reaction is occurring, the number of vortices

increases ten or twenty fold. Their physical establishment seems to depend on the use of sharp-edged microscope slides to display them, because if these are ground off, no vortices appear. The vortex has structural properties relevant to the subsequent discussion. Vortices vary in their diameter from 0. 1 to 1mm and also in their cheirality or handedness. This indicates that, at the moment of its imprinting, they spin left or right. Orientation of the drying film in various positions indicated that the axes of the vortices can take up any direction from horizontal to vertical. Some could be seen breaking up into structures which we call vectors (Reid 1980a). Some dried film preparations from a particular ambient space show only vectors rather than their parent vortices. When the film is dried in contact with matter such as a metal bar, the orientation of vortices and their vectors becomes very symmetrical. They are often disposed in rows, an arrangement which physicists call vorticeal streets.

6. The polystyrene film technique revealed another important finding. Certain types of living matter in the local space of the film over distances tested from 1-10 metres, could imprint the drying film with a faithful copy of the structure of the living organism comprising such matter. Thus living bacteria, moulds and cells of animal origin growing at a remote site, could be shown to make an imprint on the films. The image which had been copied was not only a structural replica of the living organism, but copied such attributes as its staining properties, properties which are known to be highly specific. This copying process provided a further example of the memory property of space in that the living organism need only be resident in the space concerned for minutes yet the film continued to be imprinted with its image for weeks thereafter (Reid 1988b).

Further to the fluctuations of pressure described in paragraph 4, it was found that fluctuations were enhanced in the local space of a mass of chipped ice. On the other hand, when a few milligrams of a salt such as calcium chloride was added to the ice mass the fluctuations were promptly abolished. Air temperature measurements showed that abolition of the fluctuations was not due to a temperature effect. It was theorised that the space surrounding the ice containing the salt was of a different quality from space that was more remote. To test this idea, use was made of the observation that carbon particles (in the form of india ink) suspended in water of high capacitance (see earlier discussion) in the local space of the ice mass, behaved differently to those suspended in the same water elsewhere in space. In such suspensions, it was noted that surface particles, instead of being diffused in the layer formed between water and air, aggregated to form a filament about 0.5mm diameter and of length equal to the diameter of the vessel containing the water. Moreover, the filament once formed continued to point to the centre of the ice mass even if the two vessels, ice and water, were moved about the bench. Such orientation persisted until the ice melted. In further tests of the quality of space in the vicinity of the ice vessel, it was found that the integrity of the filament which persisted as long as ice was physically melting could be altered by placing objects in this space. These objects were inserted in the space concerned on the assumption that one of the qualities of the space was that it was flowing so that with respect to the carbon-particle test system, one could refer to an up-or downstream insertion. Such insertions were made up to 50cms from the test system containing the filament. Only upstream insertions had the effect of causing a disappearance of the carbon filament into the diffuse phase within 15 seconds. This disappearance was caused by the insertion of the following two objects: first a vessel containing water of high capacitance and secondly one containing ordinary tap water covered with a very thin surface film of oil. When the active biochemical, prostaglandin was dissolved in the oil, no disappearance of the filament occurred no matter how long this vessel was resident upstream (Reid 1988c).

Interim Conclusions from these Investigations

The following conclusions were drawn from these observations.

1. Interactions involving matter more especially that in the form of growing crystals and biomatter, but possibly including all matter, cannot be considered apart from the ambient space in which these interactions are occurring.

2. The space concerned can be spoken of as having properties or qualities and some of these are memory and mimicry. They may even be said to have the ability to support actions occurring over distances measured in hundreds of metres. These distances are well beyond those which may be accounted for by presently known precepts and practice in physics.

3. The effects of these qualities of space manifest themselves as an ability to change growth patterns in crystals and living cells; to cause minute atmospheric pressure changes; to cause subtle changes in the disposition of particulate matter at the surface of water; and, to change certain features of the electrical properties of water. All this occurs at a distance measurable from millimetres to tens of metres.

4. A generalisation emerges as to the nature of a stimulus to these

phenomena. It is often associated with the building up or breaking down of order in matter. Order is a term used to indicate that adjacent building blocks, atoms or molecules are nearly the same or identical as occurs in a crystal or a homogeneous polymer. Experimentally demonstrated examples are the breaking down of the molecules stacked in a chain or polymer of cellulose, of those stacked in an ice crystal during melting or of the atoms in a metal following its dissolution by acid.

One could summarize these tentative conclusions by saying that the experimental results would be explainable if the space in which they were obtained had both structure and function. Further, these properties result in a force which both affects matter and is in turn affected by matter; especially ordered matter. The remainder of this chapter is an attempt to reconcile these conclusions with current knowledge on the content and function of space. We will describe this content and its properties as being unavailable for scrutiny by the five senses. In as far as the scientific method has traditionally relied on the use of the five senses, the origins of this perceived knowledge must reside in the realm of intuition. If, in fact, some or all observable phenomena are non-sensible (referred to as non-observable) in nature, then large philosophical, cultural and epistemological problems loom. We will refer to these problems and their bearing on investigations of the paranormal later. Meanwhile, the disciplines which explain the attributes of space will be reviewed in order to develop a reconciliation with the observations. A briefer historical perspective must first introduce this complex and often confounding topic.

The Structure and Function of Space — Historical

Different cultures have varied in their grasp of the nature of space content from the void to the plenary. In classical Greece, the plenary concept held sway and the term aether was used to mean a medium in which events occurred which often accompanied the corresponding event in matter. The aether concept was developed in Newtonian times as a vehicle for light and subsequently by the nineteenth century physicist-mathematicians as a non-sensible correspondent of many real properties of matter such as electrical fields, inertia and cohesion (Swenson 1972). This happy association of the aether idea with science came to an abrupt halt with the arrival of the first Einstein papers at the opening of the century when, after a grudging acceptance of relativity and its vindication by experimental observation, most physicists joined Einstein in regarding the aether concept as superfluous. More recently, the venerable aether concept has reappeared in a new guise, namely the zero point energy.

Whilst the aether as a concept has tended to be the property of the physicists, pure mathematicians have also been concerned with structure in space. In the middle of the last century, Riemann was one of the first to begin altering the classical straight-line co-ordinates of Euclidean origin by which space was considered. He developed the mathematics of a space whose co-ordinates were curved. Curved space reappeared in the Einstein mathematics. One of the other mathematical properties of space was its invariance which, in metaphorical terms, could be likened to an outline drawn on a sheet of rubber. In spite of tension exerted on the rubber with different force, and in different directions, the outline persists or is invariant. If the speed of light is regarded as an invariant or constant quality, the earliest accommodation of its constancy was mathematically to warp or curve space. Experimental observations vindicating such warping were to supply the first hints that Riemann's concepts may not have been purely theoretical. Space was not just a continuous void but indeed, had structure. It is then not a giant step from accepting the warp to recognising that there must exist some property to be warped. The stage was thus set earlier this century for ceding to space a considerable complexity; a complexity which may underlie some of the experimental results we have been describing.

Quantum Physics

The mathematical study of space became inextricably involved with pursuing the smallest particle of matter. Toward the end of last century, the discovery of the electron made it apparent that the atom was not the smallest particle. Thus began the search for the origins of other subatomic particles. Attempts were made to measure the energy of these particles and to record their interactions. This led to the establishment of quantum mechanics. However, a paradox emerged. It became obvious that this real energy and real matter had its origin in a non-observable, purely abstract, world. Such an origin was inevitably the result of the mathematics used in its development. In other words, the elusive origin of the nature of existence was not in the atom, but in subatomic particles. These, in turn, found their origin in a non-observable enery sea. The paradox was heightened in that this sea had an energy value even when temperature has disappeared. Clearly, in the absence of a temperature relationship, this could be no ordinary sort of energy. This term, in the equations of the quantum mechanics era, was known as the zero point or vacuum enery. From the perspective of this essay, this zero temperature energy-containing mathematical abstraction can be seen as space itself. Quantum theory was beginning to accord space with structure (in its warping) and function.

A big advance followed the elaboration of the equations of the quantum mechanics phase of quantum theory by Dirac and others (Dirac 1962). They began incorporating into their equations the mathematics not only of subatomic energy interactions but of space structure itself. Termed the second quantisation, this elaboration permitted refining the idea of the origin of matter in space by focussing mathematically on the quality of space. We should make a brief note in passing that much of this advance was enabled by a consistent use of what mathematicians call 'imaginary numbers'. Philosophically minded mathematicians like Bochner (1966) have commented on conceptual advances which have accompanied the use of imaginary numbers on various occasions in the history of science. This has been nowhere truer than in their use of the formalism relating to space-atomic particle interactions of the second quantisation. We can briefly enumerate a few of the remarkable conclusions which have resulted from the introduction of this formalism only a few decades ago.

1. It is possible to conceive of the subatomic world as matter that is composed of particles that are at the same time waves of probability. This means that the smallest units of matter have a corresponding or counterpart existence in the world of imaginary numbers.

2. There is no energy as classically known in the 'imaginary world'. Still the result of omnipresent motion in this imaginary world is to produce energy-like effects of such correspondence with the observable world that they are often termed 'forces.' These forces are related to a real force such as pressure in the observable world.

3. Mathematical terms for time and for distance disappear in the equations of the world of imaginary numbers. In other words events happen instantaneously throughout this world (which is co-extensive with space as popularly conceived) and they happen at a distance equally co-extensive with space in the same way.

The transmission of these results from mathematicians and theoretical physicists to the workaday world of the physicist and various scientists is understandably tardy. Yet scientists ever mindful of the historical prescience of mathematics, have turned to the laboratory. Already, there is limited agreement that, experimentally, one aspect of these incredible implications is demonstrable. I refer to action-at-a-distance.

We are now in a position to refer to the central argument of this chapter which avers that many experimental results relate to their correspondence with identical phenomena in a purely abstract world. This proposal explains the clear experimental demonstration of action-at-a-distance. Explanations of other phenomena are also possible. For example, acoustic waves are closely connected with pattern formation in biological objects (Hagan and Reid 1980). Their existence is known by quantum physicists to cause movement of objects in a vacuum ; that is, movement in space. These movements are of both attractive and repulsive kind, suggesting that the special pressure waves of space have a close correspondence with their counterpart in the real world.

It is logical to ask about the existence of a special sort of pressure in space. Just what is it in space causing such pressure? We have already stated that it cannot be considered as equivalent to energy in the directly observable world. In casting about for an answer, we have recourse to the experiments which demonstrated the existence and close involvement of vortices with actions occurring at a distance. If we compare this finding with the evidence that mathematicians have for centuries linked aether with vortex motion, we have a conceptual basis for speaking of pressure-like phenomena. Vortices have many properties of relevance to those of the aether of the imaginary world, and one of immediate concern is interminable motion or spin. The axial structure of the vortex allows both cheirality involving left or right spin, as well as progression along the axis as in the corresponding mechanical device of a screw. The interminable movement can have many vectors with many spins. In fact, it is considered by theoretical physicists that the usual state of space is 'symmetrical' wherein the vectors and spins are totally random. Strictly speaking, no vectors exist and therefore, opposed spins result in an overall cancellation. The equations are symmetrical. Vortices of like spin and vector direction can stack colinearly. This colinearly stacked 'object' is dubbed a vortex 'street' and the resulting coherence provides for an increase in potential (it is illegitimate to refer to energy in this abstract world). Vortices can also stack one inside the other providing for variation in vorticeal volume. These arrangements alter the random behaviour of the vortices, and the symmetry state is now said to be 'broken'. Terms in the equations are no longer symmetrical in form.

Rearrangements of vorticeal pattern in the non-observable world from the randomness of symmetry to streets and sheets of streets, that is symmetry-breaking, is accompanied by the acquisition of real energy terms by the system as it enters the world of matter.

We have argued that the correspondence of real and imaginary numbers, foreseen by mathematicians, can be used to propose that the world of real matter and its function is underlain (the mystics of religion would say overlain) by a corresponding structure and function in an abstract world. An exponent of this position is Bohm (1980). Referring to a paradox of the unavailability of this world to the five senses of modern man coupled with its proposed content of structure and function, Bohm uses the term 'information' world. The information of this world contains structures which are potential or infolded; that is, present in form only for subsequent incarnation at the moment of symmetry-breaking.

Bohm's very advanced views are, not surprisingly, received with bemusement and reserve by the physicists. This attitude is encouraged by the great difficulty of the sort of experimentation necessary in such a field. Given the results of the biological experiments mentioned earlier, it is possible that Bohm's ideas may be more easily vindicated by biology-type experiments rather than those of a purely physical character. To obtain forms or virtual images of chemical, microbial or mammalian cell nature from space, as clear cut faithful real images, was not all that difficult and certainly inexpensive.

Some Practical Implications of Biology viewed as Macroscopic Quantum Effects

Bohm derived his mathematics for presenting the idea of action at a distance from quantal potentials as has been outlined. Not only is this abstract world recognisable by its correspondence with the observable world, but its structure may be actually manipulable by methods familiar to the engineer. As discussed, in a world of imaginary parts, it is not proper to refer to these parts as having real direction or vectors as we have done. Rather they must be considered as what mathematicians know as scalar terms. Scalar potentials of one sign can build up as we have discussed for vortices. But, they are cancelled by a scalar of opposite sign so that no real energy appears. Bearden (1983) has discussed the engineering of these scalars to build up 'forces' in the abstract world which, by their reciprocal property with real energy, can be made manifest in the real world. He has written extensively on the use of such 'energy' of limitless source for offensive or weaponry purposes.

The manifestation of 'energy' in the non-observable world as real energy, such as heat or pressure, means that quantal energy can be manifest as gross macroscopic energy. There is an accompanying tendency in recent physics literature to refer to these manifestations as macroscopic quantal effects. We suggest that macroscopic properties of biosystems (movement, irritability and so forth) are conveniently considered as macroscopic quantal effects. On this assessment, they are the direct result of the interaction between the non-observable world with matter. This means that the key feature of this interaction, which we call life, resides in the very special properties of the arrangement of matter in the biosystem. Let us consider the possibility that the non-observable world is a ceaseless movement of vortices following scalars in a maze of interconnections. As we have discussed, the quantum physicist terms this state symmetry, but some commentators on this work refer to it as a 'cosmic dance' (Zukav 1979). If the non-observable world corresponds to this description, then its interaction with equally complex matter of the biosystem is a question for much future study.

Aside from a complexity of real structure which affords a maximum possibility for the interplay with non-observable force, biomatter has a remarkable ability to relate to electric fields with which it makes contact. The ability of the field within matter to be influenced by the properties of an electrical field imposed from without is known to the electrical engineer as permittivity. It is a recent and surprising finding that the permittivity of biological materials are extraordinarily high compared with those of non biological materials (Schwan 1985). This means that the former are especially responsive to electric fields in their vicinity. In as far as there must exist a correspondence between real electrical and non-observable fields of the type sustaining paranormal phenomena, these remarkable permittivity differences are of great significance. Permittivity studies of biomatter will thus go hand in hand with research into its property to exhibit paranormal phenomena.

With these events in mind, it is possible to consider briefly results of experiments from the author's laboratory. Their design was prompted by the possibility that space can be manipulated using the reciprocity of observable and non-observable worlds. It was thought that matter (such as chemical substances) inserted into the flow upstream would cause target matter components downstream to assume a particular pattern or configuration. The matter inserted upstream would differ in nature according to its experimentally demonstrable ability to affect events in the non-observable world. The idea was that these events conducted in the observable world appear reciprocally in the non-observable world where they are transmitted over space to affect a given target set up to monitor the effect. The success of early experiments toward this end attest the probable validity of Bearden's contention that the full scale attention of engineers drawn to the possibilities could produce some striking results (Reid 1988c, Bearden 1983).

Because this chapter is biologically orientated, it will be proper here to move from the macroscopic field of the engineer to the ultramicroscopic of the molecular biologist. This is to say, to the biopolymers themselves. From their demonstrably important position in biology, the nucleic acids are worthy of consideration in this context. The renowned example is DNA which, as a helical chain, is a sort of constant diameter vortex, a veritable permanent vortex street. It could afford a particularly appropriate conduit for the flow of non-observable 'energy' Nucleic acid chemistry in concerned with the effects of varying the composition of the helix, which is effect varies the sequence of its building blocks introduced into the chain as being inserted up/or downstream of a site on the helix under study.

Implications for the Paranormal

The practical implications that have been briefly considered refer to the inward workings of the biosystem. However, to the layman and scientist alike, the topic of this book, the paranormal, often refers to extra-organismal phenomena: extrasensory perception, telepathy, clairvoyance and psychokinesis such as the bending of metallic objects. It is therefore our intention to relate the results of our research to their specific connections with extra- organismal phenomena. There is, however, a further tenet of late twentieth century physics and chemistry which can provide for the observation, quite acceptable to the student of the paranormal, that ambient energy suffuses matter including biomatter. This tenet was derived from an adaptation of classical thermodynamics which, among other things, provides a usable theory for how heat engines work.

The Belgian chemist Prigogine, investigating the growth of certain crystal systems, found that the mathematics involved fitted better with observation if the system was not closed but was continuously allowed to interchange with its ambient space (Prigogine and Nicolis 1977). Prigogine's work has by now taken its place in a milieu which sees natural engines such as crystal growth and the biosystem as inevitably reliant for both their original growth and their maintenance on a free interchange of their contained energy with that of their environment or space. Prigogine's novel approach to the energy flux of natural systems means, in effect, that there now exists a sound mathematical basis for maintaining that energy flows through the system. It would then not be surprising if, given a critical role for the structuring and maintenance function of this flow, there were not highly complex channels available for its entry and departure. Such channels form the basis for much theory and practice of various forms of early medicine. For example, a popular term in Chinese medicine for the channel is a meridian.

The energy referred to by the thermodynamicists is real energy, such as heat. Referring back to previous discussion, this real form must inevitably be accompanied by non-observable force which means that afferent and efferent streams of this latter force permeate the living organism. Efferent streams thus occur and can, if provided with a suitable target and because of their non-observable world status, exhibit action-at-a-distance and simultaneity. Although the former phenomenon is well attested in the paranormal literature, so far as the author is aware, there have been no attempts to quantify or otherwise characterise the time aspect of action at the target.

The unreal 'energy' which is present in an efferent stream from certain individuals must be considerable as the metal bending observations with such people demonstrate. Strain gauge measurements of the metal, as well as electron microscopic study revealing disturbed orientation in the metallic crystalline lattice, attest to the considerable forces generated in various targets (Hasted, 1979). The architecture of striped muscle and of bone must present themselves for future study in this respect. Indeed there is some extant evidence from kinesiology wherein the voluntary exhibition of contraction in upper shoulder and leg musculature is compromised if the subject is in close proximity to a patient with a tumour of cancerous type. As another example, in the author's laboratory, a psychic healer in healing pose of the hands 10-12cms from a film of drying polystyrene, produces tears in the formed film of linear parallel disposition oriented at 90 degrees to the motion of the hands. Such a picture was not produced by other subjects chosen at random with no history of evidence of healing power (McGarry 1987).

As we have already discussed, numerous problems beset research into the paranormal not the least of which is the problem of repeatability. This is compounded by relative infrequency of those in whom paranormal powers are demonstrable. Although researchers say that this problem is often overstated and that the distribution of paranormal powers is more widespread, the study of the paranormal promises to shed light on the above findings related to the passage of energy through the biosystem.

Thus, an important research topic for the future may be to answer the question: why are paranormal powers not universal? Practitioners of forms of primitive medicine which involve the use of energy channels go about their craft supposing that the channels are subject to blockage, and that a common cause of the blockage is a disease state. The investigation of the disease state in these terms may afford clues as to the nature of the conduits and thus the nature of the impairment to their function. That the answer will not come easy is indicated by the existence of different skews in the distribution of paranormal abilities occurring in different populations. When it is considered that the lore of the Kalahari bushmen and the Australian Aborigine are bound up with the widespread appreciation of subtle energy flows, it is not surprising that one finds a wider distribution of paranormal powers in primitive communities. One may ask what happened to eclipse or shield these powers in modern man.

The whole topic of energy through-flow, together with its blockage or shielding as it permeates the living system will prospectively be of great interest not only academically but for problems in clinical practice. Obdurate diseases (such as chronic arthritis, atherosclerosis and cancer) may increasingly be treated by methods presently regarded as having 'fringe' status since they rely on a detailed knowledge of energy permeation. This can only mean that investigations of paranormal phenomena may play an important part in future medical research in elevating presently regarded fringe practices to mainstream medicine. On this basis, blockages in the energy flows of the biosystem in a given subject may affect both the ability to display paranormal powers and the maintainence of health.

Summary

1. Despite considerable historical antiquity, paranormal phenomena have never attracted the interest of researchers as have normal phenomena. The reason for this well recognised reluctance has aroused the curiosity of many people. It is possible that this attitude of orthodox science may be changing ever so slowly in the latter part of this century.

2. Over the centuries there has been no lack of description of the paranormal. Important ingredients in these descriptions have always been the inconsequence of distance and very possibly of time. Simultaneity and action-at-a-distance as topics have appeared in the history of physics with indifferent acceptance. They have reappeared this century in the guise of quantum physics where they have been derived solely from mathematical considerations of the nature of the structure and possible function of space.

3. Closer study of the mathematics phase in the history of physics points up the origins of the formalism in imaginary numbers. A key feature is the correspondence or reciprocity between terms in the non-observable world described by imaginary numbers.

4. A key factor in the manifestation process is the meeting or interface of the information with the observable world. In the case of matter with highly complex arrangements of its microscopic parts (such as occurs in biomatter), it has been shown that there are

manifestations that result from meeting these arrangements immediately or directly which produce movement and irritability, or
response, to stimuli.

Even more remarkable than the structural properties of biomatter
to afford an interplay with space is the electrical structure more
specifically the permittivity of biomatter. The extraordinarily high
values of permittivity recorded for biomatter fit it for an especially tight
association with fields existing in its nearby space.

5. With a grasp of the previous conclusions it is possible to design
experiments using arrangements of matter in the laboratory as key
variables. We assume, as do the mathematicians, ceaseless movement
or flow of the non-observable or information world in order to gain
insight about the nature of events at the interface. These experiments
have been briefly described. No qualitative conceptual leaps are
necessary to view efferent streams from a living organism as having
much more striking effects than those leaving inert matter. These
streams may well underlie more typically recognised paranormal
phenomena including extrasensory perception, clairvoyance and
metal bending.

6. It is quite likely that the results of further study and exploitation of
even our present meagre understanding of these arcane subtle or
esoteric forces will dwarf results of present technology based on real
world phenomena no matter how spectacular these are.

References

Anderson, H. E. , & Reid, B. L. (1984), Vicinal Long Range and Extremely
    Long Range Effects on Growth of Sodium Chloride Crystals from Aqueous
    Solutions Containing Protein. *Applied Physics Communications*, 4, 217-
    239.
Bearden, T. E. (1983), *Toward a New Electromagnetics (Part III): Clarifying the
    Vector Concept.* California, Telsa Book Co.
Bochner, S. (1966), *The Role of Mathematics in the Rise of Science.* Princeton,
    Princeton University Press.
Bohm, D. (1980), *Wholeness and the Implicate Order.* London, Routledge &
    Kegan Paul.
Dirac, P. A. M. (1962), *The Principles of Quantum Mechanics.* 4th ed. Oxford,
    Clarendon Press.
Hagan, B. E. , Reid, B. L. (1980), *The Mathematical Transformation of Growth
    and Form.* Medical Hypothesis, 6,559-609.
Hasted, J. B. (1979), 'Paranormal Metal Bending', in Puharich, A., (Ed.), *The
    Iceland Papers.* Wisconsin, Essentia Research Associates.
McGarry, J. (1987), 'Mesmerism Versus Hypnosis : A Comparison of
    Relaxational Responses and Evaluation of Mental and Psychophysio-
    logical Outcome.' *Australian Journal of Clinical Hypnotherapy and
    Hypnosis*, 8, 7-36.

Prigogine, I., & Nicolis, G. (1977) *Self-Organisation in Non-Equilibrium Systems*. New York, Wiley.

Reid, B. L. (1986), 'Propagation of Properties of Chemical Reactions Over Long Distance in the Atmosphere as Seen by Crystal Growth Pattern Changes.' *Australian Journal of Medical Laboratory Science*, 7, 30-35.

Reid, B. L. (1988a), 'On the Nature of Growth and Newgrowth Based on Experiments Designed to Reveal a Structure and Function for Laboratory Space', Medical Hypothesis, In Press.

Reid, B. L. (1988b), 'The Causation of Cervical Cancer: A Different View' in G. di Palo, (Ed.) *Herpes and Papilloma Viruses*. New York, Raven Press. In Press.

Reid, B. L. (1988c) 'Effects of Very Long Range Forces on Filament Formation in India Ink Particle Preparations in Water'. *Journal of Biological Physics*. In Press.

Schwan, H. P. (1985), 'Dielectric Properties of Cells and Tissues', in Chiabrera, A., Nicolini, G., & Schwan, H.P., (Eds.), *Interaction Between Electromagnetic Fields and Cells*. New York, Plenum.

Zukav, G. (1979), *The Dancing Wu Li Masters*. New York, Bantam.

SECTION IV

DEBATING THE PARANORMAL

The study of the paranormal arouses intense conflict, controversy and feeling in lay and scientific communities alike. This section is concerned with the debate between believers and non-believers in the paranormal. In some chapters this debate is dealt with in terms of how community attitudes quickly polarize into two schools of thought — believers and skeptics — in response to news about unusual phenomena such as the Sasquatch/Bigfoot sightings in South Dakota in 1977. In other chapters the debate about the paranormal can be followed through argument between various contributors about conceptual or methodological issues.

James R. Stewart in Chapter 17 approaches the study of the paranormal from the point of view of one who assumes that most paranormal beliefs are delusionary in nature. He provides a convincing examination of a rash of alleged Bigfoot sightings in north central South Dakota as an episode of collective delusion using Smelser's value-added theory of collective behaviour.

Stewart's arousal of our skepticism towards the paranormal is balanced by the next contribution from Harvey J. Irwin. While Stewart is concerned to explain belief in the paranormal, Irwin asks why some people do *not* believe in the paranormal. Irwin, in exploring the roots of skepticism, points out that the adoption of skeptical attitudes towards the paranormal is sometimes driven less by scientific standards of examination than by fear of the paranormal.

The next two chapters take the debate on the paranormal into the philosophical realm. Central to both chapters is consideration of David Hume's argument on miracles. The first of these two chapters is by Antony Flew and it deals with the problem of what constitutes acceptable evidence under circumstances where the occurrence claimed strains belief. Flew's chapter is confined to discussion about evidence for psi-phenomena. He is skeptical about the evidence so far claimed.

John Beloff takes up Hume's argument as well. Beloff's contribution incorporates references to Flew's chapter which he saw in advance of submitting his final draft. This gives the exchange between Flew and Beloff the true character of a debate. Beloff deals with the problem of credibility in the context of discussion of a selection of notable historical instances of 'extreme phenomena' such as, for instance, levitation. Beloff argues that it is not necessarily any more rational to disbelieve than to believe in a given 'extreme phenomenon'.

The final two chapters by Helmut Loiskandl and John Schumaker are concerned with debate about the role of paranormal belief in institutional and personal life. The focus of Loiskandl's contribution is the manner in which the Catholic Church accommodates belief in miracles. In discussing the Church's response to 'miracles' Loiskandl makes the point that belief in the paranormal is apt to challenge structures of institutional power. He notes that it is not surprising that the Christian Churches have retained the advice that saints should be venerated but not imitated.

John Schumaker, an absolute unbeliever, provides the final chapter in the book. This chapter is a cost-benefit analysis of paranormal beliefs in personal life. For Schumaker paranormal beliefs, which are defined broadly to include religion, are indispensable tools in one's journey through life. They are a means of coping with the harsher aspects of reality. At the same time, however, they exact a price of blunting self-awareness and compromising rationality.

It is instructive to observe how heated the debates are between believers and unbelievers in the paranormal as represented in this section. Indeed it is difficult to find a contribution which could be regarded as occupying a 'middle ground' in the debate. Nevertheless, the fact that this volume was put together by editors from both sides of the fence shows that collaboration is possible and suggests that such collaboration may ultimately lead to a helpful clarification of issues in the area.

CHAPTER 17

SASQUATCH SIGHTINGS IN SOUTH DAKOTA: AN ANALYSIS OF AN EPISODE OF COLLECTIVE DELUSION

James R. Stewart

Without begging the question about the veracity of all and every paranormal belief, it appears reasonable to assume that a fair proportion of such beliefs are delusionary in nature. The following chapter is an examination of an episode of collective delusion using Smelser's value-added theory of collective behavior. A rash of Bigfoot sightings swept through a small Indian reservation community in north central South Dakota in the autumn months of 1977. Although panic is too strong a term to describe the behavioral response of residents, there was widespread concern and considerable interest among local persons. The episode lasted for approximately 3 months during which hunting patrols scoured the area on an almost daily basis. They, of course, found no monster, but the episode attracted considerable media attention and put the community 'on the map' if only temporarily. Data from the episode was gathered from area newspapers, national magazines, and a limited number of personal interviews.

Although Sasquatch/Bigfoot sightings have been fairly common in the Pacific Northwest during the last one hundred years, there have been only isolated and infrequent reports of sightings in the Upper Midwest. It was, therefore, somewhat surprising when a rash of sightings occurred in extreme north central South Dakota in the late summer and fall of 1977. The episode centered in a small community located on the Standing Rock Indian Reservation. The eye witness descriptions of the Bigfoot monster were colorfully varied but generally depicted a 6-8 foot hairy man-like beast with long arms, dark fur and a foul odor. The first sightings were treated lightly by local townspersons and community officials, but as the reports increased and tracks were sighted, the town became embroiled in frenzied activities related to hunting, capturing or avoiding the mythical creature. The community enjoyed national limelight for a brief period as area newspapers and radio and television stations reported daily updates of the story. National television and magazine reporters were also dispatched to cover the story and scores of curious outsiders flocked to the community to join in the hunt. The episode lasted approximately three months and gradually diminished as disappointed searchers failed to discover any evidence which could substantiate the existence of Bigfoot.

During the episode the community was polarized into two schools of thought — believers and skeptics. The believers, drawing upon the rich culture lore surrounding Bigfoot, thought that he was the missing link between apes and man. Driven out of the Pacific Northwest by forest fires, Bigfoot had become disoriented and he along with his mate and possibly one offspring, had wandered into South Dakota. The skeptics, supported by the fact that Sasquatch had never been captured, killed or found, labeled the whole episode as nonsense. They depicted believers as naive, gullible victims of either hoaxes or overactive imaginations. Persons who reported sightings were often ridiculed as crackpots or heavy drinkers whose imaginations had been fueled by the appearance at a neighboring town's theatre a few months earlier of the 'B-grade movie', Sasquatch. Although the episode has ended, its legacy remains with sightings being reported at a rate of about one per year. The most recent sightings, however, are generally ignored and the local residents appear to have no inclination to participate in a repeat performance of 1977.

Based upon the available evidence (or rather lack of it) this research must conclude that this episode was a classic example of mass hysteria, or more accurately collective delusion. For the purposes of this research mass hysteria has been defined as the contagious spread among individuals of physical symptoms such as convulsions, fainting spells, seizures or hyperventilation. These episodes are typically confined to relatively small close-knit groups such as school classes or work groups. In contrast, episodes of collective delusion usually have much wider participation of disparate individuals and characteristically involve the adoption of a system of delusionary beliefs to explain situations or events about which no readily available scientific or rational explanation is adequate. While some of the individuals who reported sightings did manifest heightened anxiety levels, for the most part, the episode involved no physical maladies and was restricted to the growth and spread of the idea that a large, hairy monster was making sporadic appearances throughout the area.

Similar accounts of collective delusion have been reported in Seattle, Washington (Medalia and Larsen, 1958), Mattoon, Illinois (Johnson, 1945), Taipei, Taiwan (Jacobs, 1965) and eastern South Dakota (Stewart, 1978). These seemingly diverse episodes involving windshield pits, phantom anesthetists or slashers and mutilated cattle revolve upon a common theme. For largely inexplicable reasons, persons adopt a bizarre, extraordinary interpretation of routine or mundane events. Events which are virtual everyday occurrences (i.e. nicks in windshields, cuts on children's feet, or dead cattle) are attributed to mysterious, and to some degree anxiety-producing, causes. These extraordinary definitions of the situation usually defy logical or scientific refutation and become increasingly popular as an explanation of the events. The failure or inability of authorities to squelch the initial reports or sightings tends to legitimize and lend credibility to the unconventional explanations. As the episode develops, more and more persons adopt the delusionary belief system. Skeptics persist, however, in advancing their naturalistic explanation and eventually the episode dies when believers are unable to produce solid evidence to support their care. The popularity of the collective delusions declines as the 'flock wearies of the message' and the episode usually fades away in a quiet and inconspicuous manner.

Value-Added Theory

In the following narrative the Bigfoot sightings that occurred in South Dakota in 1977 are chronicled. The evidence upon which the research is based consists of magazine and newspaper stories, radio and T.V. accounts and a few personal interviews. As an analytical model, this study will employ the value-added theory of collective behavior (Smelser, 1962:12-22). The theory provides an excellent method of organizing the data and presenting it in a coherent manner. It offers students of collective behavior a guide for understanding the elemental features of episodes of collective behavior and how they combine to produce the event.

The value-added theory is an identification of six basic conditions or determinants which are present in all episodes of collective behavior. The theory is similar to previous 'natural history' models of revolution (eg Brinton, 1936; Edwards, 1920 or Hopper, 1950). These models were derived by studying detailed histories of particular revolutions and abstracting a pattern which included features which the individual revolutions were found to have in common. These stages typically followed a temporal sequence and, in effect, represented an 'ideal type' of revolution as a social phenomenon. In a similar fashion, Smelser breaks down episodes of collective behavior into the following crucial elements or determinants:

1. *Structural Conduciveness*. These are factors in the natural or social environment which allow episodes of collective behavior to occur. The

existence of the stock market, for instance, is a conducive feature for a possible economic panic or craze. These conditions do not cause the subsequent episodes of collective behavior, instead they create an environment in which episodes may develop assuming the other determinants combine in a certain manner. The possibility of communication between actors is likewise a conducive feature for all episodes of collective behavior. It, too, does not directly cause episodes; however, communication channels must be present for an episode to occur. Conducive features function to establish broad parameters within which outbreaks of collective behavior become possible.

2. *Structural Strain*. Straining features act as underlying causes of outbursts of collective behavior. Racial discrimination and police brutality, for instance, are generally concluded to have partially caused urban riots in the 1960's. In episodes of hysteria or delusion the strain elements are typically features which produce anxiety, uneasiness, or boredom among potential actors. Absence of 'believable' knowledge or ambiguous and conflicting knowledge generally confuses persons and increases their vulnerability of succumbing in an episode of collective delusion.

3. *The Growth and Spread of the Generalized Belief*. The generalized belief consists of the recognition of straining factors by potential participants and the processes by which these beliefs are internalized. In instances of collective delusion, often times a society's cultural lore will provide the general guidelines in the formation of the generalized belief. Continuing traditions with respect to the existence of mythical animals or UFOs, for example, provide persons with ready-made answers to events which, at least temporarily, defy a rationalistic explanation. Another component of this determinant is the identification of networks through which the delusionary beliefs are communicated among persons.

4. *Precipitating Factors*. These seemingly insignificant events act as triggering mechanisms for the growth of the episode. Typically, events which serve as precipitating factors give vividness and legitimacy to the rather nebulous fears and anxieties aroused by the straining features and identifed by the generalized belief.

5. *Mobilization of Participants for Action*. This determinant analyzes the growth patterns of the episode after the occurrence of the precipitating factor. It discusses the processes involved as the behavior/belief is adopted by increasing numbers of persons in the affected area.

6. *The Operation of Social Control*. While not being an essential condition

of the value-added process, the operation of social control determines whether any episode of collective behavior will take place. If social control mechanisms are adequate, no outbreak will occur. However, the fact that an episode has occurred is evidence of the breakdowns in mechanisms of social control. If social controls are effective, they act to deflect, deter or even suppress an episode. The interaction between the elements of the determinants influences not only the likelihood of occurrence, but also the form or type of episode that will emerge.

Structural Conduciveness

As stated earlier, structurally conducive determinants include features of the geographical or social environment which allow collective behavior episodes to develop. In this particular outbreak there appear to have been three conducive elements: (1) the nature of the geographical terrain; (2) the structure of the local community; and (3) prestige gleaning mechanisms which operate in our society.

Contrary to the popular stereotype, which depicts South Dakota as an endless flat prairie, this particular area has a great deal of variety in geographical terrain. Deep ravines and wooded areas along local rivers and creeks provide numerous potential hiding places for monsters. Large portions of the area are also virtually inaccessible by motor vehicles and thus prevented a local posse from following tracks or sightings of the monster. These features are conducive to a monster sighting episode because they provide hiding places and various possible avenues of 'escape'. The same is true of the Pacific Northwest. Deep woods and mountains provide a haven or refuge for the numerous Bigfoots which have been purportedly sighted in the last 100 years or so. It would be a virtual impossibility for a Bigfoot sighting craze to occur in a geographical area which did not provide hiding places or escape routes. This is probably why Bigfoot sightings concentrate in areas where pursuit is difficult or impossible and are virtually nonexistent in desert areas or flat prairie lands which contain no hiding places for reported monsters.

Another conducive feature for this episode was the high potential for rapid and blanket communication of the anxiety created by the generalized belief. The central community is a typical small, rural community and contains numerous informal gathering places, especially the local trading post, where newsworthy topics are discussed and disseminated very quickly. Friends and neighbours serve as the most important sources of information in this type of community and were frequently mentioned by persons interviewed in newspapers and magazines. In addition to the informal networks of information exchange, most households contain radios, television sets and subscribe to either local or regional newspapers. Once a rumor about the existence of a monster is started it is likely to be passed on with great rapidity to virtually everyone in the immediate area.

Another conducive element which played a role in this episode is typically found not in panics but in crazes. It focuses upon the mechanisms used in gaining prestige or notoriety. Despite mild ridicule which was heaped upon the persons who were the first to report Bigfoot sightings, it became evident during the height of the episode that seeing Bigfoot or passing on rumours became the 'in' thing in the local area. Persons who reported sightings became the center of attention both among their fellow townspersons and regional and national reporters. Seeing Bigfoot became a way of gaining prestige and living in the limelight, at least temporarily. As in similar episodes, participation in the outbreak of Bigfoot sightings was similar to wish fulfillment and the possibility of being granted prestige and attention served as a strong motivating factor which greatly encouraged persons to 'see' Bigfoot. This desire to be 'the first on the block to see Bigfoot' probably served to stimulate many of the sightings. The motivation to participate operated in the same manner that has been observed in fashion crazes or other fads which give prestige to the joiners. The positive aspects of playing the sick role in hysterical contagions has been noted (Gehlen, 1977) and Rose (1982:35) also discussed the application of the craze model of wish fulfillment to episodes of pseudo disaster.

These features then constituted the structurally conducive elements of the Bigfoot delusion. They combined to make any subsequent episode possible. They provided general outlines within which the episode could develop and only when combined with structurally straining features did they become instrumental factors in the determination of the Bigfoot episode.

Structural Strain

The most important sources of structural strain in an episode of collective delusion revolve around the lack of reliable information about the cause of the mysterious events and socio-economic factors which influence the perceptual frameworks of individuals in the community. The latter factors, while not necessarily part of the value-added process, nonetheless serve an important function because they influence the 'world-view' of area persons. In particular, they heighten the likelihood that persons will believe the bizarre interpretation rather than the rationalistic/scientific explanation of the episode.

The primary source of strain, therefore, resided in the situational ambiguities surrounding the sightings and the lack of believable explanation about what the people were actually 'seeing' in their reported sightings. Authorities were at a loss to explain the sightings and could not provide adequate answers which refuted the purported sightings of monsters. This inability to explain away or dismiss the sightings as resulting from pranks, hoaxes or overactive imaginations contributed to the increasing anxiety of area residents. When a sighting was reported to authorities, they, of course, investigated it. Their inability to provide reassuring explanations and answers increased the mysterious aspects of the sightings and actually, although not deliberately, gave credence to the extraordinary explanation (i.e. that the area was being visited by a monster or monsters unknown). When control agents/agencies cannot adequately explain the case of something unknown, they unwittingly are placed in the position of being accomplices to those who 'believe' in the fantastic interpretation. Just as ignorance of battlefield situations predisposes soldiers to flee in war, the lack of reliable, satisfactory information about 'what those people actually saw' strongly influenced some area residents to adopt the bizarre explanation.

The other important source of straining factors resides in the socio-economic composition of the community. It has been generally concluded that females apparently are more susceptible to hysteria or delusion than males (Johnson, 1945; Moss and McEvedy, 1966; Schuler and Parenton, 1943 and Stahl and Lebedun, 1974), less educated persons more susceptible to anxiety than better educated persons (Smelser, 145-146; Cantrol, 1947; Johnson, 1945 and Medalia and Larsen, 1958) and persons from lower-economic levels seem to be more prone to participation in hysteria or delusionary episodes (Cantril, 1947; Johnson, 1945; Medalia and Larsen, 1958 and Stewart, 1980). In addition, minorities appear to be more susceptible to anxiety than members of the dominant group (Moore, 1958). These factors apparently influence the process by which an individual defines a situation. They combine to produce an orientation which is less scientific and a world view which perceives some events as mysterious and incomprehensible. In episodes of collective delusion, the possession by persons of these socio-economic characteristics predisposes them toward adopting a bizarre explanation of events while eschewing a naturalistic/scientific one. Carson County tends to be over-represented in the socio-economic characteristics which have traditionally been associated with persons who are more likely to succumb to either hysteria or the adoption of a delusionary set of beliefs.

In sum, the inability of authorities to disprove the monster interpretation of the sightings with a believable alternative explanation couples with the predispositions of area residents toward a threatening definition of the situation to produce a stressful environment, in which the episode grew, could grow.

The Growth and Spread of the Generalized Belief

The function of this determinant of collective behavior is that of identifying and operationally defining the straining features. Uncertainty and ambiguity were the most common mental states following the intial reports of the Bigfoot sightings. These occurred because of a lack of satisfactory natural explanation regarding the objects of the sightings. The resulting anxiety caused persons to search for answers which structured the situation into believable terms. The form and shape of the new explanation seemed to be largely a function of existing cultural myths, legends or lore. The legend of Sasquatch has been a part of the general culture for approximately one century and a cultural component of various Native-American tribes even before that. Since social control agents could offer neither an acceptable scientific interpretation for the sightings, nor could they prove the sightings were hoaxes, the belief in the Bigfoot explanation gained in popularity. The assimilation of the initial reportings into a Sasquatch framework was accomplished with relative ease. The popularity of Bigfoot sightings has increased in recent years and the geographically affected area has spread to encompass virtually the entire nation. There have even been formed clubs and organizations which monitor and investigate Bigfoot reports and summarize their findings in a newsletter. The most recent addition to this phenomenon was the production of a 'B-grade movie' which purported to scientifically scrutinize the reported sightings and reached the conclusion that Bigfoot-type monsters were real animals and probably represented a link between Homo Sapiens and apes. This conclusion was supported by numerous photographs and film footage of previous sightings. This movie entitled, *Sasquatch*, played in a neighbouring town approximately 3 months prior to the first reported sighting. This movie more than any single factor was probably responsible for the 'Bigfoot interpretation' of the original sightings by area residents. Not only did it provide a ready-made explanation for the events, but it also undoubtedly heightened the awareness and imagination of those area residents who were already predisposed to such forms of belief.

The role of the news media was paramount in both the formation and spread of the Bigfoot mystery. While informal communication networks were predominantly important within the local community, the news coverage by area newspapers was responsible for enlarging the geographical scope of the event. As a result of the media barrage, what would probably have remained a local episode, mushroomed into an event which received nation-wide coverage.

In episodes of hysteria or delusion the generalized beliefs are characterized by fear or anxiety. Although the emotional reaction of Little Eagle's residents never approached panic there was certainly widespread apprehension. People were warned to stay in at night and a few persons even left town during the height of the episode. At the same time, however, there was also a carnival-type atmosphere which pervaded the community. Persons eagerly gathered each morning at local businesses to discuss the most recent developments. Daily cares and concerns were temporarily forgotten as the local residents became preoccupied with the episode. The perceived danger from phantom gassers, mutilated cattle or Bigfoot sightings is generally not viewed as immediately life threatening. In fact, it usually gives a certain amount of vicarious excitement to the community residents. As mentioned earlier there was prestige to be gained from having reporters visit the local community and finally there was a resultant heightened sense of communal spirit which derived from the identification of an outside threatening, malevolent force. Bigfoot played that role.

Precipitating Factors

According to newspaper accounts the episode began in late August with the first reported sighting. A Native-American youth was doing repair work on the home of a relative when he glanced up to see a 'big, dark-brown, hairy thing' emerging from the tree-lined banks of a river approximately a quarter of a mile away. He attempted to show the 'thing' to a co-worker but it had disappeared by the time they returned from the other side of the house. The same thing happened a short time later and once again the co-worker observed nothing. These first sightings were dismissed by most residents as the 'wild imaginings of youth'. However, about a week later another sighting was reported by a 17 year old Native-American boy. He was startled by the 'Monster' while walking home late one night. He raced home and began talking wildly of a 'big, hairy man' who had jumped out of the bushes and scared him. The youth was then reported to have gone into convulsions and had to be taken to the local community health representative. One week later he was given a ceremonial sweat bath to exorcize any evil spirits which may have possessed him as a result of the encounter with the monster.

These two sightings acted as precipitants for the subsequent rash of reports which afflicted this community for the next two months. These initial sightings set the stage for the mild hysteria which swept the county and made the small community the center of national attention for a brief period of time. These two sightings, however, acted only as the first precipitating factor and in isolation were probably not sufficient to trigger the rest of the episode. Most area residents, both white and Native-American, still remained skeptical about the existence of any monster. This situation is similar to the findings of Kerckhoff, Black and Miller (1965) who conclude that epidemics frequently begin with persons who are less well integrated in the social relationships of the community. The epidemic grows very rapidly when the socially integrated persons in the community began to adopt the hysteria/delusion. The two reports by Indian youths apparently were not credible enough to be believed by most of the persons in the area. Newspaper coverage was scant and the episode would probably have died quitely if another pair of related events had not occurred.

Approximately two weeks after the first sightings a white rancher and his brother were feeding cattle when they observed 'him' standing in a ravine about one-half mile away. They watched for approximately 5 minutes and described their monster as being seven or eight feet tall with wide shoulders and a coat of heavy, black hair. They attempted to get closer but the monster quickly jumped into the ravine and disappeared. This report acted to give more credibility to the Bigfoot interpretation of the sightings because the brothers were respected members of the area and not given to the telling of wild tales. Prior to their report, Bigfoot sightings were confined also exclusively to the Native-American community and largely dismissed by area whites. However, the sighting by the white ranchers tended to legitimize the earlier sightings and made the Bigfoot episode a bi-racial phenomenon.

Another significant event occurred about the same time as the ranchers' report. The owner of the local trading post discovered 'tracks' in the mud along the banks of the Grand River. They were deeply embedded in the muddy soil and were approximately 12-18 inches in length with five distinct toes. Their depth indicated to locals that the monster must weigh over 500 pounds and had a stride of 6-8 feet. Plaster casts were made and later authenticated by an 'expert' Bigfoot hunter who came to join in the foray. The tracks were reported to the local Bureau of Indian Affairs police chief who found himself at a loss to explain them. Both of these individuals were highly respected in the community by both white and Native-Americans and their discoveries added significantly to the momentum of the episode. The area newspapers devoted only 40 column inches to the reports when they were confined largely to the Native-American community; however, when the white ranchers reported their sightings and tracks were discovered, the event became more newsworthy and attracted far more attention. The use of newspaper column inches as a barometer of interest and growth of an episode has been accepted in previous studies (Medalia and Larsen, 1958 and Stewart, 1978). While the researcher has no longitudinal survey evidence regarding the growth of the number of believers or the decrease in the number of skeptics during the episodes, it appears reasonable to assume that newspaper coverage of an event is a crude indicator of the growth of the episode itself.

Mobilization for Action

During the later part of September the episode gathered impetus and the next two months were a period of frenzied activity in the area. The local county sheriff and the police force of the Bureau of Indian Affairs were inundated with reported sightings and it was estimated that over 100 separate incidents were brought to the attention of law enforcement personnel, newspapers and radio and television stations by the time the episode had subsided. Descriptions of the Bigfoot monster grew more and more detailed as subsequent sightings seemed to incorporate information from previous reports into an increasingly vivid description. The monster was described in somewhat vague terms by the early reports, but as sightings became more common the nature of the descriptions became remarkably detailed. From the big, dark man-like creature reported in late August, the monster now was described as being eight feet tall, covered with black thick fur and resembling a large ape-like creature. The monster had a simian-type face and long arms which reached to its knees. It's movements were said to resemble those of a monkey and 'it smelled like rotten eggs'.

As descriptions of the monster became increasingly vivid, they also became increasingly ominous. Bigfoot was accused of molesting local livestock and pets and in one instance was thought to be responsible for the deaths of a few cattle and pigs. There was never any proof to substantiate these claims, but they served to add excitement to the whole episode. About the same time a missing person report was filed on a young man and this was also attributed to Bigfoot. The youth's body was later found but an autopsy indicated that he had died of exposure and not from injuries sustained from an encounter with the monster. There was, in addition, a report of a Bigfoot sighting which caused a heart attack in an elderly male. This too was later demonstrated to be false, but the macabre theme developed in these rumors illustrated the elevated anxiety of area residents during the height of the episode.

The reason for Bigfoot's anomalous appearance in South Dakota did not strain residents' imaginations. Some persons thought that forest fires in Northern California has chased him out of that area into the northern plains. Others maintained that Bigfoot was looking for his mate. This version gained credibility because the tracks attributed to Bigfoot became greatly varied in size and some locals became convinced that they were being visited by a Bigfoot family — father, mother and one child. Later in the episode an 'undisclosed news source' told reporters that he had obtained proof that Bigfoot was actually brought to earth by flying saucers. The 'source' concluded that this visitation was part of a resettlement program from Bigfoot's home planet, which was a cold place, to an area which had a similar climate.

The area was invaded during this time by groups of outsiders who wanted to assist in the hunt for the elusive monster. During the months of October and November a posse was organized and nightly vigils were conducted as the search intensified. A number of 'Bigfoot experts' also offered their assistance to local persons. A national magazine, *Saga*, sent a copy of the recording which they claimed to be the sounds of previously sighted monsters in Pennsylvania. After listening to the tape residents quickly concluded that the recordings and the nightly screams heard in the area were the same.

According to a local source, an 'outside expert' even convinced some residents that Bigfoot was attracted to females and seemed to be especially drawn to menstruating women. These conclusions were based upon his own research of previous sightings and served as the basis for two traps which were planned to catch Bigfoot. The first involved a van with loudspeakers and an all night record-playing session using only the voices of women singers. This scheme was designed to catch the curious Bigfoot when he was drawn to the sounds of the female vocalists. Not unsurprisingly most of the participants in the all night session managed to convince themselves that Bigfoot had come close to the van, but warily lurked in the shadows instead of coming forth. The second, even more bizarre, scheme involved the use of what could only be described as 'used menstrual accoutrements (sic)'. These 'items' were placed in a plastic bag, which had holes punched in it, and suspended from a limb of a tree. A group of armed men surrounded the area and lay in wait all night, hoping to surprise and capture Bigfoot who would be inexorably drawn to the site by the odors emanating from the bag. This effort, too, proved a disappointing failure when Bigfoot failed to show. There was also a third plot to entrap the monster which never got out of the planning stage. Local enthusiasts toyed with the idea of digging large pits in areas which Bigfoot was known to frequent. When Bigfoot stumbled into the pit, he could then be tranquilized with drugs and taken to a cage where he could be easily displayed and studied by skeptical scientists. This idea was abandoned along with another scheme which involved dropping a large net from an airplane.

As anxiety grew as a result of increased sightings, residents and curious outsiders began increasingly to arm themselves and band together in a posse. The increased use of firearms was the result of two factors: the desire to protect oneself and family against attacks by Bigfoot and the desire to kill or wound the monster and prove conclusively that it existed. Area law enforcement personnel made strident pleas to stop carrying firearms and at one point the local tribal court considered issuing an injunction against the carrying of all firearms on reservation property. The injunction was not issued because it happened to be the annual hunting season and the ban would have infringed upon the rights of legitimate deer and pheasant hunters. There were a few instances where hunting parties inadvertently fired upon one another when members of the groups were mistaken for Bigfoot. There was even a report by one hunter that he had shot and wounded Bigfoot, but a thorough search of the area failed to produce any evidence. As hunting parties continued to fail in their efforts to find the monster, the number of participants dwindled. Most of the disappointed hunters decided to wait until the first snowfall before continuing their efforts. They concluded that tracking the monster would be much easier in snow; unfortunately, the arrival of the first seasonal snowfall also coincided with the end of the episode. The fresh snow failed to yield any new tracks and disappointed hunters concluded that Bigfoot had gone into hibernation. Skeptics, however, used this situation to strengthen their case and offered it as proof that Bigfoot had never existed.

The placid life of the local community underwent drastic changes during this period. The presence of outsiders and especially news media personnel disrupted what had been a 'routine small town' life style. Local persons were frequently interviewed by radio, T.V., newspaper or magazine reporters and willingly provided and, in some instances, probably embellished their account of what was happening. As is the case in most episodes of this nature the role of the media in fostering the episode cannot be understated (Rosengren, Arvidson and Sturesson, 1975 and Miller, Mietus and Mathers, 1978). Instead of objectively and skeptically reporting events, media personnel frequently became part of the 'hype atmosphere' surrounding the episode. The headlines mentioned previously are hardly indicative of objective journalism. Stories about monsters apparently 'sell' in the media while skepticism and investigative reporting have assumed a secondary role.

Residents responded to the interest and attention from the outsiders by complaining about the disruption of their daily routine. Although skeptical locals suspected that their credulous neighbours were basking in the limelight. In fact, some of the local persons who enjoyed most of the publicity were accused of, if not creating the entire episode, at least of sponsoring it by playing hoaxes on the outsiders. They were accused of profiteering on 'Bigfootism' and charges were in particular directed against the owner of the trading post who seemed to be at the centre of most Bigfoot discoveries.

Persons in a neighbouring town were also quick to cash in on the event. Since Little Eagle has no accommodations the outsiders were forced to stay in the neighbouring town of McLaughlin. Within a short period of time Bigfoot t-shirts went on sale in local stores. In addition, local eating establishments offered 'Bigfoot pancakes' and 'Bigfoot-long hot dogs' to their customers. Bumper stickers were also sold to commemorate the event.

The episode peaked in the latter part of October and early part of November. Daily updates were offered by the media and the interest culminated with the appearance of representatives from *Saga*, *Argosy*, and *Newsweek* magazines. A brief report of the episode also made the national nightly news on the N.B.C. television network.

Eventually, as in all episodes of collective delusion, it began to wane in intensity. Fewer people paid attention to any new reports while outsiders drifted away as efforts to prove the existence of Bigfoot continued to produce nothing substantial. Repeated reports by the same persons tended to undermine their credibility and new reports were often ignored by authorities. The last sighting which received media attention occurred in early December and received only a very small write-up in area papers. Eventually all reports stopped. Local skeptics sighed with relief as apparently the community had regained its senses, while local believers explained the end of the episode in one of two ways: either Bigfoot had gone into hibernation or he had been chased out of the area by all of the search activities. Although there have been a few isolated reports of sightings in the years since 1977, none has been able to rekindle the excitement and enthusiasm of the original.

Operation of Social Control

The very occurrence of an episode of this type indicates that there was a partial breakdown of social control (Rose, 1982; Turner & Killian, 1972). In episodes of collective delusion, the most salient failure of social control resides in the inability of social control agents to refute the bizarre or extraordinary beliefs which people adopt as an explanation of the events. Local law enforcement personnel were suddenly confronted with an unusual situation which was not adequately covered by accepted procedures. Since Bigfoot sightings were new to this area, they lacked experience in dealing with them. Not only did law enforcement officials not refute the initial sightings, but some of them actively participated in the episode. The Bureau of Indian Affairs police chief's active participation and leadership in the searches served inadvertently to lend legitimacy to the monster interpretation of the sightings. Those whose function it was to offer

TABLE 1: A comparison of explanations offered by 'Believers' and 'Skeptics' about events in the Bigfoot episode.

	Believers	Skeptics
The original sightings	Observations by persons who saw real animals.	Hallucinations because of that 'silly' movie or pranks.
Subsequent sightings	Continuing proof that Bigfoot was in the area.	Gullible people falling victims to their imaginations.
Discovery of Bigfoot's tracks	Conclusive evidence of the existence of the monster.	Result of a hoax or the natural enlargement of human tracks by the weather.
Varied sizes of the footprints	Result of at least three different monsters of varying sizes.	Evidence that the tracks or footprints could be from virtually any animal.
Abrupt disappearance of Bigfoot	Went into hibernation or evacuated the area.	People finally had come to their senses and stopped reporting every thing that seemed suspicious.
Failures of search parties	Bigfoot was highly intelligent and not easily captured.	Hunting parties were chasing rainbows.
Outside experts offering concurrence	Experienced people who were familiar with Bigfoot's habits.	Outside 'crackpots' who had no legitimate credentials or degrees.

reasonable explanations, were unable to do so and actually joined in activities of the believers. The local county sheriff, it should be noted, remained skeptical throughout the entire episode and went so far as to refuse to investigate the reports. His skepticism, however, seems to have fallen upon deaf ears since it seemed to accomplish little to stem the tide of delusion. A local veterinarian also voiced skepticism about the existence of Bigfoot, but unintentionally lent credibility to the extraordinary interpretation by offering his plane and tranquilizing rifle to the searchers when a reliable sighting was next reported.

It has become increasingly evident to this researcher that episodes of collective delusion are actively fueled by the mass media. Media personnel appear to exploit the desire of some persons to fool themselves. Tabloid-type journalism seems to feed upon a naive public and willingly accommodates persons who desire to add a little mystery and excitement to an otherwise routine and, perhaps boring, life style. News media do not create episodes of collective delusion; they do, however, have a penchant for amplifying those that are brought to their attention.

Informal social control mechanisms seemed to be most effective in this outbreak. Local skeptics disparaged the tales of the believers and generally acted as dampers throughout the entire episode. The following is a comparison of the explanations which both groups gave to various aspects of the Bigfoot phenomenon.

In sum, the episode dies a 'natural death'. The failure of believers to produce even a shred of credible evidence regarding the existence of Bigfoot eventually caused interest and enthusiasm to wane. Outbreaks of collective delusion seem to have within them the 'seeds of their own destruction'. When the basic assumption of the episode (i.e. the existence of a monster) rests upon a delusion evidence other than that of a circumstantial nature can never be presented. Eventually people tire in their efforts, their zeal diminishes and the episode quietly disappears.

Conclusions

The research can draw only one conclusion from the investigation — that the Bigfoot sightings episode was, in fact, nothing more than an outbreak of collective delusion. Although Bigfoot sightings occur with surprising frequency throughout the country, this regularity of Bigfoot 'appearances' adds nothing to prove its existence. A far more plausible explanation for the sightings stems from the increased sensitization of the public in the area of Bigfoot lore. Some organizations and a few isolated 'experts' devote much of their time and resources in an attempt to prove the existence of Bigfoot. Their periodic newsletters and updates serve to keep alive the legend of Bigfoot. When a public is increasingly subjected to a barrage of information regarding the existence of Bigfoot monsters, eventually, there will occur idiosyncratic sightings. These, in turn, are offered as continuing proof of the original assumption — that Bigfoot exists. The circularity of this pattern was common in the 1950's with the UFO phenomenon.

In this episode it is likely that highly suggestible people fell victim to the Bigfoot legend as it was most recently portrayed in the movie a few months before the outbreak. The initial sightings struck responsive chord among others in the community who also began to 'see' monsters. These derived sightings were magnified by the media and the episode gathered steam. However, the inability of searchers to uncover any real proof regarding Bigfoot's existence caused the 'happening' to decline in intensity and eventually stop altogether. As activities ceased most area residents breathed a collective sigh of relief. There remained, however, a hard-core of believers who adhered to the delusionary beliefs. They will continue to keep the Bigfoot legend alive and well and may even function in the role of 'expert' in outbreaks which crop out in other parts of the country, but it is highly unlikely there will ever be a resurgence of 'Bigfootism' in this area.

References

Brinton, C. (1965), *The Anatomy of Revolution*, New York, Vintage Books.

Edwards, L. P. (1927), *The Natural History of Revolution*, Chicago, The University of Chicago Press.

Gehlen, F. (1977), 'Toward a revised theory of hysterical contagion,' *Journal of Health and Social Behavior*, 18, 27-35.

Hopper, R. D. (1950), 'The revolutionary process: A frame of reference for the study of revolutionary movements', *Social Forces*, 28, 270-279.

Jacobs, N. (1965), 'The phantom slasher of Taipei: Mass hysteria in a nonwestern society', *Social Problems*, 12, 318-328.

Johnson, D. (1945), 'The phantom anesthetist of Mattoon: A field study of mass hysteria', *Journal of Abnormal and Social Psychology*, 40, 175-186.

Kerckhoff, A. C., Black, K., & Miller, N. (1965), 'Sociometric patterns in hysterical contagion', *Sociometry*, 28, 2-15.

Lake, B. (1978), 'Something big and hairy visits Little Eagle', *Human Behavior*, September, 25-26.

Medalia, N. & Larsen, O. L. (1958), 'Diffusion and belief in a collective delusion: The Seattle windshield pitting epidemic', *American Sociological Review*, 23, 221-232.

Miller, D., Mietus, K. J. & Mathers, R. A. (1978), 'A critical examination of the social contagion image of collective behavior: The case of the Enfield monster', *Sociological Quarterly*, 19, 129-140.

Moss, P. & McEvedy, C. P. (1966), 'An epidemic of overbreathing among schoolgirls', *British Medical Journal*, 26, 1295-1300.

Rose, J. D. (1982), *Outbreaks*, New York, The Free Press.

Rosengren, K. E., Arvidson, P. & Sturesson, D. (1975), 'The Barseback panic: A radio programme as a negative summary event', *Acta Sociologica*, 57, 309-314.

Schuler, E. & Parenton, V. J. (1943), 'A recent epidemic of hysteria in a Louisiana high school', *The Journal of Social Psychology*, 17, 221-235.

Smelser, N. (1962), *Theory of Collective Behavior*, New York, The Free Press.

Stewart, J. R. (1978), 'Cattle mutilations: An episode of collective delusion', *Heuristics*, 8, 55-68.

Stewart, J. R. (1978), 'Collective delusion: A comparison of believers and skeptics', Paper read before the Midwest Sociological Society, Milwaukee, Wisconsin.

Turner, R. & Killian, L. M. (1972), *Collective Behavior*, Englewood Cliffs, NJ, Prentice-Hall.

U. S. Bureau of the Census (1980a), *U. S. Census of Population: United States Summary*, Part 1, Washington: U. S. Government Printing Office.

U. S. Bureau of the Census (1980b), *U. S. Census of Population: South Dakota*, U. S. Government Printing Office.

CHAPTER 18
ON PARANORMAL DISBELIEF: THE PSYCHOLOGY OF THE SCEPTIC

Harvey J. Irwin

Other contributions to this book explore the scope of people's beliefs in paranormal phenomena and some of the factors that could underlie such beliefs. In this chapter I want to examine the other side of the coin, that is, to consider why some people do *not* believe in the paranormal. Specifically, what are the roots of scepticism?

One significant element of a sceptical attitude to the paranormal lies in the perceived quality of the scientific evidence. Sceptics feel the available experimental data of clairvoyance, telepathy, precognition, psychokinesis (PK), out-of-body experiences and allied phenomena simply are not convincing (e.g., Alcock 1981). Nor are sceptics alone in this respect. A recent international survey by Blackmore (1988) indicates that some parapsychologists also deem the experimental literature of their field to be inconclusive for the existence of paranormal processes. (To make my own position quite explicit this is the view that I, a professional parapsychologist, espouse.) There is of course, no denying that people have experiences which seem to incorporate extrasensory, psychokinetic or other psychic qualities. But the sceptical position is that parapsychological research has yet to demonstrate satisfactorily the need to appeal to paranormal concepts rather than orthodox psychological ones in accounting for these experiences. The validity of that assessment is a matter of vigorous debate (e.g., see Honorton 1985; Hyman 1985; Hyman & Honorton 1986) but is not a focal concern here. For present purposes it is sufficient to acknowledge that sceptics maintain they have taken due account of the relevant experimental work and that the perceived insufficiency of these studies is at the core of the sceptical stance.

Some disbelievers in the paranormal also appeal to various philosophical justifications of their perspective. It commonly is argued for example, that because there is no widely endorsed theory of the paranormal the existence of these phenomena can not be accepted (Flew 1980). Another justification is the alleged incompatibility of parapsychological hypotheses with mainstream science (Alcock 1981); closer scrutiny of this claim suggests it is little more than a rhetorical device used by sceptics in their case against parapsychology, although some parapsychologists have made a tactical error in this context by seeking to portray their research as ideologically revolutionary (Winkelman 1980). The low level of replicability of parapsychological experiments also is often cited in support of the belief that paranormal processes do not really exist (McClenon 1984).

Be that as it may, dispassionate examination of the evidence and its conceptual status is surely not the basis of the vehemence and belligerence of sceptics' attacks on parapsychology, particularly those launched by members of the Committee for the Scientific Investigation of Claims of the Paranormal (CSICOP). A society of scientists, magicians and other people, CSICOP was founded in 1976 originally to evaluate objectively the evidence for paranormal phenomena. Its subsequent activities however, have represented an implacable crusade against parapsychological research (Hansen 1987). On one occasion CSICOP even resorted to deceit in covering up unfavourable data from its own experimental programme (Pinch & Collins 1984), an affair that led to the resignation of many of its more evenhanded members. Additionally, CSICOP commonly uses ridicule in its attacks. Parapsychological phenomena are derided as nonsensical and primitive folk beliefs, 'A reversion to a pre-scientific religio-mystical tradition' (Moss & Butler 1978, p. 1077). Parapsychological research is belittled as occultism is pseudoscientific garb (Alcock 1981) and its practitioners as 'closet occultists' (Romm 1977) and 'mystery-mongers' (Scott 1985). Sceptics such as Diaconis (1978), Hansel (1980), Gardner (1981) and Randi (1982) have portrayed parapsychologists as dishonest or incompetent. One CSICOP Executive Council member (Randi 1983a, b) sought to demonstrate the ineptitude of a team of parapsychologists by arranging for two young conjurers to present themselves to the laboratory as psychics and to set out to circumvent the researchers' methods of experimental control. While CSICOP's exposure of fraudulent psychics has been deemed commendable many parapsychologists were outraged by the transgression of professional scientific ethics in Randi's project. In the *Humanist* and in CSICOP's own periodical the *Skeptical Inquirer* the tactic of 'guilt by association' is pursued by discussing parapsychology in the same context as the Bermuda Triangle, UFOs, popular astrology, pyramid power, witchcraft, the Abominable Snowman, the Tarot and the like. Sceptical groups also have pressured universities and colleges to cancel scheduled courses in parapsychology (Hansen 1987; McCormick 1987), despite these institutions' nominal endorsement of the principle of academic freedom. There is evidence too that parapsychologists' access to orthodox sources of publication is impeded (Collins & Pinch 1979, pp. 257–258; McClenon 1984, pp. 114–118; Rockwell 1979).

Although these sceptical responses to parapsychological research do have some rational foundations their style is unequivocally belligerent, and many parapsychologists have taken umbrage at the deviation from conventional standards of scientific debate. Rockwell (1979) for example, has complained that the sceptics' approach is contrary to the principles and spirit of scientific endeavour, where differences of opinion should be resolved by further experimentation within co-operative research programmes. But there is a significant disparity between scientific ideals and scientific practice. As Feyerabend (1975) notes, the resolution of a controversy comes not so much from the weight of evidence as from the rhetorical skills and political influence of advocates for each side. The rhetorical aspect of the parapsychology debate is examined in some depth by Collins & Pinch (1982) and McClenon (1984). In evaluating the activities of CSICOP it should be remembered too that scepticism now is more a social movement than a scientific one (Hansen 1987). CSICOP's public allegiance to scientism therefore can not be assumed to imply that sceptics would be bound by scientific ethics and practices.

Still, the underlying question remains: What is the nature of the strong emotional component of sceptics' disavowal of paranormal beliefs? One approach to this issue is to consider the path by which sceptics may have reached their disbelief.

Personal experience may be a relevant factor here. Many parapsychologists have had anomalous experiences themselves and are inclined to attribute their paranormal beliefs at least in part to such personal experience (McConnell 1977, p. 213; McConnell & Clark 1980). A similar if converse process might operate for sceptics. Over a third of sceptics surveyed by Alcock (1981, p. 36) cited a lack of personal parapsychological experience as a reason for their disbelief. There may of course be response biases underlying these data. Believers may construe chance events as parapsychological and subsequently attribute their belief to experience rather than experience to belief (Benassi, Singer & Reynolds 1980); conversely, disbelievers may encounter genuinely paranormal phenomena but dismiss them as events with undetermined causes and subsequently deny having had any parapsychological experiences at all. Research into these confounding effects is warranted, although the logistics of obtaining useful data on sceptics' part anomalous experiences are no simple matter. If asked if they had had an extrasensory experience for example, sceptics who reject the possibility of ESP can hardly be expected to respond positively. Perhaps more valid information could be obtained by asking about experiences described by the investigator in a noncommittal way and noted as being 'regarded by some people as extrasensory'. When this procedure is followed a small percentage of disbelievers in a given parapsychological concept do admit to having had the corresponding experience themselves (Irwin 1985a); on average however, about 90 per cent of disbelievers continue to deny such experiences. As Alcock (1981, p. 36) observes, it is feasible that lack of personal experience is a post hoc rationalization of paranormal disbelief rather than an effective cause of disbelief. Most probably, experience and belief interact in a mutually supportive fashion, with beliefs affecting the interpretation of experience and personal experience selectively used to buttress beliefs. In any event it seems implausible that a lack of personal parapsychological experiences would provide the emotional energy apparent in the vehemence of sceptics' attacks on parapsychology.

Education does have a substantial effect upon our beliefs. Might this also be so for paranormal belief and disbelief? There are some indications that formal tertiary education in general can reduce belief in ESP (Moss & Butler 1978), although no such relationship was observed either by Haraldsson (1981) or by Sobal & Emmons (1982). Belief in other parapsychological phenomena does not appear to be related in a simple fashion to level of general education (e.g., Irwin 1985b, pp. 183–186). Education in scientific disciplines however, may enhance paranormal disbelief (Valentine 1936); social scientists emerge from their training as the most sceptical group, followed by natural scientists and then others in the humanities, arts and education (McClenon 1984; Wagner & Monnet 1979). The result for social scientists of course, to some extent may be due to the fact that they are the people most likely to have been exposed to specific instruction about parapsychological claims. Investigations of the effect of specific educational programmes lend support to this interpretation. Banziger (1983), Emme (1940), Gray (1985) and McBurney (1976) report that students' declared paranormal belief can be attenuated by a sceptically-oriented course. A study by Irwin (1985a) suggests however, that such courses might affect merely the students' expression of paranormal beliefs rather than tacit adherence to them. The enhancement of scepticism through tertiary education therefore may be a process of socialization in attitudes to the paranormal expected to be expressed by people in various social roles. Perhaps this is most starkly illustrated by McClenon's (1984) survey of 'elite' scientists, individuals who are prominent in the determination of policy decisions in the scientific establishment; this group reportedly showed the highest level of scepticism of any sample of academics surveyed in the last two decades. The notion that paranormal disbelief is governed in part by the perception of social roles can be held to account for some of the implacability of sceptical responses to parapsychological research; elite scientists for example, may tend to see themselves in the role of a crusader intent upon ridding science of subversive purveyors of irrational superstition.

Now, crusaders can become so committed to a cause that they occasionally resort to extreme measures against their opponents. By the same token, even the idea of isolated instances of 'overkill' by crusaders does not accommodate the emotional tenor of sceptics' motivation and behaviour. The nature of this behaviour indeed suggests the presence of some very strong unconscious emotional conflict. Several writers have speculated on the bases of this conflict. An appeal frequently is made to the concept of cognitive dissonance, the generation of great psychological tension when we try to maintain two incompatible beliefs; one means of reducing the level of this tension is through a vehement cathartic attack on the sources of one of the beliefs. LeShan (1966) for example, argues that the security of our personality or ego structure is rooted heavily in a stable view of an orderly physical world governed by uniform laws. For some people the evidence of apparently paranormal processes is not compatible with their worldview and a state of cognitive dissonance thereby may be generated. McConnell (1977) similarly proposes that cognitive dissonance can arise from the incompatibility of our parapsychological experiences in everyday life and our awareness of the possibility that parapsychologists' experimental data are due to procedural artifacts and fraud. The hysterical quality of sceptics' identification of parapsychology with primitive superstitiousness is interpreted by Wren-Lewis (1974) in terms of the paradoxically religious status of scientists' anti-religious materialism; according to Wren-Lewis, conformity to this philosophy has taken on all the features of a collective obsessional neurosis and consequently the sceptics' behaviour is quite literally hysterical.

Other interpretations of the hypothesised underlying emotional conflict are more psychodynamic in character. Several of these focus on the possibility that paranormal belief stirs certain repressed fantasies and perceptions of our early childhood. Tart (1982) proposes that the young child extrasensorially may detect its mother's feelings of hatred toward it when she is under considerable stress. Because this perception is unacceptable the child represses both it and the possibility of ESP. Confrontation with evidence for the paranormal may in adulthood threaten to bring these repressed memories to the surface. The individual's reaction against this evidence then may be fuelled by the substantial psychic energy associated with repression and thereby can be highly exaggerated. Eisenbud (1946) also suggests that evidence of apparent 'mind over matter' effects can rekindle repressed childhood thoughts of killing or destroying a parent; in this circumstance the évidence for paranormal processes must vigorously be rejected.

The anxieties evoked in some people by the possible existence of the paranormal evidently are substantial, whether or not they are appropriately depicted in psychoanalytical terms. An endeavour to identify these anxieties more precisely has been undertaken by Tart (1982, 1984; Tart & LaBore 1986). His technique comprises a 'belief experiment'; participants are asked to imagine that a scientist discovers a means of making ESP work very well and then to describe their gut-feelings about this situation. Tart has observed that some people have very real fears about the existence or, more precisely, the operation of psi (ESP and PK). Control over extrasensory experiences is a commonly expressed concern: people fear if they had ESP their mind could be flooded by someone else's thoughts. Other doubts related to their capacity to utilize an extrasensory ability in a responsible and sensitive way, the threat to people's privacy, and the possible irreversibility of the scientists' technique for promoting ESP. A survey by Irwin (1985c) showed further that scepticism towards parapsychological research tended to be associated with increased fear of psi.

Although additional research is needed it would appear that for sceptics the existence of the paranormal is unacceptable very largely for emotional reasons. The parapsychology debate therefore is confounded not only by gullible superstitiousness but by prejudicial fear as well. Techniques for dealing with the fear of psi have been described by Tart (1984). It is unlikely however, that sceptics would have the inclination to work through this fear: with some notable exceptions, sceptics to date have shown little real concern to maintain an objective and evenhanded perspective in their dealing with parapsychology. This is not to point the finger of blame at the sceptics alone. After all, the sceptics' responses are needlessly inflamed by parapsychologists who insist on presenting their research as a pursuit of the paranormal rather than as a study of the actual bases of anomalous experiences. Nevertheless it seems inevitable that the controversy will not be resolved by rational discussion between opponents. Rather, there is a real possibility that one side will suffer a loss of most of its perceived credibility in the scientific arena. And whoever the victor, this would be a sad state of affairs because ultimately parapsychologists and sceptics each have something positive to contribute to the progress of science.

References

Alcock, J.E. (1981), *Parapsychology: Science or Magic? A Psychological Perspective*, Oxford, Pergamon.

Banziger, G. (1983), 'Normalizing the paranormal: Short-term and long-term change in belief in the paranormal among older learners during a short course', *Teaching of Psychology*, vol. x, 212–214.

Benassi, V.A., Singer, B. & Reynolds, C.B. (1980), 'Occult belief: Seeing is believing', *Journal for the Scientific Study of Religion*, vol. xix, 337–349.

Blackmore, S. (1988), 'A survey of parapsychologists and sceptics', paper submitted for publication.

Collins, H.M. & Pinch, T.J. (1979), 'The construction of the paranormal: Nothing unscientific is happening', *in* R. Wallis, ed., On the margins of science: The social construction of rejected knowledge, *Sociological Review Monograph*, No. 27, 237–270.

Collins, H.M. & Pinch, T.J. (1982), *Frames of Meaning: The Social Construction of Extraordinary Science*, London, Routledge & Kegan Paul.

Diaconis, P. (1978), 'Statistical problems in ESP research', *Science*, vol. cci, 131–136.

Eisenbud, J. (1946), 'Telepathy and problems of psychoanalysis', *Psychoanalytic Quarterly*, vol. xv, 32–87.

Emme, E.E. (1940), 'Modification and origin of certain beliefs in superstition among 96 college students', *Journal of Psychology*, vol. x, 279–291.

Feyerabend, P. (1975), *Against method*, London, Verso.

Flew, A. (1980), 'Parapsychology: Science or pseudo-science?' *Pacific Philosophical Quarterly*, vol. lxi, 100–114.

Gardner, M. (1981), *Science — Good, bad and bogus*, Buffalo NY, Prometheus.

Gray, T. (1985), 'Changing unsubstantiated belief: Testing the ignorance hypothesis', *Canadian Journal of Behavioral Science*, vol. xvii, 263–270.

Hansel, C.E.M. (1980), *ESP and Parapsychology: A Critical Re-evaluation*, Buffalo NY, Prometheus.

Hansen, G.P. (1987), 'CSICOP and scepticism: An emerging social movement', paper presented at the 29th Annual Convention of the Parapsychological Association, Edinburgh.

Haraldsson, E. (1981), 'Some determinants of belief in psychical phenomena', *Journal of the American Society for Psychical Research*, vol. lxxv, 297–309.

Honorton, C. (1985), 'Meta-analysis of psi ganzfeld research: A response to Hyman', *Journal of Parapsychology*, vol. xlix, 51–91.

Hyman, R. (1985), 'The ganzfeld psi experiment: A critical appraisal', *Journal of Parapsychology*, vol. xlix, 3–49.

Hyman, R. & Honorton, C. (1986), 'A joint communiqué: The psi ganzfeld controversy', *Journal of Parapsychology*, vol. 1, 351–364.

Irwin, H.J. (1985a), 'A study of the measurement and the correlates of paranormal belief', *Journal of the American Society for Psychical Research*, vol. lxxix, 301–326.

Irwin, H.J. (1985b), *Flight of Mind: A Psychological Study of the Out-of-Body Experience*, Metuchen NJ, Scarecrow.

Irwin, H.J. (1985c), 'Fear of psi and attitude to parapsychological research', *Parapsychology Review*, vol. xvi (6), 1–4.

LeShan, L. (1966), 'Some psychological hypotheses on the non-acceptance of parapsychology as a science', *International Journal of Parapsychology*, vol. viii, 367–385.

McBurney, D.H. (1976), 'ESP in the psychology curriculum', *Teaching of Psychology*, vol. iii, 66–69.

McClenon, J. (1984), *Deviant science: The case of parapsychology*, Philadelphia, University of Pennsylvania Press.

McConnell, R.A. (1977), 'The resolution of conflicting beliefs about the ESP evidence', *Journal of Parapsychology*, vol. xli, 198–214.

McConnell, R.A. & Clark, T.K. (1980), 'Training, belief, and mental conflict within the Parapsychological Association', *Journal of Parapsychology*, vol. xliv, 245–268.

McCormick, D.L. (1987), 'A lawsuit in Hawaii', *American Society for Psychical Research Newsletter*, vol. xiii, 14.

Moss, S. & Butler, D.C. (1978), 'The scientific credibility of ESP', *Perceptual and Motor Skills*, vol. xlvi, 1063–1079.

Pinch, T.J. & Collins, H.M. (1984), 'Private science and public knowledge: The Committee for the Scientific Investigation of the Claims of the Paranormal and its use of the literature', *Social Studies of Science*, vol. xiv, 521–546.

Randi, J. (1982), *Flim-Flam! Psychics, ESP, Unicorns and Other Delusions*, Buffalo NY, Prometheus.

Randi, J. (1983a), 'The Project Alpha experiment: Part 1. The first two years', *Skeptical Inquirer*, vol. vii (4), 24–33.

Randi, J. (1983b), 'The Project Alpha experiment: Part 2. Beyond the laboratory', *Skeptical Inquirer*, vol. viii (1), 36–45.

Rockwell, T. (1979), 'Pseudoscience? Or pseudocriticism?', *Journal of Parapsychology*, vol. xliii, 221–231.

Romm, E.G. (1977), 'When you give a closet occultist a Ph.D., what kind of research can you expect?', *Humanist*, vol. xxxvii (3), 12–15.

Scott, C. (1985), 'Why parapsychology demands a skeptical response', *in* P. Kurtz, ed., *A Skeptic's Handbook of Parapsychology*, Buffalo NY, Prometheus.

Sobal, J. & Emmons, C.F. (1982), 'Patterns of belief in religious, psychic, and other paranormal phenomena', *Zetetic Scholar*, No. 9, 7–17.

Tart, C.T. (1982), 'The controversy about psi: Two psychological theories', *Journal of Parapsychology*, vol. xlvi, 313–320.

Tart, C.T. (1984), 'Acknowledging and dealing with the fear of psi', *Journal of the American Society for Psychical Research*, vol. lxxvii, 133–143.

Tart, C.T. (1986), 'Attitudes toward strongly functioning psi: A preliminary survey', *Journal of the American Society for Psychical Research*, vol. lxxx, 163–173.

Valentine, W.L. (1936), 'Common misconceptions of college students', *Journal of Applied Psychology*, vol. xx, 633–658.

Wagner, M.W. & Monnet, M. (1979), 'Attitudes of college professors toward extra-sensory perception', *Zetetic Scholar*, No. 5, 7–16.

Winkelman, M. (1980), 'Science and parapsychology: An ideological revolution', *Re-Vision*, vol. iii, 59–64.

Wren-Lewis, J. (1974), 'Resistance to the study of the paranormal', *Journal of Humanistic Psychology*, vol. xiv (2), 41–48.

CHAPTER 19

THE PROBLEM OF EVIDENCING THE IMPROBABLE, AND THE IMPOSSIBLE

Antony Flew

Introduction — The Special Case of Parapsychology

One thing has to be said with emphasis at the start. It is that the cause of parapsychology is quite different from most of the others falling within the scope of the Committee for the Scientific Investigation of the Claims of the Paranormal (CSICOP)[1]. It is quite different, that is to say, from the factitious, but to some richly profitable, mysteries of the Bermuda Triangle and of the Chariots of the Gods, from astrological prediction, from the extraterrestrial identification of Unidentified Flying Objects, or from most of the other affairs dealt with so faithfully in that Committee's useful and entertaining *The Sceptical Enquirer*[2]. It is quite different in two ways.

(i) The first, and for present purposes, the less important of these two differences is the general wretchedness of the available evidence for the actuality of those other putative wonders. For the moment that anyone truly concerned to discover the truth, rather than to cook up a best-selling, allegedly real-life mystery story, began strenuously to investigate the business of the Bermuda Triangle it became apparent that there is no sufficient reason to believe that more ships and aircraft vanish without trace in that area than anywhere else with comparable traffic densities and comparable natural hazards. Again, there just is no good reason to believe that there have been any close encounters of the third kind; nor indeed of the first or second either. The truth here is that the content of normal visions, dreams, and misperceptions is always in part a function of the wishes, beliefs, and expectations of the subject. So Chinese, under old Emperors, used to dream dreams of dragons and confucian officials; but not of Red Guards, chanting doubleplusgood Chairman Mao-think. So too Bernadette Soubirois in her nineteenth century French village had a vision of the Blessed Virgin, as represented in pictures and images in her local church; but not of Shiva the Destroyer, as represented in Indian temple sculptures. So, again and likewise, when contemporary North American readers of science fiction misperceive celestial phenomena, what they believe they have seen is neither gods nor a dragon but a spaceship. Such false identifications are, in one of the finest phrases of Karl Marx, 'the illusion of that epoch' (Marx and Engels, 1964, p.51).

But parapsychology, defined as the study of the psi-phenomena[3], is a horse of an altogether different colour. The men and women who in 1882 came together in London to found the original Society for Psychical Research (SPR) were models of high-minded integrity and quintessential Victorian respectability. Nor has anyone ever accused the SPR of being either idle or frivolous in its investigations. Again, catchpenny sensation-mongering is just about the last charge which could plausibly be levelled against those conducting parapsychological experiments. William James, who was himself a leading figure in the American Society for Psychical Research, once remarked that experimental psychology 'taxes patience to the uttermost, and could hardly have arisen in a country whose natives could be *bored*. Such Germans as Weber, Fechner, Vierordt, and Wundt obviously cannot . . .' (James, 1890, p.192; author's emphasis). this is perhaps even more true of quantitative experiments in card-guessing and dice-willing; and of the experimental parapsychologists who are, as it happens, predominantly Americans.

(ii) The nature of the second major difference between the case of the psi-phenomena and that of those other alleged wonders can perhaps best be brought out by referring to C.D. Broad's classical paper on 'The Relevance of Psychical Research to Philosophy'[4]. He began by noticing how often it is said that the occurrence of any psi-phenomenon would be incompatible with the laws of physics. Yet it is not easy to think of any particular named law of nature — such as Boyle's Law, or Snell's Law, or what have you — which would be, or is, contradicted by the occurrence of ESP of psychokinesis[5]. Broad next proceeded to point out that what such occurrences would contradict is certain principles much more fundamental and elementary than any such named laws — principles generally accepted by all those thinking of themselves as 'men of sense' both before and after the growth of modern science. They are still employed almost all the time by almost everyone, both in most everyday affairs, and in all ordinary scientific work. These Broad christened Basic Limiting Principles (BLPs).

His own formulations were characteristically abstract and complicated. More significantly, and equally characteristically, they were also Cartesian. They made, that is to say, certain extremely questionable assumptions, which he himself did not recognize as being either assumptions or questionable. They were: that people are composed of two radically disparate elements, their flesh and blood bodies and their immaterial minds and souls; and that it is these latter which are the truly human agents, the subjects of every kind of consciousness. The significance of this is that it points to the one positive common characteristic shared by all the actual or merely alleged phenomena of psychical research. This uniting principle was clearly perceived by all the Founding Fathers. Most of them approached their investigations in hopes of finding here — what seemed to be altogether absent from the mainstream orthodox sciences — scientific support for a dualistic and Platonic-Cartesian view of the nature of man — opposed to any monistic and Aristotelian alternative.

PSI Phenomena and the Laws of Physics

Let us now try to represent Broad's BLPs in more concrete terms, and without any prejudicial commitment to controversial Cartesian conclusions. The crux is that psi-phenomena are, or would be, phenomena whose occurrence we all of us — including, most of the time, the believing parapsychologists themselves — would with complete confidence rule out as physically (or practically, or contingently) impossible. This point has in a way been recognized by all those who have insisted that psi-phenomena are (or would be) inconsistent with (what are currently believed to be) the laws of physics. this is, I believe, part of what J.B. Rhine and others have had in mind when they have claimed that psi-phenomena are (or would be) *non*physical[6].

(i) Suppose, for instance, that there has been yet another security leak in Washington or Bonn, Canberra or London. Then everyone, or almost everyone, assumes that some hostile agent must have had some form of direct or indirect sensory access to the Top Secret material that is now secret no longer. It never seriously enters most people's heads that the material might have been telepathically or clairvoyantly 'read' by an agent who at no time came within normal sensory range. ESP is thus in practice ruled out as impossible. That information can be acquired without employment of the normal senses is thus precluded by a Basic Limiting Principle.

(ii) Suppose, again, that there had actually been an explosion in the nuclear power station at Three Mile Island; and that it had not been true — as the Republican bumper stickers had it — that 'More people died in the back of Ted Kennedy's car than at Three Mile Island'. Then no one, or almost no one, would have dared seriously to suggest that this might have been a case of PK sabotage, achieved by one of the many agents of the KGB and allied secret services known to be operating under the cover of jobs at embassies in Washington and in and around the UN Building in New York. That too is precluded as physically (or practically, or contingently) impossible by another BLP.

PSI Phenomena and Established Experience

We have to reckon with two further truths about BLPs, in addition to the facts that they are both more familiar and more fundamental than any of the named laws of physics.

(i) The first is that to appeal to them as reasons for dismissing some alleged occurrence as physically (or practically, or contingently) impossible is not — any more than to appeal in a similar context to some named law of established physics — to dismiss such allegations dogmatically and apriori.

Many contributors to *The Sceptical Enquirer*, including some Fellows of CSICOP, are quite unnecessarily embarrassed by, while making dreadfully heavy weather of, such charges of apriori dogmatism. Certainly, since none of us is infallible, we ought to be always ready to consider any strong evidence suggesting that some proposition we had believed to express a true BLP or a true law of nature is, after all, false. Yet it is simply grotesque to complain, in the absence of any such decisive falsifying evidence, that these appeals to the BLPs and the named laws of established physics are exercises in apriori dogmatism. For what the word 'apriori' means is: prior to and independent of experience. But in both of these kinds of cases we have an enormous mass of experience supporting our present beliefs and our present incredulities.

(ii) The second of the present supplementaries amounts in reality to little more than an underlining of what was previously distinguished as the second of the two main differences between the psi-phenomena and those other truly miscellaneous wonders. The point is that ESP and psychokinesis are almost by definition ongoings which we have very strong experiential reason to dismiss as physically (or practically, or contingently) impossible. Of course it is always conceivable that we have been wrong all along: we are none of us infallible. But, in order to demonstrate that we have been in error, it will, surely, be necessary to deploy quite exceptionally powerful evidence; and that, as we shall go on to argue in Part II, evidence of one particulary and peculiar kind?

By contrast, the other putative wonders, which are not perceived as involving psi, appear to constitute a genuine miscellany. Their only common characteristic seems to be strictly negative; that they are indeed not perceived as involving psi. Of course in some cases it will be argued that those other wonders too are for some good reason physically (or practically, or contingently) impossible; and where this can be made out, we should insist upon similarly strong and quite exceptionally demanding evidential requirements. For instance: it might be argued that any Loch Ness Monster would have to be the sole survivor from some ruinously inbreeding colony; and that in any case the waters of the Loch are not sufficiently rich in possible food to have supported such a colony through the millenia. But, where there is no demonstrated impossibility, there the existence of the wonder is only very, very, improbable, not impossible. So, in order to determine whether or not these other wonders have actually occurred, or do actually occur, it becomes both necessary and sufficient to weigh up the conflicting probabilities and improbabilities; which is often a matter, as everyone knows, as difficult as it is disputatious.

DAVID HUME'S ARGUMENT ON MIRACLES

Hume and Factual Necessity

So here at last we reach the sixty-four thousand dollar question: 'What sort of evidence should we demand as sufficient to show that we had been mistaken in dismissing all alleged psi-phenomena (both ESP and PK) as physically (or practically, or contingently) impossible? When, back in 1955, G.R. Price made the first attempt to deploy Hume's argument 'Of Miracles' as a challenge to parapsychology, Price called not for a demonstration *type* but a demonstration *token*[7]. He demanded not an algorithm for producing psi-phenomena at will, whenever and wherever required, but rather a single, once-and-for-all-decisive, knock-down falsification of one or all of the precluding BLPs. In this, Price revealed that he had not appreciated the full richness and strength of the argument suggested by Hume.

'Suggested', rather than 'proposed' or 'urged', is the right word. For Hume's discussion 'Of Miracles' is not, what it has often been misdescribed as being, a separate essay. Instead it is Section X of his *Inquiry concerning Human Understanding*. But, earlier in that first *Inquiry*, he disqualifies himself from making in his own name what is going to be the crucial distinction: between, on the one hand, a marvellous and enormously improbably occurrence; and, on the other hand, an occurrence which, whether or not perceived as marvellous, is authentically miraculous. Hume does this by denying that we have any experience of the physically (or practically, or contingently) impossible, and hence concluding that we cannot have any legitimate idea of either an impossibility or a necessity of this sort. So when we assert a law of nature of a BLP, perhaps uninstructedly believing that these laws or principles refer to natural necessities and natural impossibilities, really we are only projecting the felt force of our own habits of association out onto the universe around us; a Humian universe in which, although there are everywhere regularities of conjunction and succession, nothing ever brings about or prevents anything else.[8]

The only kinds of necessity and of impossibility which Hume was prepared to admit were what we but not he would distinguish as logical, and would define in terms of self-contradiction and entailment. Whereas the conjunction of the proposition p with its contradictory not-p is, in this sense, impossible, this follows necessarily from that if to assert this while denying that is to contradict yourself.

By redefining our other kind of necessity — factual necessity — as involving nothing else but a regular succession of events, Hume was able to execute a 'reconciling project' for resolving the ancient antimony between liberty and necessity.[9] By thus extruding the notion of bringing about from his account of causation Hume has in our own day encouraged a time-reversed, backwards analogue; a fresh-minted concept with the help of which some might aspire to explain both paranormal precognition and some striking teleological phenomena.[10]

When is Testimony Believable?

Section X of *An Inquiry concerning Human Understanding* provoked in his own lifetime more protest and controversy than most of the rest of Hume's published work put together. He believed that he had 'discovered an argument . . . which, if just, will, with the wise and learned, be an everlasting check to all kinds of superstitious delusion, and, consequently, will be useful as long as the world endures. For so long, I presume, will the accounts of miracles and prodigies be found in all history, sacred and profane.'

Hume himself, like his contemporary critics, was most interested in 'the accounts of miracles and prodigies' found in what in those days people still distinguished as 'sacred history'. Here our own primary concern is with the phenomena, or putative phenomena, of parapsychology as they appear, or appear to appear, in an entirely secular context. So far, no one seems to have appreciated the full significance for parapsychology of Hume's argument. For those who prefer big words, it is an epistemological rather than an ontological argument. It is directed not at the question of whether miracles occur but at the question of whether — and if so, how — we could know that they do, and when and where they have.

(i) Having made this plain Hume begins: 'Though experience be our only guide in reasoning concerning matters of fact, it must be acknowledged, that this guide is not altogether infallible . . . A wise man, therefore, proportions his belief to the evidence . . . To apply these principles to a particular instance; we may observe, that there is no species of reasoning more common, more useful, and even necessary to human life, than that which is derived from the testimony of men, and the reports of eye-witnesses and spectators'.

From here Hume goes on to notice that there may be a 'contrariety of evidence . . . Suppose, for instance, that the fact, which the testimony endeavours to establish, partakes of the extraordinary and the marvellous; in that case, the evidence, resulting from the testimony, admits of a diminution, greater or less, in proportion as the fact is more or less unusual . . . The very same principle . . . which gives us a certain degree of assurance in the testimony of witnesses, gives us also, in this case, another degree of assurance against the fact, which they endeavour to establish; from which contradiction there necessarily arises a counterprize, and mutual destruction of belief and authority. 'I should not believe such a story were it told me by Cato', was a proverbial saying in Rome . . . The incredibility of a fact, it was allowed, might invalidate even so great authority'.

(ii) So far, so good. However, Hume continues, 'in order to increase the probability against the testimony of witnesses, let us suppose that the fact, which they affirm, instead of being only marvelous, is really miraculous . . .' But now, 'A miracle is a violation of the laws of nature; and, as a firm and unalterable experience has established these laws, the proof against a miracle, from the very nature of the fact, is as entire as any argument from experience can possibly be imagined'.

To be 'really miraculous', as opposed to being 'only marvelous', is to be physically (or practically, or contingently) impossible, as opposed to being an event merely very rare, unusual, or surprising. It is precisely and only because (it is believed that) it would be in this everyday sense impossible for any power within the universe, human or nonhuman, to bring about a 'really miraculous' event that religious people would say that, were it to occur, it would have to be the self-revelatory work of some supernatural power.

Hume was of course offering this argument only as an *argumentum ad homines*. It was to be 'an everlasting check to all kinds of superstitious delusion . . . which must at least silence the most arrogant bigotry and superstition and free us from their impertinent solicitations'. So perhaps he may be forgiven for not noticing — or, at any rate, not mentioning — that he had earlier disqualified himself from making in his own name the vital distinction between the 'only marvelous' and the 'really miraculous'. Certainly we ought never to abandon our own claims to employ it.

Critical History and Testimony for PSI Phenomena

What does need to be remembered at this point is that already, when publishing his first *Inquiry*, Hume had for some time been intending to devote himself in future to the writing of history: the Catalogue of the British Library still puts our greatest philosopher down as 'Hume, David, the historian'. Nevertheless it is sometimes thought that there is no more to this 'everlasting check' than a trite reminder that, because the occurrence of a miracle must be very improbable, it needs to be quite exceptionally well evidenced. But C.S. Peirce, who seems never to have exploited it fully, had the vital clue in his hands when he remarked: 'The whole of modern 'higher criticism' of ancient history in general . . . is based upon the same logic as it used by Hume'.[11] The section 'Of Miracles' is thus, among other things, an examination of the methods and the presuppositions of critical history. It is, therefore, at one and the same time a contribution to both the philosophy of religion and the philosophy of history (Wiener, 1958, pp. 292-293).

In effect Hume's thesis here is that the detritus of the past can only be interpreted as historical evidence — and, as such, employed to tell us what actually happened — by applying to it everything we know, or think we know, about what is probably or improbably, possible or impossible. We cannot even begin, by construing certain marks on old sheets of paper as a record of testimony, without assuming that it is impossible for such legible signs to be produced by anything other than human agency. Nor can we hope to identify conflicts of testimony without reference to what we know, or believe we know, about what sorts of events are copossible and coimpossible. The authority claiming that the cavalry were here then, and the authority claiming that the same force was there a day later, cannot — we argue — both be right; since it would have been impossible for men on horses to get from the one place to the other in the time available. And so on.

Confronted therefore with any story about the occurrence of a miracle, or of anything else which he knows, or believes that he knows, to be impossible, the critical historian is by his cloth required to reject it as a fiction. Hume himself gives an example of sound historical practice the reaction of the famous physician De Sylva to the story of the miraculous recovery of Mademoiselle Thibaut: 'The physician declares, that it was impossible she could have been so ill as was proved by witnesses; because it was impossible she could, in so short a time have recovered so perfectly as he found her. He reasoned, like a man of sense, from natural causes.'

What, regrettably, Hume did not recognize was the possibility that later historians, following the same sound methodological principles, but having the advantage of further scientific findings, might have to admit that some of the stories in question had after all been true — although the events thus truly recorded were not miraculous. For instance, the stories of supposedly miraculous cures wrought by the Roman Emperor Vespasian in Egypt, stories ridiculed by Hume and all like-minded contemporaries, would, in the light of advancing knowledge of psychosomatic possibility, appear to have been true.[12]

The moral for us is that any supposedly once-and-for-all-decisive yet not-in-practice-repeatable demonstration of the reality of psi-phenomena has to be, as such, rejected. It has to be rejected in the same emphatic way, and for the same excellent reasons, that critical historians reject stories of what they know, or believe they know, to be physically (or practically or contingently) impossible. So to the objection that there are some rare phenomena that, though not repeatable at will, are admitted by science, the correct and properly crushing reply should be that these are not phenomena for which we have the strongest or indeed any very good reasons for thinking impossible. Until and unless we have — at inordinately long last — a fully repeatable demonstration of the reality of psi-phenomena the conclusion of the 'wise man', who 'proportions his belief to the evidence', cannot, at best, be stronger than 'Not proven'.

The Necessity for Repeatability:

Agreeable though it would be to end with that peculiarly and appropriately Scottish verdict, there is still something more to be said. For there are three further reinforcing reasons why we have to demand full repeatability, refusing to accept any substitute.

(i) In the first place, parapsychology is by now a fairly old subject. The (original, British) Society for Psychical Research was founded in 1882. Serious work has been going on for more than a century, while the amount done each year appears still to be increasing. Nevertheless, the long sought repeatable demonstration of any psi-phenomenon seems to be as far away as ever. It is still stubbornly the case the those best-informed about the field automatically assume that anyone claiming to demonstrate psi-capacities, with night-after-night regularity must be some sort of fraud, achieving their effects by mere conjuring tricks.[13] As long as this situation continues, there will every year be better and better reason to close the books, concluding that the whole business was a wild-goose chase up a blind alley.

Another dampening and damaging feature of the history of the subject is the ever lengthening succession of shameful, shabby cases — cases that at one time and to many people had seemed to constitute

EXPLORING THE PARANORMAL

knock-down demonstrations of the reality of these putative phenomena but have since been definitively discredited as fraudulent. Here it is both salutary and sufficient to refer to Dr. S.G. Soal's once famous but now notorious work on Gloria Stewart and Basil Shackleton; originally hailed by the extremely tough-minded Broad as, without hesitation or qualification, 'The Experimental Establishment of Telepathic Pre-cognition' (Broad, 1944).[14]

(ii) The second reason for reviewing the whole business with the deepest suspicion, and the second reason reinforcing the demand for repeatibility or nothing, is the fact that no one has been able to think up any halfway plausible theory accounting for the occurrence of any psi-phenomenon. This is important, because a plausible theory relating these putative phenomena to something that undoubtedly does occur would tend both to explain and to make probable their actual occurrence. That said, it should not seem a lapse into anti-empiricist, apriori dogmatism to conclude the paragraph with a maxim attributed to Sir Arthur Eddington, a leading British physicist of the period between the wars: 'it is also a good rule not to put overmuch confidence in the observational results until they are confirmed by theory'.

(iii) Third, and finally, there are the reasons arising from the fact that all the psi-concepts are negatively defined. This important truth is often overlooked because such expressions as 'by telepathy' and 'by psychokinesis' sound like expressions 'by telephone' and 'by psychoanalysis'. But the fact is, of course, that all the psi-terms refer rather to the absence of any means or mechanism, or at any rate to the absence of any normal and understood means or mechanism. Although parapsychologists sometimes talk of psi-processes, and of psi itself as a causal factor, there is not in this case any presently identifiable analogue of the wires or of the radio waves by which telegraphic and telephonic signals are detectably transmitted.

One consequence is that no sense has been given to a distinction between single hits achieved by ESP and single hits due to chance alone. Only when it turns out, after a series of guesses (or whatever) has been made and has been scored up against the targets, that there have been significantly more hits than we could have expected by chance alone are we entitled to begin to talk of psi, or of a psi-factor. The phenomenon, therefore, is — so far, at least — defined as essentially statistical. Furthermore, and despite some protests to the contrary, the same applies not only to the experimental work but also to the supposed spontaneous or sporadic phenomena. If, for instance, someone has a dream of a maritime disaster 'on the night when the great ship went down', then there is no way of identifying this dream as a psi-phenomenon by summing single items of correspondence between dream and reality and arguing that there are too many correspondences and too few noncorrespondences for the whole incident to be put down to chance alone.

Rhine once remarked: 'The most revealing fact about psychokinesis is its close tie up with ESP'.(Rhine, 1947, p.230) It is indeed; and *vice versa* too. It seems to have been quite uncritically assumed that, because a cards-and-statistics method is appropriate for the investigation of ESP so, and as it were analogously, a dice-and-statistics method method must be appropriate for the study of psychokinesis. Presumably this assumption was mediated by an unthinking association of ideas: just as some too regularly lucky poker-players may owe a part of their prosperity to ESP, rather than to orthodox cheating; so there might be, when their other skills fail them, something comparable coming to the assistance of successful professional dice-gamblers.

Yet, however strong that unthinking association of ideas, the two cases are in a relevant way different. For even to begin to demonstrate the reality of ESP it is essential to show: not merely, as is only to be expected, that some guesses are hits; but also that, even in conditions that preclude cheating, the hits are significantly more numerous than can comfortably be accounted for by chance alone. Hence any design for an experiment has to provide targets that — thanks to their number or to their individual complexity, or to both — give sufficient purchase to calculations of statistical significance.

By contrast there is no obvious reason for expecting psychokinesis to manifest itself only in ways similarly statistical. For, if people really were able to exert force at a distance on other objects at will, then we should have expected this to be demonstrated by the use of some extremely delicate and very carefully shielded apparatus. If the subject's willings were always followed by the occurrences of the movement willed, and that movement was one that we had taken every care to ensure would not otherwise occur, then we would be home and dry; and, presumably, we should in this have a repeatable demonstration.

But the actual 'dice work' has been different. In fact, it is once again essentially statistical. A batch of dice are tossed mechanically, and the subject is told to will them all to come up on one particular side. The procedure is repeated *ad nauseam*, and well beyond. The experimenter's hope is that he will find significantly more willed sides turning up than chance alone would lead us to expect. If that hope is fulfilled, that experimenter reports a psychokinetic effect. So, once again, no operational sense is in fact given to the notion of a single psychokinetic hit, as opposed to a run of falls suggesting the operation of a psychokinetic factor.

Now the first thing to be said about this is that, after the event, it is fairly easy to think up various reasons why these theoretical differences may in practice be irrelevant. The crux, however, is not that there is not or cannot be a good case for solid concentration on the 'dice work' and on other psychokinetic experiments which can be assessed only statistically. It is, rather, that the failure of the experimenters in Rhine's laboratory ever on their own initiative to take account of the obvious possibility of looking for non-statistical evidence must constitute yet one more reason for questioning their general competence, and therefore the reliability of any of their reports of positive results in parapsychology.

The second and further consequence of all this is that there is no way of decisively identifying even a single run in which a psi-factor was operating. Since no identifiable means or mechanism is being employed, it must remain always possible to say that any single run was no more than a statistical freak — however improbably, not impossible. There is therefore once again no substitute for what there is ever less reason for expecting we shall in fact get — namely a repeatable demonstration, showing psi-phenomena being produced and inhibited at the will of the experimenters and/or their subjects. Only this would really demonstrate that the targets actually are causing the subjects to come up with correct guesses and/or that subjects actually are influencing the fall of the dice.

Concomitant Variation and the Reality of PSI Phenomena

Perhaps the commonest everyday way of checking whether we really are faced with a causal connection is to seek what J.S. Mill christened 'concomitant variations'. Suppose we wonder whether this is the switch which controls that light. Then there is an easy way of discovering whether or not there is any connection between our operating the switch and the coming on or going off of the light. If when we operate the switch at random the comings on and goings off correlate pretty well perfectly with our switchings, then there is. If not, not.

What is so depressing about the evidence for the reality of the psi-phenomena is the apparently near total lack even of claims to have detected experimentally any such concomitant variations. In face of this it becomes almost irresistibly tempting to dismiss as some sort of improbably but still possible statistical freaks all those correlations which cannot be attributed to either fraud or some more venial kind of experimenter fault.

Everyone, presumably, is employing a causal concept of PSI.[15] So no one would want to maintain that, in order to establish the reality of ESP, it would be sufficient to demonstrate a purely statistical effect: namely, that, under the tightest possible conditions, some star guessers score sky high. It must on the contrary be necessary also to show that the targets were somehow causing the guessers to make their guesses in senses which later turned out to be correct. But now, in so far as this is granted, it becomes not just remarkable but scandalous that experimenters having enjoyed the good fortune of finding star subjects, have not made a practice of randomly, and without telling them, stopping the provision of targets for their guessing. Suppose that these star subjects reacted by somehow collapsing or, better, by refusing to continue guessing. Then this would indeed be a very strong reason for believing that the targets had been playing a part in causing the guessers to guess in the senses in which they did guess. But if not, not.[16]

Footnotes

1. This was set up now several years ago on the initiative of Professor Paul Kurtz of the State University of New York at Buffalo, then editor of *The Humanist*, in hopes of doing something to stem the rising tide of popular credulity.

2. Formerly *The Zetetic*, now edited by Kendrick Frazier from 3025 Palo Alto Drive, NE Albuquerque, New Mexico 87111, and published from P.O. Box 229, Buffalo, New York 14215.

3. Mainly Extrasensory Perception (ESP), under either telepathic or clairvoyant conditions, and Psychokinesis (PK).

4. This was first published in 1949 (Broad, pp. 291-309). The immediately relevant parts are perhaps most conveniently to be found in Flew (1987, pp. 37-52).

5. For proof tests, see pp. 14ff. of the 'Introduction' to Flew (1987). For some account of the historical conflict between these two rival traditions, and of their different implications see Flew (1964).

6. Rhine (1937 and 1947) insists on describing the guesswork of his experimental subjects in prejudicially Cartesian terms. He is thus misled into an inclination to believe: both that he has propounded at least the beginnings of an explanatory hypothesis; and that his experiments have confirmed the correctness of his own Platonic-Cartesian view of the nature of man. Compare, for instance, Chapter IX, 'Describing and explaining', in Flew (1953, pp. 111-134). There is an improved version in Ludwig (1977).

7. The key paragraphs of this debate in Part IV of Broad (1949, pp. 241ff).

8. See Flew (1982, pp. 487-494) and compare Chapters 2 and 5 of Flew (1986).

9. Compare Chapter 8 of Flew (1986).

10. Compare Dummett (1954, pp. 27-44). The successor contribution to that symposium (Flew, 1954, pp. 45-62) definitively disposes of Dummett's speculation. Since the explanatory power of the traditional concept of cause resides exclusively in the familiar fact that causes do bring about their effects, a backwards cause would: either have to make not to have happened something which had already happened; or make to happen something which has not, in fact, happened. How could anything be more manifestly self-contradictory? For further discussion of notions of cause in the context of paranormal precognition see Part III of Flew (1987).

11. It is a noteworthy illustration of the way in which academic compartments can constrict a scholar's vision that R.G. Collingwood never mentioned this section of Hume's first *Inquiry* (Collingwood, 1946). Presumably he took it for granted that, because the section contains a contribution to the philosophy of religion, it could not also be relevant for the philosophy of history.

12. For a full critical account, see Flew (1961, Chapter 8).

13. It is doubtfully correct to speak of psi-capacities, as is so often done, when these putative capacities are so little under the control of those to whom they are attributed. For when we say that certain people possess the capacity to do this or that we usually imply that they are able to do it, or not to do it, as they choose.

14. For the evidence that Soal was in fact faking the records, see Markwick (1985, pp. 287-311) as well as further references in the same volume (Kurtz, 1985). Soal's self-righteous response to G.R. Price's redeployment of the Humian challenge makes wry reading today.

15. It is important to notice both the immediate and the wider implications of this observation. It is obvious — or at least it is once we have mastered the argument about backwards causation — that, in so far as this observation is correct, the putative concept of paranormal precognition becomes an incoherent pseudo-concept. As such it cannot serve any constructive scientific purpose, whether descriptive or explanatory. Less directly, the same observation must raise a question about the scientific value of the remaining, genuine, concepts concerning ESP.

16. One of the reasons why some of us — before his fraudulence was exposed — were so impressed and excited by Soal's experiments with Shackleton was that Soal, with his wholly innocent colleague Mrs K.M. Goldney, reported that several times, in experiments in 'precognitive telepathy', the agent was secretly instructed to stop turning up and looking at the target cards. Whenever she thus ceased to learn the values of those target cards it was afterwards found, although Shackleton has given no sign of awareness that anything was amiss, that his scores had dropped to the levels of mean chance expectation.

References

Broad C.D. (1942), 'The experimental establishment of telepathic precognition', in *Philosophy* vol. xix, pp. 261-275.

Broad C.D. (1949), 'The relevance of psychical research to philosophy', in *Philosophy* vol. xxiv, pp. 291-309.

Collingwood R.G. (1946), *The Idea of History*, Oxford, Clarendon.

Dummett M.A.E. (1954), 'Can an effect precede its cause?', Symposium contribution in *Proceedings of the Aristotelian Society*, Supp. vol. xxviii, pp. 27-44.

Flew A. (1953), *A New Approach to Psychical Research*, London, C.A. Watts.

Flew A. (1954), 'Can an effect precede its cause?', Symposium contribution in *Proceedings of the Aristotelian Society*, Supp. vol. xxviii, pp. 45-62.

Flew A. (1961), *Hume's Philosophy of Belief*, London, Routledge & Kegan Paul.

Flew A., ed., (1964), *Body, Mind and Death*, New York and London, Macmillan and Collier-Macmillan.

Flew A. (1982), 'Another idea of necessary connection', in *Philosophy*, vol. lvii, pp. 487-494.

Flew A. (1986). *David Hume: Philosopher of Moral Science*, Oxford, Iackwell.

Flew A., ed., (1987), *Readings in the Philosophical Problems of Parapsychology*, Buffalo, New York, Prometheus.

Hume D. (1955), *An Inquiry Concerning Human Understanding*, New York, Liberal Arts Press, (first published in that form and under that title in 1758).

James W. (1980), *The Principles of Psychology*, vol. 1, London, Macmillan.

Kurtz P., ed., (1985), *A Skeptic's Handbook of Parapsychology*, Buffalo, New York, Prometheus.

Ludwig J.K., ed., (1977) *Philosophy and Parapsychology*, Buffalo, New York, Prometheus.

Marwick Betty (1985), 'The establishment of data manipulation in the Soal-Shackleton experiments', in Kurtz P., ed., *A Skeptic's Handbook of Parapsychology*, Buffalo, New York, Prometheus.

Marx K. and Engels F. (1964), *The German Ideology*, trans. Dutt C., Moscow, Progress.

Rhine J.B. (1937), *New Frontiers of the Mind*, New York, Farmer and Rinehart.

Rhine J.B. (1947), *The Reach of the Mind*, New York, Sloane.

Wiener P.P. (1958), *Values in a Universe of Chance*, New York, Doubleday Anchor.

CHAPTER 20
EXTREME PHENOMENA AND THE PROBLEM OF CREDIBILITY

John Beloff

The Problem of Credibility

From time to time one comes across a claim about which one can say only that it makes one gasp. It goes so far beyond anything in one's experience, it makes such a mockery of all one's presumptions about what sort of a world it is that one is living in, one is at a loss for words. At the same time one can see no easy way of dismissing it as mere fantasy. Our ancestors might have called it a miracle or, if they disapproved of it, witchcraft or sorcery; I prefer a less loaded word so I shall call such cases extreme phenomena.

The problem of deciding what is to be regarded as credible and what as incredible is a problem that has exercised philosophers since antiquity. The Greek sceptics were preoccupied with it and were able to find reasons for doubting everything. But, as with a number of perennial problems in philosophy — e.g. the problem of causation or the problem of personal identity — it is in the writings of the great 18th century Scottish philosopher, David Hume, that we find its classic formulation. Hume, moreover, brought it to bear directly on the question of extreme phenomena. His solution to the problem has already been discussed at some length by Antony Flew in his contribution to this volume. There he quotes Hume as saying:

> 'A miracle is a violation of the laws of nature; and, as a firm and unalterable experience has established these laws, the proof against a miracle, from the very nature of the fact, is as entire as any argument from experience can possible be imagined'.

Hume could hardly be more positive and yet we must understand that he is not denying that a miracle might occur. Indeed, it was he, after all, who pointed out that we can have no proof that the laws of nature will hold from one day to the next! What he does insist on is that we could never be *justified* in accepting a miracle at its face value — not, at any rate, unless we could first be sure that it would be an even greater miracle if those who vouched for it were telling a lie. But, given the unreliability of human testimony, such would never be the case. And, to drive home his point, he imagines what he would do if he were to find that all the competent authorities agreed that Queen Elizabeth of England, a month after she had been buried, returned to life, reascended the throne and reigned for a further three years. Would he then, as a conscientious historian (and, in his day, as Flew reminds us, he was esteemed more as an historian than as a philosopher) be forced to admit that here, at any rate, was one genuine miracle? By no means, 'I would still reply' he tells us 'that the knavery and folly of men are such common phenomena, that I should rather believe the most extraordinary events to arise from their concurrence, than to admit so signal a violation of the laws of nature' (Hume, 1748).

Although Hume's Essay on Miracles did not go unanswered by critics who seized upon various weaknesses and inconsistencies in his argument, by and large most self-styled rationalists since then have been content to follow Hume's line. Hence we find Antony Flew reiterating the Humian position when he now declares: 'Confronted, therefore, with any story about the occurrence of a miracle, or anything else which he knows to be impossible, the critical historian is, by his cloth, required to reject it as a fiction'

In what follows, I shall try to show, first, that Hume — much as we revere him in Edinburgh — was mistaken and that it is not necessarily any more rational to disbelieve than to believe in a given extreme phenomenon. I shall then consider whether there are, in fact, any actual instances of extreme phenomena to which one could justifiably lend credence and I will describe in this connection a number of notable historical cases that have so far resisted demolition. Finally, I shall discuss some of the consequences of taking such cases on board as part of our intellectual baggage if we were to do so.

Let us start, then, with the Humian argument. Obviously, to acknowledge a claim that runs counter to so much that we normally take for granted is a much riskier proposition than to dismiss it from one's thoughts without more ado. At the same time, if the facts demand that we acknowledge it, it would be sheer intellectual cowardice and evasiveness to refuse to do so. Now Hume argued, for the reasons we have mentioned, that the facts are never such as to make assent obligatory. To do justice to Hume's argument would require a chapter on its own. Here I shall confine myself to what I would regard as its most serious defect. It is an argument which, whatever else may be said in its defence, cannot carry any weight with someone who has actually witnessed an extreme phenomenon — if, indeed, there are any such! I am not in this privileged position and that probably also goes for many of my readers. Nevertheless, it would not be difficult for any of us to think up a scenario in which we not only witnessed an extreme phenomenon but were in a position to satisfy ourselves, to our heart's content, that we were not the victim of any kind of trick or illusion. As an Empiricist, Hume would have to agree that there can be no better evidence than the evidence of our own senses. Hence, since he could not deny that miracles might occur, and, hence, that some people might have direct experience of them, he would have to say that such people must, at all costs, be disbelieved no matter how impeccable their previous reputation or credentials! Yet, if a rule is valid, it should be valid for all cases, real or hypothetical. It should not lead us to opposite conclusions depending on whether our knowledge of the event in question is at first or at second hand. Hume's argument amounts to an epistemological solipsism whereby only one's own experience is allowed to count. Such a prescription cannot, I submit, be regarded as rational.

Extreme Phenomena

Before we proceed to discuss some concrete examples, I want to make a few general points about how one might deal with them. There are, it seems to me, three pertinent questions that we should always ask and in the following order: (1) Could there be some normal explanation for what is alleged to have happened? If the answer to this first question is 'yes' we need proceed no further but if the answer is definitely 'no' then (2) Could the witnesses have been deceived or mistaken about what they thought they had observed? If the answer to this second is still 'no' then (3) Could the witnesses, or those who report their testimony, be lying? Only if the answer to this third question is a firm 'no' do we reach what I shall hereafter refer to as a 'credibility impasse'. I shall present in due course five such cases but, first, let us see how Hume acted to some actual cases that came to his attention.

Like the good philosopher he was, the only escape from such an impasse was to plead that the evidence was incomplete and that if we had all the facts at our disposal the situation would appear in a very different light. The plea of ignorance can always be invoked to sustain any position which appears to contradict the facts but it should be recognized for what it is, a desperate expedient. It is certainly one way of escaping from a credibility impasse but we would do well to remember that dodging a problem is not the same as getting rid of it.

So far, all I have done is to argue that if we had good evidence for an extreme phenomenon, we would not need to discount that evidence on a priori grounds, be they Humian or otherwise. It is now time to turn to the more exciting question as to whether history supplies us with any cases that bring us to the brink of a credibility impasse. Like the good philosopher that he was, Hume did not try to make things easy for himself, as an inferior polemicist might have been tempted to do, by dwelling only on miracles that were plainly risible. He was aware, for example, that, only shortly before the time he was writing, a whole clutch of miracles, mostly having to do with healing, had been taking place in Paris, of all places, the then undisputed cultural capital of Europe. They were all connected with the tomb of François Paris, the revered and saintly Jansenist priest who had been buried in the cemetery of St. Medard. Now the fact that Paris had been a Jansenist, and thus a heretic in the eyes of the Church, made such claims a test case since the authorities, egged on by the Jesuits, did everything in their power to suppress or discredit them, even going so far, eventually, as to close down the cemetery, thereby provoking Voltaire's jibe that it had now become a case of no miracles by order! We must remember, therefore, that anyone testifying to such a miracle was risking persecution. Yet, in spite of this, scores of people came forward to add their own testimony. No wonder Hume was driven to exclaim: 'Where shall we find such a number of circumstances agreeing to the corroboration of one fact? And what have we to oppose to such a cloud of witnesses?' But then, immediately, he answers his own rhetorical question in the way with which we are familiar. 'The miraculous nature of such claims' he asserts 'is sufficient reason to dismiss them' since 'when men are heated by zeal and enthusiasm, there is no degree of human testimony so strong as may not be procured for the greatest absurdity'.

So long as we are content, like Hume, to stick to generalities, we may feel secure. Let us focus, therefore, on one specific case and see whether it, too, can be dismissed as the product of an overheated imagination.

1. The Case of Louise Coirin

The case in point is that of a Mlle Louise Coirin, not one, incidentally that Hume mentions in his essay. Her story, as it has come down to us, is, briefly, as follows: She lived with her mother and stepfather (the mother having remarried after her father died) at Nanterre on the outskirts of Paris. Her two brothers, like their father before them, were officers in the Royal household. In 1716, at the age of 31, she developed a cancer of the left breast which gradually destroyed the nipple and flesh leaving her with a suppurating wound whose odour was said to have rendered her almost unapproachable. In 1718, to compound her misery, she became completely paralysed down her left side. The following year two local surgeons recommended a mastectomy, as the last slender chance of saving her life, but she declined. By 1731 — she was now 47 — she had had reached the brink of death and had already received the last sacraments on several occasions. It was only then — on August 9th to be precise — that she decided to seek supernatural aid. As she was too ill herself to make the pilgrimage to St. Medard, she persuaded a pious woman of the neighbourhood to undertake the mission for her. The woman was to bring back a clod of earth from around the tomb and her chemise after it had been in contact with the tomb. The following day, after annointing herself with the clod of earth and after putting on the chemise her recovery commenced. Before the end of the month she had regained perfect health, and more to the point, her breast was whole again.

The Jesuits lost no time in putting out rumours that a relapse had occurred and that her cancer and paralysis had returned. To scotch these slanders, Mlle Coirin went in person to Paris to make a deposition before a notary stating the full facts of her case. More important for us is the fact that one of the royal surgeons, risking the displeasure of the court, went in person to the same notary and testified that no trace of the cancer remained and he laid special stress on the fact that her left nipple was now so perfectly formed at to be indistinguishable from her right nipple.

Let us apply now to this case our three key questions. Could the phenomenon have a normal explanation? Spontaneous remissions in cases of cancer are, after all, not unknown to the medical literature. Indeed, they complicate the evaluation of some of the Lourdes cases. However, though I speak as a layman, I would suppose that the complete regeneration of a breast and its nipple must be unique. Could the witnesses, including a number of medical practitioners who are mentioned by name, have been mistaken about what they saw? Only, presumably, if some other woman, some look-alike, had impersonated Mlle Coirin during the medical examinations. However, the fact that Louise Coirin was then able to resume her normal life among her family and friends makes such an hypothesis not only far-fetched but quite untenable. There remains, then, only one last possibility, namely that the entire story is a fabrication on the part of the writer on whose authority the case is known to us. This is by far the most attractive hypothesis from the standpoint of a sceptic since, so far as I know, there is only one extant source for this story, as for so many other of the St Medard cases, namely the three volume work by Carre de Montgeron (Montgeron, 1745).[1] Who, then, was this Montgeron?

Even Hume had to admit that Montgeron was no ignorant fanatic but a man of substance and repute. He was, in fact, a nobleman, a magistrate and a member of the Paris Parliament. Prior to his encounter with these events he had had the reputation of being something of a sceptic in matters of religion. But there are at least two facts that make it extremely unlikely that he had invented this case. In the first place he mentions by name in this connection a number of notabilities and public figures included churchmen and physicians — some of the royal doctors are mentioned by name. Secondly, even if he could have got away with such a fabrication, he had nothing to gain by it. On the contrary, in the event he had to pay dearly for his audacity in publishing a work of such a controversial nature so that, although he took the precaution of dedicating the book to the King (Louis XV), he was promptly interned in the Bastille. Even this, however, did not teach him a lesson since he managed to bring out two further volumes of cases while in prison. This is hardly what one would expect from a writer of fiction!

2. The case of Joseph of Copertino

For our next exhibit we must go back another century to a case that still ranks as among the most remarkable of all time. This is the case of the levitating friar, Joseph of Copertino (Cupertino). The late Eric Dingwall devoted a chapter to him in his Human Oddities (Dingwall, 1947) from which I have freely drawn and, more recently, Stephen Braude has again drawn attention to this case in his The Limits of Influence (Braude, 1986). Here are the main incidents of his life as far as we know them:

Guiseppe Desa was born in 1603 to an impoverished family. He was resented by his mother who was soon widowed but she had him apprenticed to a shoemaker. By the age of 17 he had decided to devote his life to religion. He was then taken on as a lay Capuchin but was dismissed again after only eight months for clumsiness and stupidity. However, the Franciscans took him in first as a servant but he was admitted as a novice in 1625 and, despite his lack of scholarship, was duly ordained in 1628 (Delaney, 1980). As a monk he became notorious for his extreme asceticism and for the severity of the mortifications he would inflict on himself. What alone makes him memorable, however, was his habit of going into a rapture and then levitating, sometimes to a considerable height and, sometimes, suspended just above the ground for considerable periods of time. These levitations took place in broad daylight, sometimes in a church, sometimes in the open air. In all there are some seventy recorded instances of such levitations. His most spectacular feats were his flights to images placed high above the altar and the assistance he gave to workmen attempting to erect a Calvary Cross 36 foot high. It was said that he would lift it into place in mid-air after ten men had failed to lift it (Farmer, 1987). There is even a story that, on one occasion, he carried a fellow monk up with him into the rafters of a church (Haynes, 1970) but that could be apocryphal![2] What we do know is that Joseph constantly apologized for his levitations calling them his 'fits of giddiness'.

I shall mention one incident which strikes one as more evidential than most if only because it occurred during his final illness when two named doctors were in attendance. A certain Dr. Pierpaoli was in the process of cauterizing Joseph's right leg when he noticed that he had gone into a trance and was sitting a few inches above the seat of his chair. To make absolutely sure that this was not an illusion, both doctors went down on their knees to get a better look. When this had gone on for about fifteen minutes, Joseph's superior, Fr. Evangelista, entered the room and was able to bring Joseph back to his senses — and to terra firma! — by calling out his name.

Joseph died in 1663 at the age of 60. Within three years of his death an official inquiry was instituted with the aim of establishing the true facts of his career and, more especially, obtaining sworn depositions from those who had actually witnessed the levitations. On this basis a biography was eventually published in 1722 by one, Domenico Bernino. This, in turn, led to Joseph becoming a candidate for beatification and a Process was set in train by the Congregation of Rites, the body responsible for adjudicating these matters. It is noteworthy, from our point of view, that the person in charge of the Process, the so-called *promotor fidei*, was Cardinal Prospero Lembertini who was noted for his enlightened views — he even corresponded amicably at one time with Voltaire! (Haynes, 1970) — and was the author of what became the standard work on canonization. Lambertini, whose role here was to play devil's advocate, does not seem to have raised any serious doubts about the levitations. He was more concerned about some of the more outrageous aspects of Joseph's life style, for he had little sympathy for such extreme asceticism. Nevertheless, in 1753, by which time Lambertini had become Pope Benedict XIV, beatification was duly decreed. Canonization then followed in 1767 — just over a century after Joseph's death — and so it was that Giuseppe Desa became, for all the world, St Joseph of Copertino.

Now let us ourselves play devil's advocate and see whether, from our sophisticated vantage point, we can puncture this pious tale. The first thing that will strike us, now that some three centuries have elapsed, is that nothing remotely like this has ever happened again! Of course, in every generation, there have been claims that someone, somewhere, has levitated. Most of the best known physical mediums are credited with occasional self-levitations — one thinks, inevitably, of Daniel Home — but, still, nothing on this scale or of this magnitude.

One's first impulse may be to regard this as another particularly glaring example of the natural human tendency to exaggerate. One is reminded of the stories that used to circulate about the dancer Nijinsky. It was said that he must have been able momentarily to defy gravity and he even seems to have believed this himself. So, perhaps, Joseph was in the habit of leaping up and down when he became excited and the legend took off from there and eventually got out of hand? I am afraid such speculations cannot get us very far. There would have had to be massive collusion to have produced this amount of documentary evidence.

More promising, from the sceptical standpoint, is that Joseph was the stooge or puppet in a fiendish counter-reformation plot to bring heretics back into the fold of the one true Church. This might account for what happened to Johann Friedrich, the Duke of Brunswik, a Lutheran, who is now remembered only as the patron of the philosopher Leibnitz. The Duke visited Assisi in 1651 and, while there, expressed a wish to meet Joseph. With his two companions he was conducted to a chapel where, without being aware that he was being observed, Joseph was saying mass. After a while he was heard to utter a loud cry and was seen to rise into the air in a kneeling position. The Duke was so intrigued that he begged permission to go again the next day. This time Joseph was seen to rise just a few inches but then to remain floating above the altar steps for about a quarter of an hour. This was too much for the poor Duke who then and there decided to become a Catholic.

Had he been ensnared by some adroit piece of conjuring or illusionism? Contrary to what some people imagine, the Catholic Church has always been extremely wary of exploiting miracles associated with living individuals — the treatment of the late Padre Pio would be a case in point. So far from lending himself to such machinations, Joseph was all his life an embarrassment to his superiors. On no less than three occasions he was summoned to defend himself before the Inquisition[3] and, for much of his life, he was under strict orders to remain in his cell where he could least attract attention.[4] Of course we are heavily dependent on his biographer, Bernino, for our knowledge of his career — Dingwall relied mainly on this source — but Bernino names so many eminent personages that there would have been a limit to what he would have dared to invent or embroider. He cites, for example, three cardinals each of whom was willing to testify to having see Joseph levitate. There there is the incident when the Father General of the order of St. Francis arranged for Joseph to kiss the feet of the then Pope, Urban VIII. As often happened when Joseph got too excited, he rose into the are and remained suspended there for some time until the Father General recalled him to his sense — to the amazement of the Pope (New Catholic Encyclopedia, 1967). How easy would it be, one wonders, to invent an incident like this about a named Pope? I do not know but, all things considered, I am inclined to agree with Dingwall when he says: 'For my part I do not find it easy to believe that Cardinals, Bishops, Superiors, monastic physicians and lay visitors were all lying or engaged in a system of deceit for the apparent purpose of bolstering up the reputation of a fraudulent friar or the Order to which he was attached.' (Dingwall, 1947).

3. The case of 'Margery'

From the middle of the 19th century onwards, the Spiritualist movement provided the power-house for generating paranormal claims. My remaining three exhibits are all drawn from the careers of physical mediums who flourished during the present century. My choice was partly dictated by the fact that each has recently been the subject of biographical studies which have come to my attention. Now, physical mediums, unlike saints, have a murky reputation and, to the uninitiated, this alone is sufficient reason for dismissing, or at least playing down, any claims that are made on their behalf. One could argue, with perhaps more logic, that the more suspicious a medium the more vigilant will be the investigators — no one, after all, enjoys being taken for a ride! Fortunately, both arguments are irrelevant when one understands that the critical question in such cases is never whether the individual involved would cheat but, only, whether he or she could have cheated in the conditions specified. It is their ability, never their morals, that are on trial.

These remarks are specially pertinent because my next exhibit concerns a medium who was, surely, one of the most tempestuous and controversial characters in the whole stormy history of psychical research. I allude to Mrs. Mina Crandon, nee Stinson, known to the literature, and to all the world, simply as 'Margery'. Few mediums can have caused quite as much havoc in their time as did Margery. The American Society for Psychical Research split in two on her account (Tietze, 1985) causing W.F.Prince to set up a rival organization; the Boston Society for Psychical Research. J.B. Rhine was so quickly disillusioned with her after only a single sitting (Brian, 1984; Matlock, 1987) that he never again wanted to have any further dealings with mediums, not, at any rate, unless, like Mrs Garrett, they were willing to play it his way and guess cards. Hence one could say that Margery was instrumental in launching the new experimental parapsychology. Yet, in fairness, despite the revulsion which many decent people felt towards her, it must be said that she submitted meekly and indefatigably to the tedious and strenuous tests that were imposed upon her, perhaps, in the end, at the cost of her sanity. Ostensibly, she put up with it all for the sake of her deceased brother Walter, who had been killed as a young man in a raiload accident, and whose passive vehicle she has now become. At all events, whatever was really going on, she undoubtedly produced phenomena that still remain baffling.[5]

I shall here confine myself to a single phenomenon of Margery's multifarious mediumship, namely her 'rings'. A seamless linkage of solid rings — a manifest topological miracle — is one of the rarest of extreme phenomena. Yet it appears that, during the 1930s, Margery produced a whole series of such linkages. Since none has survived it may seem a waste of time discussing them but we still have to make sense of the documentary and photographic evidence. Some of the component rings have survived — I have examined one such pair — they are substantial wooden objects. Care was taken that each rink in a linkage should be made from different timber so as to preclude the possibility that the entire linkage might have been carved from a single block of wood. According to the records of the seances at which 'Walter' engineered these linkages, some dematerialisation and rematerialisation of the wooden rings seem to have been involved. At all events, we have a photograph of one intact linkage that is said to have been on display at one time at the office of the American Society for Psychical Research in New York and we have the text of a letter from an outside expert affirming that the linkage has been X-rayed but that 'nothing resembling an artifically concealed cut or break could be detected' (Nester, 1985). Unfortunately, with the perversity that is so typical of extreme phenomena Margery's linkages regularly (but paranormally) became unlinked. It is as if 'Walter' could get no further than creating a semi-permanent paranormal object.[6] The whole case, as you will note,

EXPLORING THE PARANORMAL

bristles with these absurdities but who are we, after all, to deny that reality may at times come to resemble a theatre of the absurd?

4. The Case of Indridason

My next exhibit may strike the reader as even more absurd. It is certainly more obscure. In this case, the protagonist, far from being world-famous (or infamous) is someone whose very name was unknown to me until just recently and is unlikely to be known to my readers unless, that is, they happen to be Icelanders! Indridi Indridason was rescued from obscurity when, at the instigation of Erlendur Haraldsson, of the University of Iceland, his student, Loftur Gissurarson, wrote a monograph on him for his B.A. Thesis. A new version of this monograph is soon to appear as an issue of the Proceedings of the Society for Psychical Research (Gissurarson and Haraldsson. In Press) Indridason's mediumship first manifested in 1905 — there had been no previous mediums in Iceland — but died from tuberculosis in 1912 at the early age of 29. He never left Iceland and thus never came to the attention of those who were most experienced at dealing with physical mediums.

In some respects the investigation of his mediumship compares unfavourably with the best work of this kind being done in Europe. Except on rare occasions the sittings were conducted in darkness apart from the occasional striking of matches when permission was given. No attempts were made to use flashlight photography as had been done in the case of Palladino and others. Assessment of the case is further hampered by the fact that all the contemporary seance notes in possession of the so-called Experimental Society have been lost. On the other hand, the case has some very positive aspects in its favour. In the first place the group who undertook the investigation were prominent persons in the community, writers, academics, scientists. They were not militant spiritualists seeking to propagate a creed; they concentrated throughout on the one key issue, namely whether the effects they observed were truly paranormal or just trickery. The most distinguished member of the group who, after 1908, took charge of the investigation, was Gudmundur Hannesson who was Professor of Medicine at the University of Iceland from 1911 to 1946 as well as being twice president of the University and, for a time, a member of parliament. Gissurarson and Haraldsson say of him that: 'he had a greater reputation as a scientist in Iceland than any of his contemporaries and was known for his integrity and impartiality'. He was, furthermore, a man of a markedly sceptical outlook. Most of the sittings took place in a small building specially built for this purpose by the Experimental Society but many were also held in Hannesson's own house where the medium was obliged to wear Hannesson's clothes. In the end, all the investigators without dissent, not least Hannesson himself, came round to the view that fraud was not involved and that the phenomena they had witnessed were, indeed, inexplicable.

During the four years, 1905-1909, during which Indridason was the subject of intensive study, he produced virtually all the classic phenomena associated with physical mediumship: raps, levitation of objects, self-levitations, strong breezes, luminous phenomena, unaccountable odours, direct voices, apports, the remote playing of musical instruments and even, on a few occasions, full form materialisations. However, the particular incident that I want to discuss, although not one of the best attested — it pertains to the period before Hanesson took charge — is one that, just because of its bizarre and almost farcical character raises the problem of credibility in its acutest and most uncomfortable form. It involves nothing less than the temporary disappearance of Indridason's left arm!

It happened for the first time at a sitting on the 19th December 1905 and then on two subsequent occasions in the course of that winter. On the third occasion, we are informed, no less than seven witnesses were present each of whom signed a document at the end stating that they had not been able to feel or to find Indridason's left arm and were willing to certify this under oath. We are further informed that, at one point, Indridason stood in full light but still no arm was visible until it as suddenly reappeared half an hour later. The ostensible reason for this strange incident, as provided by Indridason's control personality speaking through the medium, was that the powers on the other side were getting ready to bring about a full form materialisation. This was, in fact, a reported feature of his later seances.

So what are we to make of this story? An obvious ground for suspicion is that the investigators were never allowed to undress the medium. From the published account we cannot even be sure whether the medium wore his jacket throughout or was in his shirt-sleeves. Even so, it is not easy to fathom how anyone, however crafty, could manage to conceal an arm from seven inquisitive individuals whose one and only aim was to find it! No doubt the disciples of Batcheldor will see in this a further confirmation of the Batcheldorian doctrine that, unless some element of ambiguity is allowed, nothing paranormal can ever happen (Batcheldor, 1984).[7]

5. The Case of Helen Duncan

All paranormal phenomena are, by definition, 'impossible' but some, one is tempted to say, are more impossible than others! Nothing, I think, in all the literature of psychical research taxes one's credulity so severely as the phantoms of the seance chamber. There one has, at one moment, creatures that, for all the world, resemble living, talking human beings; at the next they have ceased to exist! It is fitting, therefore, that, for my last exhibit, we take a look at this ultimate extreme phenomenon and the example I shall discuss is one associated with the Scottish Medium, Helen Duncan, who died in 1956 at the age of 58. In making this choice I may appear to be putting my own credibility at risk for there is no disguising the fact that she had an unsavoury reputation. If miracles were the prerogative of persons of saintly character — or even of moderate refinement — poor Helen Duncan would be nowhere in the running. To be blunt, she was an uneducated woman of gross appearance whose mannners and language were anything but ladylike. More seriously, both she and her husband-manager were deeply involved in fraud. Nevertheless, she has two important advantages from my point of view. First, whereas we can no longer interrogate those who witnessed St. Joseph's levitations, Mrs. Duncan's phenomena are close enough to us in time for me to have met and corresponded with a fair number of those who *did* witness them. Secondly, my friend, Manfred Cassirer has done his home-work on her case and has produced a hefty monograph which he has lodged with the Society for Psychical Research (Cassirer. Unpubl.). If there were others like her at the present time I would not need to bother with such a tarnished case but alas, as with all my previous exhibits, there simply is nothing comparable at the present time.

The witnesses with whom I have spoken or corresponded, all persons whose sanity I have no reason to doubt — indeed two of them are good friends of mine and prominent members of the Society for Psychical Research — all tell much the same story. They all speak of watching figures emerging from the cabinet or sometimes taking shape out of swirling masses of amorphous ectoplasm, sometimes they are of recognisable individuals whom the sitter had known in life, sometimes they engage in conversation, but, invariably, they soon disappear by sinking through the solid floor. On this last point there is, according to Cassirer, virtual unanimity. It must be said, however, that these spectacular phenomena were reserved for her clients who attended her seances. The phenomena she produced for psychical researchers, such as Harry Price or Mollie Goldney, were much less impressive, mainly copious quantities of ectoplasm whose paranormal origin remained problematical.

Eventually, Mrs. Duncan made legal history by becoming the last person ever to be tried under the 'Witchcraft Act'. This was an archaic statute, introduced in the reign of George II, which stated that: 'anyone pretending to exercise or use any kind of witchcraft, sorcery, enchantment or conjuration could be committed to prison for one year'. Her trial at the Old Bailey, in March 1944, became something of a cause celebre in wartime London (Bechofer Roberts, 1945; West, 1946). It lasted seven days, capturing the headlines in the daily press, at the end of which the jury of seven men and one woman, with little hesitation, found her guilty and she was duly sentenced to nine months in prison. Her defence counsel, during the trial, made a bold offer to stage a seance for the benefit of the jury who, after all, knew nothing about such matters, but, although the judge was willing to give his permission, the jury turned down the offer. That, too, might have made legal history but it was not to be. Perhaps the jury thought it would be less confusing to condemn the wretched woman without first seeing what it was she claimed to be able to do!

The defence did, however, produce a long string of witnesses. One of these who made a specially good impression on the court because she seemed to be a sensible, matter-of-fact sort of a woman, was Janet Rust, a retired municipal midwife and a widow who described, at length, her experiences at a sitting with Helen Duncan at Portsmouth only some two months before the trial on January 17th, 1944. She told the court how she had there met and embraced her deceased husband and how she had felt the knobbly knuckles of his rheumatic hands, how she was able to identify her deceased mother by the two moles on her face, the one in the hollow of her chin, the other above her left eyebrow and, finally, how her aunt Mary appeared and spoke to her in Spanish with a Gibraltarian accent saying 'I would have come sooner but they did not understand'.

Was all of this just a pack of lies? But, then, why should a professional woman of unblemished reputation want to perjure herself to no purpose? Was she, perhaps, deeply hallucinated during that seance? That is more plausible and yet the only way I know whereby such hallucinations could be induced is by hypnotising someone and making the appropriate verbal suggestions. If Helen Duncan could do this without speaking or leaving her cabinet this, in itself, would suggest paranormal ability, albeit not of a physical nature. Of one thing, only, we can be certain. This could not have been the result of Mrs. Duncan regurgitating cheesecloth, a common accusation.

Conclusions

This concludes my selection of extreme phenomena. To recapitulate, we have discussed Louise Coirin with her new breast, St. Joseph of Copertino sitting on his cushion of air, Margery's impossible object, Indridason's missing left arm and, finally Helen Duncan with her troups of phantoms. The literature of psychical research affords an endless variety of such cases and readers may enjoy compiling their own list of favourites. The common factor in all such cases is that they serve as intellectual irritants or conundrums. They contrive to disturb us and make us feel giddy but we can see no easy way of getting rid of them. I cannot go along with Flew who urges us to dismiss them, in principle, as fictions. To disbelieve on principle is not a mark of rationality but of an immutable conservatism.

My critics are welcome to make what they can of the fact that I have had to delve deep into history for my examples. If I were forced to choose a contemporary and ongoing example, I think I would plump for the Chinese children. They are credited with clairvoyant powers far surpassing anything we have known in the West. I have now read three separate accounts about them, each written by a Western scientist of Chinese extraction who knew the language after a visit to the People's Republic. Each was allowed complete freedom to devise his own targets — pictures or inscriptions were used. Each was allowed to administer the test in his own preferred way. In each case the results were phenomenally successful and each scientist returned to the West satisfied that the children could not have tricked him (Jen, 1982; Kiang, 1982; Teng, 1981). But, of course, this is no more than an appetizer and, until better communication is possible between the People's Republic and the West it would be rash, indeed, to draw any conclusions.

Finally, what lessons am I asking the reader to take away from this recital of the incredible? While I am, I must admit, fascinated by such extreme phenomena, I do not wish to gloat about them. On the contrary, I am fearful about what might happen if such phenomena ever became more frequent or more widely credited. Indeed, the irony of my position is that I am still, ideologically speaking, on the side of David Hume. I consider that excessive credulity does far more harm than excessive incredulity. Perhaps the greatest menace that confronts us at the present time is still, as it was for Hume, superstition, irrationality and fanaticism. The recent world-wide resurgence of religious fundamentalism underscores my point. Survivalists will, no doubt, find in some of these extreme phenomena a vindication of their position as they are, no doubt, entitled to do. For my part, however, it puzzles me why those on the other side should seek to communicate with us in quite such a queer and unseemly fashion! And yet I am bound to confess that I find it no less puzzling that such cataclysmic disturbances of the natural order should be a product of a medium's private unconscious. So we may have to entertain the notion that something like a transpersonal force or cosmic mind is being harnessed in these exceptional situations.

To be a rationalist does not mean agreeing that everything will, in the end, be susceptible to rational analysis even though we may hope that this will prove to be the case. There may be some things that the human intellect will never understand and some phenomena that will never be explained. All that is demanded of a rationalist is that reason should never be abandoned in favour of some supposed short-cut to truth, whether we call this faith, intuition or whatever. At first blush these extreme phenomena that I have been discussing may appear to take us right away from the orderly world of science and plunge us back into the dark chaotic world of magic. On further reflection, on the other hand, the situation may not be quite so bleak. If you accept, as I do, that parapsychology, alone among the sciences, studies the influence of mind on matter, then, perhaps, it is no longer so unthinkable that every once in a while, mind overreaches itself with the consequences we have been discussing.

Footnotes

1. I am much indebted to Dr. Ian Stevenson for procuring a photocopy of the relevant chapter from the Bibliotheque Nationale in Paris. As a medical man, Dr. Stevenson queried the diagnosis of cancer since, ordinarily, a young woman afflicted with breast cancer would not be expected to survive more than a few years if it went untreated. He therefore consulted a colleague of the Department of Pathology of the University of Virginia who suggested that this might well have been a case of tuberculosis. None of this, of course, goes any way to explaining the subsequent regeneration of the affected breast which is the phenomenon in question.
2. Stories such as these earned him the nickname 'the flying friar' and he is today revered as the patron saint of air-travellers!
3. The Neapolitan Inquisition accused him of 'drawing crowds after him like a new Messiah through prodigies accomplished on the ignorant who are ready to believe anything' (Farmer, 1987). This may suggest a sceptical attitude on the part of the Neapolitan inquisitors but it certainly contradicts the idea that he was being exploited by his superiors.
4. Joseph constantly apologized for his levitations calling them his fits of giddiness. They were, indeed, so disturbing to his superiors that for some 35 years he was not allowed to celebrate Mass or attend choir and refectory

within his own community (Farmer, 1987). In 1653 the Inquisition of Perugia sent him to an isolated Capuchin friary where he was completely cut off from the outside world for the next four years when he was allowed to rejoin his own order at Orismo near Assisi.

5. We may be in a better position to evaluate her mediumship when Marian Nester has completed her book about Margery. Mrs Nester is the daughter of Mark Richardson, one of the principal investigators, and was a young woman when these events were taking place.

6. It is tantalizing to speculate on what might have been the consequences if such an object *had* survived. For the special virtue of a 'permanent paranormal object' from the credibility angle is that it transfers the onus of proof from the claimant onto the critic. It is then up to those who wish to challenge its paranormality to demonstrate how it could have been faked.

References

Batcheldor, K.J. (1984), 'Contributions to the theory of PK induction from sitter-group work', *Journal of the American Society for Psychical Research*, 78, 105-122.

Bechhofer Roberts, C.E. (1945), *The Trial of Mrs. Duncan*, London, Jarrolds.

Braude, S. (1986) *The Limits of Influence: Psychokinesis and the Philosophy of Science*, London, Routledge & Kegan Paul.

Brian, D. (1982), *The Enchanted Voyager: The Life of J.B. Rhine*, Englewood Cliffs, NJ, Prentice-Hall.

Cassirer, M. (Unpublished), 'Witchcraft at Portsmouth: A reassessment of the mediumship of Mrs. Duncan', Archives of the Society for Psychical Research, London.

Delaney, J.J. (1980) *Dictionary of Saints*, Tadworth, Surrey, Kaye & Ward.

Dingwall, E.J. (1947), *Human Oddities: Studies in the Queer, the Uncanny and the Fanatical*, London, Home and Van Thal.

Farmer, D.H. (1987), *Oxford Book of Saints* (2nd Edit.) Oxford: Oxford University Press.

Gissurarson, L.R. & Haraldsson, E. (In Press), 'The Icelandic medium Indridi Indridason', Proceedings of the Society for Psychical Research.

Haraldsson, E. (1987), *Miracles are My Visiting Cards: An Investigative Report on the Psychic Phenomena Associated with Satya Sai Baba*, London, Century.

Haynes, R. (1970), *Philosopher King: The Humanist Pope Benedict XIV*, London, Weidenfeld & Nicolson.

Hume, D. (1948), *An Enquiry Concerning Human Understanding*, Section X Of Miracles.

Jen, C.K. (1982), 'Some demonstrations on extraocular image in China', in R. McConnell (Ed.), *Parapsychology and Self-Deception in Science*, Pittsburg, PA, R. McConnell.

Kiang, T. (1982), 'Report on investigations into exceptional human body function in the People's Republic of China', *Journal of the Society for Psychical Research*, 51, 304-307.

Matlock, J.G. (1987), 'Cat's paw: Margery and the Rhines', *Journal of Parapsychology*, 51, 229-248.

Montgeron, Carre de (1745), *La Verite des Miracles Operes par l'Intercession de M. de Paris et Autres Appelans*, Cologne, Nouvelle Edition, Vol. I.

Nester, M.L. (1985), 'The Margery mediumship: I was there', *Fate*, April, 78-89.

New Catholic Encyclopedia (1967), 'Entry: Joseph of Cupertino, St.'

Teng, L.C. (1981), 'Letter to the Editor', *Journal of the Society for Psychical Research*, 51, 181-183.

Tietze, T.R. (1985), 'The Margery affair', *Journal of the American Society for Psychical Research*, 79, 339-379.

West, D.J. (1946), 'The Trial of Mrs. Duncan', *Proceedings of the Society for Psychical Research*, 48, 32-64.

CHAPTER 21
CHRISTIAN SAINTS AND THE PARANORMAL

Helmut H. Loiskandl

Saints in Christianity, and especially in the Catholic Church, have been part of the contention that transcendent power has been and is still permeating normal life. This perception is by no means just an outgrowth of Christian ideas about powers beyond everyday experience; all religions are fertile ground for paranormal experiences and beliefs since fascination and fear, attitudes characteristic of religion, surround occurrences so outstanding and unusual as to be seen beyond human capacity or endeavour. Numerous religions identify certain persons as the focus of such close encounters, from shamans in simple societies to the saints of Islam and Christianity and the Bodhisattvas of Buddhism.

Some controversy surrounds the history of Christian saints. Many writers, from then contemporary pagans to protestants and anti-clericals, claimed pagan origins for these successors to the gods and heroes of paganism. One example frequently cited is the shrine of Cosmas and Damian at Cyrrhus in Syria which was a continuation of a shrine devoted to Asclepius and characterized by the same method of healing. However more than a few catholic scholars have argued that the process involved was one of opposition rather than osmosis. As Wilson (1983) puts it: 'Even where it was agreed that pagan elements were present in the cult of saints, this was very often seen as a necessary compromise with mass converts or gross peasants and as a departure from an originally purer and more exclusive Christian practice. What we teach is one thing, declared St Augustine, what we tolerate is another; and what we are obliged to put up with is yet another.

It is certainly true that in early Christianity the term *saint* was applied in a more general manner than is now the custom in the Catholic Church where it denotes a person officially declared worthy of public cult; a declaration based on often lengthy research into life, virtues and miracles of the persons in question. Thus, two proven miracles are still required for the juridical process of canonization. Initially the early church applied the term to all baptized church members and to the faithful departed, as they were regarded to have become part of Christ in baptism and as such part of a new creation. Eventually people were singled out who were thought to have embraced this new life in an exemplary way. Historically, the first type of the cult-saint was the martyr. While the ideological justification is essentially Christian (having been united with the death and resurrection of Christ), the forms of cult developing were too close to paradigms of an order to be replaced to keep the official guardians of faith very happy. A good example of this is the longdrawn fight of Augustine of Hippo against what he considered excesses in the cult of miracle-working saints.

As the period of persecution ended, new concepts of sainthood developed. Asceticism became a central concept; to spread the gospel among pagan nations and to govern the church was regarded as special participation in the work of Christ. The approval of the papacy was eventually added to the process of designating saints. The first papal canonization was that of St Ulric of Augsburg in 993. As papal approval became an exclusive procedure, ousting local or episcopal canonization altogether from 1234, the influence of pressure groups prsent at the Roman Curia increased. Their influence grew with the establishment of elaborate bureaucratic procedures at the papal court; and it was especially religious orders who constantly tried to increase their share of saints. In the Eastern Christian Churches where synod and council remained the instrument of canonization, the number of canonizations has dwindled as we move to the present time. This is not the case in the catholic west, contrary to Sorokin's famous postulate that the rationalization of society means the end of saints. According to the formal canonization statistics, saints are being produced at a steady rate; and the present Pope seems to have some pleasure in presenting countries visited with new local saints at a rather impressive rate. Research also shows that devotion to saints is very much alive in contemporary Europe (Wilson, 1983; Sachis, 1983).

Around the life of saints has developed a literary tradition which carries literary forms from an early period into our times. This tradition got established in the hagiographical accounts dealing with the ascetic saints of the post-persecution period, but reaches back to the acts of martyrs. Patlagean (1983) has shown that this early model of a saintly life always includes the rejection of the societal-cultural sphere and its powers as well as the rejection of the purely natural. By becoming powerless in these two spheres, the saint gains power over them. That is to say he acquires paranormal power. Patlagean writes: 'Ascesis begins with two modes of separation: the saint leaves human society at an early age to go into the desert, and he abstains from sexual relations. In other words, he leaves the field of culture to rejoin that of nature, whose limits he then reaches and at which he carries on his struggle; sexual abstinence is usually combined with abstinence from food' (1983, p. 106). He not only reaches the limits of nature, he goes beyond. The final proof is the encounter with the reality behind nature, with the world of demons. Demons are real for late antiquity and the early middle ages. These paranormal forces take over humans and turn them into violent negators of social rules when possessed, or they just attack them with blows or by throwing stones at them or via real or imaginary poisonous or harmful animals. Illness is caused by these negative forces, as are attacks on man's possessions. By transcending the biological limits of nutrition, sleep, pain, equilibrium and motion, the saint exposes himself to the demonic world as final proof of having overcome the normal.

Once this training period is over, the saint returns to the world, remaining an outsider but a man more powerful than anybody relying on the normal power of society, culture, or nature. His miracles are signs; they show that the saint is now free of the limitations of time and space and of the impact of elements, demons, hunger and wild beasts. He heals illnesses and infirmities, he throws out demons, he raises people from the dead, calms storms, multiplies bread and fish.

Needless to say that this model of saintly performance was very much shaped by the example of Christ in the gospels; the life of the Saint is presented as 'imitatio Christi'.

An impressive line of miracles is reported in the gospels; miracles worked by Jesus (exorcisms, healings, raising from the dead, epiphanies, rescue miracles, gift miracles and rule miracles), miracles worked on Jesus (incarnation, virgin birth, temptation, transfiguration and resurrection) and post-Easter miracles (appearance of the risen Lord, Ascension, Pentecost, miracles in the name of Jesus by Peter, Philip, Paul and Barnabas). The powerful deeds of Jesus legitimate him in his mission, give plausibility to his demands and provide the legitimation-basis for his claim to an authority surpassing the traditional and rational one of priests and scribes. The exercise of paranormal power thus challenges structures of power established by history and rational deliberation, by qualification-exercises and legal claims. The writers of the gospels take great pains to provide Jesus with a semblance of traditional and legal legitimacy. These included: the claim to be king, made on Davidic origin (over Joseph who supposedly had no biological relation to Jesus); the claim to be priest, based on Mary's cousin Elizabeth who was married to a member of the priestly tribe; the claim to be teacher, founded on the story that the boy Jesus already was so insightful that the rabbis in the temple were impressed. Nonetheless, it is easy to understand the concern of people occupying the established structures of authority. The claim of a new way of life is a potent threat to any established order of interaction. To quote

Theissen (1983); 'whereas healing and oracular sites are concerned with the maintenance of the accepted order and way of life, and sorcery and magic represent an individualistic reaction to growing social disintegration, belief in charismatic miracles embodies the claim of a new way of life. This process is on the one hand shaped by social forces and on the other fuelled by social intentions' (p. 264). Miracle stories can thus be seen as symbolic actions in which a new way of life is opened up.

No wonder that the Christian churches have retained the advice that saints should be venerated but not imitated. These imitators of Jesus are not only a challenge to a sinful nature and to a self-content culture and society, but very often also to the church which has become part of the web of societal and cultural interactions. This is true for their life as well as for their place in symbolic interaction systems. Some saints like Hildegard of Bingen were excommunicated at some stage in their life, others like Francis of Assisi were seen as the counter heroes of the dispossessed and thus the writing about them was strictly controlled and they themselves had to spend time in enforced custody. Saints though did not just question societal vestiges in the church; they openly attacked the power-structures of society. The 'holy fools' of Russian tradition played this role, as did Thomas of Canterbury in medieval England. But the lives of saints are not just history; they are symbols structuring ongoing interaction. As symbols their influence does not end with their physical death; distance enhances their power. The Christian churches never declare a living person to be a saint, in the sense of being the object of an official cult; the efficacy of the saint is the influence as recollected by others. As Delooz (1983) puts it: 'only the dead can be saints. And so sainthood is automatically situated in recollection. If someone is the object of an official cult today, it is because he is a saint; but he is a saint now because it is believed that he was during his lifetime, in the past, and because one is assured that he was indeed so. Sainthood therefore depends on a community's recollection of a dead person's past existence' (p. 194). However, sainthood also depends on continuing paranormal power. And, as long as this power can be experienced, it is not of much concern to the believer if the life story of the saint 'was indeed so' as Delooz wrote.

But in modern times the question of historical truth has become more important, even in regard to the figure of Jesus and to his miracles. On the one hand Lattke (1985) admits that 'some fundamental theologians, treating the miracles as facts produced by supernatural (divine) power within the limits of space and time, regard the miracles worked on and by Jesus as proof for his being the Messiah and Son of God, or even the decisive criterion of revelation. There is no doubt that this official catholic view can be traced back to the patristic age' (p. 62). On the other hand, he asks if these miracles ascribed to Jesus of Nazareth really happened and if the laws of nature were really broken. His answer is that, today, the whole idea of miracles has to come under question. Not all biblical scholars agree with a central attack on the possibility of the paranormal, but even the official church has become more circumspect in regard to wonder and miracles of saints. There has been some talk about real and constructed miracles and about real and constructed saints. To quote Delooz (1983) again: 'All saints are more or less constructed in that, being necessarily saints for other people, they are remodelled in the collective representation which is made of them. It often happens, even, that they are so remodelled that nothing of the real origin is left, and, ultimately, some saints are solely constructed saints simply because nothing is known about them historically: everything, including their existence, is a product of collective representation' (Delooz, 1983 p. 195).

Lack of historicity does not interfere with the ability of these constructed saints, though, to activate paranormal powers in the believers. A good example is that of St Philomena, a saint who was unknown up to 1802, when a body was found in the catacombs in Rome. The educated guess at the time was that the remains were that of a martyred virgin; miracles took place, and the new saint became popular. At least here was a skeleton; on the other hand Catherine of Alexandria probably was never a real person at all. Still, the believers experienced miracles, and maybe it is fitting that eventually she became the patron saint of philosophers. One could argue that the saint's role is only in eliciting the faith necessary to activate paranormal powers. The archives of Rome are full of the applications of candidates for canonization who were not popular enough to awaken the faith required to effect a miracle. As already mentioned, miracles are still one of the preconditions for canonization. In our present time Rome did not only clear the calendar of constructed saints — St George was one of the losers widely bemoaned — the criteria for the recognition of miracles were made more stringent as well. The canonization of Elizabeth of Portugal in 1742 was based on two cases of women who were able to suckle again after prayer to the saint, one case of mouth ulcer disappearing after the inflicted had kissed the bier used to carry the saint's body, one of a crippled old nun able to walk again, and one an event in which a carpenter had fallen from a roof, invoked the saint and found himself on the roof again. These cases might not be enough of established miracles today. After the second Vatican Council some miraculous healings recognized before were excluded in pending beatification processes; the case of Josef Freindemetz had to wait for an 'Ersatzwunder' ('Auxiliary Miracle') before the beatification took place in 1975 (Reuter 1986). Today the official church is clearly weary of constructed saints and constructed miracles, but still insisting that there exist real saints and real miracles, an approach shared by some sociologists of religion like Delooz (1983).

Clearly this approach is too hesitant for some groups in the church; and one has to keep in mind that even the official cult of saints is not a matter of general enforcement but of free choice. Thus the cult itself can become the focus of conflict between a church administration schooled in the bureaucratic requirement of rationality and a flock of faithful shaped by symbolic interaction based on the paradigm of transcendent power. History is full of stories how more enlightened members of the clergy had fought against folkloric elements in many a saint's cult, but the fact that these fights were reiterated down the centuries suggests that the construction of miracles and saints had rather strong roots. Even a number of modern Marian apparitions (from La Salette, Fatima, Garabandal to Yugoslavia) can illustrate the same principle: There is a discrepancy between the rational spirit present in bureaucratic church organization and the expectancy of superhuman manifestations of power by the faithful. Weber once said in a slightly different context: 'No one knows who will live in this cage in the future, or whether at the end of this tremendous development entirely new prophets will arise, or there will be a great rebirth of old ideas and ideals' (1958 p. 182). He speaks of course of our world of modern rationality. Within the legal-rational structures of church organization at least the openness to real or constructed prophets and messengers of transcendent power does not need to be reborn.

References

Delooz, P. (1983), 'Towards a Sociological Study of Canonized Sainthood in the Catholic Church', in S. Wilson (ed.), *Saints and their Cults*, Cambridge, Cambridge University Press.

Lattke, M. (1985), 'New Testament Miracle Stories and Hellenistic Culture of Late Antiquity'. *Listening 20*, 54–64.

Patlagean, E. (1983), 'Ancient Byzantine Hagiography and Social History', in S. Wilson (ed.) *Saints and their Cults*, Cambridge, Cambridge University Press.

Reuter, J. (1986), 'Geschichte der Verehrung des seligen Josef Freindemetz', *Verbum SVD*, 2, 173–185.

Sanchis, P. (1983), 'The Portuguese Romarias' in, S. Wilson (ed.) *Saints and their Cults*, Cambridge, Cambridge University Press.

Theissen, G. (1983), *The Miracle Stories of the Early Christian Tradition*, translated F. McDonagh. Edinburgh, T. & T. Clark.

Weber, M. (1958), *The Protestant Ethic and the Spirit of Capitalism*, translated by T. Parsons. New York, Charles Scriber's Sons, Cambridge University Press.

Wilson, S. (1983), (ed.) *Saints and their Cults*, Cambridge, Cambridge University Press.

CHAPTER 22

PARANORMAL BELIEFS: OUR SALVATION AND PUNISHMENT

John F. Schumaker

The words of the wise are like spears and nails. — Ecclesiasticus, 12:11[1]

Pascal, in *Pensees*, captures our contradictory natures so beautifully:

> What a chimera then is man!
> How strange and monstrous!
> A chaos, a subject of contradictions, a prodigy.
> Judge of all things, yet a stupid earthworm;
> Depository of truth, yet a cesspool of uncertainty and error;
> The glory and the refuse of the universe, who will unravel this tangle?

The contradictions that seem to offset efforts to understand ourselves are, in fact, an integral part of our unusual natures and constitute the clues we need to fashion an image in our own likeness. I want to argue in this paper that paranormal beliefs are at the very heart of our chimera-like makeup. I will place this argument in the context of Tolstoy's insight from his 1890 work *Kreuzer Sonata* that 'both our salvation and our punishment lie in our ability to befog ourselves', and to show that paranormal believing probably is a necessary adaptation, but one that carries with it certain costs to us on an individual and collective level. However, before proceeding, I should state my theoretical leanings and clarify the way in which I use the term 'reality', since I will be explaining paranormal beliefs as a mechanism by which to cope with the harsher aspects of this reality. Paranormal experiences, like paranormal beliefs, will, in this chapter, be construed as results of human suggestibility.

Psychologists are in an especially awkward position to define 'reality' since we have a long tradition of using that word promiscuously and acting as if we know what it means without much concern about ontological philosophies. Have we not even recommended that certain individuals be institutionalized for being too much 'out of touch' with reality? However, the word 'reality', as part of our professional nomenclature, tends to refer to those behaviors and perceptions shared by the majority, a meaning entirely different from the one I intend here. I use the term 'reality' to refer to certain irrefutable exigencies of the human condition and, in particular, those that could lead us to take refuge in paranormal belief. This usage is consistent with that of Ernest Becker (1973) who, in his classic *The Denial of Death*, commented that terror should be the *normal* psychic state for people in touch with, and bearing the full emotional brunt of, 'reality'. Specifically, he believed that our knowledge of inevitable death haunts us and, if not defended against, generates anxiety that threatens to undermine mental health.

As an 'absolute unbeliever', a philosophy which is well described by Connolly (1980), I in no way accept, or wish to refer to, an ultimate or transcendent reality. Rather, the term is used here to specify the intellectual and emotional responses that would probably derive from an intact mind employing critical reflection and rational evidence not transcending empirical order or the basic limiting principles of science. Death awareness would constitute one aspect of this reality. However, this concept will be expanded in the following section where I try to explain paranormal beliefs as the *normal* consequence of our being 'mugged' by this and other aspects of reality, as well as a more general sense of chaos that would pervade human experience. After that, I will outline some benefits and costs of the psychological sanctuary I believe we take when we engage in paranormal believing.

Let me also note that I will not make a distinction between religious and nonreligious paranormal beliefs. Clark (1977) and LeShan (1966), for example, point out that religious and other paranormal beliefs do not differ significantly in their basic principles and methods of communication; in their concepts involving separation of body, mind and soul; or in the view that our reality is not the true or the only one.

Furthermore, this chapter is based on the premise that currently available evidence for paranormal phenomena is insufficiently conclusive to accept, at present, the validity of claims for paranormal capacities. Like any person, the author may be proved wrong by further research findings.

Paranormal Beliefs in Evolutionary Perspective

Henri Bergson (1935) described the origins of two types of religious paranormal belief. I believe his analysis of 'static' or conventional, in contrast to 'dynamic', religious beliefs, can serve as a model for the development and maintenance of the entire range of paranormal beliefs that we hold to varying degrees. This views intelligence as a less than ideal basis for natural selection. While increased brain capacity undoubtedly enabled our species to adjust, and thrive, in a changing primordial environment, 'pure intelligence' would have resulted in what Rank (1936) called 'too much reality'. Somewhere in our evolutionary history we had to brace ourselves for the impact that would result from the collision of consciousness and reality. We needed to become believers, and specifically paranormal believers.

In his work on the psychodynamics of belief, Kennedy (1977) made the point that we are, first and foremost, 'a believing phenomenon who must believe in order to live at all' (p. 29). He wrote that believing is as vital to us as air and water and that is critical for full personality integration. Conversely, he added that an individual's failure to exercise his or her capacity to believe will prove destructive to personal growth and development, a conjecture that, as we will see, has a reasonable empirical basis. Kennedy (1977) maintained that very few can escape belief and that almost everyone believes in something beyond the 'normal', even those who on the surface appear to be unbelievers.

Dobzhansky (1965) attempted to put religious paranormal beliefs in the perspective of evolutionary biology. He agreed that such paranormal belief systems were of survival value at the point in our evolutionary history where self-awareness made its debut as part of expanding brain capacity. Dobzhansky reasoned that death awareness was an unfortunate by-product of, or sequel to, the development of self-awareness. Whereas self-awareness held obvious survival advantages, death perception and subsequent knowledge of our 'fragmentariness' did not, according to Dobzhansky. But, most evolutionary adaptations have relatively minor disadvantages that can be absorbed by the increased survival potentialities carried by the primary adaptation. Dobzhansky wrote that death awareness was probably compensated for by the distinct advantages of self-awareness. For example, this later facility enabled us to perceive relationships between process and events and to determine the consequences of our actions. Dobzhansky maintained that self-awareness also came to form the basis for the development of human social organization. Nonetheless, he suggested that paranormal belief systems emerged as a reaction to the death awareness that inevitably accompanied self-awareness.

In all likelihood, the difficulty posed by the big brain and its functioning included the realization of death and other unpleasantries of the human condition that generate anxiety and thereby threaten productivity and, ultimately, reproductivity. But, a lot more than immortality would have been frightening and much more than death would have failed to make logical sense. Nothing would have made much sense to a purely rational perceiver. Ortega y Gasset (1957) may have been correct in saying that life is initially a chaos in which one is lost. Then, one can readily imagine value in the ability to invent order and to disguise objective reality with what he termed a 'curtain of fantasy'. These beliefs could serve to iron out this chaos and solve the perplexing randomness that would normally impede a manageable, albeit fictitious, understanding of the world.

Although it seems such an obvious next step to speculate about diametrically opposed brain-level processes that are designed to both construe and misconstrue the world around us, Bergson (1935) is one of the few writers to develop this concept extensively. Bergson defined these 'static' paranormal beliefs as 'a defensive reaction against what might be depressing for the individual, and dissolvent for society, in the exercise of intelligence' (1935, p. 194). These fictions 'guard against certain dangers of intellectual activity without compromising the future of intelligence' (1935, p. 99). In this model, when intelligence threatened to impinge deleteriously on our emotional makeups, a need was established for myth-making and some form of 'voluntary hallucination' (1935, p. 186). Bergson used the terms 'counter-intelligence' and 'counterfeit experience' in describing this innate process that 'confronts intelligence and stops it from pushing too far the conclusions it deduces from a true experience' (1935, p. 99). According to Bergson, we then became 'the only creature endowed with reason, and the only creature to pin its existence to things unreasonable' (1935, p. 92).

But, how does a 'reasonable' and intellectually gifted creature come to believe such 'unreasonable' things? In all likelihood, the specific mechanism that evolved to provide the necessary overriding of logic to enable an otherwise rational organism to adopt and maintain such beliefs is suggestibility, one of the least studied and most poorly understood of all human abilities. Although the term is usually automatically associated with hypnotism, still another little under-stood phenomenon, suggestibility is quite simply defined as the extent to which an individual is influenced by suggestions from an external source. Actually, suggestibility need not be considered so mysterious since it is probably an all pervasive component of our individual and shared perceptions of the world around us. The same is true of hypnosis for, as Ferenczi (1916) realized, we are dependent on a certain degree of auto-suggestion, or self-hypnosis, in the mental working of everyday life. Furthermore, what is stereotypically regarded as the hypnotic state may only be a more dramatic expression of the 'common everyday trance' (Rossi, 1982, 1986) in which we paranormal believers languish by necessity. While an in-depth analysis of this fascinating aspect of human behavior is well beyond the scope of this paper, I will refer to some evidence that points to a relationship between suggestibility and paranormal believing. This will be done while attempting to point out some of the benefits and liabilities that accompany the marvel of paranormal belief.

Paranormal Beliefs as Our Salvation

If paranormal beliefs serve to limit the potentially damaging effects of 'pure intelligence', we must operate from the premise that they are a useful evolutionary invention for basic survival purposes. While Freud (1927/1961) may have been accurate in noting that humans are inclined to give the unreal precedence over what is real, his equating of religious paranormal beliefs with childhood neurosis failed to em-phasize the vital role played by such belief systems. On the contrary, the extraordinary importance of paranormal beliefs is underscored when one recognizes that they are one of only a few human characteristics that is truly universal in the strictest sense of the word. Cultural anthropologists and cross-cultural psychologists have yet to find a single culture without extensive and well-developed sets of paranormal beliefs. This tempts one immediately to speculate that paranormal believing, as a process, has relatively more evolutionary advantages than disadvantages.

Although literature reviews paint a very confusing picture of the relationship between paranormal believing and psychological func-tioning, a sizable body of research supports the thesis that paranormal beliefs are associated with overall adjustment. This is especially true if the belief systems fall clearly into accepted cultural ideology, such as traditional religion. For example, McClain (1978), Ness and Wintrob (1980), and Sturgeon and Hamley (1971) reported that individuals with strong religious paranormal beliefs were less prone to emotional and psychological distress than others, while McClure and Loden (1982) found that these beliefs and their associated activities were correlated with overall happiness and life satisfaction. Some studies have demonstrated lower rates of suicide among religious than nonreligious groups (Maris, 1981; Martin, 1984). Tobacyk and Milford (1983) reported an inverse relationship between fear of death and belief in traditional religious dogma, although no such correlation was found among a group of adolescents (Mahabeer & Bhana, 1984). It is interesting that some systems of religious paranormal belief appear to be more effective than others at controlling death anxiety levels. Kubler-Ross (1975), Schumaker, Barraclough, and Vagg (1988), and

Westman and Canter (1985) found that people with 'eastern' religious beliefs, such as those in Hinduism and Buddhism, had significantly lower death anxiety levels than their counterparts from 'western', or more specifically, christian religions. This was explained in terms of the manner in which such 'eastern' religions view death as 'an incident of on-going existence' (Westman & Canter, 1985, p. 419), as well as the belief that the best way to conquer death is to regard it as a primary fact of life. This was contrasted with more materialistic western religious belief systems in which death of body is frequently equated with death of self.

Other studies suggest that traditional religious paranormal beliefs are not conducive to psychological well-being. Vine (1978) reported that religious belief tends to promote emotional instability. Cowen (1954), Francis (1978), Roberts (1965) and Wilson and Miller (1968) found that individuals with strong religious beliefs were more likely to have low self-esteem, and to suffer from anxiety and other neurotic symptoms. Francis (1985), however, proposed that sex differences could explain such correlations between religious belief and neuroticism. Women have been found in a number of studies to be more religious than men and also to have higher levels of neuroticism. This taken together could create a false positive correlation between religious belief and measures of neurotic behavior.

I recently compared the mental health ratings of a group of atheists with those of a group of individuals with strong traditional religious beliefs (Schumaker, 1987). Atheists were found to experience significantly more symptoms of psychological disturbance than their believing counterparts, a finding that was not explainable by sex differences. This would be expected if religious paranormal beliefs do, in fact, have prophylactic properties that serve to ensure mental health in the manner described above. In this same study, I attempted to determine if the atheists would compensate for their lack of religious paranormal beliefs by adopting a greater number of other non-religious paranormal beliefs (eg. witchcraft, superstition, precognition, etc.). It was predicted that the atheists would compensate for their deficit of socially sanctioned religious beliefs. Indirect evidence for belief compensation came from a study by Caird and Law (1982) who reported that individuals who accepted nonconventional religious belief and practices, as opposed to traditional religion, had multiple group memberships more frequently than traditionally religious people. Contrary to expectations, those with strong religious beliefs were somewhat more inclined than the atheists to believe in nonreligious paranormal beliefs. This was consistent with Bainbridge's (1981) research on belief in ESP in which he reported that subjects with religious paranormal beliefs were more likely to believe in ESP than nonreligious subjects. Also, Randall and Desrosiers (1980) found that those accepting one paranormal belief were more likely to hold other additional paranormal beliefs.

Regarding the relative advantages of less conventional paranormal beliefs, the research findings are also somewhat mixed. Blum and Blum (1974) showed that superstitious beliefs served to mitigate feelings of anxiety, while Tobacyk (1984) reported that belief in witchcraft, superstition, and spiritualism related to higher death anxiety levels. Adorno, Frenkel-Brunswick, Levinson, and Sanford (1950) and Maller and Lundeen (1933) found that these types of paranormal beliefs were positively correlated with emotional mal-adjustment, but a later study by Jones, Russell and Nickel (1977) found no such relationship.

The equivocal findings related to the possible benefits of religious and nonreligious paranormal beliefs may be due, in part, to the well known psychological phenomenon in which already psychologically disturbed individuals frequently drift toward various paranormal belief systems, and their related rituals, in an effort to obtain 'magical' conflict resolution and stave off further emotional deterioration. I have seen many examples of this quest for 'magic' in the various clinical settings in which I have worked over the years. If it were possible to eliminate this confounding factor from paranormal research, it is possible that a more dramatic positive relationship would be found between paranormal beliefs, both religious and nonreligious, and measures of overall adjustment and life satisfaction. Nonetheless, while research clearly demonstrates the advantages of socially sanctioned religious paranormal beliefs, additional studies are necessary to establish the relationship between overall adjustment and other paranormal belief systems.

Additional empirical evidence for the merits of being able to 'befog' oneself comes from an award-winning study by Martin, Abramson and Alloy (1984). They found that people who are proficient at creating self-deceptions and similiar 'self-serving cognitive biases' are less prone to become depressed than those who are less able to perceive events and life situations with a 'rosy glow'. This further highlights the previously mentioned therapeutic value inherent in the capacity to distort and cognitively 'bias' objective reality in certain desirable directions, as well as the unfortunate repercussions in failing to do so effectively.

The Psychological Costs of Paranormal Beliefs

Casualties of the System. Not everyone is equally adept at fishing out of culture's grabbag of paranormal armaments the quantity and/or quality of belief that can, as Ortega y Gasset (1957) said, serve 'as scarecrows to frighten away reality' (p. 157). So, one might speak in terms of casualties in the system and give as one disadvantage that paranormal believing, as a process, cannot work well in all cases. The expected individual differences in the ability to adopt and retain paranormal beliefs may determine, in part, the degree to which a person will achieve 'adjustment' within a unique condition that requires one to by-pass and over-ride our reasoning and critical thinking ability.

Some maintain that the casualties, that is, those who fail to impose sufficient 'cognitive bias' on reality, are vulnerable to neurosis. Becker (1973) described neurosis itself as the 'miscarriage of clumsy lies about reality' (p. 248). By 'lies', of course, Becker was referring to all paranormal myths, the purpose of which is to convince ourselves of a second, or expanded, reality and to thereby limit ourselves to a 'safe dosage of life' (1973, p. 201). Otto Rank (1936, 1941), who inspired Becker's *Denial of Death*, had also proposed that neurosis ensued when a person was exposed to too much of 'the painful truth' and when they refused to adopt 'the illusions important for living' (1936, p. 251). As seen earlier, some empirical evidence does suggest that people with less developed paranormal belief systems are, in fact, more likely to suffer from various forms of psychopathology, including depression and even suicide in some cases.

Loss of Self-Awareness. One body of research suggests that paranormal believing may have a negative impact on extent of insight and self-knowledge. This evidence stemmed from repeated observations that individuals with well developed religious paranormal beliefs scored significantly higher on the 'lie' scales of such tests of personality as the Minnesota Multiphasic Personality Inventory (Dahlstrom & Welsh, 1960) and the Eysenck Personality Questionnaire (Eysenck & Eysenck, 1975). High scores on this scale are typically interpreted as indications of defensive denial behavior and a lack of self-insight. Crandall and Gozali (1969), who reported significantly higher 'lie' scores in religious 8-17 year olds, argued that religious paranormal beliefs interfere with self-awareness as the result of concomitant repression and a denial of certain thoughts and behaviors. Francis, Pearson, and Kay (1983) obtained similar findings and also accepted that a lack of insight was indicated by the elevated 'lie' scores which they observed in religious subjects. However, they explained these results somewhat differently, proposing that the more insight people have into their own thoughts and behavior the less likely they are to be favorably disposed to religious paranormal beliefs. Eysenck, Nias, and Eysenck (1971) took still another position and maintained that insight and self-knowledge are signs of maturity. Therefore, it is also possible, as Pohier (1965) had postulated earlier, that religious paranormal beliefs promote, and are an expression of, emotional and intellectual immaturity.

The Risks of Suggestibility. The anthropologist, Melford Spiro (1965), argued that paranormal beliefs, including traditional religious ones, can themselves be considered symptoms of insanity since they clearly represent 'impairment of psychological functioning' (1965, p. 104). In fact, it may be that paranormal beliefs 'require psychiatric rather than sociocultural analysis' (1965, p. 100). Spiro labeled our species 'homo religiosus' (1965, p. 103) and maintained that, while these reality-snubbing beliefs serve as culturally constituted defense mechanisms in much the way as described above, they also involve significant cognitive, perceptual and affective distortions.

Although these 'distortions' may be insane by strict definition, it may prove more useful to consider any psychological expenses connected with suggestibility; that beguiling process underlying and facilitating these distortions and paranormal believing generally. More specifically, we might consider the psychological repercussions that become manifest when suggestibility, as the possible linchpin of paranormal belief, works too well.

Sargent (1973) wrote that 'we need to be suggestible, but our suggestibility is dangerous' (p. 199). This can be understood in the same way that we need paranormal beliefs, even though those too bring with them certain risks. The origins of my own interest in paranormal belief stem, oddly enough, from my long standing interest in eating disorders and, in particular, anorexia nervosa. Several years ago, I began to suspect that anorexia nervosa was a 'problem of religion', that is, an aberrant manifestation of the normal suggestibility process that facilitates all forms of paranormal belief, including religion. The conceptual bridge between that mysterious disorder and suggestibility and religion was a long and untraveled one and I did not take that link too seriously until I began to run across writing and research that helped to bridge the theoretical gap.

Haraldsson (1985), for example, found a positive relationship between suggestibility and extent of belief in the paranormal. This was successfully predicted with the rationale that suggestibility involves an information processing style that relies heavily on an external frame of reference and involves lower levels of *self*-consciousness. Even closer to my own thinking was the work of Kaffman (1981, 1984) who observed that hypersuggestibility characterized individuals with anorexia nervosa and other autosuggestive or 'monoideistic' forms of psycho-pathology. Monoideisms are defined as singular motivations that involve preoccupations with one particular constrictive content of thought, such as the anorexic's all-consuming preoccupation with thinness. Bliss (1982) also hypothesized that auto-suggestion was involved in the development and maintenance of anorexia nervosa and observed that anorexic individuals frequently have perceptual distortions and dissociative experiences typically associated with hypnotic-like states. Earlier behavioral descriptions of the anorexic as 'programmed' and 'robot-like' (Bemis, 1978; Selvini, 1974) added further credence to the association between monoideistic psycho-pathology and misdirected and/or elevated suggestibility. Bliss (1983) studied anorexics directly and found that they had significantly higher levels of suggestibility than non-anorexic individuals.

Recently, I theorized that fully developed monoideistic symptoms, such as those found with anorexia nervosa, may serve to 'absorb' errant and/or excessive suggestibility and recommended the study of individuals in high-risk, but pre-onset, stages of such conditions (Schumaker & Groth-Marnat, 1987, 1988). This led to a study in which we isolated 'sub-clinical' anorexic women who appeared to be at risk of developing the disorder and compared their suggestibility scores with a group showing little inclination to behaviors associated with anorexia nervosa (Groth-Marnat & Schumaker, 1988). It was predicted that individuals with elevated suggestibility levels would be the most likely to adopt what is probably the most dominant culturally-based suggestion for young western women, namely that 'one should be thin'. High suggestibility subjects did, in fact, show significantly more signs of sub-clinical anorexia nervosa. Kaffman (1984) postulated that an entire class of psychopathology, including obsessions, compulsions and paranoia, as well as anorexia nervosa, may be tied to the human suggestibility process. If suggestibility is the mechanism by which paranormal belief is made possible, it may be that certain types of psychological disturbance can be understood in terms of the paranormal belief imperative. These same disorders may then be considered another potential cost that must be registered to the paranormal belief adaptation.

Although this area of study is obviously in its infancy, one could step back and, keeping in mind Haraldsson's (1985) reported correlation between suggestibility and paranormal belief, reconsider the afore-mentioned prospect that suggestibility is the *necessary* process that has evolved to facilitate *necessary* paranormal beliefs that enable one to cope with consciousness and 'reality'. With that as a possibility, it may be that a range of monoideistic mental disorders, with their ritualistic behaviors that have their counterpart in many religious practices, could be deviant 'spiritual' expressions by members of 'homo-religiosus' who, for some reason, came off the cultural track of belief. Attempting to locate the factors that make suggestibility 'dangerous' in the form of maladaptive manifestations of suggestibility and the normal paranormal believing process would be a rich area for research in psychology and related disciplines.

The Promotion of Evil. Becker's (1974) final, but unfortunately uncompleted, book *Escape From Evil* went beyond an expose of our rejection of reality and the self-deceptions he believes come to be mistaken for mental health. He elaborated on how it is that our appetite for illusion enables us to transcend reality at the expense of transcending ourselves and how this self-transcendence inevitably generates evil to the extent of jeopardizing our very futures. Becker's thinking was influenced by Arthur Koestler who, like Bergson, focused on the 'schizophysiology built into our species' (Koestler, 1954, p. 286). This adaptation makes possible a 'closed' cognitive structure by which logic and reality are distorted and otherwise unbelievable paranormal beliefs made believable in order to 'keep the deluded mind happy' (Koestler, 1967, p. 262) and to protect these illusions from 'the intrusion of reality' (Koestler, 1954, p. 121). However, he also referred to the 'mistake' that is built into the evolutionary making of the brain as the source of human natural selection, as well as the fact that 'the tragedy of man is not his truculence, but his proneness to delusions' (1967, p. 235).

Although our beliefs enable us to 'successfully offend our reasoning faculties' in becoming 'cheerful ostriches' (Koestler, 1967, p. 240), the self-transcendence involved in this valuable trick causes a perilous dimming of awareness and a lowering of the subjective experience of personal freedom. Hoffer (1951) also described how, in escaping our self in order to embrace belief, we simultaneously distance ourselves from the rational and the obvious. Koestler compared the self-transcended paranormal believer to robots and machines because the 'un-selfing of the self' (1967, p. 218) diminishes self-consciousness and impedes self-understanding. This theoretical stance has some support in the previously mentioned studies that show an inverse relationship between certain paranormal believing and extent of self-knowledge. Becker and Koestler described the entire range of evil and destruction, including war, as the end product of the 'integrative tendency' associated with self-transcending belief systems. One could point to examples of destructive and genocidal behavior, such as the Crusades or Jonestown, that are closely tied to a defense, or elaboration, of paranormal beliefs. On the other hand, one could just as easily argue that many of the beliefs incorporated into many prevalent systems of religious belief are pro-social and focused on love and acceptance of our fellow man.

The quantitative studies dealing with this issue are somewhat indirect and concerned primarily with the relationship between religious belief and involvement and extent of prejudice and intolerance for others. However, the direction of the findings is unmistakable. Batson and Ventis (1982), in an extensive research review, were able to isolate 44 studies that examined this issue. Of those, 34 reported a positive relationship between traditional religious belief/involvement and prejudice as measured by a number of assessment devices. Eight studies showed no correlation between these two factors. Only two of the 44 studies found a negative correlation between degree of prejudice and adherence to religious beliefs and practices, and those were ones that used preadolescents and/or adolescents. Batson, Schoenrade and Pych (1985) make the 'very clear, if unsettling conclusion... that religion is not associated with increased love and acceptance but with increased intolerance, prejudice and bigotry' (p. 189).

Other research has determined that religious belief and affiliation are also associated with personality characteristics frequently regarded as precursors to destructive and cruel behavior. Kirkpatrick (1949) demonstrated that people with strong religious beliefs advocated more punitive measures than nonreligious individuals toward various categories of criminal offenders. Religious people in America have also been found to be more prejudiced against blacks (Allport & Kramer, 1946) and to be more intolerant of those with different political persuasions (Stouffer, 1955), and different sexual preferences (Hong, 1984). Adorno, et al, (1950) reported greater authoritarianism and ethnocentrism among religious than nonreligious individuals.

Batson, Schoenrade and Pych (1985) cautioned against an over-simplified interpretation of such findings, since religious orientation styles vary greatly and thus preclude any sweeping indictments of religious beliefs and practices, or paranormal believing generally. Additionally, far more research in this fascinating area is needed before any detailed conclusions can be drawn. Still, these preliminary findings are highly provocative and do lend support to the theoretical speculation offered by people like Becker and Koestler. One particularly fruitful route of investigation would involve establishing the relationship between more direct measures of aggression and destructiveness and a much wider range of paranormal belief.

Conclusions

I have argued, however crudely, that our conspicuous propensity for paranormal belief can be understood as an evolutionary response to a high degree of intelligent awareness. The ability to distort reality cognitively undoubtedly carried potential evolutionary pitfalls. As previously mentioned, most evolutionary adaptations have disadvantages that are compensated by overall adaptational advantages. This chapter was organized around that idea and an attempt was made to compare the relative benefits and costs of paranormal belief.

While that discussion was by no means exhaustive, certain evidence was provided to support the view that paranormal belief is a mixed blessing. The disadvantages of diminished self-awareness, irregularities of suggestibility, and individual system casualties seem slight in relation to the important prophylactic properties these beliefs have in relation to emotional and psychological health. The greatest cause for concern is voiced by people like Becker and Koestler. They assert that human destructiveness is the result of the self-transcendence that inevitably accompanies all forms of reality distortion. The potentially destructive aspect of paranormal belief is particularly worrying when we consider the extremely advanced technology we now have for destroying each other.

I have not tried to hide the fact that I am not a believer in the paranormal. However, that does not necessarily mean that I think paranormal beliefs are not a useful survival tactic. Rather, I would agree with Wagner (1981) that there are 'many kinds of magic whose measure of acceptance and usefulness is not their literal content, but whether they *work* . . . that is, whether one can believe in them' (p. 89). If paranormal beliefs are essential to human survival, as some suggest, one can only hope that they continue to 'work' and that we go merrily along in our translated realities.

Footnotes

1. Thanks to my colleague G. K. Zollschan for supplying a translation from the original Hebrew.

References

Adorno, T., Frenkel-Brunswick, E., Levinson, D., & Sanford, N. (1950), *The Authoritarian Personality*, New York, Harper.

Allport, G. W. & Kramer, B. M. (1946), 'Some roots of prejudice', *Journal of Psychology*, 22, 9-30.

Bainbridge, W. S. (1981), 'Biorhythms: evaluating a pseudoscience', in K. Frazier (Ed.), *Paranormal Borderlands of Science*, Buffalo, NY, Prometheus.

Batson, C. D. & Ventis, W. L. (1982), *The Religious Experience: A Social-Psychological Perspective*, New York, Oxford University Press.

Batson, C. D., Schoenrade, P.A., & Pych, V. (1985), 'Brotherly love or self concern?: Behavioral consequences of religion', in L. B. Brown *Advances in the Psychology of Religion*, New York, Pergamon Press.

Becker, E. (1973), *The Denial of Death*, New York, The Free Press.

Becker, E. (1974) *Escape From Evil*, New York, The Free Press.

Bemis, K. M. (1978), 'Current approaches to the etiology and treatment of anorexia nervosa', *Psychological Bulletin*, 5, 593-617.

Bergson, H. (1935), *The Two Sources of Morality and Religion*, Westport, Conn, Greenwood Press.

Bliss, E. L. (1982), 'The psychology of anorexia nervosa', in M. Gross (Ed.), *Anorexia Nervosa*, Lexington, Mass, Collamore Press.

Bliss, E. L. (1983), 'Multiple personalities, related disorders and hypnosis', *American Journal of Clinical Hypnosis*, 26, 114-123.

Blum, S. H., & Blum, L. H. (1974), 'Do's and don't: an informal study of some prevailing superstitions', *Psychological Reports*, 35, 567-571.

Caird, D. & Law, H. (1982), 'Nonconventional beliefs: Their structure and measurement', *Journal for the Scientific Study of Religion*, 21, 152-163.

Clark, W. (1977), 'Parapsychology and religion', in B. Wolman (Ed.), *Philosophy and Parapsychology*, New York, Van Nostrand Reinhold.

Connolly, J. R. (1980), *Dimensions of Belief and Unbelief*, New York, University Press of America.

Crandall, V. C. & Gozali, J. (1969), 'Social desirability responses of children of four religions - cultural groups', *Child Development*, 40, 751-762.

Cowen, L. (1954), 'The negative concept as a personality measure', *Journal of Consulting Psychology*, 18, 138-142.

Dahlstrom, W. G. & Welsh, G. S. (1960), *An MMPI Handbook*, Minneapolis, Minn., University Press.

Dobzhansky, T. (1965), 'Religion, death, and evolutionary adaptation', in M. Spiro (Ed.), *Context and Meaning in Cultural Anthropology*, New York: Free Press.

Eysenck, H. J. & Eysenck, S. B. (1975), *Manual of the Eysenck Personality Questionnaire*, London, Hodder and Stoughton.

Eysenck, S. B., Nias, D. K. & Eysenck, H. J. (1971), 'Interpretation of children's lie scale scores', *British Journal of Educational Psychology*, 41, 23-31.

Ferenczi, S. (1916), 'Introjection and transference', in S. Ferenzci, (Ed.), *Contributions to Psychoanalysis*, London, Phillips.

Francis, L. J. (1978), 'Attitude and longitute: A study in measurement', *Character Potential*, 8, 119-130.

Francis, L. J. (1985), 'Personality and religion: Theory and measurement', in L. B. Brown, (Ed.), *Advances in the Psychology of Religion*, New York, Pergamon Press.

Francis, L. J., Pearson, P. R. & Kay, W. K. (1983), 'Are religious children bigger liars?', *Psychological Reports*, 52, 551-554.

Freud, S. (1927/1961), *Future of an Illusion*, translated by J. Strachey. New York: W. W. Norton & Co.

Groth-Marnat, G. & Schumaker, J. F. (1988), 'Suggestibility, eating attitudes, and concern for body size', Unpublished Manuscript.

Haraldsson, E. (1985), 'Interrogative suggestibility and its relationship with personality, perceptual defensiveness and extraordinary beliefs', *Personality and Individual Differences*, 6, 765-767.

Hoffer, E. (1951), *The True Believer*, New York, Harper & Row.

Hong, J. (1984), 'Australian attitudes towards homosexuality', *Journal of Psychology*, 117, 89-95.

Jones, W., Russell, D. & Nickel, T. (1977), 'Belief in the paranormal scale: an objective instrument to measure belief in magical phenomena and causes', *JSAS Catalog of Selected Documents in Psychology*, 7, 100, (Ms. No. 1577).

Kaffman, M. (1981), 'Monoideism in psychiatry: Theoretical and clinical implications', *American Journal of Psychotherapy*, 35, 235-243.

Kaffman, M. (1984), 'Inflexible belief-constructs in families of paranoid patients', *International Journal of Family Psychiatry*, 3, 487-500.

Kennedy, E. (1977), *Believing*, Garden City, NY, Doubleday.

Kirkpatrick, C. (1949), 'Religion and humanitarianism: A study of institutional implications', *Psychological Monographs*, 63, No. 304.

Koestler, A. (1954), *The Invisible Writing*, London, Hutchinson.

Koestler, A. (1967), *The Ghost in the Machine*, London, Hutchinson.

Kubler-Ross, E. (1975), *Death: The Final Stage of Growth*, Englewood Cliffs, NJ, Prentice-Hall.

LeShan, L. (1966), *The Medium, the Mystic, and the Physicist*, New York, Viking Press.

Mahabeer, M. & Bhana, K. (1984), 'The relationship between religion, religiosity and death anxiety among Indian adolescents', *South African Journal of Psychology*, 14, 7-9.

Maller, J. & Lundeen, G. (1933), 'Superstition and emotional maladjustment', *Journal of Education Research*, 27, 592-617.

Maris, R. W. (1981), *Pathways to Suicide: A Survey of Self-destructive Behaviors*, Baltimore, Johns Hopkins University Press.

Martin, R. W. (1984), 'Religiosity and United States suicide rates', *Journal of Clinical Psychology*, 40, 1166-1169.

Martin, D. J., Abramson, L. Y. & Alloy, L. B. (1984), 'Illusion of control for self and others in depressed and nondepressed college students', *Journal of Personality and Social Psychology*, 46, 125-136.

McClain, E. W. (1978), 'Personality differences between intrinsically religious and non-religious students - factor analytic study', *Journal of Personality Assessment*, 42, 159-166.

McClure, R. F. & Loden, M. (1982), 'Religious activity, denomination membership and life satisfaction', *Psychology*, 19, 12-17.

Ness, R. C. & Wintrob, R. M. (1980), 'The emotional impact of fundamentalistic religious participation', *American Journal of Orthopsychiatry*, 50, 202-215.

Ortega Y Gasset, J. (1957), *Man and People*, New York, Norton.

Pascal, B. (1658/1952), *The Provincial Letters, Pensees, Scientific Treatises*, Chicago, Encyclopedia Britannica.

Pohier, J. M. (1965), 'Religious mentality and infantile mentality', in A. Godin, (Ed.), *Child and Adult Before God*, Chicago, Loyola University Press.

Randall, T. M. & Desrosiers, M. (1980), 'Measurements of supernatural beliefs: Sex differences and locus of control', *Journal of Personality Assessment*, 44, 493-498.

Rank, O. (1936), *Will Therapy and Truth and Reality*, New York, Knopf.

Rank, O. (1941), *Beyond Psychology*, New York, Dover Books.

Roberts, F. J. (1965), 'Some psychological factors in religious conversion', *British Journal of Social and Clinical Psychology*, 13, 157-182.

Rossi, E. L. (1982), 'Hypnosis and ultradian cycles: A new state(s) theory of hypnosis?', *The American Journal of Clinical Hypnosis*, 1, 21-32.

Rossi, E. L. (1986), 'Altered states of consciousness in everyday life: The ultradian rhythms', in B. Wolman & M. Ullman (Eds.), *Handbook of States of Consciousness*, New York, Van Nostrand Reinhold.

Sargant, W. (1973), *The Mind Possessed*, London, Heinemann.

Schumaker, J. F. (1987), 'Mental health, belief deficit compensation, and paranormal beliefs', *Journal of Psychology*, 121, 451-457.

Schumaker, J. F., Barraclough, R. A., & Vagg, L. (1988), 'Death anxiety in Malaysian and Australian Individuals', *Journal of Social Psychology*, 128, 41-47.

Schumaker, J. F. & Groth-Marnat, G. (1987), 'The prevention of anorexia nervosa in an adolescent female population', in J. Sheppard, (Ed.), *Advances in Behavioral Medicine*, Sydney: Cumberland Press.

Schumaker, J. F. & Groth-Marnat, G. (1988), 'The Role of suggestibility in the understanding and prevention of anorexia nervosa', *Corrective and Social Psychiatry*, Vol. 35.

Selvini, M. P. (1974), *Anorexia Nervosa*, London, Chaucer Press.

Spiro, M. E. (1965), 'Culturally constituted defense mechanisms', in M. E. Spiro, ed, *Context and Meaning in Cultural Anthropology*, New York, The Free Press.

Stouffer, S. A. (1955), *Communism, Conformity, and Civil Liberties*, New York, Doubleday.

Sturgeon, R. S. & Hamley, R. W. (1971), 'Religiosity and anxiety', *Journal of Social Psychology*, 108, 137-138.

Tobacyck, J. (1984), 'Death threat, death concerns, and paranormal belief', in F. R. Epting and R. A. Neimeyer, (Eds.), *Personal Meanings of Death*, New York, McGraw-Hill.

Tobacyk, J. & Milford, G. (1983), 'Belief in paranormal phenomena: Assessment instrument development and implications for personality functioning', *Journal of Personality and Social Psychology*, 44, 1029-1037.

Tolstoy, L. (1890), *The Kreuzer Sonata*, New York, Ogilvie.

Vine, I. (1978), 'Facts and values in the psychology of religion', *Bulletin of the British Psychological Society*, 31, 414-417.

Wagner, R. (1981), *The Invention of Culture*, Chicago: University of Chicago Press.

Westman, A. S. & Canter, F. M. (1985), 'Fear of death and the concept of extended self', *Psychological Reports*, 56, 419-425.

Wilson, W. & Miller, H. L. (1968), 'Fear, anxiety and religiousness', *Journal for the Scientific Study of Religion*, 7, 111.

THE CONTRIBUTORS

William Sims Bainbridge (Chapter 14) is an American Sociologist who has published extensively on religion as well as writing books on the space program and methodology textbooks incorporating micro-computer software. In collaboration with Rodney Stark, he has published two books developing a formal, deductive explanation of supernaturalism: *The Future of Religion* and *A Theory of Religion*. A believer in personal freedom, he is fascinated by the creative powers of the human mind.

John Beloff (Chapter 20) is an academic psychologist, now retired but still attached to the University of Edinburgh. The main thrust of his career, as reflected in his publications, has been his interest in the philosophical implications of psychology and in the mind-body problem. This led to his becoming deeply involved with para-psychology on which he has become a leading authority. He takes the view that, while it is still permissable to reject the evidence for the paranormal, it is intellectually dishonest to ignore the evidence.

Stephen E. Braude (Chapter 2) is Professor of Philosophy at the University of Maryland. He is author of two books and numerous articles on philosophy and parapsychology, as well as articles on the philosophy of language and logic. He is currently doing philosophical research on multiple personality and dissociation. Several articles on those topics have already appeared, and another book is forthcoming. He is also a professional pianist and composer.

Lawrence B. Brown (Chapter 15), of the University of New South Wales in Sydney, has research interests in medical and social psychology, with particular reference to the nature of health and illness, as well as religious belief and practice. He has published a number of books on the psychology of religion, and has written several papers with Dr. Thouless on the religious thinking of children and adults.

Rod S. Bucknell (Chapter 9) is a meditator/linguist/ symbologist whose research focuses on introspective meditation techniques and resulting insights. He is interested in the application of meditation in explicating altered states of consciousness and Buddhist doctrine and symbolism. Formerly a practising Buddhist monk, he now teaches eastern religions at the University of Queensland.

Ronald Conway (Chapter 6) is a Clinical Psychologist who has practised in Melbourne, Australia for thirty years. He was Senior Consulting Psychologist to St. Vincent's Hospital in Melbourne from 1959 to 1984 and was Senior Lecturer in Applied Psychology at the Royal Melbourne Institute of Technology from 1975 to 1981. He is a well-known author and social commentator on Australian manners and mores, and has been active in ecumenical religious affairs. An interest in the paranormal has existed parallel to his practice for most of his adult life.

Jule Eisenbud (Chapter 3) has taught at Columbia University and at the University of Colorado Health Sciences Center, where he is currently Associate Clinical Professor of Psychiatry. He has been interested in parapsychology for more than forty years, mainly in its spontaneous cases and 'superstar' psychics, as well as in philosophical aspects of the subject. He practices psychiatry and psychoanalysis in Denver, Colorado.

Antony Flew (Chapter 19) is a British philosopher whose first book was, with the brash impetuosity of youth, entitled *A New Approach to Psychical Research*. Everything relevant which he has since learnt is in his Editorial and other contributions to his book *Readings in the Philosophical Problems of Parapsychology*. He is both Vice-President of the Rationalist Press Association and a radical Thatcherite.

Gary Groth-Marnat (Chapter 7) is an American Clinical Psychologist who has worked as an academic as well as a private practitioner. Special interests include forensic psychology and clinical neuro-psychology. He is author of *Handbook of Psychological Assessment*, and has recently completed an extensive review of literature related to the near-death experience. Although a personal believer in the paranormal, he is professionally a skeptic.

Ralph W. Hood, Jr. (Chapter 8) is an American Social Psychologist particularly interested in the psychology of religion. He is co-author with Bernie Spilka and Richard Gorsuch of *The Psychology of Religion*. His major writings focus upon mysticism for which he has both a professional and personal interest.

Julie D. Howell (Chapter 5) is an American anthropologist, residing in Australia, who developed an interest in the paranormal through field research in Indonesia on the role of religious movements in social change. She has published on the Hindu and Buddhist revivals in Java and Bali, contemporary Javanese mysticism, and on the cross-cultural comparison of altered states accessed by shamanic, yogic and other ecstatics. Historical research for these projects was conducted in the Netherlands. She has belatedly accepted the challenge of her one-time research subjects to herself test the 'doors of perception', albeit within another cultural context.

Richard A. Hutch (Chapter 10) is a psychoanalytic thinker who has published books and articles in the areas of the History of Religions, Cross-Cultural Religious Leadership, and Psycho-Biography. His interests converge on the connection between personality formation and historical process. He has lectured in the United States, France and Australia, where he is presently employed at the University of Queensland. He is a practising husband and father, which is paranormal enough.

Harvey J. Irwin (Chapter 18) is an Australian Psychologist who has published books and numerous papers on diverse parapsychological topics. His principal teaching interests lie in parapsychology and in dying and bereavement. Currently his research focuses not so much on paranormality of parapsychological experiences as on the phenomenology of these experiences and their place in the life of the experient. In these respects he maintains that parapsychological experiences warrant scientific attention whether or not they prove to be paranormal. He interprets the aggregate data of parapsychological experiments to be suggestive of anomalous processes but not conclusive for the existence of paranormal phenomena.

Stanley Krippner (Chapter 11) is Professor of Psychology at Saybrook Institute in San Francisco. In a dozen volumes and over 600 articles, he has investigated and reported on the forefront of developments in consciousness research, education, and healing. Among the books he has authored or co-authored are *The Realms of Healing*, *Healing States*, *Human Possibilities*, *Dream Telepathy*, and *Dreamworking*. He has served as president of several national organizations including the Association for Humanistic Psychology, the Parapsychological Association, and the American Psychological Association's Division of Humanistic Psychology. He has served as Director of the Dream Laboratory at Maimoinides Medical Center in New York City for ten years, and for three years was director of the Child Study Center, Kent State University. He was the first person invited to speak on the topic of parapsychology to the Soviet Academy of Pedagogical Sciences, one of the most prestigious institutions in the Soviet Union.

Helmut H. Loiskandl (Chapter 21) is an Australian Sociologist with a background in anthropology and religious studies. He has published in the area of world religions, sociological theory and the social sciences in general. His latest research has been on local tradition, catholic clergy and nation-building in Ecuador, the Philippines and Papua New Guinea.

Peter L. Nelson (Chapter 12) is an American who conducted the research reported in this volume in Australia. He started his career in neurophysiology and computer science. His interest in consciousness eventually led him to the disciplines of psychology and religious studies and it was in the latter area he conducted an empirical study of mystical and related states. He describes himself as an 'ontological neutralist' (an 'absolute relativist') in relation to the 'normal' as well as the 'paranormal'.

Bevan L. Reid (Chapter 16) is an Australian researcher in cell and reproductive biology, as well as Embryology as related to growth and newgrowth. He has nearly one hundred scientific publications to his credit, and has been the recipient of several international science awards. The motivation for some of his recent work stems from what he sees as a growing intellectual impasse and 'omniscient reductionism' in many sectors of the scientific community. He feels there are rich spoils awaiting the believer who is willing to apply rigorous orthodox methods of study to phenomena that some consider to be outside the realm of traditional scientific investigation.

John F. Schumaker (Chapter 22) is an American Clinical Psychologist who has published in the area of cross-cultural psychology, human suggestibility, and the relationship between mental health and paranormal beliefs. He has taught and done research in Zambia, South Africa, Thailand, the USA, and Australia. He describes himself as an 'absolute unbeliever' in the paranormal.

James R. Stewart (Chapter 17) is an American Sociologist who has published numerous articles in the general area of collective delusions and mass hysteria. A self-described 'skeptic of all claims of the paranormal', he is currently professor and chairman of the Social Behavior Department at The University of South Dakota. His other research interests include collective behavior, demography, and gerontology.

Charles T. Tart (Chapter 1) is currently a Professor of Psychology at the Davis campus of the University of California, and a Senior Fellow at the Institute of Noetic Sciences in Sausalito, California. He is internationally known for his research with altered states of consciousness, transpersonal psychology, and parapsychology. Tart's books include the two classics *Altered States of Consciousness* and

Transpersonal Psychologies. In addition, he has authored *On Being Stoned: A Psychological Study of Marijuana Intoxication, States of Consciousness, Symposium on Consciousness* (with P. Lee, R. Ornstein, D. Galin, & A. Deikman), *Learning to Use Extrasensory Perception*, *Psi: Scientific Studies of the Psychic Realm*, *Mind At Large* (with H. Puthoff & R. Targ), and *Waking Up: Overcoming the Obstacles to Human Potential*, and numerous journal articles. His primary goal is to build bridges between the scientific and spiritual communities and to help bring about a refinement and integration of Western and Eastern approaches to knowing the world and to personal and social growth.

Michael A. Thalbourne (Chapter 13) is a Psychologist whose interests include the psychological variables affecting belief and disbelief in the paranormal, both in the layperson and in orthodox scientists. A student of John Beloff at Edinburgh University, he obtained his Ph.D. in experimental parapsychology, held post-doctoral fellowships at the University of Iceland and at Washington University in St. Louis. He is currently teaching and doing research at the University of Adelaide in Australia. A relative of David Livingstone, he describes himself as exploring the limits of 'mental influence'.

Greg F. Walsh (Editorial Contributions) is an Australian Social Scientist who has pursued a particular interest in religion and politics through research, lecturing, and publication in various areas of institutional and labor movement history. He is especially interested in comparative religion and in inter-denominational differences as they affect belief in the supernatural. He is a practising Catholic.

George K. Zollschan (Chapter 4) is a Sociologist who has published books in the area of social change and theories of motivation/action. He was research assistant to the noted philosopher Sir Karl Popper and has since taught in England, the USA, Canada, and Australia. Current interests include a radical reformulation of Popper's Three World View, as well as the Sociology and Demography of Paranormal Beliefs. He is a practising Jewish Mystic.